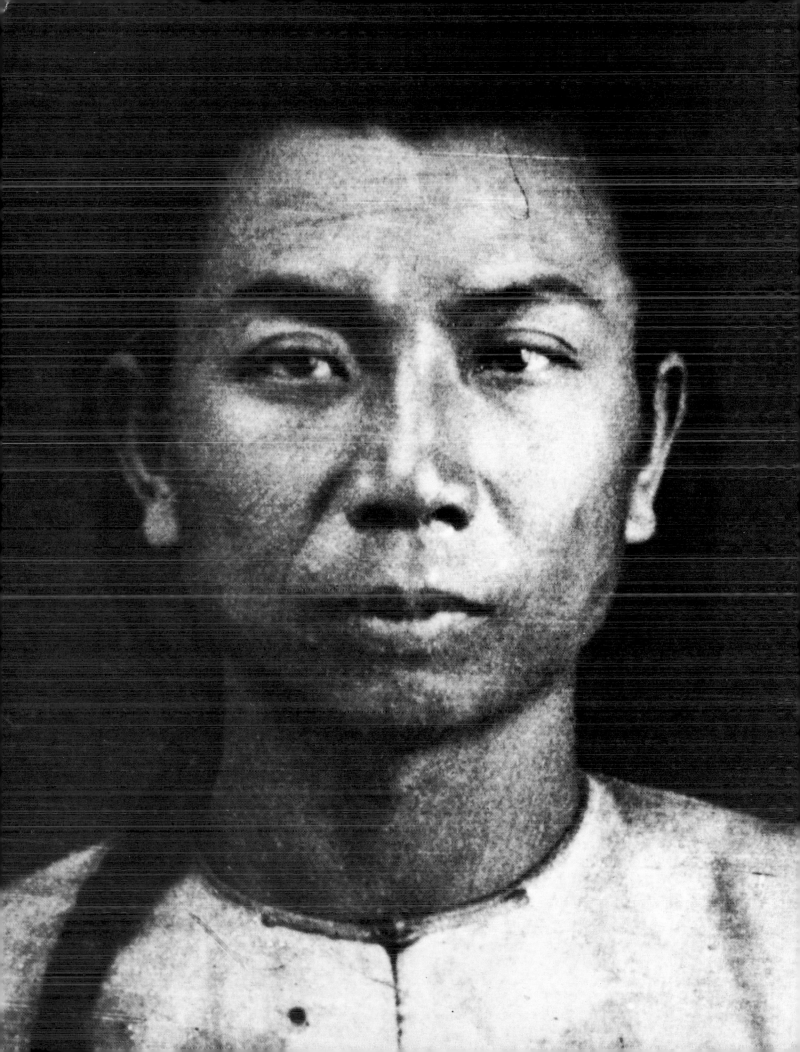

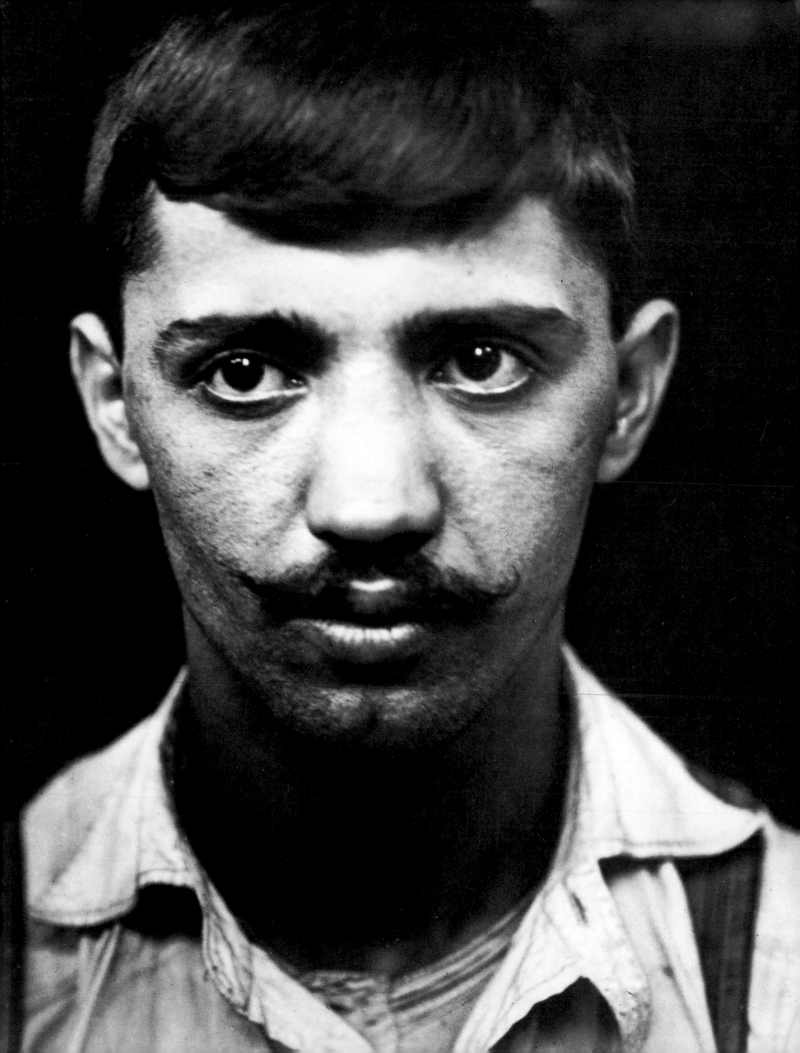

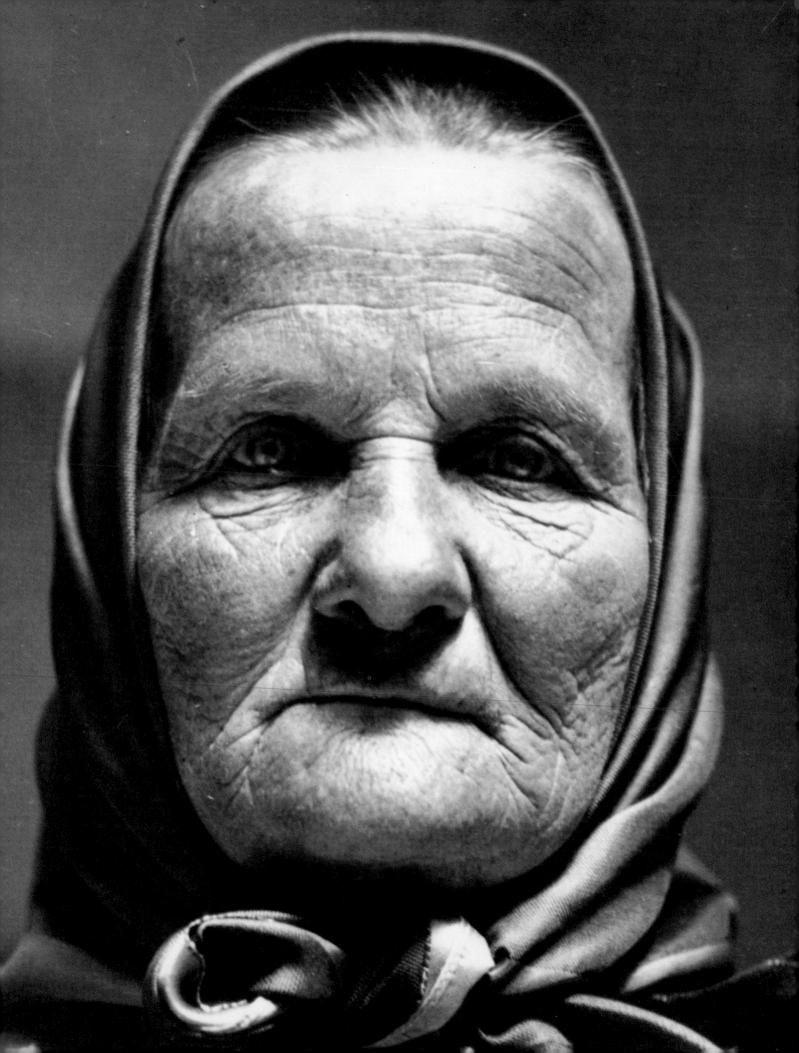

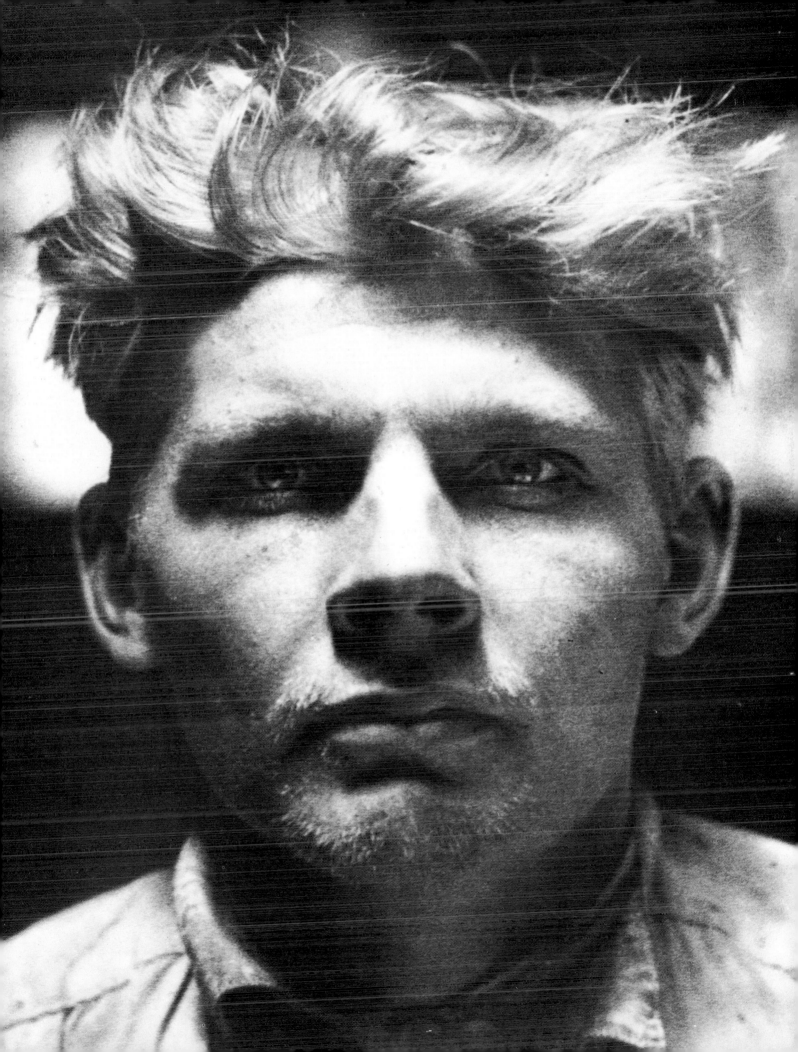

The

AMERICAN HERITAGE

History of

THE

AMERICAN

PEOPLE

By

BERNARD A. WEISBERGER

And the Editors of AMERICAN HERITAGE
The Magazine of History

EDITOR IN CHARGE MICHAEL HARWOOD

PICTORIAL COMMENTARY KRISTI WITKER

Published By

AMERICAN HERITAGE PUBLISHING CO., INC.   NEW YORK

Staff for this book

EDITOR

Michael Harwood

ASSOCIATE EDITOR

Kristi Witker

ART DIRECTOR

Richard Glassman

PICTURE EDITORS

Joanne Shapiro

Wesley Day

COPY EDITOR

Lee Culpepper

ASSISTANT EDITOR

Susan Eikov Green

CONTRIBUTING EDITORS

Beverley Da Costa

Nancy Kelly

EUROPEAN BUREAU

Gertrudis Feliu, *Chief*

AMERICAN HERITAGE PUBLISHING CO., INC.

PRESIDENT AND PUBLISHER

Paul Gottlieb

EDITOR-IN-CHIEF

Joseph J. Thorndike

SENIOR EDITOR, BOOK DIVISION

Alvin M. Josephy, Jr.

EDITORIAL ART DIRECTOR

Murray Belsky

GENERAL MANAGER, BOOK DIVISION

Andrew W. Bingham

Introduction

Americans, wrote Herman Melville, "are not a narrow tribe of men . . . No: our blood is as the flood of the Amazon, made up of a thousand noble currents all pouring into one. We are not a nation so much as a world."

Since the first European settlers in America began farming the fringes of the Indian's empire, the American people have been a perpetually changing mixture of diverse cultures. Spain and France and Holland and England and Africa; Ireland, the Germanys, Scandinavia, and China; Italy and Russia and Hungary and Poland—all these and many more contributed their noble currents of people. The cultures that found new homes in America have not truly melted into each other, except at the edges, and yet they have created a new culture peculiarly their own, including a social and political system that is inherently flexible enough to accommodate each of them. In the summer of 1969 a woman sitting on her front stoop in New York City boasted about the ethnic variety of her lower East Side neighborhood: "We're a regular United Nations here."

The accommodating nature, however, has not been consistently evident. Conflict has always been present. Nonwhites have been denied their choice of niches within the system; each great wave of immigrants met resistance from the reigning establishment. But admission of outsiders into the established order has usually resulted from two processes: America changed them, and at the same time they changed America. They became part of the national fabric without completely losing their special qualities. In the 1970s, that manner of national growing continued to offer hope of relieving the knottier problems of mutual acceptance.

The character of the American people has been reworked and replenished in each generation. It has never existed in what could be called a definitive form. Even after strict barriers to immigration were raised in the 1920s, internal migrations continued to sustain the momentum of constant, massive change. This is the story, then, of how "the American, this new man," as Crèvecoeur called him in 1782, has remained new for more than three centuries.

—The Editors

This cabinet in the library on Ellis Island held pamphlets for immigrants awaiting clearance to enter the United States.

Calm morning sea, gulls fishing, and in the air the sweet smell of land

MAGNET AND FILINGS

"AMERICA," says the title of a poem by Archibald Mac-Leish, "was promises." It has been so in every generation of the national history. "America" is imprecise as a descriptive geographical term, standing neither for a particular country nor a clearly delimited land mass. But it perfectly defines a state of expectation. It has appeared in sundry forms over the centuries and to many pairs of eyes: as a free farm in the dark interior wilderness to a German or Norwegian peasant; as a place without official restrictions on mobility to a Jew in a Czarist village; as so many dollars a day for steady work in the mills, on the railroad, or in the garment center to a hungry Irishman, Greek, or Puerto Rican; as the theater of fulfillment of God's word to a Scottish Presbyterian. It is more than milk and honey; it is, in F. Scott Fitzgerald's words, "the green light, the orgiastic future that year by year recedes before us." The green light winked to Columbus to come over the sea's edge, where others feared to go. It has been signaling ever since. It has brought the scattered American people together on their portion of a continent, to act out their common destiny.

Tradition has created a dividing moment in time when the word for a new American changes, and associations change with it. Those who came to the New World before 1776 were "colonists" and later arrivals "immigrants." But as Marcus Lee Hansen, a distinguished twentieth-century historian of immigration, wrote, "in every practical respect the settlers, old and new, were much the same. The Puritan who landed in Massachusetts Bay with his blunderbuss and Bible was an immigrant. The peasant from Eastern Europe who twenty years ago passed through Ellis Island with a pack upon his back was a colonist. They were all colonists, all immigrants. And all were engaged in providing America with ancestors."

The heart of the matter is that with one tragic exception—kidnaped Africans—the history of American settlement from the beginning was the record of people in search of castles in air. The seekers were always led on by tales, both true and misleading, of extraordinary New World gifts for the taking. These allurements sounded with special magic in the ears of Europeans beset by hardship, frustration, discontent, or the rages of ambition. They came westward to their Promised Land. Always, they found it occupied by earlier arrivals. And always, they and these predecessor Americans have then learned, in one way or another, to live and die in each other's presence and awareness, both groups being transformed in the process. That is the theme on which all else is variation. There is no special period of "immigration," somehow separate from the basic weave of American history.

One begins at the beginning, then, with the early image of America presented in travelers' tales that found their way into currency in a variety of ways—printed books, ballads and broadsides, dockside yarns, and word-of-mouth repetition of solemn reports made by sea captains to interested royal officials and directors of trading companies. Some were fundamentally factual. Some (possibly the majority) were Indian fantasies, further distorted in the imaginations of explorers often half mad with exhaustion and fever. Some were the calculated exaggerations of advertisement, set in motion by colonial promoters looking for settlers. But some were true. The astonishing thing is that in the long run the truth in the best reports outweighed the lies in the worst.

Companions of the Norse adventurer Leif Ericson, who came ashore somewhere on the New England seacoast around A.D. 1000, probably deserve the honor of being the first Europeans to catalogue America's enticements. A saga quotes them as describing a half-frozen Scandinavian's paradise with "bigger salmon than they had seen before . . . conditions . . . so favorable that the cattle would need no fodder there in the wintertime . . . no winter frosts; the grass only withered a little, and day and night were more evenly divided there than in Greenland or Iceland." But the Norsemen did not stay long enough to fertilize their discovery, and America sank into obscurity for another five hundred years. When it re-emerged in Western Europe's consciousness, Renaissance man was in full swagger, alive with carnal appetites and avid for gold.

Treasure madness inflames the reports of America that appear from 1500 onward — which is not surprising when the original goal of exploration, a short cut to the wealth of the Orient, is considered. Gold hunger was fed and increased alike by the reality of what Cortés and Pizarro took in plunder from the Aztecs in Mexico and the Incas in Peru. Thereafter, Spanish (as well as English, French, and Dutch) visions built glittering mountains of spoil whenever Indians gesticulated vaguely toward the horizon. There were broken communications; the Indian gift for metaphor, taken literally by interpreters (and probably the Indian discovery that troublesome white men might move out of a village if told of wealth farther onward), led to wild chases after golden geese. Some Indians paid dearly for the white man's disappointment. Many were tortured and slain for their inability to produce hoards that existed only in the European captains' fancies.

A Spanish history of the "Indies," read with eager curiosity (and later paraphrased) by the English entrepreneur Sir Walter Raleigh, told of the court splendors of a supposed ancestor of the "emperor of Guiana." "All the vessels of his house, table and kitchin," it was said, were of gold and silver. The royal "wardrobe" included "hollow statues of gold which seemed giants, and the figures in proportion and bignesse of all the beasts, birds, trees, and hearbes, that the earth bringeth foorth." Beside this New World pleasure dome there was an imperial garden "which had all kinde of garden-hearbs, flowers and trees of golde and silver," as if the copper-colored sovereign, Guaynacapa, were some Midas who had run his fingers over the vegetation while on a refreshing stroll through his palace grounds. Alvar Núñez Cabeza de Vaca was shipwrecked in the Gulf of

Mexico in 1528, taken prisoner by Indians, and led by them on an incredible odyssey throughout the Southwest. When he finally reached Spanish territory in 1536, he spoke excitedly of the "South Sea" (the Pacific) as being only a short journey to the west of what is now Texas; and, he continued, the Indians swore to him that on the blue coasts of that sea were "pearls and great riches, and the best and all the most opulent countries are near there."

Fired in part by such promises, Francisco Vásquez de Coronado led an expedition out from Mexico in 1540, searching in present-day Kansas and eastern Colorado for seven cities of gold — the empire of wishful legend, called Cibola. Seas of grass and herds of buffalo were awesome sights, but the jeweled palaces of the quest turned out to be a few scattered tepees. Still, when Coronado became discouraged, he could listen to the reassurances of a captured Pawnee known as "the Turk," who had met white men before. The Turk told him of some genuine wonders—"a river in the level country which was two leagues wide" (the Platte) in which there were "fishes big as horses" (catfish, perhaps, not as big as horses but impressive and some of them man-sized)—and also of things that Shakespeare might have found usable in *Antony and Cleopatra*: ". . . large numbers of big canoes with more than twenty rowers on a side, . . . they carried sails, . . . their lords sat on the poop under awnings, and on the prow they had a great golden eagle. He said also that the lord of that country took his afternoon nap under a great tree on which were hung a number of little gold bells, which put him to sleep as they swung in the air. He said also that everyone had their ordinary

COSMOGRPHIAE

Capadociam/Pamphiliam/Lidiam/Cilicia/Armē
nias maiorē & minorē.Colchiden/Hircaniam/Hi
beriam/Albaniā:et preterea mltas quas singilatim
enumerare longa mora esset.Ita dicta ab eius nomi
nis regina.

Nūc ỹo & he partes sunt latius lustratæ/& alia
quarta pars per Americū Vesputiū(vt in sequenti
bus audietur)inuenta est/quā non video cur quis
iure vetet ab Americo inuentore sagacis ingenij vi
ro Amerigen quasi Americi terrā/siue Americam
dicendā:cū & Europa & Asia a mulieribus sua sor
tita sint nomina.Eius situ & gentis mores ex bis bi
nis Americi nauigationibus quæ sequunt liquide
intelligi datur.

Hunc in modū terra iam quadripartita cognoʃ
scit:et sunt tres prime partes cōtinentes/quarta est
insula:cū omni quaqʒ mari circūdata conspiciaf.Et
licet mare vnū sit queadmodū et ipsa tellus/multis
tamen sinibus distinctum / & innumeris repletum
insulis varia sibi noīa assumit:quæ et in Cosmo
phiæ tabulis cōspiciunt/& Priscianus in tralatione
Dionisij talibus enumerat versibus.
Circuit Oceani gurges tamen vndiqʒ vastus
Qui ꝗuis vnus sit plurima nomina sumit.
Finibus Hesperijs Athlanticus ille vocatur
At Boreę qua gens furit Armiaspa sub armis
Dicit ille piger necnō Satur.ide Mortuus est alijs.

Ameri-ca

Priscia-nus.

WALDSEEMÜLLER, *Cosmographiae Introductio*, 1507, NYPL.

Martin Waldseemüller's Cosmographiae Introductio *of 1507, opposite, first suggested naming the New World for the navigator Amerigo Vespucci, who is depicted in the woodcut above.*

dishes of wrought plate, and the jugs and bowls were made of gold."

So America appears in its earliest depiction a golden land. (Almost four hundred years after de Vaca and Coronado, Yiddish-speaking Eastern European immigrants were to use that precise phrase, *ah goldeneh Land*, to describe their adopted United States, unaware of the dissonance of the images that they and the conquistadors invoked—or the similarities.) By the end of the sixteenth and the beginning of the seventeenth centuries, however, new ideas were beginning to emerge. Even the visionary Spanish temperament divined by then that the virgin continent had greater prospects than just those measurable in fine ounces of bullion. In 1598, for example, Juan de Oñate undertook a colonizing venture in New Mexico. Expectedly, he reported to the viceroy of New Spain on "the great wealth which the mines have begun to reveal," and on the possible traffic, still dreamed of then, with ports that might be established on the American shore of the South Sea. But he also noted "the wealth of the wool and hides of buffalo," and "judging from the general nature of the land, the certainty of wines and oils." Buffalo hides, wine, and oil came closer to what the Southwest could actually deliver than the far from golden Seven Cities of Cibola.

Foundations of the United States would in a few years begin to be built on the eastern coast as well, by the English in Virginia. Elizabethan merchants and ministers were second to none in their lively concern for treasure, but the real success of Great Britain as a colonizing power was eventually to rest in its ability to sustain permanent, large-scale, self-supporting "plantations" in North America. To that end, farm-hunting settlers were indispensable; and to stir their interest, there were accounts of Virginia like that from the pen of young George Percy, one of 120 men who came in three ships to "plant" Jamestown in May, 1607.

Percy and his companions were not plowmen. They were interested in mines, trade, and possibly the cultivation of such exotic products as silkworms. But the lushness of the New World seems to have distracted them somewhat and was transmitted in undiminished force in Percy's descriptions of the first springtime weeks of the first white Virginians.

At an initial stop in the West Indies, the founders saw fowl flying "over our heads as thick as drops of hail." They sailed on northward to enter "Chesupioc" Bay, and on April 26, 1607, landed amidst "fair meadows and goodly tall trees, with such fresh waters running through the woods as I was almost ravished at the first sight thereof." More than just fresh waters ran through the woods, however, and that night a party of Indians crept into Percy's encampment and wounded two men with their arrows before the newcomers drove them off. A short march brought Percy's men to a spot where "good store of mussels" lay on the ground "as thick as stones." Onward they went, passing over ground strewn not only with wild flowers but "fine and beautiful strawberries, four times bigger and better than ours in England."

As they progressed up the James River, they passed "pleasant springs which issued from the mountains" and "the goodliest cornfields . . . ever were seen in any country." Abundance rioted in an unexploited Virginia Maytime. Everyone marveled at "store of vines in bigness of a man's thigh, running up to the tops of the trees in great abundance" and at "many squirrels, conics, blackbirds with crimson wings," and birds with crimson, blue, green, and yellow feathers. There were flowers "as though it had been in any garden or orchard in England," and fragrance from cedar and cypress and other trees, out of which issued "sweet gum like to balsam." Percy's lyricism was, of course, retrospective, and may not have reflected the sentiments of his men, burdened and hot with their armor, weapons, and coarse linen clothing. "We kept on our way in this paradise," he was to write, having perhaps dreamed of going naked in it and being sustained, like Adam in the first Paradise, without toil. After all, there was fruit in abundance, "great plenty of fish," and the meadows would furnish excellent pasture for cattle. There was also "great store of deer . . . bears, foxes, otters, beavers, muskrats, and wild beasts unknown." (The fur trade would corrupt Paradise soon enough; Europe was turning to fur garments as tokens of affluence, and there was wealth to be trapped in the woods and rivers—especially in Canada, where, just a year after Percy's excursion in Eden, Samuel de Champlain was to found the city of Quebec.)

America in the seventeenth century was not merely the mines of Montezuma; it was fat and fertile soil. "A remarkably beautiful country," wrote Governor Johan Printz of New Sweden (Delaware) in 1643; and the beauty he extolled was like that of an Old Testament bride, not only pleasing to the eye but with a teeming womb. At about the same time, David De Vries wrote a similar description, calculated to bring fresh settlers to the Dutch West India Company's colony of New Netherland, which he described as a fat Hollander's Utopia: maize stalks "as high as a man can reach, and higher," together with pumpkins, watermelons, hazelnuts, chestnuts, wild grapes, elk, hares, foxes, wildcats, squirrels, minks, otters, polecats, bears, and "many kinds of fur-bearing animals which I cannot name or think of." The soil, De Vries rhapsodized, enabled "our Netherlanders" to raise good wheat, rye, barley, oats, and peas and "brew as good beer here as in our Fatherland." Forty-pound turkeys struggled through the air and fell, exhausted by their own weight, into the hands of pursuers. According to De Vries, fifteen-pound geese flew by in their thousands and were decimated for holiday tables. Meadow hens, herons, turtledoves, and the ubiquitous blackbirds darkened the sky; the waters virtually foamed with runs of pike, perch, roach, haddock, and herring, while flounder and sole carpeted the mud bottoms. The very crabs on the beach, said De Vries, had claws "the color of the flag of our Prince [of the Netherlands], orange, white, and blue, so that [they] show sufficiently that we ought to people the country, and that it belongs to us."

Thus the changing portraiture of a promised land: in one century, emperors in feathered robes drinking from golden vessels; in another, fish and grain choking smokehouses and barns, peltry piling higher and higher at the trading posts. Whatever the terms of the description, America was the opportune moment waiting to be seized. So the first settlers, the first immigrants, English, Dutch, French, Swedish, Spanish, came to seize it —and to confront trials beyond belief. For the gold, the grain, and the fur, it turned out, had to be struggled for after all. The settlers braced for and endured the arrow that flew by noonday and the pestilence that walked in darkness. They outlasted the heartbreak of slain wives and children, the torments of thirst, insects, heat, and hunger, and the frustrations of false leads, crops burned out by Indian attack, packs of furs lost as canoes over-

turned in white water. Later generations of newcomers would know other, different trials. But always hope could only be deferred, not destroyed. America was goodness to come. The stouthearted hung on, for the prize was bound to be there somewhere. That faith would be a dominant note in all of American history.

The faith was sustained for the newcomers not only by the promises ahead but by the horrors left behind, across the Atlantic. Actually, the seventeenth-century impetus to colonization was part of a general tidal shifting of human groups, running deep into a biological past when nomadic cave men roved over the continents, tied to the migration patterns of the game they pursued. But Europe, from 1600 onward, offered special motives for swarming. The century that began in that year saw England almost constantly writhing in civil disturbance, and those convulsions underlay the great exodus to the colonies responsible for determining the basically English pattern of American life.

The Continent, too, was in ferment. In a sense, the seventeenth century saw the emergence of those institutions which, in the late twentieth, are characteristic of the modern world: centralized and wholly sovereign nation-states; capitalism; individualism, secularism, and heroic grandeur in the arts; the triumphant growth of modern science with its relentless reduction of divine mysteries to a precalculated interplay of forces and effects; and European mastery of the rest of the world— America being one of the first outposts of modern imperialism to be created and one of the first to escape. For the historians of the United States, the seventeenth century is when momentum becomes measurable. Prior to 1600 few settlements were made within modern national boundaries—a Spanish salient in New Mexico and toehold in Florida; two abortive French Huguenot and English ventures in the Carolinas—these were all.

It was the post-Renaissance era which, in a sense, created "America," and that was only one of its achieve-

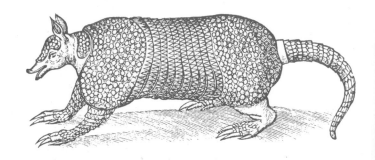

Settlers of the New World found many unfamiliar animals, such as the armadillo shown in this 1579 book illustration.
MONARDES, *Simplicium Medicamentorum*, NYPL

ments. The dynastic splendor of emergent monarchs like France's Louis XIV were reflected in Baroque palaces. The wealth of the merchant princes who founded such mighty trading companies as England's Hamburg Company (1611) or the Netherlands' Dutch East India Company (1602) was embodied in their homes and costumes and captured in expensive portraiture. It was an age of intellectual as well as terrestrial conquest, with a dazzling constellation of great names—Spinoza, Leibniz, Locke, Descartes, and Hobbes in philosophy; Rubens, Rembrandt, Velázquez in painting; Cervantes, Molière, and Milton in literature; Newton, Harvey, Kepler, and Galileo in science.

Yet there was a macabre reverse to the medallion. Royal splendor was attained at the expense of the clergy, the nobility, and the provincial towns. A crop of younger sons and hard-taxed merchants sought to replenish family fortunes under alien skies. And as usual, the pressure fell hardest on the sweated commoners at the bottom of the social ladder. Posterity may gape admiringly at the swank of an era when a single nobleman, the Duke of Lerma, could meet his future bride with 34,000 ducats' worth of jewels on his person and another 72,000 in value carried along behind him. But such opulence was made possible only by levying the most burdensome of taxes on land, crops, houses, and livestock. In 1648 a French writer registered this complaint: "The country has been ruined, the peasants reduced to sleeping on straw, after their furniture has been sold to pay taxes which they cannot raise—to maintain the luxury of Paris, millions of innocent souls are forced to live on bread, bran and oats, and cannot hope for any protection except their impotence. [That is to say, their incapacity to yield up more than the absolute limit.] These unfortunates do not possess anything but their souls, and them only because they cannot be auctioned off."

What was more, warfare, both civil and international, erupted epidemically from massive dislocations of power. France, Spain, England, and the Netherlands were almost continually in combat. The century opened with the Dutch still struggling to free themselves of Spain and ended on the threshold of a general European conflict over the succession to the Spanish throne. The Catalans and Portuguese revolted against Madrid in 1640, the latter successfully. Another revolt, in 1647 in Naples, was put down by the Spanish. Between 1648 and 1653 a civil war in which religious overtones were mingled, known as the War of the Fronde, seethed in France. The Austrians intrigued over and intervened in the German states to the north and the Italian principalities to the south, while to the east they fended off

This print of an ear of corn was made in 1535.

the Turks, who were still pounding at the gates of Vienna as late as 1683.

Seventeenth-century wars did not wreak destruction on a modern scale. The relatively primitive weapons of the time were too crude for that. But the bands of soldiers who marched back and forth over the countryside routinely commandeered wagons, animals, and foodstuffs, set houses and barns afire, tortured and murdered men suspected of hiding either money or goods, committed rape at will, and left starvation and disease to mop up behind them. The brutality of such warfare was magnified when religious zeal kindled the fighting. In the twentieth century, governments arouse men to accept the unthinkable by proclaiming rigorous political ideologies. Warring princes sought the same end three centuries earlier by enlisting God on their side. Sometimes the heretics were merely expelled. Sometimes they were massacred, becoming "slaughtered saints" in the vocabulary of their fellow worshipers.

The worst intertwining of religious and dynastic warfare was in the states of Central Europe. From 1618 to 1648 the Thirty Years' War raged, involving not only German principalities but present-day Scandinavia, Bohemia, and Poland. It ended with each prince in the miscellaneous aggregation of political splinters free to determine religious practice in his realm—and with gutted communities. In Sweden, as a later historian was to put it, "hundreds of once-fertile fields lay for years uncultivated and covered with weeds." In Württemberg the number of men capable of bearing arms dropped from 65,400 in 1623 to 14,800 in 1652, and 318 castles as well as 36,100 urban dwellings were destroyed. In a county in Thuringia, half the families disappeared. In another in Brandenburg, only 630 peasants of an estimated 1,900 remained at the war's end. In Munich the number of weavers was halved.

"These days are days of shaking . . . ," observed an English preacher in 1643, "and this shaking is universal. . . ." But even when the earth did not shake under horses' hoofs and the lumbering wheels of siege cannon, the age was brutal enough. As one historian of the Thirty Years' War, Cicely V. Wedgwood, has noted:

Bloodshed, rape, robbery, torture and famine were less revolting to a people whose ordinary life was encompassed by them in milder forms. Robbery with violence was common enough in peace-time, torture was inflicted at most criminal trials, horrible and prolonged executions were performed before great audiences; plague and famine effected their repeated and indiscriminate devastations.

The outlook even of the educated was harsh. Underneath a veneer of courtesy, manners were primitive; drunkenness and cruelty were common in all classes, judges were more often severe than just, civil authority more often brutal than effective, and charity came limping far behind the needs of the people. Discomfort was too natural to provoke comment; winter's cold and summer's heat found European man lamentably unprepared, his houses too damp and draughty for the one, too airless for the other. Prince and beggar were alike inured to the stink of decaying offal in the streets, of foul drainage about the houses, to the sight of carrion birds picking over public refuse dumps or rotting bodies swinging on the gibbets. On the road from Dresden to Prague a traveller counted "above seven score gallowses and wheels, where thieves were hanged, some fresh and some half rotten, and the carcases of murderers broken limb after limb on the wheels."

The twentieth-century reader must weigh against this *Totentanz* background New World images of dusky par-

ents flinging golden bracelets to their children for trinkets, of skies and rivers swarming with food, of clear air, smiling suns, nodding flowers. In plague-stricken cities, amid offal-choked alleys, and on burned-out farms, in chapels where the Word was preached furtively, with sentinels at the door, Europeans received such tidings as they would rain in the desert.

A theme was thus established. The New World was hope and promise. The Old, though it had the energy, wealth, courage, and yearning to unfold the New, was haunted by a bitter past from which the restless wished to fly. That, too, was a theme that would last.

The first "immigrants," like those who followed, found guardians of the Promised Land waiting for them, but with this difference: later newcomers would hold themselves inferior to the established "Americans" and would struggle to replace their "alien" ways with new patterns; but the first European settlers found the possessors of the land to be "savages," and immediately set out to impose civilization upon them.

Yet at first the transaction worked the other way. The fresh arrivals *did* learn from their untutored hosts. Willy-nilly, they were dependent on them. The Indians

This early illustration reveals the European's notion of the land of plenty and a banquet shared with friendly Indians.

An allegory of the New World by a French artist

make useful evaluations among classes and tribes within African or Asian kingdoms, confounding everything and everybody in tableaux of primitivism. This destructive ignorance has not yet worked its full mischief.)

Simplicity was non-European and therefore suspect. Columbus touchingly reported that the Indians of Bahama swam out to his ships with parrots, brightly colored threads, and other gifts. These were the offerings of children, the Spaniards thought, and in return gave childish things: "red caps and glass beads to put round their necks." Later, the faith in Indian innocence was shaken (though it kept re-emerging in noble-savage stereotypes), and what replaced it was an enduring caricature of the redskins as naked men, paint-smeared, cunning, fickle, cruel, lazy, destructive—children turned into monsters.

These first Americans, however, were not a single entity but many peoples. Some—perhaps most—were far from the Stone Age barbarism of popular belief. The Indians were themselves migrants to the New World (over a prehistoric land bridge from Asia) and had developed for centuries before they were discovered. The sophistication of the Mexican and Andean Indian empires is well known, but the North American tribesmen were not far behind them. Those who dwelt in the eastern United States (from the Atlantic to the Mississippi, from the Great Lakes and the St. Lawrence to the Carolinas) clustered in hundreds of tribal units whose names, still on the map, are the first and most mellifluous Indian contribution to American life—the Penobscots, Passamaquoddys, Narragansets, and Mohegans of New England; the Delawares, Oneidas, Eries, Pamlicos, Powhatans, Nanticokes, and Susquehannocks of the Middle Atlantic region; the Potawatomis, Ojibwas (Chippewas), Ottawas, Menominees, Sauks and Foxes, Winnebagos, Kaskaskias, and Peorias of the Midwest. The rustle of wilderness is in the syllables, even though they represent only partly successful struggles of Europeans to pronounce the names as the Indians spoke them.

"Primitives" these first Americans were, but the term is relative. About four thousand years before Columbus, the people of the Laurentian Culture, situated in eastern New York, the St. Lawrence Valley, and New England, carved animal bone into gouges, adzes, and harpoons and ground slate points and knives. About a thousand years later the Old Copper Culture in the

were the first and indispensable reception committee in America. No history of the American people—a title to which, after all, the Indians have the most legitimate claim—can omit the red men's role. They held the keys to survival. They knew the land as worshipers know divinity and lovers know each other, taking what they needed without exhausting the supply. They knew where the furs were (and the gold if there *was* gold); they knew how to track game and take fish with tools made of bone, sinew, bark, twig, and vine. They knew what strange flesh was fit to eat, which berries poisoned —and which ones cured.

They were also, as it happened, a test of the embryonic American conscience. That all but a few white men failed the moral examination was tragic but almost inevitable, given the circumstances. The assumptions of European culture virtually dictated that redskin and paleface should be enemies, only temporarily and intermittently allied for trade and profit. Men coming from the world of the Escorial, the Armada, the Papacy, Parliament, the money markets of Amsterdam, and the gardens of Versailles were bound to regard simple people as much less than equals. (They made no distinction among nonwhites, in fact, tending to regard Indians, Chinese, Africans, and Malays as uniformly backward. For the most part they did not even

OVERLEAF: *Although the universality of the human condition was Peter Breughel's subject in* The Triumph of Death, *the allegory also reflects the violence and decay of European life that compelled many to leave their countries for America.*

Great Lakes region made birchbark containers (possibly including canoes) and domesticated the dog. Mound-building cultures such as the Adena placed their dead reverently on hills, surrounded by ornaments of stone, copper, and shell.

Even before Europe hung suspended between the collapse of Roman Imperial order and the emergence of feudalism, in the so-called Dark Ages, some North American Indians had developed what anthropologists call the Hopewellian Culture. They lived in villages, worshiped in ceremonial centers, cultivated corn, squash, beans, and tobacco, and adorned their dead with objects brought to them through a sophisticated trade network: grizzly-bear teeth and obsidian from the Rockies, curly conch shells from the Gulf Coast, mica from the Appalachians, copper and lead from the Great Lakes region and the upper Mississippi Valley. Their beaded jewelry, their tools, and their pottery were decorated with floral and animal figures in intricate interwoven designs. Led by priests bedecked in gorgeous beads and shells, they danced to the music of rattles, pipes, and drums. Their craftsmen were true specialists, and hereditary ranks were attached to different specialties.

Not long before the white man came, the intricacies of some Indian clan relationships matched the quarterings and bloodlines of European nobility. Ritual and magic in Indian religious life was not altogether unlike the Latin chants of the Roman priesthood, and the exorcisms of medicine men were not so far from the incantatory curses upon imps and devils that Europeans pronounced during the witchcraft crazes that still swept over Europe long after 1492. (America's own Salem witch trials took place in the 1690s.) The use of shells (wampum), both as money and, strung together on belts, as a device for conveying messages and ideas, indicated a growing social sophistication. Elaborate political arrangements were embodied in such a structure as the Iroquois League—a delicately balanced confederation that linked clans, families, and tribes in an unbreakable network, vested much authority in women, and rested decision-making powers in representative councils. These policies argue a developing Indian life far removed from howling animalism.

The Europeans swung to extremes in judging Indian life. At first they called the chiefs they met by names both familiar and curious—princes, emperors, caciques, and werowances. Then they changed, and professed to see mere posturing wildlife in any Indians who claimed authority. In either case the end was the same. The thrust of white culture, with its demand for furs and land, and its trade bait of iron tools and pots, blankets,

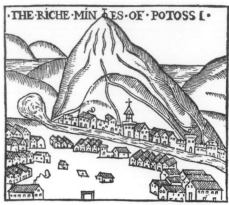

Among the first attractions of the New World were South America's gold and silver mines and high-wrought pre-Columbian treasures like the Peruvian gold mask below. Above is the first known picture of a Bolivian silver-mining town, Potosí, published in London in the late 1500s.

firearms, and the fatal whisky, broke down the self-sufficiency of the Indian world. The sad course of near-extermination ran its melancholy length.

The Indian's development was overwhelmed in the tragedy of invasion, but the record stands: the Indian was the initial American. It is not necessary to be sentimental. As Bernard DeVoto says, the romantic image of "the squash blossom in the hair" becomes a mask of falsehood in itself, disguising realities of torture and filth. But neither should it be overlooked that the Indians, functionally tied to the continent, eased the white European's first perilous entry into it. They taught him the use of snowshoes, moccasins, canoes, toboggans, and other artifacts (and arts) of wilderness survival. In possessing them, he became himself American. In 1893 Frederick Jackson Turner announced a theory of national history which asserted that American democracy was born in the leveling atmosphere of the frontier. He pointed out that one of the first signs of adaptation to the new environment on a European's part was to strip off the garments of civilization, with their class and social connotations, and wear the undifferentiated skin garments of the Indian (without the decorations, he failed to add, by which some Indians announced their own ranks and titles).

The Indian did more than communicate forest skills, however. As Alvin M. Josephy, Jr., has noted, the red man also introduced almost half the crops that make up the world's total food supply today. Corn and potatoes were his gift, and more than eighty other domesticated plants, according to one historian, "including peanuts, squashes, peppers, tomatoes, pumpkins, pineapples, avocados, cacao [and] chicle . . . and at least fifty-nine drugs as well, including coca (for cocaine and novocaine), curare (a muscle relaxant), cinchona bark (the source of quinine), cascara sagrada (a laxative), datura (a pain reliever), and ephedra (a nasal remedy). . . ."

Finally, of course, there was what Jacques Cartier described in the year 1535 as "a certain kind of herb, whereof in summer they make great provision for all the year . . . first they cause it to be dried in the sun . . . they make powder of it and then put it in one of the ends of the said cornet or pipe and lay in a coal of fire upon it, at the other end suck so long, that they fill their bodies full of smoke, till that it comes out of their mouth and nostrils. . . ."

It can even be argued that the Indian contribution does not end there, but that the New World gold, which swelled the Spanish treasury for two centuries and more after Cortés, was an involuntary Indian gift to European development. But the point need not be labored. The Indian past is vital tissue in the social organism known as the American people. If nothing else bore witness, the evidence could be found in a language enriched by such words as succotash, tobacco, chipmunk, squash, skunk, toboggan, opossum, moose, mackinaw, hickory, pecan, raccoon, cougar, woodchuck, hominy, and hundreds of others. The Indians gave. They set a model of welcome to "immigrants" not always emulated later. George Percy related that in 1607 some Indians "murmured at our planting in the country, whereupon this Werowance [Powhatan] made answer again very wisely of a savage. Why should you be offended with them as long as they hurt you not, nor take anything away by force? They take but a little waste ground, which doth you nor any of us any good."

Centuries afterward, other, white "old stock" Americans could well have used such generous attitudes instead of the restrictive ones they actually displayed. It is a pity that Powhatan's estimate of white needs was altogether too ingenuous.

The story began, then, with interaction among the continent's new and old inhabitants—the Indian "garrison" and the colonizing immigrants. The process that developed in the course of settlement was twofold: it Americanized the settler and Europeanized the land. Its results are still visible and can be seen with special clarity across the vista of more than three centuries if we examine two European settlements almost a continent apart. They are those of the Spaniards in New Mexico and the Dutch in New Netherland, now New York State. Each stamped the design and texture of an Old World way of life on an American region and a pattern on the lives of the succeeding generations who would dwell there.

The Spaniards came first. Today there is a fresh Hispanic strain among the American people. It is felt in the impact of minority groups—the Cubans of Florida, the Puerto Ricans of New York, and the Mexicans of Texas and southern California. Latin modes and accents work their way into national habits through the tortuous channels of ethnic and racial participation in politics, sports, entertainment—and in the statistics of the city ghetto. But it is a useful perspective device to see how Spaniards shaped a piece of America to their liking almost four centuries ago, when they were masters of the situation.

As the sixteenth century waned, Hispanic explorers were moving northward from Mexico, hoping to find new sources of wealth. The momentum of Spanish expansion in the East was running down. The little post at St. Augustine, Florida, remained static— an undeveloped hand reaching feebly for the fur trade; merely an appendage to Madrid's Caribbean holdings. But two thousand miles westward there was action. In 1581 Fray Agustín Rodríguez, two other friars, nine soldiers, and about sixteen Indian servants traveled the barren way from Santa Barbara, in Chihuahua, to the Rio Grande. They then continued up that river to the pueblo country around Socorro, modern New Mexico. As the expedition made its way back to Mexico to report the findings, one of the fathers was killed by Indians. Still, the news that got through inspired plans to make the Pueblo Indians colonials. These were not wretched nomads but tribes who had "well-built houses of four and five stories, with corridors and rooms twenty-four feet long and thirteen feet wide, whitewashed and painted," with "very good plazas, and . . .

streets along which they pass in good order." To colonialize such well-organized natives was a practical and laudable goal.

In 1598 Juan de Oñate's expedition moved into New Mexico, attempting to re-enact the great scenario of Cortés and freely killing Indians in the process. But Oñate looked in vain for gold and jewels amid the cactus and the sharp mountain peaks. There were only hungry Hopis and Zuñis. On subsequent quests he probed for a route to the South Sea, and finally found it in the impassable Colorado. It was a dispiriting finale to the treasure hunts. In 1606 a royal edict to the viceroy in Mexico banned further explorations for bonanzas —they had become too costly in lost expeditions, starving men, massacre, torture, and restlessness among the Indians. Spain would now try the less glamorous road to empire, that of plantation. But Oñate's expedition was not wasted. It set up a permanent Spanish lodgment in New Mexico. In 1610, with appropriate ceremony, the capital of the colony was established at Santa Fe.

The Spanish busied themselves with impressing their culture upon New Mexico. They sent their cattle, sheep, horses, and goats to graze in the haciendas—the great unfenced areas granted to them—and the pattern of American ranching was born. They learned to irrigate the desert as is done to this day and to plant life-giving wheat, oats, barley, chilies, onions, peas, beans, and melons. The Indians taught them such tricks as fishing with long nets of yucca fiber. Under Governors Peralta, Eulate, de Rosas, Mendizabel, and Bertugo, the New Mexican colonists of the 1600s prospered and pined for home. The soldiers amused themselves with traditional garrison occupations. Now and then, after finding some outlying settlements in ruins, with corpses bearing evidence of horrible torture, they enjoyed a lively foray into the countryside against marauding Apaches. There would be battles. Some Indians would hang, as salutary examples. Then back to town, the girls, the wine. They took squaws, sired children, waited for promotion and better duty, went on horseback hunting trips in mountains like those they had known at home, and behaved themselves very much as American soldiers in exactly the same circumstances and locality would do two and a half centuries later.

The friars, meantime, took on the work of converting the savages. There was an essential similarity among the fifty churches they built in New Mexico before 1625. The chief of the mission was "architect, engineer, carpenter, mason, foreman, building master to apprentices who themselves were masters of a building style," as Paul Horgan has noted in his magnificent book *Great River*. The Spaniard adopted the obvious virtues of the native Indian buildings—simple, rectangular, earth-hugging, and made of such common materials as clay and rock. He undertook the manufacture of adobes, earthen bricks as heavy as sixty pounds each, out of which rose the walls of storehouses and chapels. Scarce wood, for doorframes and beams to support roofs of branches and packed earth, was laboriously hewn and shaped by axes, adzes, saws, chisels, augers, and planes. Locks, nails, hinges, ironware of any sort, was rare and costly. The rich grillwork of Moorish-Iberian churches had to yield to something simpler. What came of it all was an American Southwestern style: stuccoed exterior, low and straight lines, and whitewashed walls (often decorated with Indian symbols), sometimes with attached walled cemeteries that filled with pink reflections and blue shadows in the hot afternoons.

The Spanish friars brought silver chalices, brocaded vestments, and golden crucifixes and candlesticks. The Indians joined to these riches the passion of their own faith (which did not scorn to break through the barriers of consciousness by the use of drugs, sleeplessness, and self-inflicted pain) and the intricate arts that expressed it. The converts needed no instruction in reverence for the spirit-informing life. They had only to transform their native mysticism into loyalty to tangible figures of Saviour, saints, and Madonna. They learned to sing hymns, to pray, even to participate in the Mass, and to hold their new beliefs in a grip that survived the vicissitudes of many years of battle between white warriors and red. And they taught the fathers themselves new lessons in evangelism.

By 1679 a valley culture of corn and oil, adobe and silver, Christ and earthen gods, was emerging. Santa Fe was laid out then much as it is today. Mountains on the north overlooked a plaza surrounded on three sides by houses. And on the northern side of that plaza stood a Palace of the Governors, long, low, and containing offices, chapel, living quarters, prison, fortress, and stables—the entire apparatus of rule. Cultivated fields stretched out on all sides. To the west were barracks. On the east was the church of St. Francis; to the south stood the chapel of St. Michael.

It was Indian in one sense; in another, Spanish—but not quite either of them. It was ultimately American. It was also vulnerable. In 1680 an Indian, Popé, outraged by the Spaniards, led an insurrection that swept them from the valley, leaving behind pillars of smoke and circling buzzards.

The Spaniards came back after a time, profoundly to affect the Southwest anew with their style—so appropriate to the stark land—of iron pride, of harshness,

New Sweden

There is no telling what the course of American history and the present composition of the American people might have been if several early settlements had continued to fly their original flags. Obviously, the pattern of American life would have been far different had Dutch control of New Netherland been viable. By the same token, the Scandinavian imprint might have been far more pronounced had Sweden's abortive attempt to maintain its settlement on the Delaware River succeeded. From its inception, New Sweden was never more than a halfhearted venture—except insofar as its non-Swedish promoters were concerned. Money, ships, and equipment were in short supply; Swedish claims to lands on or near the Delaware River had been pre-empted by earlier Dutch arrivals who were in no mood to extend a warm welcome to the interlopers; quarrels arose with Indians who claimed territory sold to the Swedish settlers by *other* Indians. Perhaps most damaging of all to the colony's prospects, few Swedes or Finns (Finland was then ruled by Sweden) were eager to emigrate—a circumstance which necessitated the forced emigration of a motley of incompetents and other undesirables, and which resulted in one colonial official's observation that "it would be impossible to find more stupid people in all Sweden."

For a time the Swedes and Dutch effected an uneasy alliance for the purpose of thwarting English designs on the region, but once Anglo-Dutch hostilities in Europe were concluded, the New Netherlanders (who had undergone the mortification of losing a Delaware garrison to the Swedes in 1654) sent in a task force under Peter Stuyvesant that outnumbered the entire population of New Sweden and took the settlement without troubling to fire a shot. Thus was deferred for at least two centuries a Scandinavian impact which might have done much to shape America's heritage but which left little trace except for the log cabin—which became the symbol, for others, of a beginning on the frontier, not of a premature end.

of self-tormenting loyalty to honor and other abstractions, of worship, and of deep dignity. The bloodshed, heartbreak, tortured acolytes, and flayed settlers were simply part of the price of migration.

The Dutch, nearly two thousand miles away, were different. (Dutch and Spanish differences, in fact, had bathed the Netherlands in blood for years when the Low Countries were a province of Spain.) The Dutch in North America were a colonial power for a relatively brief period of some fifty years. Yet they showed the variety inherent in the process of transplanting European modes of life to America. There were, the record shows, many ways of populating and characterizing a new land.

The spirit of seventeenth-century Holland was relentlessly dominated by the quest for profit. (That in itself may have been a legacy to later American life, but it came from other sources as well as from the Dutch.) In their pursuit of guilders, the Netherlanders looked unperturbed on the entire catalogue of explorers' hazards: tempests, pirates, disease, and massacre. Their energy was frightening. Throughout the century, from Hudson's Bay to Cape Horn, they were daring and busy. Despite almost constant wars at home, they set up posts in India in 1616, on Java in 1619, in Brazil in 1623, on Ceylon in 1638, and on the Cape of Good Hope in 1652. Yet their accounts of these deeds were never touched with the eager pleasure of a John Smith savoring the wonders of Virginia, or with the half-greedy, half-ecstatic aura surrounding some Spaniard's vision of gold piled in heaps around the feet of men in cuirasses. Step by step they built an empire, but never celebrated the feat in verse or paint. The empire was an investment. Art and philosophy and science—Dutch intellectual strong points—were not concerned with investments.

In creating New Netherland in 1621, however (basing their claim on Henry Hudson's 1609 explorations of the river named for him), the Dutch called on (or rather submitted to) the services of two men who stand at the head of a long line of American promoters: William Usselinx and Peter Minuit. Usselinx, the father of the Dutch West India Company, was an Antwerper who seethed with the commercial aspirations of Northern Europe and with hostility toward the Spaniards who still occupied Belgium. With a successful career in business behind him, he got the ear of Netherlands officials and besought them to form a West India trading company to furnish a Caribbean base from which to harry the Spanish. In 1621 the States-General did charter such a corporation, but by then Usselinx was disgruntled over insufficient Dutch appreciation of his genius. He traveled to several northern cities, singing commercial rhapsodies. One of his auditors was King Gustavus Adolphus of Sweden, who was so impressed that he asked Usselinx to create a Swedish company to trade with Asia, Africa, America, and "Magellanica." Usselinx' glowing dream of ships full of pepper, ivory, camphor, jewels, silks, coffee, tea, gold, and spices unloading (at an immense profit) in the Baltic never was realized. Capital for the company did not materialize from the Swedes, hard pressed by war. But his blandishments probably helped to stir up Swedish interest in a small fur-trading colony that they planted on the lower Delaware River in 1638.

Meanwhile, Usselinx' brain child, the Dutch West India Company, had set up posts at Fort Orange (Albany) in 1624, and in New Amsterdam (New York City) the next year. A year later, the original governor was replaced by Peter Minuit. Minuit, too, is an early example of Americanization. Like Samuel de Champlain or John Smith, he was a European whose own country filled no special place in his heart and who could therefore become totally attached to the promise of the New World. For seven years Minuit sweated to make New Netherland a profitable fur-trading and farming center, but he managed to accomplish little more than to enter American history books as the purchaser of Manhattan Island for an estimated twenty-four dollars' worth of trinkets.

Replaced, he returned home but could not remain downcast for long while any American prospects were in the offing. He had bought some land in the Delaware Valley, along with Samuel Blommaert, a copper and brass merchant from Amsterdam, always interested in colonial markets for his wares. After an unsuccessful attempt to get the Dutch to plant a new settlement on the Delaware, he traveled to Sweden, exercised his persuasive talents, and was hired to start *Sweden's* colony. After getting it organized, he started back to Europe for fresh recruiting and fund raising. Stopping in the West Indian harbor of St. Christopher, he went aboard a Rotterdam vessel lying at anchor for a visit. A storm arose, blew the ship out to sea, and he disappeared forever. Thus did Minuit leave his bones in the New World and his spirit to generations of land speculators and salesmen of railroad, oil, and mining stocks who came after him in American history.

Technically the Dutch settlements in the future United States were a failure. They were established on territory claimed by England at a time when Holland was not in a strong position to contest matters. The Dutch spread themselves too thin, and in arrangements bound to provoke disputes that they would lose.

Wouter Van Twiller, the governor of New Netherland who took over in 1633, established a fort at Hartford just before the English founded a number of settlements in the Connecticut Valley. Willem Kieft, who ruled from 1637 to 1647, provoked cruel and needless battles with the Indians. Peter Stuyvesant, the last Dutch governor on Manhattan, who held the position from 1647 to 1664, rashly squandered funds in overthrowing and capturing the Swedish settlement on the Delaware in 1655, though the Netherlanders themselves could not afford to take it over. All the governors quarreled bitterly with their own people in New Amsterdam —Stuyvesant so violently that when an English fleet finally appeared in the Narrows in 1664, claiming the city for the Duke of York, the splenetic one-legged governor was deserted by his own burghers. They insisted on—and obtained—surrender, when he wanted to fight.

Despite the political weaknesses of the Dutch, they set an impress on the life of Americans yet unborn. Of all the early immigrants, they made their style felt most vigorously. Although the initial settlement around Fort Orange remained tiny, a new policy in 1629 allowed colonizers to carve out great estates, known as patroonships, from choice lands along the Hudson, provided they brought (or sent) numbers of emigrants to populate them. Under that dispensation, the Dutch began to fulfill the Dutch West India Company's charter obligation of "the peopling of those fruitful and unsettled parts." The 270-odd settlers of 1628 grew in number until, by the time of New Amsterdam's capture, much of the Hudson Valley was Dutch in appearance. From as far north as Rensselaerswyck (near the present-day Troy), sloops loaded the produce of good Dutch farmsteads—beef, pork, butter, cheese, turnips, and carrots—and carried them to Manhattan markets.

The Hollanders pushed out into New Jersey, Long Island, and Connecticut like twentieth-century New York commuters. Michael Paauw bought land in New Jersey and Staten Island that he named Pavonia. It is not as well known today as Breuckelen (transformed into Brooklyn) or the Bronx (named for the tract of land once owned by Jonas Bronck) or Yonkers, an Anglicization of the Dutch *Jonker*, an estate holder. Dutch names persist everywhere in New York State (and New Jersey) like baggy-trousered, wide-hatted ghosts of Dutchmen, now gone, who once looked with satisfaction on their American lands.

New Amsterdam itself became a model Dutch town. Gabled houses turned narrow fronts to the street. Tradesmen went home, entered through brick-faced doorways and ascended to cozy rooms where, under

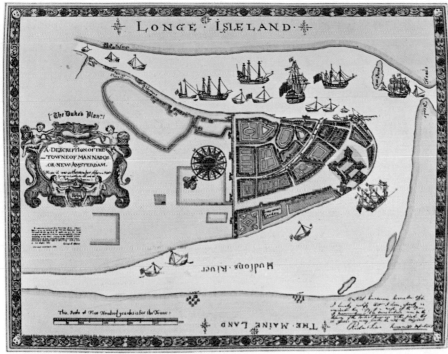

The plan of New Amsterdam, a miniature Dutch trading city, was drawn in 1661, three years before Governor Peter Stuyvesant, above, surrendered the town to the English.

tiled roofs, windows with tiny panes illuminated polished delftware. Tulips danced in back yards. Housewives proudly set out their *crullers* and *cookies*. *Scows* plied the rivers. On snowy winter days, one got around by *sleigh*, and when December arrived, children excitedly dreamed of the visit of *Santa Claus*.

But New Amsterdam was more than simply a Dutch exclave in America. The Hollanders' tolerance of dissent spread from old to New Amsterdam. True, the Dutch Reformed Church was the official, and Calvinistic, propagator of the colony's religious outlook. And the profits of the settlement were meant for Dutch bank accounts and no others. Yet from the start, New Netherland recruited from all nationalities, perhaps because the hearth-loving Dutch themselves emigrated reluctantly. The first boatload of settlers shipped to New Amsterdam were French-speaking Walloons. French Huguenots, Danes, Italians, and Spaniards soon were included in the populace. The first Jews in the area of the future United States came from Brazil to New Amsterdam in 1654 and were allowed the free exercise of their faith. (They were, however, put under certain civic restrictions; they could not, for example, serve in the town's defense forces, a deprivation of which they soon complained.)

Observers were quick to comment on the polyglot nature of the settlement. It has been claimed, perhaps improbably, that as early as 1629 some fourteen languages were spoken in the streets of the tiny village. In 1643 the French missionary Isaac Jogues

reported hearing eighteen. By the time of the settlement's fall to the English, it was a lively port city. Indians, sailors, and African slaves (the latter brought in for domestic service by the imperturbable and busy Dutch "blackbirders") jostled each other in the lanes; and despite the Dutch Reformed Church's strictures, the town was known for the presence, in Peter Stuyvesant's words, of many "rumshops and houses where nothing can be had but beer and tobacco."

In 1809 the young Washington Irving wrote his playful *History of New York . . . by Diedrich Knickerbocker*. This portrait of the outpost as a community of fat, guzzling, pipe-smoking Dutchmen is a comic distortion, but it suggests the kind of easygoing, cosmopolitan spirit that made New Amsterdam unique among early American towns, and a worthy predecessor of an internationally oriented New York City three hundred years later.

Thus, when the century of the Baroque ended, a beginning had been made in North America. Uprooted Europeans had adventured into the void of unmapped lands, looking for the realization of their various hopes. They had planted themselves and their national customs at several points in the unknown. They had outlasted grim challenges—and clung on. European flags flew over their settlements; European laws, institutions, and customs structured their lives, their beliefs, their tongues, and their decorative arts. Yet these transplanted Europeans were already demonstrating what it was like to become Americans.

Lush virgin forests greeted the land-hungry settlers from Europe.

THE ENGLISH IMPRINT

As THE NINETEENTH CENTURY entered its last years, some euphoric Americans liked nothing better than to expound on the dazzling future of what they called "the Anglo-Saxon peoples." It was a time when the spirit of Darwin hovered above the intellectual deeps, and when certain patriots marched to the cadence of a social theory that pressed biology into the service of chauvinism. The outlines of this theory were simple: the degree of a nation's success was determined by the supposed racial inheritance of its populace. The world's two most "successful" nations—those which most happily combined self-government, wealth, command of technology—were Great Britain and the United States. It was clear that this was no mere accident but a scientifically comprehensible and inevitable development. Bloodlines were the basis. England was America's "mother country." It was England's law, letters, and social patterns that had been transplanted to the colonies that became a nation. And England itself had been settled, in dark antiquity, by invading Saxons and Danes and other tribes of vaguely Teutonic origin, who mingled with the native Britons and later received strains of Norman blood to produce the final Anglo-Saxon amalgam.

It was a little murky. At one point a leading American proponent of the Anglo-Saxon gospel, the Congregational clergyman Josiah Strong, referred to the chosen race as one of "the branches of the great German family," and only a few paragraphs farther on was counting one hundred and twenty million Anglo-Saxons by using "the term somewhat broadly to include all English-speaking peoples." (It was wavering of this sort that led the Irish-American humorist Finley Peter Dunne to have his fictional bartender-philosopher, Mr. Dooley,

remark that "An Anglo-Saxon . . . is a German that's forgot who was his parents.") But there was no ambiguity in the record of Anglo-Saxon triumph or in the promise of future Anglo-Saxon glory, especially for that larger portion of the postulated race that lived in the United States. "Here, also," wrote the Reverend Mr. Strong, "has been evolved the form of government consistent with the largest possible civil liberty. Furthermore, it is significant that the marked characteristics of this race are being here emphasized most." Those characteristics included "money-making power," plus "an instinct or genius for colonizing," as well as "intense and persistent energy," perhaps "the most forceful and tremendous energy in the world." It was clear to Strong that "God, with infinite wisdom and skill," was "training the Anglo-Saxon race" for an apotheosis that, as representative of "the largest liberty, the purest Christianity, the highest civilization," and other attributes, would spread itself over the earth. Earlier in the same work, he had quoted Darwin to the effect that there was "much truth in the belief that the wonderful progress of the United States, as well as the character of the people, are the results of natural selection." In this way Strong neatly enlisted both religion *and* evolution in the service of his prophecies, making them almost irresistible to the popular mind of his day.

This glorification of the Anglo-American connection made for a striking discontinuity in the narrative of American settlement. It assumed, in effect, two classes of migrants. Those settlers who did not speak English were truly strangers in the land, but those from Britain's fast-anchored isle were unconscious agents of destiny. Born to become Americans, they merely crossed

James I as seen by the portraitist Nicholas Hilliard

the Atlantic to reach a foreordained home. It was in this version of history that the distinction between "colonists" and "immigrants" took shape, and it is significant that the line was drawn at a turn-of-the-century hour of anxiety among "old stock" Americans over the rising tide of Southern and Eastern European newcomers to the United States.

The trouble with the Anglo-Saxon formulation was that it retroactively cheated thousands of seventeenth-century Englishmen out of their humanity. It made historical puppets of suffering people who had lived out the pains of their conscious choices like all other self-uprooted wanderers. The basic mold of the thirteen American colonies *was* English, certainly. The great initial plantings were England's, and its imprint on the land was the most distinctive, the most visible, the most determinative of things to come. But the Englishmen who dared the Atlantic crossing and the added perils of the wilderness were themselves products of a Western European civilization. Their migration came at a particular moment in their own national history. The cultural and institutional baggage they brought was not packed by divine, invisible hands but by the immediate circumstances of their time: their birth, their nurture, their problems of livelihood and family rearing, no less than abstract desires for political and religious liberty.

They too were immigrants, fleeing to find opportunity abroad. They changed the land they found and were in turn changed by it, like millions who followed them. In the words of Stephen Vincent Benét:

. . . those that came were resolved to be Englishmen,
Gone to the world's end, but English every one,
And they ate the white corn-kernels, parched in the sun,
And they knew it not, but they'd not be English again.

The "immigrant experience," in short, was also an English experience. And it began as it did for all the footloose of the earth, with trouble in the national family.

It was under the Tudors that England first sent explorers to the New World—the Cabots, Hawkins, Frobisher, Drake, Gilbert, and the rest. But the actual planting of English settlements was accomplished almost entirely under the reign of the star-crossed Stuarts. James I came to the throne in 1603. Four years later Jamestown was planted, the seed from which Virginia grew. In 1681 Pennsylvania joined the family of English colonies in North America—the last save for latecoming Georgia (1732). In 1688, Parliament engineered the ouster of James II (a grandson of James I) from the kingship and the country itself, ending once and for all the Stuart claim to rule by divine right instead of by national consent through a representative body.

Between the accession of James I and the deposition of James II, the pressures that sent Englishmen swarming abroad built up relentlessly. James I, a burlesque of intelligent royalty, spent his reign in clumsy destruction of an equilibrium carefully created by Elizabeth and her ministers. True, her era had known its conflicts. The Church of England, for example, though firmly established, did not command the loyalties of great Catholic families on the one hand, or, on the other, of the Puritans who hoped to purge it of "Romish idolatry." Country squires and local officials were jealous of the powers of the nobility gathered at court in London. Lords and Commons quarreled with each other in Parliament, and both quarreled with the throne. In particular, the merchants and middling landowners represented in the Commons were eager for the right to discuss and criticize the royal ambitions and techniques for raising large revenues through taxes.

But the great Queen had astutely balanced these antiphonal zealotries and united the nation in support of her own person and the English achievements in war and trade. James started with this reservoir of good will and with the asset of being King of Scotland as well, thus terminating the traditional border conflicts. But he soon squandered these resources. He bestowed on favored friends monopolies in certain trades and industries, thus alienating important segments of the mercantile and artisan classes. He denied Puritan clergymen official status within the Church of England and further outraged them by enforcing rigid adherence to some of its detested ritual prescriptions. He rode hard on the law courts, traditional moderators of royal power, insisting that his prerogative enabled him to overrule their decisions. When, in 1616, James removed the Lord Chief Justice, Edward Coke, for insisting that the King's edicts were valid only when they added force to—and did not replace—existing law, sober Englishmen began to fear that they had to choose between two certainties that should have been harmonious, the royal will *and* the law's majesty. Finally, to compound his woes, James lavished wealth and power on certain associates like the Duke of Buckingham, and raised money through such ignoble expedients as the sale of offices and honors. When Parliament objected to such steps, the Stuart wrath thundered over Westminster. At the close of one session, James with his own hands seized the Parliamentary journal in which a "protestation" against his acts had been recorded and tore out the offending pages.

James died in 1625, but his son Charles I continued his disastrous policies. After many clashes with Parliament, he dissolved that body and tried to rule without it. But this course compelled him to resort to ever more abrasive forced loans and grants in order to sustain the cost of wars that never seemed to come to satisfactory resolutions—with the Spanish, the French, the Irish, even the Scots. Finally, after resistance to royal exactions had led to innumerable arrests, protests, angry sermons, and state trials, open fighting broke out between Parliamentary forces and those loyal to Charles. That was in 1642. By 1646 the "New Model Army," led by the fiercely Puritan country gentleman Oliver Cromwell, had defeated the King. Parliament was not of one mind about what to do with its victory; its own ranks included every shade of religious and political opinion from high-church royalists whose quarrel was with Charles, not the monarchy, to ultrademocratic groups like the Levellers, who held that "every man that is to live under a government ought first by his own consent to put himself under that government." But Charles' obstinacy and Cromwell's seizure of power finally combined to produce the unthinkable: regicide. On January 30, 1649, before a great multitude at Whitehall, Charles I of England and Scotland was beheaded.

For eleven years, England was kingless. At first the "rump" Parliament ruled the Commonwealth, as it was by then called, but the real power lay with the army, and as almost always happens, that army's commander became dictator. Cromwell, established as Lord Protector, held together the country's discordant elements until his death in 1658. Then in 1660, recognizing that only around the magnetic symbols of royalty could the particles of society cohere, Parliament welcomed

Dubious homage was paid James II on this delft plate.

back the exiled older son of the murdered sovereign, as King Charles II.

For almost a full generation thereafter, England groped toward its eighteenth-century system—a Parliament with ultimate power, and a King whose great influence and prestige made him more than a puppet but less than an absolute ruler. The road was difficult, and was made more so by the second Charles, whose attachment to the Catholic Louis XIV of France aroused deep fears of a royal drive against Protestantism at home. When Charles died without legitimate issue in 1685 and was succeeded by his brother, James II, matters came quickly to a head. James was openly Catholic and refused to renounce his allegiance to the Pope, in spite of a Test Act requiring such renunciation of all officials. The nation had to choose between a legitimate Catholic monarch (and the possibility of endlessly continuing religious strife) and a Protestant ruler who was far down in the line of succession but acceptable to the great majority of Englishmen. Parliament made its decision and offered joint possession of the throne to Mary, Protestant daughter of James II, and to her Dutch husband, William of Orange, provided they could oust James II from the country. The thing was done, and the "Glorious Revolution" of 1688 was entered into the history books. A series of acts provided that Parliament must remain free from royal dissolution or harassment, that the judiciary must remain independent, and that religious dissenters must be granted freedom of worship.

Even in such sketchy outline, the course of British

history in the seventeenth century demonstrates its solid impact on the future of America. Especially after 1688, colonial legislatures considered themselves to be little parliaments, and the royal governors to be surrogate Kings—properly kept in line on approved Whig principles. (The Whigs were the pro-Parliamentary party in English politics.) Moreover, the leaders of the American resistance to Britain after 1760 long insisted that they were claiming no more than the rights of Englishmen, established by the Glorious Revolution. Only the obduracy of London forced them finally to change that tune and demand the liberties of Americans. American constitutional democracy owes much of its form to the fact of English transatlantic migration at the very time that English democracy was assuming its own patterns. To that extent the Anglo-Saxon mythmakers were correct, except that they insisted on calling a series of historically connected events a fulfillment of divine or scientific law. They also overlooked the many contributions of European thinkers to English libertarian theory.

But there is more. The riven England of Puritanism, Parliamentary obstinacy, civil war, and regicide was the political matrix of America, and its anguish furnished the final cutting edge that severed thousands of its people from their home roots. The war itself was short. But for decades before and after, the land was in flux. The center of authority shifted erratically. A landholder, a clergyman, a scholar, a member of a guild, borough, or corporation, an "adventurer" (as an investor was called) went through years of uncertainty. Sometimes he was a friend to the party in power, and sometimes a quick turn of the wheel threatened him with expropriation, arrest, even death. The patronage of a nobleman could be a risk as well as an asset, depending on what side he took and who won. Even the justices, those guardians of stability, danced a tortured quickstep between conscience and fear of reprisal. With chronic misgivings about the future, no wonder that some men were tempted by the prospects of secure estates and freedom from harassment across what seemed an infinity of ocean.

Moreover, these conflicts took place against a background of economic revolution. Late in the sixteenth century, landowners began to react to rising prices for raw wool by "enclosing" their estates. This meant turning plowed fields into sheep meadows and driving off tenants, who thereupon became part of a mass of "idlers" flocking to the cities. There they could not be absorbed into the labor force readily because of guild restrictions, and there thousands of them languished as burdens on public charity, as potential crim-

inals, and as the prey of the press gangs that rounded up unwilling soldiers and sailors for the wars. The conviction that the country suffered from overpopulation was inescapable, and the cry of a country gentleman, John Winthrop, in 1629 was widely echoed: ". . . this lande growes wearye of her Inhabitantes, so as man which is the most pretious of all the Creatures is here more vile and base, then the earthe they treade upon: so as children, neighbours, and freindes (especially if they be poore) are rated the greatest burdens, which if things were right, would be the cheifest earthly blessings."

In an earlier, more pungent image, one clergyman had preached that "the people, blessed be God, do swarm in the land, as young bees in a hive. . . . The mightier, like old strong bees, thrust the weaker . . . out of their hives." The beehive was constantly shaken by depressions. From the opening of the century until 1603 times were hard, and again in the periods from 1619 to 1624, from 1629 to 1631, and from 1637 to 1640. In 1622 a preacher (and preachers were the most frequent public commentators on the state of the realm in that age of no journals and many pulpits) noted that the almshouses were full, that multitudes got their livelihood by begging, and what was most poignant, that "neither come these straits upon men, alwaies through intemperancy, ill husbandry, indiscretion, etc., as some thinke, but even the most wise, sober and discreet men goe often to the wall, when they have done their best. . . ."

Huddled into the cities, the poor were helpless before the plagues that swept devastatingly into their slums and then undiscriminatingly went on to lay low the proud and wealthy as well. Between 1603 and 1605 the provincial cities of Norwich, York, and Bristol each suffered about 3,000 deaths by plague (presumably the dread bubonic plague), exclusive of those who died of smallpox and other scourges. London suffered incredibly from the plague's visitations. Almost 35,000 succumbed in 1603 and a like number in 1625. In the latter year, 5,205 Londoners and another 4,000 in the suburbs of Westminster and Stepney died in a single week.

Imperiled by pestilence and starvation, many of the able-bodied men among the poor might have looked to impressment as an opportunity at least to eat and to be clothed. But they were disabused of any such notions by the facts of life as reported in the words of veterans. Typhus, scurvy, and other diseases incident to filth and improper diet ravaged the ranks as badly as enemy bullets. Of eight thousand troops sent on one expedition (to the Île de Ré in 1627), only three thousand sickly men returned. Small wonder that even "rogues" went to ghastly lengths to avoid service. In one group of impressed men, one hanged himself, another threw himself into the Thames, a third cut off the fingers of one hand, and another "put out his owne eyes with salt."

For thousands, then, life was as Thomas Hobbes had said it was for early man in his *Leviathan*, published in 1651: "nasty, brutish, and short." And those who endured it on such terms found nothing to encourage any fantasies of escape through a change in their social status. English ranks and degrees were firmly set. Each class had its particular style, and while each might have its discontents, none expected much alteration in its condition within England itself. The great landed families had little outward need for a change in their condition. They had builded themselves stately mansions, where they maintained a tradition of hospitality which required that no guest of a true aristocrat should leave until the spirit moved him. Travelers accompanied by large retinues might linger for months, eating, drinking, womanizing, gaming, gossiping, and pelting over privately owned hill and dale in pursuit of the flying deer. The host himself sometimes escaped these obligations only by going on a journey of his own, and this of course required not only a coach and outriders but also suitable expensive clothing for himself and in particular for his wife and daughters. It was all very picturesque —and its cost was staggering. (A suit for an exquisite blueblood might cost $1,000 in modern money.) Debt gnawed all too often at the most richly endowed landowner. His position rested, in many cases, on nothing more solid than title, style, manners, and insolvency. And nothing short of a spectacular piece of luck or royal preferment seemed likely to improve the situation. In a striking and fateful line of historical development, this pattern was to be faithfully and consciously emulated—

down to and including the debts—two centuries later by plantation owners in Virginia and elsewhere in the southern United States.

The country gentleman (one to whom the Heralds' College, in view of his property, had granted the right to "gentility") lived in a fashion less socially constrained than that of his titled neighbors and superiors. His home was full of the evidences of an active outdoor life, and he could, if so inclined, take a hand in the haying or harvesting of his own fields and orchards without loss of status. At worst, he might be a boorish Squire Western; at best, an Allworthy, dutifully serving as judge, social-service administrator, lay church leader, and moral pacesetter for the community. (Although *Tom Jones* was written in the mid-eighteenth century, country ways had not then changed much from Stuart times.) But the country squire, too, might be hard pressed. His religious views might bring him into trouble, and any combination of high taxes and falling agricultural prices could score his face with anxiety lines. If at such times he did not think of emigrating, his sons might well do so.

For the younger sons of country gentlemen and noblemen alike, who saw the estates of their fathers pass intact to their eldest brothers, the future presented the problem of finding socially acceptable careers. The choices might not yet have narrowed to the traditional handful—the army, the navy, the church, the bar— since in the seventeenth century none of these had quite become a profession in the modern sense. But in fact a landless young man who was neither scholarly, pious, nor martially minded was a prime candidate for a hazard of new fortunes by emigration.

Farther down the social scale, the yeoman might also try to enhance the value of his lands or the prospects

Londoners flee their city during the plague of 1630. Europe's frequent epidemics drove many to greener American pastures.

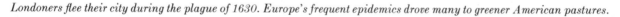

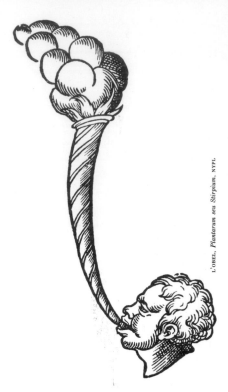

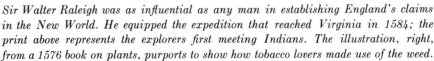

Sir Walter Raleigh was as influential as any man in establishing England's claims in the New World. He equipped the expedition that reached Virginia in 1584; the print above represents the explorers' first meeting Indians. The illustration, right, from a 1576 book on plants, purports to show how tobacco lovers made use of the weed.

of his children by taking fliers in New World ventures such as fishing and trading companies. If, in his emerging middle-class consciousness, America was not a haven for himself or his kin, he had no objection to investing his money there.

Fixed in the social mold below the landowning classes were the rural laborers, whose conditions became increasingly desperate as the era of the civil war wore on and were still a scandal as late as the nineteenth century. They lived in cottages not much different in quality, if one observer in the 1600s can be credited, from American Negro slave cabins—"no other windowes than to serve to let out the smoke, no other hangings, than what the spider affords, no other bedsteads, or table-bords, than the bare earth, no other bedding than plaine strawe, . . . no other Couches, or Chaires, or stooles, or fourmes, or benches, or Carpets, or Cushions, than what Nature hath wrought with her owne hands, the groundwork being the earth, and the greene grasse . . ." A farm worker received the equivalent of perhaps fifty to seventy-five dollars a year in modern money, and lived on a diet primarily of cheese, ale, and bread of a quality so poor that it led one Londoner to remark: "What makes the peasant grovel in his muck, humbling his crooked soul, but that he eats bread just in colour like it?" His clothes were rags; he shivered through a damp winter, worsened by a pinched supply of expensive firewood. (Not the least of America's attractions was expressed in 1629 by a settler who wrote from among its endless forests: "All Europe is not able to afford to make so great Fires as

New-England.") From this existence, no improvement on the condition of the urban poor, there was no exit for parents or children, unless a youngster became apprenticed to a craftsman and survived the risks of bad masters, floggings, and starvation to rise to artisan's rank. Even then, his social status was likely to improve little, for any attempt on his part (or that of his wife) to dress or act like his betters might well be deemed, as one writer expressed it in 1635, "pride and arrogance [which was to be] most justly rewarded with shame, reproach, and scorn."

Not that all of England groaned under oppression. There were urban and country tradesmen, estate managers, attorneys, shipowners, clerics, skilled butchers, brewers, goldbeaters, sailmakers, and the like who were at ease in Zion, untouched by political combat and even willing to adjust their religious practices to the prevailing winds. But it was also true that for the large mass of Englishmen of many classes, displaced or disaffected by civil brawls and economic upheavals, there seemed little opportunity to hew out a more satisfactory destiny. It was to such people as these that the promotional literature of the colonies came as a revelation. They were the ones whose eyes widened when they read in such pamphlets as *A Plaine Path-way to Plantations* (1624) that every emigrant might have a house "with one or two hundred acres of ground." They stirred in the pews when ministers declaimed on the text wherein God spoke to Abram and said: "Get thee out of thy country, and from thy kindred, and from thy father's house, unto a land that I will shew thee." It was to them that John Smith spoke when, after a description of the marvelous sights of Virginia and his hair-raising adventures among its beasts and savages, he asked: "Who can desire more content, that hath small meanes, or but only his merit to advance his fortunes, then to tread, and plant that ground he hath purchased by the hazard of his life? . . . what to such a minde can bee more pleasant, then planting and building a foundation for his Posteritie, got from the rude earth, by Gods blessing and his owne industrie . . . ?" The boldness of Smith in referring to hazards of life and the need of industry was matched by other writers such as Captain Christopher Levett: "I will not tell you that you may smell the corne-fields before you see the Land; neither must men think that corne doth grow naturally (or on trees), nor will the Deare come when they are called, or stand still and look on a man till he shoot . . . nor the fish leap into a kettle. . . . But certainly there is fowle, Deare, and Fish enough for the taking, if men be diligent. . . ."

These writings were among the first notes of an American challenge to the restless and bold everywhere: come here, wrestle with the rich but forbidding land for your fortune, and what you win will be not only independence but new selves and new lives. Millions of migrants would answer the call in the centuries that followed the New World's first imprint upon the consciousness of the Old. The Englishmen who went out from the realm of James and Charles were not essentially different from the other "races" that followed.

Of the eighty thousand Englishmen (close to two per cent of the population) who ventured out between 1620 and 1642 alone, not only to Virginia, New England, and Bermuda but to "Barbarie, India, Muscovie, and verie Calecute," it can be assumed that a goodly number endured the experience of some emigrants who arrived in London in need of board and lodging until their vessel sailed. They were taken in hand "by such men as we here call Spirits" and placed into boarding houses, "where once being entred [they] are kept as Prisoners untill a Master fetches them off; and they lye at charges in these places a moneth or more before they are taken away." It is also safe to guess that under the very best of conditions, the stormy Atlantic passage in small, cranky, wet, foul, overcrowded sailing ships was terrifying. The supplies of hard bread and preserved meat that were carried aboard for use after the fresh provisions gave out (in a matter of days) usually became wet, moldy, and verminous. In their close quarters, the passengers quickly passed on plague, smallpox, and respiratory diseases to each other, while scurvy, arising from the lack of fresh vegetables, was another

hazard. Sometimes, when a voyage was particularly prolonged by misfortune, discomfort escalated into nightmare. Not typical, perhaps, but always a possibility for an unlucky vessel, was the gruesome experience of the ship *Virginia Merchant*.

In 1649 she sailed for Virginia, with 350 passengers crowded into a hold designed for three hundred tons of cargo. It took her twenty-three days to reach Teneriffe. From there she labored to Bermuda. Even though some replenishment must then have been taken aboard, her provisions were so low that when she was delayed further in a gale off the Carolinas, the travelers nearly starved. The "infinite number of rats that all the voyage had been our plague," one passenger wrote, "we now were glad to make our prey to feed on. . . ." A grown rat sold for sixteen shillings. At one point a "Royalist gentleman," Colonel Henry Norwood, was put on an island with several others to fend for himself. (Whether or not this was at his own request is not clear.) One of the women in the party died. The others were advised to save themselves by eating her, which they proceeded to do. This group reached the settlements on the York River only after twenty-two weeks of this horror.

In such premonitory agonies, then, the English families who were to become "old stock" Americans—First Families of Virginia, *Mayflower* Passengers, Builders of the Bay Colony—endured the transition between hemispheres. Once they arrived on American shores, their

A 1624 print shows John Smith's most famous close call.

Adam's Grand Charter

From the start of the settlements at Jamestown and Plymouth the incoming Europeans had, among other motives, a sense of mission. Of all the many qualities and attitudes that they and the American Indians misunderstood in each other, this was one of the most important. The sense of mission on the one side and the inability to comprehend it on the other worked to the violent disadvantage of the Indians. *"Wee hope to plant a nation,/where none before hath stood,"* proclaimed a colonist-poet, home from Virginia, early in the seventeenth century:

> To glorifie the Lord tis done,
> and to no other end:
> He that would crosse so good a worke,
> to God can be no friend. . . .

Strong in the belief that they were fulfilling God's command, those who founded the wilderness villages with names that rang of home—Lancaster and Marlborough, Sandwich and Northampton and New London—expanded into the Indian domain, displacing Nipmucks, Narragansets, Pequots, Mohegans.

Their conviction was rationalized and fortified by a sermon preached in 1630 by the Reverend John Cotton. His audience was John Winthrop's Puritan company, then preparing to sail from Southampton, England. "Now God makes room for a people 3 wayes," said the Reverend Mr. Cotton:

"First, when he casts out the enemies of a people before them by lawfull warre with the inhabitants, which God cals them unto: as in *Ps. 44. 2. Thou didst drive out the heathen before them.* But this course of warring against others, & driving them out without provocation, depends upon speciall Commission from God, or else it is not imitable.

"Secondly, when he gives a forreigne people favour in the eyes of any native people to come and sit downe with them either by way of purchase, as *Abraham* did obtaine the field of *Machpelah*; or else when they give it in courtesie, as *Pharaoh* did the land of *Goshen* unto the sons of *Jacob*.

"Thirdly, when hee makes a Countrey though not altogether void of inhabitants, yet voyd in that place where they reside. . . . there is liberty for the sonne of *Adam* or *Noah* to come and inhabite, though they neither buy it, nor aske their leaves. . . . in a vacant soyle, hee that taketh possession of it, and bestoweth culture and husbandry upon it, his Right it is. And the ground of this is from the grand Charter given to *Adam* and his posterity in Paradise, *Gen.* 1. 28. *Multiply, and replenish the earth, and subdue it.* If therefore any sonne of *Adam* come and finde a place empty, he hath liberty to come, and fill, and subdue the earth there."

The early arrivals from Europe, weak in numbers, bargained with the Indians for village sites and for the right to stay. But the Indians, besides being wholly unaware of "the grand Charter given to *Adam*," had little understanding of the concept of owning land: their lives were inextricably bound to the land; it had borne them; it was a spiritual mother; the tribal group hunted and fished and farmed and lived on it and passed it on not from one individual to another but from generation to generation. When they traded or gave land to the Europeans, they believed they were giving simply the right to share the land. All at once they found themselves excluded from their "vacant" hunting grounds and fishing sites, and trouble came. And the trouble's end, as in King Philip's War of 1675–76, was "lawfull," according to the Book: *"Thou didst drive out the heathen before them."*

One encounter, painted about 1700

The pattern was repeated continuously as the frontier moved west, with the Indians unprepared to deal with the white men on terms understood by both sides—except the brutal ones of battle. Treated as heathen and driven out of their ancestral lands, or else selling what was not, in their way of living, actually salable, the Indians gave way before a tidal wave of men, sons of Adam, whose goal was to *"multiply, and replenish the earth, and subdue it."*

history tends to be absorbed into the traditional framework of institutional chronicles: the record of how communities, land-tenure systems, governments, churches, courts, and corporations were created, and of how diplomacy and war and internal migration expanded the boundaries of old settlements and inspired the creation of new ones. Yet there is another facet to the story. There is the matter of how the human material of colonies, the living souls who were "planted," chose their goals and dealt with the iron reality of their new surroundings. These first English comers were not living Anglo-Saxon ancestral portraits but restless, frightened, angry, hopeful people, trailing sundry pasts behind them. The amalgam of new-settlement society was different for the different colonies, but a few serve particularly well as paradigms for later modes of migration.

Though it did not remain one, pioneer Virginia began as a company venture. Its initial settlers were brought out by a corporation as employees of different ranks, much as Irish and Chinese labor gangs would be imported to lay rails across the Great West in the 1860s. It was several years before Virginia's promoters sounded the call for stable, family-sized groups to take up private lands and plant farms in the wilderness.

Plymouth Colony, where the "Pilgrims" landed in 1620, and Massachusetts Bay, founded in 1629, represented a different design. The leaders of both colonies were bound cohesively by shared religious sentiments. They emigrated in groups, with two purposes in mind. One was the well-advertised motive (historically speaking) of creating an atmosphere free from official harassment in matters of worship. But they were likewise eager to build a stable economic base under their communities. In the case of the Puritan gentry who established Massachusetts, they could have remained in England as investors, reaping the profits of farms and fisheries whose harvests were gleaned by the sweat and perils of others. Instead, they chose to move to the hazardous New World themselves. Both Pilgrims and Puritans were forerunners of other groups that in later centuries set out from Europe, bought virgin land in wholesale tracts, planned towns, dealt out tasks and properties to members, and set their roots in fresh soil as corporate bodies (until, almost invariably, the frontier's attraction for rampant individualism broke them up). The script is a frequently repeated one of likeminded souls, huddled together for mutual security in new surroundings.

Pennsylvania and Georgia, founded respectively in 1681 and 1732, were of mixed parentage. Both were intended to return revenue, and from the start both offered opportunities for individual planters to purchase land and settle down to propertied futures, just as earlier arrivals had been doing in the New World for decades. But both these colonies were also at least partly Utopian. They were founded by strong men of philanthropic bent, who hoped that the good impulses in the human breast might prevail over the evil, especially in an experimental setting. William Penn and James Oglethorpe shared a dream that in a new world untainted by the clotted injustices of the past, a better life could be built by fallible mortals. The human material available to both men sometimes failed them, but their vision of America as the place where the human spirit could be refined to a new purity endured as a basic theme in the continuing story of migration to America. Whether the transplanting process was company-induced, part of a voluntary group plan, nursed by philanthropy, or simply inspired by individual ambition, it rested on a kind of optimism about human prospects. Perhaps without such optimism the process would have been unendurable.

The first Virginians were living witnesses of what commercial ambition could project in the way of fantasy, given only scanty evidence to work with. The London Company, authorized to plant a colony anywhere between the 34th and 41st parallels North Latitude, had no clear idea what the land might produce. Its directors instructed the founding expedition, which left England in December of 1606, to establish a colony, look for a possible passage to the "South Sea," and explore the mineral resources of the area—which would include a search for gold. Yet the hope of turning Virginia into a gold-producing community or one that manufactured luxury goods of any kind was wildly unjustified. The initial phase of colonization was a brutal struggle for mere survival. The English "immigrants" who landed at Jamestown found themselves unprepared to survive a wilderness winter. Their inadequate supplies of food ran out, and the "bloudie Fluxe" and other diseases began to kill off the 104 men who remained after Captain Christopher Newport sailed back to England for fresh provisions, settlers, and tools. In the very midst of a land that offered, George Percy recalled, "a fruitful soile" and a great store of wild fruits and game, the adventurers who were not destroyed by disease endured famine. Their food was "but a small Can of Barlie sod in water, to five men a day, our drinke cold water taken out of the River, which was at a floud verie salt, at a low tide full of slime and filth. . . ." For five months they suffered this "miserable distresse," the living trying to shut their ears to "the pitifull murmurings and out-cries of our sick men without reliefe," several of whom died each night. ("In the morning, their bodies trailed out of their Cabines like Dogges to be buried.") Not until the Indians brought "Bread, Corne, Fish and Flesh in great plentie" was a reprieve for the group assured.

The London promoters, still hopeful, sent out German and Polish experts in the manufacture of glass, pitch, tar, and soap with the second "supply" of men and goods to Virginia. But in the face of the evidence, able observers on both sides of the Atlantic were beginning to realize that successful "plantations" required a different order of priorities. In Virginia itself, the controversial Captain John Smith, who was on the governing council from the beginning and was in charge of the new colony from September, 1608, to September, 1609, had decided that the horrors of the first year were not entirely due to God's dispensation but to bad management and laziness. "Most of our chiefest men," he reported in a hastily written pamphlet printed in England in 1608, were "either sicke or discontented, the rest being in such dispaire, as they would rather starve and rot with idleness, then be perswaded to do any thing for their owne reliefe without constraint. . . ."

Captain Smith was not reluctant to apply constraint. He put men to work planting and gathering for the common store, and kept them at work by the threat of imprisonment, whipping, and even hanging—a policy followed by subsequent governors for several years. He achieved these reforms in intervals between exploring expeditions, combats with the Indians, and a great deal of enthusiastic note-taking on the wonders of Virginia. Historians are still stung to debate by Smith. His own accounts of his colorful life include episodes that have the flavor of Baron Munchausen: captivity by the Turks when he was a soldier of fortune in Europe; an escape assisted by a lady—one of many—smitten with his charms; single combat with three Turkish champions, whose heads he cut off one after another; a journey into Russia, where he was reduced on occasion to beggary; and, of course, the famous tale of capture and condemnation by Powhatan, and rescue by Pocahontas. He may have been an inveterate liar, though the evidence is by no means clearly against him. What is certain is that his energy and drive in the early days of the Jamestown undertaking put indispensable backbone into the others present, even those who hated him. His zest for the virgin land, his absolute fearlessness in the face of its challenges, his dedication, from 1608 (when he was only twenty-eight years old) until his death in 1631, to "Virginia" and "New England," and finally his strong sense that life was spacious and inviting on the outer limits of civilization—all qualify him as a candidate for that select company of truly Americanized Europeans of the colonial era.

If Smith and his successors sensed that what Virginia needed was a more prosaic and workmanlike kind of migrant—a digger and builder, and not a simple fortune seeker—the company officials in London were beginning to react in somewhat the same way. The groups that were sent out in 1608 and 1609, the latter a contingent of settlers six hundred strong, included in their baggage many more items of hardware (andirons, tongs, spits, nails, bolts, hinges, latches, scales, and pots), supplies of such basic tools as augers, shears, knives, hatchets, hammers, and chisels, enough dried fruits and vegetables, cheeses, fish, meat, and flour to last out the first year, and seeds for the planting of cabbages, turnips, lettuce, onions, carrots, and the like against future needs. (There is no actual record of what the 1609 supply included, but inventories of later cargoes suggest the pattern.)

Still, it was touch and go whether the colony would survive. When Sir Thomas Gates, the new acting governor, arrived in May, 1610, only some sixty settlers were left, and Jamestown was in ruins. The palisades of the fort were down, the gates sagged on the hinges, empty cabins ("whose owners, untimely death had taken newly from them," Gates wrote) had been dismantled for fuel, and the Indians were "as fast killing without as the famine and pestilence within." The town was abandoned in June, but a rescue mission arrived and coaxed the enterprise back to life. Four years later a solid economic foundation was laid when the first crop of tobacco was shipped back to the mother country. From then on, a shift in the quality, or more precisely in the aims, of the incoming migrants was discernible. For a long time, those already on hand continued to complain of the poor quality of the new arrivals, thus sounding another note that would be struck again and again throughout the history of immigration to America. While one settler wrote to London denouncing his superiors for sending "lascivious sonnes, masters of bad servants and wives of ill husbands," Sir Thomas Dale wistfully asserted that "this country" would be the equal of any in Europe "if it be inhabited with good people." Changes in policy were then in the offing that would attract those defined by Dale as "good people"—family heads, landowners, and craftsmen.

In 1614, Dale, by then governor, initiated a program of land-grant incentives amounting to perhaps three acres per person. Thereafter it became more and more common to offer the bait of cheap land to would-be settlers. About 1617, the company began to encourage groups of "adventurers" to band together in associations and migrate en masse. These "hundreds" (although that was not always the number involved) were expected to outfit themselves, and to include among their numbers not only tenants to work the land but also a minister, a physician, servants, and governing officials. They would be given much larger homesteads—as many as fifty acres for each member of the party—and the right to govern their estates, provided they made no ordinances repugnant to English law or the parent company's regulations. The offer of fifty acres for each immigrant landed, a gift known as a "headright," was later made to individual family heads, ship captains, and even single men who would get themselves across the ocean, a condition sometimes met only by signing a contract of indenture to work as someone's servant for a term of years, in exchange for passage money. It was an arduous route to landownership—but one open only in the colonies, not in England itself.

In effect, the Londoners were subcontracting the task of recruiting Englishmen to go to Virginia. They themselves continued to solicit municipalities for orphans, imprisoned debtors, and other social failures at home to make up the passenger lists of Virginia-bound ships. But they were moving toward a new system, wherein the colonizers would not be employees but citizens. Symbolic was a shipment of one hundred "young and uncorrupt maids to make wives to the inhabitants and by that means to make the men more settled and less moveable." What was emerging was not merely a plantation but a society. Many years later, emigration agencies that sent entire shiploads of workers and their families to the shores of the United States would be accused of dumping "hordes" of newcomers into the national community. Yet the practice had ancient and honorable American beginnings.

By 1624, when the London Company failed and the crown authorities took over the direct administration of Virginia, some five thousand white residents were there. Almost all had arrived during the preceding five years. There is no way of knowing how many had endured hunger, pestilence, and Indian attack as part of their personal experience of transplantation. Yet together they had created a community and written the first chapter in the record of the making of Americans.

The story of the small group known as the Pilgrims has been told so often, so inaccurately, and so sententiously that it seems impossible to endow it with a spark of novelty. Though it is not often considered typical of the immigration process, the leaders of the venture were Englishmen whose discontents at home led them along a rocky road of dislocation and severance from

JOHN BULMER

In 1571, William Brewster, his wife, and their four-year-old-son, William, moved to the village of Scrooby, Nottinghamshire. The elder William became bailiff and postmaster for Scrooby Manor, a vast complex of farms and villages belonging to the Archbishop of York. After his father's death in 1590, young William, founder of the Pilgrim Church, continued the same duties and lived, as had his father, in a venerable mansion at Scrooby Manor. King James's 1604 ordinance against private religious meetings compelled the dissenters—who called themselves the Scrooby Separatists—to meet secretly at Scrooby Manor until 1608, when Brewster lost his job as postmaster and the Separatist group soon set out for Holland. The mansion was finally torn down in 1637, and from its ruins the farmhouse shown above was built.

This nineteenth-century painting by William Halsall shows the
Mayflower, *covered with spray ice, at anchor in Plymouth Harbor,*
while a small boatload of Pilgrims heads for shore. The ship re-
mained at anchor for several months, providing shelter for many
Pilgrims while their houses were being built. The first English
child born in New England, Peregrine White, slept in the wicker
cradle at right. His name comes from the Latin word "peregrinus,"
or "stranger," from which the name "Pilgrim" is also derived.

known patterns to the ultimate haven in a new land.

They were not huddled masses yearning to breathe free. Their story began in the little town of Scrooby, where William Brewster was postmaster at the beginning of the seventeenth century. It was not a lowly office. Brewster was charged with accommodating and expediting travelers on government business as they picked their horse-drawn way along the main route to and from London. The safe conveyance of official dispatches was his responsibility, and to its exercise he brought an unfinished Cambridge education and experience as an aide to Sir William Davison, one of Queen Elizabeth's secretaries of state. Politically speaking, Brewster was a loyal subject. In religious terms, however, he was a rebel in the eyes of English officialdom. Like his close associate, Pastor John Robinson, and a number of other Scrooby folk, Brewster was a Separatist. The Separatists went further than the Puritans; whereas Puritanism hoped to save the Anglican Church from corruption and heresy by the zeal of reform from within, Separatism advocated that its followers leave the Church of England entirely and form self-governing congregations of "saints," owing allegiance to no bishop, archbishop, or any ecclesiastical official. To Englishmen who regarded church and state as inseparably joined props of the social order, such views were untenable. In repeated efforts to impose conformity, the law officers kept a close watch on the houses of the Scrooby Separatist congregation and even imprisoned a number of them. Such persecution drove many Separatists to flight, though it might mean the abandoning of homes and occupations.

One memorable flight occurred in 1608, according to the recollections of William Bradford, who lived to become a governor of Plymouth Colony and to record his experiences in *Of Plimmoth Plantation*. Bradford and a number of his coreligionists fled to the Netherlands, at that time a model of tolerance to religious refugees (just as nineteenth-century England was to offer sanctuary to political fugitives from all over the world). They settled first in Amsterdam and then in Leyden, where they practiced such homely trades as brewing, baking, and brickmaking, followed the leadership of community pillars like Brewster and Bradford, and for more than a decade enjoyed "much sweete and delightful societie and spiritual comforte together in the wayes of God."

But even in the Promised Land there were the surrounding Canaanites. The Leyden Separatists appreciated the hospitality of their Dutch hosts, but life was hard for *émigrés* and strangers; moreover, the younger people were falling, as Bradford noted, "into extrava-

Edward Winslow, who made the Pilgrims' first treaty with the Indians, sat for this portrait in 1651, five years after he and his son, Josiah, had returned to England. The picture is the only known authentic portrait of a Mayflower *Pilgrim.*

gante and dangerous courses, getting the raines off their neks. . . ." The elders of the congregation regarded the extravagant courses as essentially Netherlandish. What they were facing, without quite realizing it, was the possibility of assimilation into their new milieu, and, like many small and zealous religious communities in the later United States—the Amish, for example—they resisted it. The course of resistance, for them, lay in further flight. After due and solemn deliberation, they made arrangements to move in a body to Virginia. The Separatist community consisted at this point of the original Scrooby migrants plus others who had joined them in the Netherlands. Not all the faithful, however, proved willing and able to undertake the risks of the journey or life in the wilderness, so that by the time of the departure for America less than fifty of them actually took ship.

In the textbooks, religious liberty looms as the only consideration in the minds of the Pilgrim leaders as the year 1620 approached. In fact, they were occupied with more mundane considerations. Not only was it necessary to secure permission from the Virginia Company and its various offshoots to establish a settlement in "Virginia," but it was likewise imperative that they accumulate a stake to get themselves settled and devise some form of activity that would render their colony self-supporting. The problem was one that racked thousands of later migrants. The Pilgrims' solution was to rely on fishing as "the cheife, if not the only means to doe us good," and to raise funds by a method that was a compromise with an unholy world.

They made an agreement with a company, numbering some seventy partners, in England. Shares were sold to some merchant-investors who would never leave England. Some of the Pilgrims themselves were able to buy shares. And finally, as plans for departure matured, a number of people were added to the passenger manifest who were neither shareholders nor veterans of life in Leyden, but who were simply going out to increase the labor supply of the prospective settlement. Thus the initial company of settlers contained a smaller number of "saints" from Leyden than of "strangers," many of them willing communicants of Anglicanism, who were seeking in the New World "not spiritual salvation but economic opportunity," according to a recent historian of the voyage. There was some sharp bargaining between the religious leaders and their business-minded sponsors over how much time the migrants might spend in working for the company and how much on their own account, and on how the joint property of all the shareholders—those who stayed and those who went—should be divided at the end of the contract period of seven years. But in the end it was all settled, and the gist of the agreement was that the Pilgrims plunged themselves into debt for seven years in order to win title to their New World estates, just as individual indentured servants in other colonies sometimes labored seven years for a master to pay off a passage and earn a "headright." (The *Mayflower* carried some of them, too.) Or, as the Pilgrims themselves might have pointed out, just as Jacob served Laban seven years in order to win Rachel.

With such details settled, the group left England in August on two ships—the *Mayflower*, of 180 tons burden, and the sixty-ton *Speedwell*. The *Speedwell* was so leaky and unseaworthy that the expedition was forced to return to port and abandon her. One hundred and one passengers then crowded aboard the *Mayflower*, along with a crew of about fifty, and set out September 16, 1620, on their historic voyage. It was probably a better one, on the whole, than many later immigrants were to have. It took sixty-six days, during which the Pilgrims undoubtedly grew tired of constant wetness, unchanged clothing that must have reeked after the first fortnight, and a monotonous diet of bread, salt, beef, and beer. But the ship was clean, and only three or four crew members and one passenger died of illness, which was remarkable for the time. A boy, Oceanus Hopkins, was born at sea, and another, Peregrine White, on shipboard just before the landing in present-day Massachusetts. The saints and strangers had their quarrels, and the Pilgrims were especially disturbed by the profanity of one member of the crew. When he died suddenly of disease, they regarded it as "ye just hand of God upon him."

The details of the first landing on Cape Cod and the later disembarkation on the site of present-day Plymouth make up the prelude to a story much like that of the agony of Jamestown. During the relatively mild first winter, the men worked doggedly, putting up cabins of squared and sawed timber, storing food, and planting their few cannon. Weakened by their exertions and by an unbalanced diet, they fell prey to scurvy and typhus, and endured a ghastly period in their huts, during which the sick died off while the well performed the "homly and necessarie offices" they required. In March of 1621 an Indian came into camp, saying, "Welcome, Englishmen," a phrase he had learned from seasonal fishermen in Maine. Regaled with ship's biscuit, cheese, butter, wild duck, and brandy—and given a knife, bracelet, and ring—he departed to take the greetings of the Pilgrims to the Wampanoags. Subsequently the chieftain, Massasoit, appeared and made the acquaintance of the new settlers, who ultimately were taught the techniques of survival in New England.

By 1628 the colony was laid out on the slope of a hill along which two broad intersecting streets ran past houses, gardens, and stockades. It was patterned after an English village, predominantly lower-class (or at least lower middle-class) in flavor, with few formally educated men, ordained ministers, or evidences of schooling (though Brewster left a library of four hundred volumes at his death, and Bradford eighty). Yet they governed themselves more or less successfully. They were neither the saints they believed themselves to be nor figures in a pageant, but real people who had bootstrapped themselves into self-sufficiency in a wild new environment. They were the basic stuff out of which centuries of migration would be made.

Most of the leaders of the Puritan migrants to the Boston area in 1629 and later were wealthier and better educated than the Pilgrims, but the problems and processes there and in the other early colonies were similar. By the time the benevolent founders of Pennsylvania and Georgia undertook their plantings, the English migration was being mingled with other strains.

To a New World

William Penn once remarked that he wished all "my dear Country-Folks" who might have it in mind to emigrate to America would first "consider seriously the premises. . . ." These premises, Penn indicated, included "the present inconveniences" of moving to a new and largely unknown land every bit as much as they did the expectations of "future ease and Plenty. . . ." Consider them, he admonished his readers, "so that none may move rashly or from a fickle but [from a] solid mind. . . ." That would be good advice for all future migrants, but it was particularly so for those who mulled over the idea in the seventeenth and early eighteenth centuries. The ocean they would have to cross was hostile; the ships that bore them were slow and crowded and pestilent; the shore that greeted them presented unfamiliar challenges—however rich in possibilities it might also be. As is evidenced by some of the letters, articles, and narratives on the following pages, colonists frequently complained that the new life did not measure up to the advance billing of the promoters—that in fact getting there, besides meaning the risk of one's life, was expensive, the colonial managers sometimes dreadfully inept, the immigrants physically and emotionally unprepared, the Indians often terrifying, and starvation all too common. However, as with later groups of newly arrived Americans, there were many tenacious people among them, people who forced the land to accept their roots, and then bloomed children, farms, industries, and thriving communities.

MAGNUS, *Historia de Gentibus Septentrionalibus*, 1555, NYPL

"Pressing and Oppressing"

Three major forces—political oppression, religious persecution, and economic hardship—motivated the mass emigrations from England to America in the early seventeenth century. Accentuating these were the mounting strains of overcrowding, unemployment, undernourishment (and outright famine), disease, and the chronically high death rate of infants and mothers. Indeed, there probably were almost as many reasons for leaving as there were individuals who left. In the end the decision was a personal one, but one which, according to the testimony of many of those who migrated, was spurred by the realization that the future held less and less promise in "Merrie England."

During the sixteenth century the rising profits derived from the sale of raw wool impelled many landowners to convert their plowed fields into sheep pastures, thereby creating both a rise in food prices and widespread unemployment. In 1516 these acts of "enclosure" were vigorously attacked by Sir Thomas More in Utopia, Book I.

Your sheep, that were wont to be so meek and tame, are now become so great devourers and so wild that they eat up and swallow down the very men themselves. They consume, destroy, and devour whole fields, houses, and cities; for look in what part of the realm doth grow the finest, and therefore dearest wool, there noblemen and gentlemen, yea, and certain abbots, holy men, God wot! not contenting themselves with the yearly revenues and profits that were wont to grow to their forefathers and predecessors of their lands, nor being content that they live in rest and pleasure—nothing profiting, yea, much annoying the weal publick—leave no ground for tillage; they enclose all into pastures, they throw down houses, they pluck down towns, and leave nothing standing but only the church to be made a sheephouse. And, as though you lost no small quantity of ground by forests, chases, lands, and parks, those good holy men turn all dwelling places and all glebe lands into desolation and wilderness, enclosing many thousands acres of ground together within one pale or hedge [while those who formerly lived on the land,] poor, silly, wretched souls, men, women, husbands, wives, father-

The ratcatcher was kept busy.

less children, widows, and woeful mothers with young babes, were starving and homeless. And where many labourers had existed by field labour, only a single shepherd or herdsman was occupied.

In a promotional tract thought to have been written around 1620 by Robert Cushman, deacon and business agent of the Leyden congregation, the author described the grim life that was lived by most Englishmen.

Was there ever more suits in law, more envie, contempt and reproch then now adaies? *Abraham* and *Lot* departed asunder when there fell a breach betwixt them, which was occasioned by the straightnesse of the land: and surely I am perswaded, that howsoever the frailties of men are principall in all contentions, yet the straitnes of the place is such, as each man is faine to plucke his meanes as it were out of his neighbours

throat, there is such pressing and oppressing in towne and countrie, about Farmes, trades, traffique &c. so as a man can hardly any where set up a trade but he shall pull downe two of his neighbours.

The Townes abound with young trades-men, and the Hospitals are full of the Auncient, the country is replenished with new Farmers, and the Almeshouses are filled with old Labourers, many there are who get their living with bearing burdens, but mo[r]e are faine to burden the land with their whole bodies: multitudes get their meanes of life by prating, and so doe numbers more by begging. Neither come these straits upon man alwaies through intemperancy, ill husbandry, indiscretion, &c. as some thinke, but even the most wise, sober, and discreet men, goe often to the wall, when they have done their best. . . .

Overcrowding and unemployment forced London and even small English towns to deal with their own immigrant problem, by fining anyone who housed a stranger without first putting up security. The churchwardens of the village of Steeple Ashton promulgated these stringent rules.

It is ordered by this vestrie that ev'ry person or persons whatsoever which shall lett or sett any houseinge or dwellinge to any stranger and shall not first give good security for defending and saving harmeless the said inhabitants from the future charge as may happen by such stranger comeing to inhabite within the said parish and if any person shall doe to the contrary Its agreed that such person soe receiving such stranger shall be rated to the poor to 20s. moncthlie over and above his monethlie tax. . . .

When members of the Scrooby church emigrated to Holland in 1608, William Bradford was among them. Years later, after serving as governor of Plymouth Colony, Bradford recalled, in his History of Plimmoth Plantation, *the pressures borne by the Pilgrims in England and in Holland.*

[Unable to worship freely,] they could not long continue in any peaceable condition, but were hunted and persecuted on every side, so as their former afflictions were but as flea-bitings in comparison of these which now came upon them. For some were taken and clapt up in prison, others had their houses besett and watcht night and day, and hardly escaped their hands; and the most were faine to flie and leave their howses and habitations, and the means of their livelehood. Yet these and many other sharper things which affterward befell them, were no other than they looked for, and therfore were the better prepared to bear them by the assistance of Gods grace and spirite. Yet seeing them selves thus molested, and that there was no hope of their continuance ther, by a joynte consente they resolved to goe into the Low-Countries, where they heard was freedome of Religion for all men. . . .

Being thus constrained to leave their native soyle and countrie, their lands and livings, and all their freinds and famillier acquaintance, it was much, and thought marvelous by many. But to goe into a countrie they knew not (but by hearsay), wher they must learne a new language, and get their livings they knew not how, it being a dear [i.e., expensive] place, and subjecte to the miseries of warr, it was by many thought an adventure almost desperate, a case intolerable, and a miserie worse than death. Espetially seeing they were not acquainted with trads nor traffique, (by which that countrie doth subsiste,) but

Two men locked in the stocks—a common punishment in England

had only been used to a plaine countrie life, and the inocente trade of husbandrey.

Thomas Shepard, who with his wife and son set out from Harwich for New England in 1634, afterward recounted his London experiences in his Autobiography.

While my father & mother lived when I was about 3 yeare old there was a great plague in the Town of Towcester which swept away many in my fathers family, both sisters & servants; I being the youngest & best beloved of my mother was sent away the day the plague brake out; to live with my aged grandfather & grandmother in Fossecut, . . . I was left fatherles & motherles when I was about 10 yeares old. . . .

A sham cripple and the chief of his gang

The reasons which swayed me to come to N:E: [New England] were many; 1: I saw no call to any other place in old England nor way of subsistence in peace & comfort to me & my family; 2: diverse people in old England of my deare freends desired me to goe to N:E: there to live together & some went before & writ to me of providing a place for a company of us, one of which was John Bridge; & I saw diverse families of my Christian friends who were resolved thither to goe with me; 3: I saw the Lord departing from England when mr Hooker & mr Cotton were gone, & I saw the hearts of most of the godly set & bent that way & I did thinke I should feele many miseries if I stayd behind, 4: my judgement was then convinced not only of the evill of Caeremonies but of mixt communion & joyning with such in sacraments tho I ever judged it Lawfull to joyne with them in preaching, 5: I saw it my duty to desire the fruition of all gods ordinances, which I could not enjoy in old England; 6: my deare wife did much long to see me settled there in peace & so put me on to it; 7: although it was true I should stay & suffer for Christ yet I saw no rule for it now the Lord had opened a doore of escape; otherwise I did incline much to stay & suffer especially after our sea stormes; 8: tho my ends were mixt & I looked much to my own quiet, yet the Lord let me see the glory of those Liberties in N: England. . . .

51

Canaan Land

The mounting anxieties and unsettled conditions of their lives convinced growing numbers of Englishmen that their one hope was to leave England. But the Great Migration of a previously stay-at-home population occurred only when the forces driving men away from England were matched by forces drawing them to the New World. Beginning with the sermons and promotional tracts of the Virginia Company in 1609, an all-out advertising campaign was instituted "to educate the English public" in the "wonders of the New World called America." Given impetus by the reports of early colonists, the promotion soon succeeded in influencing thousands to seek new opportunities in America.

In this passage from a 1656 pamphlet, John Hammond, who lived in Virginia for nineteen years and in Maryland for two, wrote enthusiastically of America.

The Country [of Virginia] is not only plentifull but pleasant and profitable, pleasant in regard of the brightnesse of the weather, the many delightfull rivers, on which the inhabitants are settled (every man almost living in sight of a lovely river) the abundance of game, the extraordinary good neighbourhood and loving conversation they have one with the other. . . .

Several ways of advancement there are and imployments both for the learned and laborer, recreation for the gentry, traffique for the adventurer, congregations for the ministrie (and oh that God would stir up the hearts of more to go over, such as would teach good doctrine, and not paddle in faction, or state matters; they could not want maintenance, they would find an assisting, an imbracing, a conforming people). . . .

It is knowne (such preferment hath this Country rewarded the industrious with) that some from being wool-hoppers and of as mean and meaner imployment in England have here grown great merchants, and attained to the most eminent advancements the Country afforded. If men cannot gaine (by diligence) [es]tates in those parts (I speake not only of mine own opinion, but divers others, and something by experience) it will hardly be done, unless by meere lucke as gamesters thrive, and other accidentals in any other part whatsoever.

In Some Account of the Province of Pennsilvania, *William Penn used Scripture, heroic history, and colonial experience to prove the advantages of emigration.*

Colonies then are the Seeds of Nations begun and nourished by the care of wise and populous Countries; as conceiving them best for the increase of Humane Stock, and beneficial for Commerce.

Some of the wisest men in History have justly taken their Fame from this Design and Service: We read of the Reputation given on this account to Moses, Joshua and Caleb in Scripture-Records; and what Renown the Greek story yields to Lycurgus, Theseus, and those Greeks that Planted many parts of Asia. . . .

Those that go into a Foreign Plantation, their Industry there is worth more than if they stay'd at home, the Product of their Labour being in Commodities of a superiour Nature to those of this Country. For Instance; What is an improved Acre in Jamaica or Barbadoes worth to an improved Acre in England? We know 'tis threetimes the value, and the product of it comes for England, and is usually paid for in English Growth and Manufacture. . . .

John Smith's A Description of New England *optimistically argued the practicality of planting an English colony.*

Worthy is that person to starve that heere cannot live; if he have sense, strength and health: for there is no such penury of these blessings in any place, but that a hundred men may, in one houre or two, make their provisions for a day: and hee that hath experience to manage well these affaires, with fortie or thirtie honest industrious men, might well undertake (if they dwell in these parts) to subject the Salvages, and feed daily two or three hundred men, with as good corne, fish and flesh, as the earth hath of those kindes, and yet make that labor but their pleasure: provided that they have engins, that be proper for their purposes.

Who can desire more content, that hath small meanes; or but only his merit to advance his fortune, then to tread, and plant that ground hee hath purchased by the hazard of his life? If he have but the taste of virtue, and magnanimitie, what to such a minde can bee more pleasant, then planting and building a foundation for his Posteritie, gotte from the rude earth, by Gods blessing and his owne industrie, without prejudice to any? If hee have any graine of faith or zeale in Religion, what can hee doe lesse hurtfull to any; or more agreeable to God, then to seeke to convert those poore Salvages to know Christ, and humanitie, whose labors with discretion will triple requite thy charge and paines? What so truely sutes with honour and honestie, as the discovering things unknowne? erecting Townes, peopling Countries, informing the ignorant, reforming things unjust, teaching virtue; and gaine to our Native mother-countrie a kingdom to attend her; finde imployment for those that are idle, because they know not what to doe: so farre from wronging any, as to cause Posteritie to remember thee; and remembring thee, ever honour that remembrance with praise? . . .

When the Portugale and Spanyard had found the East and West Indies; how many did condemn themselves, that did not accept of that honest offer of Noble Columbus? who, upon our neglect, brought them to it, perswading our selves the world had no such places as they had found: and yet ever since wee finde, they still (from time to time) have found new Lands, new Nations, and trades, and still daily dooe finde both in Asia, Africa, Terra incognita, and America. . . .

Now he knowes little, that knowes not England may well spare many more people then Spaine, and is as well able to furnish them with all manner of necessaries.

In the same treatise, Smith went on to point up a moral: the success of the industrious Hollanders as opposed to the frequent disasters of the get-rich-quick conquistadors.

What an Army by Sea and Land, have they [the Dutch] long maintained in despite of one of the greatest Princes of the world? And never could the Spaniard with all his Mynes of golde and Silver, pay his debts, his friends, and army, halfe so truly, as the Hollanders stil have done by this contemptible trade of fish. . . .

Herring, Cod, and Ling, is that triplicitie that makes their wealth and shippings multiplicities, such as it is, and from which (few would thinke it) they yearly draw at least one million and a halfe of pounds starling. . . .

Some enthusiasts never left home. While Michael Drayton sat snug in England, he urged his compatriots to cross the sea.

You brave heroic minds,
Worthy your country's name,
   That honour still pursue,
   Go and subdue,
Whilst loitering hinds
Lurk here at home with shame.

Britons, you stay too long,
Quickly aboard bestow you,
   And with a merry gale
   Swell your stretchèd sail,
With vows as strong
As the winds that blow you.

Your course securely steer,
West and by South forth keep;
   Rocks, lee shores, nor shoals,
   When Eolus scowls,
You need not fear,
So absolute the deep.

And cheerfully at sea
Success you still entice,
   To get the pearl and gold,
   And ours to hold
VIRGINIA,
Earth's only paradise!

NOVA BRITANNIA.

OFFERING MOST

Excellent fruites by Planting in
VIRGINIA.

Exciting all such as be well affected
to further the same.

LONDON
Printed for SAMVEL MACHAM, and are to be sold at
his Shop in Pauls Church-yard, at the
signe of the Bul head.
1609.

Title page from a 1609 promotion tract

In one of the many pamphlets published in London, a List of Privileges outlined advantages for prospective Carolina settlers.

First, There is full and free Liberty of Conscience granted to all, so that no man is to be molested or called in question for matters of Religious Concern; but every one to be obedient to the Civil Government, worshipping God after their own way.

Secondly, There is freedom from Custom, for all Wine, Silk, Raisins, Currance, Oyl, Olives, and Almonds, that shall be raised in the Province for 7 years. . . .

Thirdly, Every Free-man and Free-woman that transport themselves and Servants by the 25 of March next, being 1667 shall have for Himself, Wife, Children, and Men-servants, for each 100 Acres of Land for him and his Heirs for ever, and for every Woman-servant and Slave 50 Acres, paying at most ½d. per Acre, *per annum*, in lieu of all demands, to the Lords Proprietors. . . .

Fourthly, Every Man-Servant at the expiration of their time, is to have of the Country a 100 Acres of Land to him and his heirs for ever, paying only ½d. per Acre, *per annum*, and the Women 50 Acres of Land on the same conditions; their Masters also are to allow them two Suits of Apparrel and Tools such as he is best able to work with, according to the Custom of the Countrey. . . .

Such as are here tormented with much care how to get worth to gain a Livelyhood, or that with their labour can hardly get a comfortable subsistance, shall do well to go to this place, where any man what-ever, that is but willing to take moderate pains, may be assured of a most comfortable subsistance, and be in a way to raise his fortunes far beyond what he could ever hope for in England. Let no man be troubled at the thoughts of being a Servant for 4 or 5 year, for I can assure you, that many men give money with their children to serve 7 years, to take more pains and fare nothing so well as the Servants in this Plantation will do. Then it is to be considered, that so soon as he is out of his [indentured] time, he hath Land, and Tools, and Clothes given him, and is in a way of advancement. . . .

If any Maid or single Woman have a desire to go over, they will think themselves in the Golden Age, when Men paid a Dowry for their Wives; for if they be but Civil, and under 50 years of Age, some honest Man or other, will purchase them for their Wives.

Out of Egypt

Appealing as the New World propaganda might sound, emigration was still a terrifying step into the unknown. Besides making the emotional and intellectual commitment to leave his home, his relatives, and his friends, the prospective colonist had to raise money for his passage and somehow transport himself and his possessions to one of the ports of embarkation. There he might require cheap lodging for weeks—or even months—while he bargained with ships' masters. Finally he faced a voyage at least five weeks long, and the probability of acute discomfort: there would be storms; he might go hungry, or fall ill. And one of every ten like him died before reaching America.

For England's religious nonconformists, leaving their native land was made difficult by a decree that forbade unlicensed emigration. Forced to travel clandestinely, the Pilgrims were often victims of extortionist sea captains, many of whom, as Governor William Bradford described in his History of Plimmoth Plantation, *cruelly betrayed their prospective passengers.*

There was a large companie of them purposed to get passage at Boston in Lincoln-shire, and for that end had hired a ship wholly to them selves, and made agreement with the master to be ready at a certaine day, and take them and their goods in, at a conveniente place, where they accordingly would all attende in readiness. So after long waiting, and large expences, though he kepte not [the appointed] day with them, yet he came at length and tooke them in, in the night. But when he had them and their goods abord, he betrayed them, having before hand complotted with the searchers and other officers so to doe; who tooke them, and put them into open boats, and there rifled and ransacked them, searching them to their shirts for money, yea even the women further then became modestie; and then carried them back into the towne, and made them a spectackle and wonder to the multitude, which came flocking on all sids to behold them. Being thus first . . . rifled, and stripte of their money, books, and much other goods, they were presented to the magistrates, and messengers sente to informe the lords of the Counsell of them; and so

they were commited to ward. Indeed the magistrates used them courteously, and shewed them what favour they could; but could not deliver them, till order came from the Counsell-table. But the issue was that after a months imprisonmente, the greatest parte were dismiste, and sent to the places from whence they came; but 7 of the principall [William Brewster was one of them] were still kept in prison, and bound over to the Assises. . . .

After several months, the Pilgrims arranged for passage on a Dutch ship. To shelter the women and children as they waited, they placed them aboard a bark.

But so it fell out, that they were there a day before the ship came, and the sea being rough, and the women very sicke, prevailed with the seamen to put into a creeke hardby, where they lay on ground at low water. The nexte morning the ship came, but they were fast, and could not stir until about noone. In the mean time, the ship master, perceiving how the matter was, sente his boate to be getting the men abord whom he saw ready, walking aboute the shore. But after the first boat full was gott abord, and she was ready to goe for more, the Master espied a great company, both horse and foote, with bills, and guns, and other weapons; for the countrie was raised to take them. The Dutch-man seeing that, swore his countries oath, "sacremente," and having the wind faire, weighed his Ancor, hoys[t]ed sayles, and away. But the poore men which were gott abord, were

in great distress for their wives and children, which they saw thus to be taken, and were left destitute of their helps; and them selves also, not having a cloth to shifte them with, more then they had on their backs, and some scarce a penny aboute them, all they had being abord the barke. It drew tears from their eyes, and any thing they had they would have given to have been ashore again; but all in vaine, there was no remedy, they must thus sadly part.

In Wonder-working Providence, *Captain Edward Johnson, a founder of Woburn, Massachusetts, bewailed the exorbitant cost of settling New England.*

And now they enter the Ships, should they have cast up what it would have cost to people New England before hand, the most strongest of Faith among them would certainly have staggered much, and very hardly have set saile. But behold and wonder at the admirable Acts of Christ, here it is cast up to thy hand, the passage of the persons that peopled New England cost ninety five thousand pounds; the Swine, Goates, Sheepe, Neate and Horse, cost to transport twelve thousand pound besides the price they cost; getting food for all persons for the time till they could bring the Woods to tillage amounted unto forty five thousand pounds; Nayles, Glasse and other Iron-worke for their meeting-houses, and other dwelling houses, before they could raise any meanes in the Country to purchase them, Eighteene thousand pounds: Armes, Powder, Bullet and Match, together with their great Artillery, twenty two thousand pounds: the whole sum amounts unto one hundred ninety two thousand pound, beside that which the Adventurers laid out in England, which was a small pittance compared with this, and indeed most of those that cast into this Banke were the chiefe Adventurers. Neither let any man thinke the sum above expressed did defray the whole charge of this Army, which amounts to above as much more. . . .

New World settlers suggested items to be brought along by future colonists. Below is a list of such necessities published in a 1635 pamphlet, A Relation of Maryland.

Fine Wheate-flower, close and well packed, to make puddings, etc. Clarret-wine burnt. Canary Sacke. Conserves, Marmalades, Suckets, and Spices. Sallet Oyle. Prunes to stew. Live Poultry. Rice, Butter, Holland-cheese, or old Cheshire, gammons of Bacon, Porke, dried Neates-tongues, Beefe packed up in Vinegar, some Weather-sheepe, meats baked in earthen potts, Leggs of Mutton minced, and stewed, and closed packed up in tried Sewet, or Butter, in earthen pots: Juyce of Limons, etc.

In 1656, a promoter described the sea voyage to Virginia as time "pleasantly passed away, though not with such choice plenty as the shore affords." Letters home from emigrants, however, depicted the crossing as anything but pleasant. Here, Lady Margaret Wyatt, wife of Sir Francis, the governor, complains bitterly to a stay-at-home sister in a letter written in 1623.

Deare Sister eare this you should have heard from me, had not th'extremitie of sickness till now hindered me. For our Shippe was so pestered with people and goods that we were so full of infection that after a while we saw little but throwing folkes over board: It pleased god to send me my helth till I came to shoare and 3 dayes after I fell sick but I thank god I am well recovered. Few else are left alive that came in that Shipp: for here have dyed the Husband, wife, children & servants: They tould me they sent the Shipp less pestered for me, but there never came Shipp so full to Virginia as ours. I had not so much as my Cabin free to my selfe. Our Capt[ain] seemed to be troubled at it, and . . . to make the people amendes dyed himselfe. Our Beer stunke so I could not endure the deck for it: This was our fortune at the Sea, and the land little better, for as well our people as our Cattle have dyed, that we are all undone, especially we that are new commers, and except our Freindes help us it will goe hard with us next Wynter, and who besides your selfe to send to, I know not: my Mother beeing so farr off that she could give me none when I came away: [your help] did me a great pleasure so did my [other] Sisters: butter & Bacon which if she talke of sending me a token, desire her from your selfe [that] it may [rather] be Butter & Cheese, for since th'Indyans & we fell out we dare not send a-hunting but with so many men as it is not worth their labour. . . .

Richard Norwood did not enjoy the voyage any more than did Lady Wyatt. He described his macabre crossing to his father.

It was the first of Aprill before we came to Virginia, & we were halfe starved for want of Victualls: for we were kept with stinking Beer & water: One pound of Bread & a quart of pease porridge was th'allowance for 5 men a day: which caused 9 or 10 of our Passengers to leave the Shipp and to stay in the West Indies (at St. Vincents) and XX dyed and all sick except 3 or 4. But we came well to or Journeyes end where we find victualls scarce & deare a Hen 15 s[hillings]: a Hogg X [pounds]: Meale XV [pounds] a hogshead. . . .

In a report to his friend Sir Simonds D'Ewes, who was considering emigrating, the Reverend Edmund Browne described a 1638 voyage that was relatively lucky.

We were often put into some feare of pyrates or men of warre, but our God preserved us. When wee had bin 3 weekes at sea the contagious Pox struck in amongst us, yet ordered by the Lords power, as if it had not bin infectious; I suppose some 30 had it, yet directly I think but one or 2 dyed. It was confined within one division in our ship, [the] middle decke, the gunroome being free unless some 2 or 3 children which had them sparingly, and all other roomes . . . were free & injoyed health.

A Voyage to Virginia:
OR,
The Valliant Souldier's Farwel to his Love.

Unto *Virginia* he's resolv'd to go,
She begs of him, that he would not do so;
But her Intreaties they are all in vain,
For he muft plow the curled Ocean Main:
At length (with forrow) he doth take his leave
And leaves his deareft Love at home to grieve.
To the Tune of, *She's gone and left me here alone.*

This broadside, printed about 1709, expressed the sentiments of many who had to leave their loved ones behind.

"The Naturals"

In 1584 Captain Arthur Barlowe rhapsodized over his first encounter with the natives of the New World—a "people most gentle, loving, and faithfull, void of all guile, and treason. . . ." Not all later colonists shared the captain's view. Their opinions varied widely, depending on the location of their settlements, the experiences of the natives with earlier pioneers, and the treatment of the Indians by the other settlers. Almost all colonists, however, shared an intense interest in the Indians whose lands they would sooner or later seize. Although some genuine trust developed between the two races, there remained mostly enmity—an enmity that would haunt both for centuries to come.

In writing of a 1606 voyage to Cape Ann, the French explorer Samuel de Champlain dismissed the Indians as racially inferior.

It would seem from their appearance that they have a good disposition, better than those of the north, but they are all in fact of no great worth. Even a slight intercourse with them gives you at once a knowledge of them. They are great thieves and, if they cannot lay hold of any thing with their hands, they try to do so with their feet, as we have oftentimes learned by experience. I am of the opinion that, if they had any thing to exchange with us, they would not give themselves to thieving. They bartered away to us their bows, arrows, and quivers, for pins and buttons; and if they had had anything else they would have done the same with it. It is necessary to be on one's guard against this people, and live in a state of distrust of them, yet without letting them perceive it.

The instructions carried on Captain Christopher Newport's 1606–07 Virginia voyage hardly were calculated to inspire amity between settlers and the native inhabitants.

You must have great care not to offend the naturals, if you can eschew it, and employ some few of your company to trade with them for corn and all other lasting victuals . . . , and this you must do before that they perceive you mean to plant among them. . . . Your discoverers that pass over land with hired guides must look well to them that they slip not from them, and for more assurance let them take a compass with them, and write down how far they go on every point of the compass, for that country having no way or path, if that your guides run from you in the great woods or desert, you shall hardly ever find a passage back. And how weary soever your soldiers be, let them never trust the country people with the carriage of their weapons, for if they run from you with your shot which they only fear, they will easily kill *them* [i.e., you] all with their arrows. And whensoever any of yours shoots before them, be sure that they be chosen out of your best marksmen, for if they see your learners miss what they aim at, they will think the weapon not so terrible, and thereby will be bold to assault you.

Above all things, do not advertise the killing of any of your men [so] that the country people may know it. If they perceive that [you] are but common men, and that with the loss of many of theirs they may diminish any part of yours, they will make many adventures upon you. . . . You shall also do well not to let them see or know of your sick men, if you have any. . . .

In a tract published in 1644, Johannes Megapolensis gave his impressions of the Mohawk Indians of New Netherland.

The people and Indians here in this country are like us Dutchmen in body and stature; some of them have well formed features, bodies and limbs; they all have black hair and eyes, but their skin is yellow. In summer they go naked, having only their private parts covered with a patch. The children and young folks to ten, twelve and fourteen years of age go stark naked. . . .

They likewise paint their faces red, blue, etc., and then they look like the Devil himself. They smear their heads with bear's-grease, which they all carry with them for this purpose in a small basket; they say they do it to make their hair grow better and to prevent their having lice. . . .

Describing the Indians of Virginia, Hugh Jones, like many early colonists, found causes for both admiration and contempt.

They are frequently at War with all their Neighbours, or most of them, and treat their Captive Prisoners very barbarously; either by scalping them (which I have seen) by ripping off the Crown of the Head, which they wear on a Thong by their Side as a signal Trophee and Token of Victory and Bravery. Sometimes they tie their Prisoners, and lead them bound to their Town, where with the most joyful Solemnity they kill them, often by thrusting in several Parts of their Bodies scewers of Light-wood which burn like Torches. . . .

They are so wonderfully quick-sighted, that they will swiftly pursue by *Eye* the Track of any Thing among the Trees, in the Leaves and Grass, as an Hound does by the Scent, where *we* can't perceive the least Mark or Footstep. . . .

Their Children almost as soon as born, are ty'd flat on their Backs to a Board; and so may be flung on the Ground, or put to lean against any Thing, or be slung over the Neck in Travelling, or hung upon a Bough, as Occasion requires.

This occasions them to be exactly strait; so that it is a Miracle to see a crooked or deformed *Indian*. . . .

An Instance of their resolute Stupidity and Obstinacy in receiving a new Custom, I have seen in the prodigious Trouble of bringing them to sell their Skins, and buy Gunpowder by Weight; for they could not apprehend the Power and Justice of the Stilliard [balance scale]; but with the Scales at Length they apprehended it tolerably well; though at first they insisted upon as much Gunpowder as the Skin weighed, which was much more than their Demand in Measure. They have Geographical Notions, as to the Situation of their own Country, and will find the way to very remote Places in a surprizing Manner. . . .

A Relation of Maryland, *published in London in 1635, wisely admonished future settlers to treat the natives decently.*

Experience hath taught us, that by kind and faire usage, the Natives are not onely become peaceable, but also friendly, and have upon all occasions performed as many friendly Offices to the English in Maryland, and New-England, as any neighbour or friend uses to do in the most Civill parts of Christendome: Therefore any wise man will hold it a far more just and reasonable way to treat the People of the Countrey well, thereby to induce them to civility, and to teach them the use of husbandry, and Mechanick trades, whereof they are capable, which may in time be very useful to the English; and the Planters to keepe themselves strong, and united in Townes, at least for a competent number, and then noe man can reasonably doubt, either surprise, or any other ill dealing from them.

One of the earliest drawings of an Iroquois, by a Frenchman in Canada around 1700

By 1679 the Indians of New York had been generally accepted into the colonial community and—as Jasper Danckaerts recorded in his journal—were preyed upon by tradesmen given to sharp practices.

I must here remark, in passing, that the people in this city who are most all traders in small articles, whenever they see an Indian enter the house, who they know has any money, they immediately set about getting hold of him, giving him rum to drink, whereby he is soon caught and becomes half a fool. If he should then buy any thing, he is doubly cheated, in the wares, and in the price. He is then urged to buy more drink, which they now make half water, and if he cannot drink it, they drink it themselves. They do not rest until they have cajoled him out of all his money, or most of it; and if that cannot be done in one day, they keep him, and let him lodge and sleep there, but in some out of the way place, down in the ground, guarding their merchandise and other property in the meantime, and always managing it so that the poor creature does not go away before he has given them all they want.

Abundance

The immigrants came, Sir Walter Raleigh said, "to seek new worlds for gold, for praise, for glory." Whatever the reasons, their first impressions of the land itself were usually exhilarating. Enticed by America's bountiful forests and grasslands, the settler from crowded Europe glimpsed a new life that also seemed to promise unbounded opportunities—to forget his past, to commit himself to the future, and to accomplish anything his own talents and energies permitted. The basic materials were there, but their use often proved very difficult. "Some of the newcomers," wrote one clergyman, "are almost at a stand, and do sigh to see how many trees they have to fell. . . ."

Any distress suffered on the voyage to America apparently was soon forgotten by one Master Graves, who sent this ecstatic report to old England from the New.

Thus much I can affirme in generall, that I never came in a more goodly Country in all my life, all things considered: if it hath not at any time beene manured and husbanded, yet it is very beautifull in open Lands, mixed with goodly woods, and againe open plaines, in some places five hundred Acres, some places more, some lesse, not much troublesome for to cleere for the Plough to goe in, no place barren, but on the tops of the Hills, the grasse & weedes grow up to a mans face, in the Lowlands & by fresh Rivers abundance of grasse and large Meddowes without any Tree or shrubbe to hinder the Sith [scythe] . . . every thing that is heere eyther sowne or planted prospereth farre better than in Old England: the increase of Corne is here farre beyond expectation, as I have seene here by experience in Barly, the which because it is so much above your conception I will not mention: And Cattell doe prosper very well, and those that are bredd heere farr greater than those with you in England. Vines doe grow heere plentifully laden with the biggest Grapes that ever I saw, some I have seen foure inches about, so that I am bold to say of this countrie, as it is commonly said in Germany of Hungaria, that for Cattel, Corne, and Wine it excelleth. We have many more hopefull commodities here in this countrie, the which time will teach to make

good use of: In the meane time wee abound with such things which next under God doe make us subsist, as Fish, Foule, Deere, and sundrie sorts of fruites, as Musk millions, water-millions, Indian-Pompions [pumpkins], Indian Pease, Beanes, & many other odde fruits that I cannot name, all which are made good and pleasant through this maine blessing of God, the healthfulnesse of the countrie which farre exceedeth all parts that ever I have beene in: It is observed that few or none doe heere fall sicke, unlesse of the Scurvy that they bring from aboard the Shippe with them, whereof I have cured some of my Companie only by labour.

SMITH, *Twee Scheeps-Togten* . . . , LEYDEN, 1707, NYPL

A German's version of bountiful Virginia

In a 1630 pamphlet, New-Englands Plantation, *one happy colonist waxed effusive over the health-bestowing climate.*

The Temper of the Aire of New-England is one speciall thing that commends this place. Experience doth manifest that there is hardly a more healthfull place to be found in the World that agreeth better with our English Bodyes. Many that have beene weake and sickly in old England, by comming hither have beene thoroughly healed and growne healthfull and strong. For here is an extraordinarie cleere and dry Aire that is of a most healing nature to all such as are of a Cold, Melancholy, Flegmatick, Reumaticke temper of body. None can more truly speake hereof by their owne experience than my selfe. My Friends that knew me can well tell how verie sickly I have been and continually in Physick, being much troubled with a tormenting paine through an extraordinarie weaknesse of my Stomacke, and abundance of Melancholike humors; but since I came hither on this Voyage, I thanke God I have had perfect health . . . and therefore I thinke it is a wise course for all cold complections to come to take Physicke in New-England: for a sup of New-England Aire is better than a whole draught of old Englands Ale.

. . . you have heard of the Earth, Water and Aire of New-England, now it may bee you expect something to bee said of the Fire proportionable to the rest of the Elements.

Indeed I thinke New-England may boast of this Element more than of all

the rest: for though it bee here somewhat cold in the winter, yet here we have plenty of Fire to warme us, and that a great deale cheaper then they sel Billets and Faggots in London: nay, all Europe is not able to afford to make so great Fires as New-England.

Thomas Newe hoped to emulate the careers of many successful Carolina colonists, first amassing capital through trade and then becoming a planter. These are his first impressions of Charles Town.

Most Honourd Father:

The 12th of this instant by the providence of God after a long and tedious passage we came to an Anchor against Charles town at 10 in the night in 3½ fathom water. . . . As for the Countrey I can say but little of it as yet on my one [own] knowledge, but what I hear from others. The Town which two years since had but 3 or 4 houses, hath now about a hundred houses in it, all which are wholy built of wood, tho here is excellent Brick made, but little of it. All things are very dear in the Town; milk 2d a quart, beefe 4d a pound, pork 3d, but far better than our English, the common drink of the Countrey is Molossus and water, I don't hear of any mault that is made hear as yet. The English Barly and Wheat do thrive very well, but the Indian corn being more hearty and profitable, the other is not much regarded. I am told that there is great plenty of all things in the [back] Countrey, whither I intend to go as soon as conveniently I can dispose of my goods, which I fear will not be soon, nor to such advantage as we expected. Several in the Country have great stocks of Cattle and they sell so well to new comers that they care not for killing, which is the reason provision is so dear in the Town, whilst they in the Country are furnisht with Venison, fish, and fowle by the Indians for trifles, and they that understand it make as good butter and cheese as most in England. . . . This is the first opportunity I have had to write since I came from England but I hope to find more opportunityes here, then I had at Sea. . . .

This ballad, composed about 1623 by a whimsical member of the Plymouth Colony, was passed along in spoken form until 1767, when the words—as remembered by a ninety-four-year-old woman—were at last committed to paper. It was published in the Massachusetts Spy *in 1774.*

The place where we live is a wilderness wood,
Where grass is much wanting that's fruitful and good.
Our mountains and hills and valleys below
Being commonly covered with ice and with snow;
And when the northwester with violence blows,
Then every man pulls his cap over his nose;
But if any's so hardy and will it withstand,
He forfeits a finger, a foot, or a hand.

When the spring opens we then take the hoe,
And make the ground ready to plant and to sow;
Our corn being planted and seed being sown,
The worms destroy much before it is grown;
And when it is growing, some spoil there is made
By birds and by squirrels that pluck up the blade;
E'en when it is grown to full corn in the ear
It is often destroyed by raccoons and deer.

And now our garments begin to grow thin,
And wool is much wanted to card and to spin;
If we can get a garment to cover without,
Our other in-garments are clout [patch] upon clout;

Our clothes we brought with us are often much torn,
They need to be clouted before they are worn;
But clouting our garments they hinder us nothing,
Clouts double, are warmer than single whole clothing!

If flesh meat be wanting to fill up our dish,
We have carrots and pumpkins and turnips and fish;
And, when we've a mind for a delicate dish,
We repair to the *clam-bank* and *there* we catch fish.
Instead of pottage and puddings and custards and pies,
Our pumpkins and parsnips are common supplies;
We have pumpkin at morning and pumpkin at noon;
If it was not for pumpkin we should be *undoon.*
If barley be wanting to make into malt,
We must be contented, and think it no fault;
For we can make liquor to sweeten our lips
Of pumpkins and parsnips and walnut tree chips.

Now while some are going, let others be coming,
For while liquor's boiling it must have a scumming;
But we will not blame them, for birds of a feather,
By seeking their fellows are flocking together.
But you whom the Lord intends hither to bring,
Forsake not the honey for fear of the sting;
But bring both a quiet and contented mind
And all needful blessings you surely will find.

"Miserable and Pittiful"

The initial excitement over arriving in the New World often soon gave way to despair. Instead of receiving a warm welcome, the travel-weary settlers stepped off their ships to face an untamed wilderness. Inadequate equipment, supplies, and skills, ill-chosen town sites, and divided leadership hindered their progress, while famine, imported pestilence, and Indian attacks threatened their very existence. But if the colonist found the Promised Land a disappointment, there was almost nothing he could do about it. Homesickness was a genuine and painful malady. An unhappy settler wrote of Virginia that "more do die here of the disease of theire minde than of theire body."

One wretched newcomer, Richard Ffrethorne, was sold by his parents into servitude with the Virginia Company. In March, 1622, he sent this letter to England.

Right Worshipfull this is to lett you understand that I am in a most miserable and pittiful Case both for want of meat and want of cloathes for we had meale and provision for twenty and there is ten dead, yett our provision will not laste till the Seaflower come in, for those servants that were there before us were allmost Pined [wasted away], and then they fell to feedinge soe hard of our provision that itt killed them that were ould Virginians as fast, as the scurvie & bloody fluxe [dysentery] did kill us new Virginians: for they were in such a Case by reason of the murder done all over the land that they Could not plant anythinge att all, and att everie Plantacion all of them for the most part were slaine and theyr howses & goods burnt. Some, the Indians kept alive and tooke them awaie with them, and nowe theise two Indians that they [we] have taken doe tell us that the Indians have 15 alive with them thus through theyr Roguery the land is ruinated and spoyled, and itt will not bee soe stronge againe not this 12 yeares. . . .

In 1623 Edward Hill described the conditions of the preceding year in Virginia and set forth his fears for the immediate future.

Now for the state of this Contrey, There was the first Massacre killd of our Eng-

lish 400 and odd persons: since [then] at tymes there have ben killd XX and odd And in this last Massacre there was cutt off by th'Indians a Pinnace, a Shallopp, and a small Boate with 26 men all in compleat Armour the 27 of March 1623. So the truth is we lyve in the fearefullest age that ever christians lyved in: And to speak the truth I stay to gett what I have lost and then god willing I will leave the Contrey: for this is the worst yeare here that ever I saw like to bee. . . .

Butter, cheese, and women—in that order —would have made life more endurable for Thomas Niccolls, according to his 1623 letter to an official of the Virginia Company.

If the Company would allow to each man a pound of butter and a pound of Cheese weekely they would find more comfort therein then by all the Deere, Fish & Fowle is so talked of in England of which I can assure you yor poore servants have not had since their coming into the Contrey so much as the scent: Wherefore it must neede follow that Oatemeale and Pease and bread & water have ben their food in sicknes & in health. It may appeare to be want of comforts and no way through the ill disposicion of the Clymate or ayre of the Contrey. Women are necessary members for the Colonye, but the poore men are never the nearer for them they are so well [paid], for I myselfe have ever since my coming payd 3 pounds sterling per annum for my washing &

find [supply the] sope. A hard case not having had for all the service I have done the Company not one pipe of Tobacco consideracion. I am sure for all these women yor poore Tenants that have nothing dye miserablie through nastines & many departe the World in their owne dung for want of help in their sicknes. Wherefore for prevention I could wish women might be sent over to serve the Company for that purpose for certayne yeares. . . .

During the 1620s William Rowlsley wrote from Jamestown to his brother in England, begging provisions to ensure his survival.

The Contrey is fullie determyned this Somer to sett mainly [forcefully] upon th'Indians which if it please God to prosper we shall have againe a plentiful Contrey; but in the meane tyme we shall want if our Frendes in England doe not stand to us. If it be possible send me a Hoggeshead of Beife, & some Neates Tongues for here is not a bitt of flesh to be had at any Rate For the woods are so dangerous we dare not goe abroad: And for tame Cattle there have so many died and ben killd otherwayes that there is no more to be had. . . .

Jonas Michaelius, a New Netherlander living on Staten Island, complained of conditions that he found there in 1628.

As to what concerns myself and my household: I find myself by the loss of my good and helping partner very much hindered and distressed,—for my two little daughters are yet small; maidservants are not here to be had, at least none whom they advise me to take; and the [female] Angola slaves are thievish, lazy and useless trash. The young man whom I took with me, I discharged after Whitsuntide, for the reason that I could not employ him out of doors at any working of the land, and, in doors, he was a burden to me instead of an assistance. . . .

The promise which the Lords Masters of the Company had made me to make myself a home . . . is wholly of no avail. For their Honours well know that there are no houses, cows nor laborers to be obtained here for money.

The country yields many good things for the support of life, but they are all to be gathered in an uncultivated and wild state. It is necessary that there should be better regulations established, and people who have the knowledge and the implements for gathering things in their season, should collect them together, as undoubtedly will gradually be the case. In the meanwhile I wish the Lords Managers to be courteously inquired of, how I can have the opportunity to possess a portion of land, and at my own expense to support myself upon it. For as long as there is no more accommodation to be obtained here from the country people, I would be compelled to order everything from Fatherland at great expense, and with much risk and trouble. . . .

Adriaen Van der Donck, a former lawyer, charged the Dutch West India Company with mismanagement in a 1649 document.

As we shall speak of the reasons and causes which have brought New Netherland into the ruinous condition in which it is now found to be, we deem it necessary to state first the difficulties. We represent it as we see and find it, in our daily experience. To describe it in one word, (and none better presents itself,) it is *bad government*, with its attendants and consequences, that is, to the best of our knowledge, the true and

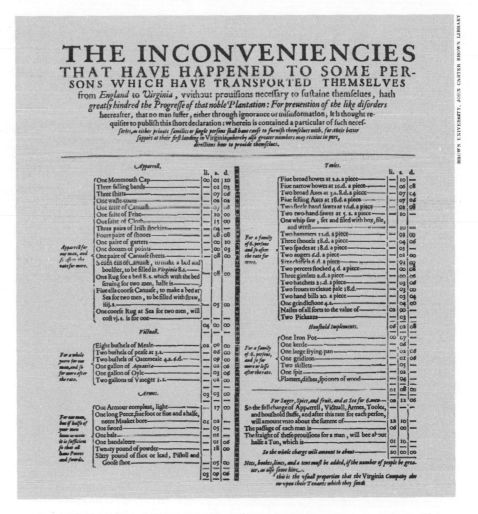

To spare future colonists "inconveniencies," this 1622 broadside lists necessary supplies.

only foundation stone of the decay and ruin of New Netherland. This government from which so much abuse proceeds, is twofold, that is; in the Fatherland by the Managers, and in this country. . . .

In 1624 Captain John Smith wrote this agonizing, even horrific, account of the "Starving Time" in Jamestown in 1609.

As for corne provision and contribution from the Salvages, we had nothing but mortall wounds, with clubs and arrowes; as for our Hogs, Hens, Goats, Sheepe, Horse, or what lived, our commanders, officers and Salvages daily consumed them, some small proportions sometimes we tasted, till all was devoured; then swords, armes, pieces, or any thing, wee traded with the Salvages, whose cruell fingers were so oft im-

brewed in our blouds, that what by their crueltie, our Governours indiscretion, and the losse of our ships, of five hundred [colonists] within six moneths after Captaine Smiths departure, there remained not past sixtie men, women and children, most miserable and poore creatures; and those were preserved for the most part, by roots, herbes, acornes, walnuts, berries, now and then a little fish. . . . Nay, so great was our famine, that a Salvage we slew and buried, the poorer sort tooke him up againe and eat him; and so did divers one another boyled and stewed with roots and herbs: And one amongst the rest did kill his wife, powdered [salted] her, and had eaten part of her before it was knowne; for which hee was executed, as hee well deserved: now whether shee was better roasted, boyled or carbonado'd, I know not; but of such a dish as powdered wife I never heard of.

Embellishments

Despite the perilous beginnings of the colonies, European immigrants kept arriving in North America. By 1642, partly because of the great Puritan migration, nearly thirty thousand colonists were settled along the Atlantic seaboard. While the great majority of newcomers cleared the land as the earlier settlers had, the late seventeenth century saw cities begin to flourish. As the colonists' energies—formerly expended on mere survival—were directed increasingly toward the acquisition of greater comforts and a more stable economy, they set about re-creating the world they had left behind. Whether for Southern planters or New England tradesmen, the problems were similar.

Municipal authorities kept close watch on public conduct. In 1647, after a drunken brawl, this order was posted for the instruction of all New Amsterdamers.

Therefore, by the advice of the late Director-General and of our Council and to the end, that instead of God's curse falling upon us we may receive his blessing, we order all brewers, tapsters and innkeepers, that none of them shall upon the Lord's day of rest by us called Sunday, entertain people, tap or draw any wine, beer or strong waters of any kind and under any pretext before 2 of the clock, in case there is no preaching or else before 4, except only to a traveller and those who are daily customers, fetching the drinks, to their own homes,—this under the penalty of being deprived of their occupation and besides a fine of 6 Carolus gilders for each person who shall be found drinking wine or beer within the stated time. We also forbid all innkeepers, landlords and tapsters to keep their houses open on this day or any other day of the week in the evening after the ringing of the bell, which will be rung about 9 o'clock, or to give wine, beer or strong waters to any, except to their family, travellers and table boarders under the like penalty.

Albany's city fathers seemed displeased with the deportment of the community's youth when they issued this ultimatum.

Whereas ye children of ye said city do very unorderly to ye shame and scandall of their parents ryde down ye hills in ye streets of the said city with small and great sleighs on the lord day and in the week by which accidents may come, now for pventing ye same it is hereby publishd and declard that it shall and may be lawful for any Constable in this City or any other person or persons to take any sleigh or sleighs from all and every such boys and girls rydeing or offering to ryde down any hill within ye said city and breake any sleigh or sleighs in pieces.

By the late seventeenth century, struggle— at least for some dwellers on the Eastern seaboard—had been replaced by a life of ease. Here, William Fitzhugh describes the estate of a wealthy Tidewater plantation owner, while incidentally noting the presence of a number of native-born blacks.

The plantation where I now live contains one thousand acres at least, seven hundred acres of which are a rich thicket, the remainder good hearty plantable land without any waste . . . and upon it, there are three quarters well furnished with all necessary houses, grounds and fencing, together with a choice crew of negroes at each plantation, most of them this country born, the remainder as likely as most in Virginia, there being twenty-nine in all with stocks of cattle and hogs in each quarter. Upon the same land is my own dwelling house furnished with all accommodations for a comfortable and gentle living, with rooms in it, four of the best of them hung, nine of them plentifully furnished with all things necessary and convenient, and all houses for use furnished with brick chimneys, four good cellars, a dairy, dove cot, stable, barn, henhouse, kitchen and all other convenienceys, and all in a manner new, a large orchard of about 2500 apple trees, most grafted, well fenced with a locust fence, which is as durable as most brick walls, a garden a hundred foot square well paled in, a yard wherein is most of the foresaid necessary houses pallisadoed in with locust puncheons, which is as good as if it were walled in, and more lasting than any of our bricks, together with a good stock of cattle, hogs, horses, mares, sheep, necessary servants belonging to it for the supply and support thereof.

Thomas Paschall, a tradesman from Bristol, appeared to be well satisfied with William Penn's domain. In a 1683 letter written several months after his arrival, he commented on his new life and on the prevalence of earlier immigrants in the region.

Here is a place called Philadelphia, where is also a Market kept, as also at Upland [now Chester]. I was at Bridlington [Burlington, New Jersey] fair, where I saw most sorts of goods to be sold, and a great resort of people; Where I saw English goods sold at very reasonable rates; The Country is full of goods, Brass and Pewter lieth upon hand, That which sells best is Linnen cloath, [and] trading Cloath for the Indians; I bought Kersey [a coarse, ribbed wool] and it doth not sell, Broad Cloath is wanting, and Perniston [another coarse wool], and Iron-pots; and as for the Swedes, they use but little Iron in Building, for they will build, and hardly use any other toole but an Ax; They will cut down a Tree, and cut him off when down, sooner than two men can saw him, and rend him into planks or what they please; only with the Ax and Wooden wedges, they use no Iron; They are generaly very ingenous people . . . have lived here 40 Years, and have lived much at ease, having great plenty of all sorts of provisions, but then they were but ordinarily Cloathd; but since the English came, they have gotten fine Cloaths, and are going proud. . . .

The River is taken up all along, by the Swedes, and Finns and some Dutch, before the English came, near eight score miles, and the Englishmen some of them, buy their Plantations, and get roome by the great River-side, and the rest get into Creeks, and small rivers that run into it, and some go into the Woods seven or eight Miles; Thomas Colborne [a Quaker from England] is three miles in the Woods . . . and hath about fourteen Acres of Corne now growing, and hath gotten between 30 and 40 pounds by his Trade, in this short time. I have hired a House for my Family for the Winter, and I have gotten a little House in my Land for my servants, and I have cleared Land about six Acres; and this I can say, I never wisht my self at Bristol again since my departure. I live in the Schoolkill Creek, near Philadelphia, about 100 Miles up the River. Here have been 24 Ships with Passengers within this Year, so that provisions are somewhat hard to come by in some places, though at no dear rate. . . .

In 1697, after fifteen years in Pennsylvania, Welshman Gabriel Thomas presented this picture of the community.

Poor People (both Men and Women) of all kinds, can here get three times the Wages for their Labour they can in England or Wales.

I shall instance in a few, which may serve; nay, and will hold in all the rest.

The first was a Black-Smith (my next neighbour), who himself and one Negro Man he had, got Fifty Shillings in one Day, by working up a Hundred Pound Weight of Iron, which at Six Pence per Pound (and that is the common Price in that Countrey) amounts to that Summ.

And for Carpenters, both House and Ship, Brick-layers, Masons, either of these Trades-Men, will get between Five and Six Shillings every Day constantly. As to Journey-Men Shooe-Makers, they have Two Shillings per Pair both for Men and Womens Shooes: And Journey-Men Taylors have Twelve Shillings per Week and their Diet. Sawyers get between Six and Seven Shillings the Hundred for Cutting of Pine-Boards. And for Weavers, they have Ten or Twelve Pence the Yard for Weaving of that which is little more than half a Yard in breadth. Wooll-Combers, have for combing Twelve Pence per Pound. Potters have Sixteen Pence for an Earthen Pot

which may be bought in England for Four Pence. . . .

In the said City [Philadelphia] are several good Schools of Learning for Youth, in order to the Attainment of Arts and Sciences, as also Reading, Writing, etc. Here is to be had on any Day in the Week, Tarts, Pies, Cakes, etc. We have also several Cooks-Shops, both Roasting and Boyling, as in the City of London. . . .

All sorts of very good Paper are made in the German-Town; as also very fine

An Indian and a gentleman adorn this tobacco label, used for advertising.

German Linen, such as no Person of Quality need be asham'd to wear; and in several places they make very good Druggets, Crapes, Camblets, and Serges, besides other Woollen Cloathes, the Manufacture of all which daily improves: And in most parts of the Countrey there are many Curious and Spacious Buildings, which several of the Gentry have erected for their Country-Houses. . . .

The Servant Problem

The desire to better one's lot was, of course, the motivating force that brought most European immigrants to America. Whereas in Europe a man born into a given social level was destined almost irrevocably to remain there, the new continent afforded the imaginative, the industrious, and the lucky a chance to break through traditional barriers. In these circumstances—a situation that provided every man with an opportunity to make his fortune —it was only natural that few newcomers who could do otherwise would settle permanently for subservient roles. Thus the scarcity of domestic help, except for slave labor, was a real and pressing problem for would-be employers.

Of all people, members of the renowned Winthrop family should have had their choice of the best servants. Judging, however, from this letter of 1717 written by one of the lesser-known John Winthrops to his father, neither he nor his wife was pleased with an Irish maid who was indentured to them for four years.

It is not convenient now to write the trouble and plague we have had with this Irish creature the year past. Lying and unfaithfull; w'd doe things on purpose in contradiction and vexation to her mistress; lye out of the house anights and have contrivances w'th fellows that have been stealing from o'r estate and gett drink out of ye cellar for them; saucy and impudent, as when we have taken her to task for her wickedness she has gone away to complain of cruell usage. I can truly say we have used this base creature w'th a great deal of kindness and lenity. She w'd frequently take her mistresses capps and stockins, hankerchers etc., to dresse herselfe and away without leave among her companions. I may have said some time or other when she has been in fault that she was fitt to live nowhere but in Virginia, and if she w'd not mend her ways I should send her thither tho I am sure nobody w'd give her passage thither to have her service for twenty yeares she is such a high-spirited pirnicious jade. Robin has been run away neare ten dayes as you will see by the inclosed and this creature know of his going and of his carrying out 4 dozen bottles of cyder, metheglin and palme wine out of the cellar among the servants of the town and meat and I know not w't. The bottles they broke and threw away after they had drunk up the liquor, and they got up o'r sheep anight, killed a fatt one, roasted and made merry w'th it before morning.

A great many colonists found themselves on American soil by way of indenture. Most were laborers willing to work two to seven years in order eventually to become independent landowners or tradesmen. This bond of indenture of a young house servant is typical of the colonial period.

This Indenture witnesseth that Aulkey Hubertse, Daughter of John Hubertse, of the Colony of Rensselaerwyck deceased hath bound herself as a Meniall Servant, and by these presents doth voluntary and of her own free will and accord bind herself as a Meniall Servant unto John Delemont of the City of Albany, weaver, by and with the consent of the Deacons of the Reformed Dutch Church in the Citity of Albany, who are as overseers in the disposal of the said Aulkey Hubertse to serve from the date of these present Indentures unto the full end and term of time that the said Aulkey Hubertse shall come to Age, all which time fully to be Compleat and ended, during all which term the said servant her said Master faithfully shall serve, his secrets keep, his lawful commands gladly everywhere obey, she shall do no Damage to her said Master nor see it to be done by others without letting or giving notice thereof to her said Master: she shall not waste her Master's goods or lend them unlawfully to any. At Cards, Dice, or any unlawful Game she shall not play whereby her said Master may have Damage: with her own goods or the goods of others during the said Term, without License from her said Master she shall neither buy or sell: she shall not absent herself day or night from her Master's service without his Leave, nor haunt Ale-houses, Taverns, or Play-houses, but in all things as a faithful servant, she shall behave herself towards her said Master and all his during the said Term. And the said Master during the said Term, shall find and provide sufficient Wholesome and compleat meat and drink, washing, lodging, and apparell and all other Necessarys fit for such a servant: and it is further agreed between the said Master and Servant in case the said Aulkey Hubertse should contract Matrimony before she shall come to Age then the said Servant is to be free from her said Master's service by virtue thereof: and at the expiration of her said servitude, her said Master John Delemont shall find provide for and deliver unto his said servant double apparell, that is to say, apparell fit for to have and to wear as well on the Lords Day as working days, both linning and woolen stockings and shoes and other Necessarys meet for such a servant to have and to wear, and for the true performance of all and every of said Covenant and Agreements the said parties bind themselves unto each other by these presents.

Within a year of its first publication in 1732, Benjamin Franklin's *Poor Richard's Almanac* had become the second most popular book in the colonies, surpassed only by the Bible. His maxims and sayings were read as eagerly as was his information on weather, tides, sunsets, and medical remedies. These engravings are from *Bowles's Moral Pictures; or Poor Richard Illustrated, Being Lessons for the Young and Old, on Industry, Temperance, Frugality, &c* (1795). They stressed that anybody—even the lowliest indentured servant—could rise in the world by practicing the virtues that Franklin praised.

From Ulster to Pennsylvania to the Shenandoah Valley, the hardy Scotch-Irish pushed ever farther into the wilderness.

THIS NEW MAN

IN 1782 A FORMER SOLDIER OF FRANCE, lately a resident of Orange County, New York, published a book that he modestly entitled *Letters from an American Farmer*. In it he posed and answered a question that was of particular import during the transition from colonialism to nationhood in America:

What then is the American, this new man? He is either an European, or the descendant of an European, hence that strange mixture of blood, which you will find in no other country. I could point out to you a family whose grandfather was an Englishman, whose wife was Dutch, whose son married a French woman, and whose present four sons have now four wives of different nations. . . . Here individuals of all nations are melted into a new race of men, whose labours and posterity will one day cause great changes in the world. . . . The American ought therefore to love this country much better than that wherein either he or his forefathers were born. Here the rewards of his industry follow with equal steps the progress of his labour. . . . The American is a new man, who acts upon new principles; he must therefore entertain new ideas, and form new opinions.

Thus did Michel-Guillaume Jean de Crèvecoeur, who had first come to North America to fight under Montcalm, lay his finger on the fundamental significance of the American experience. A new nation was emerging, without historic boundaries, ancient traditions, or a single, binding folk culture. The American future, like the westward-stretching continent itself, was an uncharted terrain of innumerable hazards and limitless possibilities. The American past was a patchwork quilt, made up of the customs, habits, taboos, visions, and memories of men and women drawn from a variety of national stocks. Most of them had been in the new land

for less than three generations, scarcely time enough for new behavior patterns to sink roots below the level of conscious choice. Somehow, England's plantations had become colonies, settlements had become communities, companies of pilgrims and adventurers had become participants in a society. Thanks to a steady westward flow of transatlantic migration, that society was, as Crèvecoeur perceived, neither English nor European. "American" would do as a term for it, but the word was as yet not precise and definitive; rather it was suggestive and elastic, a white space on the map of mankind marked "Unexplored."

The tendency of classroom-taught history has long been to deal with immigration as a force in American life mainly after 1850. It will therefore come as a surprise to many to learn that perhaps a third of all colonial Americans in 1760 either were born abroad or had foreign-born parents. Accurate records were not kept, but the total colonial population in 1760 was about 1,600,000—a fourfold increase from 1713, when the Treaty of Utrecht opened a long period of peace. In that nearly fifty-year span, hundreds of thousands of Germans and Ulstermen (Protestants of Scottish descent, from the northern counties of Ireland) came over. Of the estimated 200,000 blacks brought to American shores in the eighteenth century, perhaps half were landed during this period. (It is an unaccustomed twist of thought to consider a captive Negro, plantation-bound, an "immigrant." Yet in demographic terms such a treatment has its uses. For the settlement of "America" was a westward transatlantic shift of population groups in massive numbers, and of this movement a Fanti tribesman, groaning with seasickness in the foul hold of a slave ship, was a part as surely as any Puritan yeoman embarking with John Winthrop.)

Add to these numbers reasonable proportions of recent arrivals among the Huguenots, Acadians, Catholic Irish, Jews, Scots, Swedes, Hollanders, and other "foreigners" in Great Britain's North American mainland colonies on the eve of the Revolution, and it is a fair guess that at least half a million had made the ocean passage within the span of a lifetime.

This surge of newcomers had been a critical element in the great transformation of the provinces. The open sea lanes from Europe and Africa, as well as the open frontier, had effectively reshaped worship, deference, speech, the getting and spending of wealth, and the taking of ease. The political and juridical structure of the colonies remained essentially English, but the society was cosmopolitan.

An immigrant of 1760 debarked in a land where the early days of simple struggle for survival, the agonies of Jamestown and Plymouth, were only memories. Now he found cities, newspapers, courts, schools, legislatures, churches, roads, postal services, bookshops, finely furnished houses. Some of them were built and maintained by his countrymen, and his own presence continued to remold institutions. The thrust of German or Ulster Scot migration into western Pennsylvania transformed the life of that colony in ways that could not

have been envisioned by William Penn. The impact of slavery on the economy of the South was measureless. In the compact, yeasty colonial cities, a handful of Scottish, Jewish, or French families with important mercantile connections could radically affect the distribution of social and political patronage. (Boston in 1740 had only 16,000 inhabitants, Charleston 6,800, Philadelphia 13,000, and New York 11,000.)

The motives, the drives, the particular distresses, and the "contributions" of each immigrant group are part of a kaleidoscopic pattern. But when the threads are unraveled, some gleam fresh and in distinct colors. The Germans—and in particular the Germans of Pennsylvania, where they constituted about a third of the populace in 1766—were the most conspicuous non-Britannic element in the colonies. Their mixture of piety and efficiency, mystic yearning and worldly realism, in matters of farming and business formed one important theme of future Americanism. The Ulster Scots brought to the back country, where they flocked, a toughness and Calvinistic communitarianism bred of their own troubled past. Both qualities stamped the future of a major American church—the Presbyterian —and the many colleges that it nurtured. Many colonial Jews and Huguenots were a commercial force in the port towns. Like the printers, ironmasters, and papermakers of German origin, they helped to diversify

In 1681, as payment of a debt to the late Sir William Penn, King Charles II granted Penn's son, William, a charter for a large tract of land in America (see reproduction below). At right is the title page from an almanac for 1756 published in Germantown.

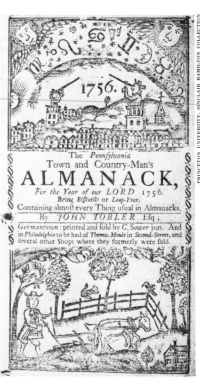

PENNS TREATY with the INDIANS made 1681 with out an Oath, and never broken. The foundation of Religious and Civil Liberty in the U.S. of AMERICA.

This idealized Penn's Treaty with the Indians *was painted by a Quaker, Edward Hicks, in the early nineteenth century. Penn made several treaties with the Indians, paying them for their land and protecting their rights. He appears below right in a charcoal pastel, the only authentic contemporaneous portrait.*

the colonies' soil-based economy. And as for the forced immigrants, the slaves, by 1760 they were already the bedrock of the Southern economy. To consider the story of all these groups is to feel the texture of American life as it took shape before political revolution confirmed the economic and cultural separation from Europe.

For America's Germans, the counterpart of the *Mayflower* was a roomy and seaworthy vessel of the West Indian service named the *Concord*, which dropped anchor in Philadelphia harbor on October 6, 1683. The families aboard were not the first Germans in the English colonies. Among individual settlers of Germanic origin who had appeared on the scene earlier, Jacob Leisler was already one of the wealthiest citizens of New York in 1684, with an estate of fifteen thousand guilders acquired by trade with the Indians. In 1689 he would become involved in a revolt against royal authority in the province, and on a cold, wet May day in 1691 he would be hanged on a spot where Pearl and Centre Streets now meet in downtown Manhattan. But the *Concord*'s passengers were part of a group migration—the vanguard of armies of German, or *Deutsch*, newcomers, whose name would be corrupted by American tongues to "Dutch." Their John Smith, their Winthrop, their Bradford, was Francis Daniel Pastorius.

Their voyage probably had its origin in 1677, when William Penn traveled to Germany to make converts to Quakerism. He found a sympathetic audience among many German Pietists—believers like himself in a religion of inward vision, brotherly harmony, and worship undefiled by churchly ritual, pomp, and office. In 1681 Charles II of England gave Penn a province in America in lieu of sixteen thousand pounds owed to Penn's late father. Hoping to put his ideals into practice there,

Penn published *Some Account of the Province of Pennsilvania* in the same year. The book was almost immediately translated for German readers, some of whom then formed a company to buy Pennsylvania land, and among those who heard their appeals for support was Pastorius.

A thirty-year-old graduate in law and theology from Altdorf University who had also studied at Strasbourg, Basel, and Jena, Pastorius could have applied his gifts to the pursuit of a comfortable career at home. But the prospective emigrants' descriptions of the idealized Pennsylvania-to-be, he later wrote, "begat a desire in my soul to continue in their society and with them to lead a quiet, godly, and honest life in a howling wilderness." Soon he himself was playing a leading role in recruiting German colonists for the Frankfurt-based company, and in the spring of 1683 he took ship for Pennsylvania to make advance arrangements. On shipboard he had a symbolic immigrant experience in meeting a Welsh physician, Thomas Lloyd, late of Jesus College, Oxford. Pastorius then knew no English and Lloyd no German, but the two America-bound scholars conversed amiably, in the tossing cabin, in Latin!

Penn's agents had sold the Frankfurt adventurers about forty-three thousand acres, and the newly landed settlers took part of the purchase in a tract about six miles north of Philadelphia. On it they began to build a city to be known as Germantown. It was the first American showcase for German orderliness, diligence, common sense about cash, and beehive closeness.

For thousands of Germans, careful attention to the sharp responsibilities of this world mingled with a mystical concern over the proper way to prepare for the next. German religious communities, harassed by au-

The Pennsylvania Dutch brought with them the whimsical style of art shown in the decoration of the eighteenth-century pottery shaving basin, pie plate, and wooden splint box above.

thority in the homeland, migrated wholesale to await the Second Coming in the liberal air of Pennsylvania, where, Gottlieb Mittelberger reported, "not only is everyone allowed to believe what he wishes; he is also at liberty to express these beliefs publicly and freely." There were the Mennonites, whose founder, Menno Simons, taught them that true Christians shunned participation in government, refused to lift up their hands to slay others in war, dressed in a style that rejected worldly vanities, and swore no oaths. A colony of Swiss Mennonites settled near Lancaster in 1710. (The Amish folk of Pennsylvania are ultraconservative schismatic Mennonites.) There were the Dunkards, members of a sect of baptizers by total immersion, founded in Westphalia in 1708. Some time after their arrival at Germantown in 1719, the secession of some members led to the foundation of the Cloister of Ephrata, whereupon robes, tonsures, and liturgical rites appeared in the hospitable wilderness. Near Goshenhoppen, now Bally, were clusters of Schwenkfelders, originally a group of true believers from Silesia. Shortly before 1740, a colony of Moravians, or United Brethren, settled on a tract on the Lehigh River, purchased for them by their leader, Count Nikolaus Ludwig von Zinzendorf. There they built a community like that which they had formed on the count's estate at Herrnhut, in Saxony. To it he gave the Scriptural name of Bethlehem, and administered it through officials with the apostolic titles of elder, overseer, monitor, and, simply, teacher. Zinzendorf optimistically sent Moravian missionaries into the western wilderness as far as present-day Ohio, where they earnestly attempted with German polysyllables to bring God's word to the red-skinned savages.

The more firmly established German churches had representation in Pennsylvania, too. By 1733, Lutheran congregations in Philadelphia and elsewhere were requesting European-educated pastors. The German Reformed Church, essentially Lutheran, counted forty-six congregations in America in 1751. The German churches filled the settlements with their own jangle of religious argument (some of it printed on German presses) and also with the new sound of Baroque and classical music. Bach and Haydn came to America in the tongues and hands of German choristers and organists; Haydn's *The Creation* and *The Seasons*, for example, had American premieres in Bethlehem. And the religiosity and superstition of some uneducated Germans were reflected in the folk art that even today imprints its bright colors and intricate designs on rugs, furniture, pottery, wagons, barns, and farmhouses in the hilly countryside of "Dutch" Pennsylvania.

German colonists were sometimes brought over in

Vision and Reality

To Alexis de Tocqueville, the secret of America lay in the fact that it was a nation of immigrants—a society of people who dared to give up their settled existences and build new lives in a strange, wild country, unbound from Old World restrictions and traditions. And yet this freedom was not quite what the European planners of colonies had in mind; they attempted to fulfill special blueprints of their own—to force patterns on the virgin continent. But the success of both early and later American immigrants came from taking advantage of the space around them, and from the flexibility of a society in the making; rigid adherence to European philanthropic ideals could, in fact, impede success in America.

Georgia, the last of the thirteen colonies, was founded on a vision. And just as the experience of the older colonies had often proved to be a far cry from English expectations, so too, for Georgia, did the hopes of well-intentioned London trustees run afoul of the facts of life in a colony thousands of miles distant, and afoul of the possibilities apparent in the new land. Georgia was planned in true Utopian spirit by two men who resolved to make no profit from the venture—John, Viscount Perceval, later Earl of Egmont, an aristocrat with a generous enthusiasm for good works, and James Edward Oglethorpe. Oglethorpe had been an Oxford student and a soldier, and was a member of Parliament; tempestuous, a lover of adventure, he had "uncommon vivacity of mind and variety of knowledge" –in Boswell's phrase– and, said Alexander Pope, a "strong benevolence of soul." Perceval and Oglethorpe had served on a Parliamentary committee investigating English jails; the experience left them shocked at the deplorable treatment of imprisoned debtors. With Perceval's support, Oglethorpe rallied nineteen other public-spirited Englishmen to join them as trustees for a colony where such victims of society could start anew. King George II granted the land between the Savannah and Altamaha Rivers, and the trustees set out to publicize their "Macedonia crying for help" and to attract settlers. As the colonists were chosen, however, the conflicts between the ideal and the possible began to appear. Founded for "the poor persons of London" who had failed to make a living, the colony was also intended to be a sound economic venture; ultimately, very few debtors were selected to go to Georgia. Farmers and soldiers were not encouraged to join, yet the colony was to exist on agriculture and had to defend itself against the Spanish in Florida and against the Indians. Here the trustees did not bow to the practical: the first group, which sailed with Oglethorpe on November 17, 1732, was described by Perceval as "about forty able, sensible men, the rest women and children," but only three of the men were acquainted with farming; most were merchants and artisans, unused to hard physical work.

The trustees hoped to create a co-operative and highly moral community. They sharply restricted the possession, exchange, sale, and inheritance of land— in a wilderness; they forbade the slave trade and made selling liquor a crime. They expected the colony, despite an insufficiency of local mulberry trees, to make silk its major industry. Oglethorpe, said a visitor in 1733, "is extremely well beloved by all his people; the general Title they give him is Father. . . . [He] keeps a strict Discipline. . . . There are no Idlers. . . ." As it happened, that very spring he had to face a storm of objections to the rules. But, having staked his dreams, his reputation, and much of his fortune on the venture, he refused to acknowledge that his idealism denied the colony some of the things it needed. So did the trustees: "The Board will always do what is right," they pontificated in 1735, "and the people should have confidence in us." Not many did. Settlers poured out of Georgia, seeking the freedom of other colonies. In 1752, a year before the charter was scheduled to expire, the disillusioned trustees turned Georgia over to the crown. Most of the benevolently inspired restrictions had already been gradually repealed over the years, and under royal rule the still struggling colony at last began to thrive.

OGLETHORPE UNIVERSITY

James Edward Oglethorpe

David Rittenhouse, Philadelphia clockmaker, invented astronomical instruments.

groups by royal officials eager to add them to the always inadequate supply of labor. In 1710, for example, Governor Robert Hunter of New York recruited some three thousand "Palatines" (from the region known as the Rhenish Palatinate) whom he intended to settle in the Mohawk and Hudson Valleys to produce naval stores—tar, pitch, rosin, and turpentine—for the Royal Navy. Their saga was painful. Nearly fifteen per cent of them died of fever they contracted in the convoy that brought them across. Then they quarreled with Robert Livingston, on whose vast estates they had been settled. The issues were high rents and delays in permitting the eventual outright purchase of farms in the Schoharie Valley, which the Germans had been promised. Some of them, indignant and courageous, struck out for western New York on their own. In March, 1713, one settler, Conrad Weiser, chronicled, "did . . . the people (tho' treated by the Governor as Pharaoh treated the Israelites) proceed on their journey, and by God's assistance travel'd in a fortnight with sledges thro' the snow—which there covered the ground above three foot deep—cold and hunger . . . [to] the promised land of Schoharie." That particular Promised Land was plagued with frequent and fiery visits from the children of Canaan, the Indians, but the migrants endured it all. Promoters brought German and German-Swiss groups to still other colonies—to Germanna, Virginia, to New Bern, North Carolina, and to Purysburg, South Carolina, where they were variously supposed to smelt iron, weave cloth, produce silk, and cultivate vineyards.

Thousands of Germans continued to cross the Atlantic on an individual basis. Some paid their own passage, but others became part of a brutal flesh traffic in "redemptioners." A redemptioner was an immigrant who had no money for passage or subsistence. When he reached America, the ship's captain "sold" him as a servant for a term of years to whatever buyer would pay the accumulated cost—according to the captain's reckoning! Unlike some immigrants who signed contracts of indenture while still in Europe or England, where they had some bargaining power with recruiting agents, the redemptioner, a prisoner aboard ship until he was redeemed, was at the mercy of the captain. And the ship, by the end of the crossing, was apt to be a chamber of horrors.

The reason lay in the greed of shipowners who packed their passengers into the hold like herring—four to six hundred to a small vessel. What ensued was bitterly described by Gottlieb Mittelberger, one of that forgotten breed of immigrants who came, found the milk and honey lacking, and returned. Most of the passengers had exhausted their own provisions and pocket money in the long, exasperating, delay-filled journey down the Rhine to Holland and across to England, where they boarded their ships. They had no alternative to being jammed into dark, dank holds in bunks two feet by six feet; no effective means to protest against putrescent meat disguised by heavy salting, "fresh" water thick with filth, biscuits full of spiders' nests and worms.

With murder in his heart, Mittelberger, a schoolmaster and organist, held prayer meetings on deck when weather allowed, baptized five children, and commended to God's mercy the souls of those who died and were thrown over the side. At journey's end the redemptioners—starving, sick, exhausted—were in no position to resist any terms offered by the colonists who "liberated" them and carried them off as farmhands, domestics, and apprentices, with children and parents often going to different masters in permanent separation.

Yet the survivors—and every immigrant was, in a sense, a survivor of exile—persevered and endured. By the outbreak of the Revolution, it was estimated that there were as many as 225,000 "inhabitants of German blood" in the colonies. They had been in the new land, in substantial numbers, for more than a century by that time—longer than the majority of Poles, Italians, or Russian Jews and all their descendants were in the United States of the 1960s. And they had left a solid impress. Dr. Benjamin Rush—patriot, pioneer in psychiatry, exponent of equal education for women, and combative publicist, among other things—wrote, in 1789, a description of Pennsylvania's German inhabitants. He praised their well-built homes, their tight fences, their thoroughly cleared acres, and their well-tended gardens, noting that Pennsylvania was "indebted to the Germans for the principal part of her knowledge in horticulture." He admired their deep and

German immigrants who swarmed to Pennsylvania in the eighteenth century struggled to preserve their language and culture from Anglicizing influences. Above, a Pennsylvania Dutch christening certificate, dated 1803, is enlivened by German art.

Kurtze Nachricht von einigen evangelischen Gemeinen . . . 1744, NYPL

In the picture above, a group of pacifist Moravians hold a joint marriage ceremony before their departure for America.

solid farm wagons, under whose white tops the German farmers loaded the bushels of wheat and barrels of flour that they brought to market in such quantities as to make Pennsylvania the national breadbasket in the late eighteenth century.

They were at ease in Zion, belonging to the land. Many of their number would go on to distinguished careers as assimilated Americans. But it should be noted also that some of them added color to the national life by remaining entrenched behind traditional walls, too. They planted and pruned by conjunctions of the stars and phases of the moon, sought water with divining rods, and were not above begging talismans and incantations from witchlike crones to make the pumpkins fatter or the cows' udders fuller. In schools and churches they often clung to the mother tongue—successful, adjusted, and yet still solidly German.

The Scotch-Irish, to give them one of their names, were immigrants of a somewhat different breed. Even in the Old World they were borderers—fighting families sent out to hold a frontier against enemy aliens. About the time when the Jamestown settlers were starving and shivering with malaria, Scottish migrants were being settled on another "plantation," in Ulster, for the purpose of civilizing or at least containing the Irish, who even then were a thorn in the flesh of England, for reasons described by Francis Bacon in 1601: "barbarous laws, customs . . . habits of apparel, their poets or heralds that enchant them in savage manners, and sundry other dregs of barbarism and rebellion." Sir Arthur Chichester, Lord Deputy of Ireland, had a method for dealing with the poetry-drunk rebels. Certain of their lords had lately risen in resistance to England. They were defeated, and their estates, largely in

the northern counties collectively known as Ulster, were forfeited to the crown. Chichester decided that the settling of "colonies of civil people of England and Scotland" on these lands would plant the seeds of Protestantism and fidelity to London in the tough Irish soil.

So it was done, and by 1641 approximately 120,000 Britons had been "planted" in Ulster. The great majority of the settlers were Scots, not Englishmen, and were variously called Ulster Scots, Ulstermen, Scotch- (or Scots-) Irish, and sometimes (especially in emigration records and to the confusion of history) simply "Irish." They were not all "civil people" as Chichester had planned, either, which was possibly just as well in an undeveloped land with few roads and less law, as a contemporary saying had it. It was noted that many "from debt, or breaking and fleeing from justice, or seeking shelter, came hither, hoping to be without fear of man's justice," and that "iniquity abounded."

But the righteous had their supporting forces. As a historian of the Ulster settlement noted, the wicked might haste across the Irish Sea, but "God followed them when they fled from Him." Their righteous neighbors needed a certain measure of contentiousness themselves in order not to perish. God's pursuing agents were Scottish Presbyterian preachers, armored in a Calvinism that was stern even by seventeenth-century standards. More than a religion, Calvinism was a buckler against the world's snares. Holding man to rigid moral accountability before an angry God who had predestined him to damnation or salvation, it celebrated accumulation and diligence, and thundered against vanity and the flesh.

The Ulstermen took their Presbyterianism with them, and therefore tended to live in closely knit communities, led in the paths of duty by their ministers. They wrestled hard with Satan, losing spectacularly when they fell and agonizing more loudly when they repented, than Christians of milder temperament were accustomed to witness. They were a tough breed, as hard on themselves as on their enemies, and they had need to be sinewy, for enemies encompassed them. From Cromwell's era through the Glorious Revolution, Ireland was constantly a battleground of Protestants and Catholics. The Ulstermen won bloody victories at Enniskillen and Londonderry over forces loyal to the Catholic James II and also planted the seeds of hatred between "green" and "orange" Irishmen that still bears bitter fruit.

Then, at the moment of Protestant victory, the English government turned against the Ulstermen, who had begun to establish themselves as successful farmers, dairymen, sheep raisers, and weavers. English landowners and merchants secured the passage of laws forbidding the importation into England of Irish beef, meal, grain, wool, linen, woven goods, and many other manufactured items. The ports of Ireland were excluded from any sort of participation in the profitable colonial trade. Prices fell drastically in Ulster, and landlords attempted to make up the loss by raising rents. A calculated policy of keeping imperial profits exclusively in the hands of English merchants tightened the screws of adversity on the Scotch-Irish, and as depression fell like a rain of iron on the land, they began to swarm to America.

Sometimes whole congregations followed their preachers to the docks, after being inspired by sermons that promised goodly land to Abraham and his seed. The movement was heaviest between 1717 and 1785, with occasional peaks in years of bad harvests and consequent famines. Around 1750 it was estimated that nearly 12,000 Ulster Scots were reaching just Pennsylvania each year. For 1771–73 the total lay somewhere between 25,000 and 30,000, not including a heavy inflow from Scotland proper. Dr. Samuel Johnson and James Boswell, touring Scotland at that time, observed a rural dance in which the couples one by one joined a whirling circle, symbolizing "how emigration catches, till all are set afloat." Those who joined the overseas movement were, as the traveler Arthur Young saw it, probably the boldest and hardiest of their tribe—and also "probably the most mischievous." As it happened, they turned out to be superbly suited for the task that fell to them, that of subduing the colonial frontier.

Some went to New England, where a religious atmosphere congenial to their own might have seemed to guarantee a welcome. But the Lord's anointed had already filled up the greenest valleys there, and the Scotch-Irish were driven to the mountainous terrain of western Massachusetts, New Hampshire, and the future Vermont and Maine. (In New Hampshire they left a mark in the town of Londonderry, which produced six governors of the state, nine members of Congress, and five justices of the state Supreme Court.) But to the southward the younger colonies of Pennsylvania and the Carolinas begged for settlers, and the Scotch-Irish flowed readily into the so-called Great Valley, running from northeast to southwest, which forms a trough in the Appalachians and from which rise the rivers that flow down to the sea in Pennsylvania, Maryland, Virginia, and the Carolinas.

They were not always scrupulous about land titles. James Logan, secretary of Pennsylvania Province— that is, agent for the proprietors, the Penn family— complained in 1730 of their "audacious and disorderly manner" in squatting on choice tracts such as the fifteen-thousand-acre Conestoga Manor, reserved by the Penns for themselves. Spokesmen for the Scotch-

In 1706 seven ministers who had fled to Philadelphia seeking religious freedom formed that city's first presbytery, a court of ministers and elders; below is a page from their minutes.

Irish, Logan wrote, replied that it "was against the laws of God and nature, that so much land should be idle while so many Christians wanted it to labor on and to raise their bread." Making a virtue of necessity, Logan wrote to his employers that it might be a good idea to populate the Indian-threatened frontier with the sons of those who had fought so gallantly in Ireland. Meanwhile, the Carolinas offered tracts for the taking, not yet pounced on by large companies or by favored friends of the governors or other speculators. Consequently, many Ulstermen moved on from Pennsylvania in long Biblical caravans—horses, hogs, oxen, kine, wives, children, and menservants and maidservants trudging ever further into the wilderness. In 1764 Salisbury, North Carolina, alone witnessed the passage of a thousand wagons, bound away for the mountains.

Once more the Ulstermen were strangers in a hard environment, and they developed enduring protective ways. It was the Scotch-Irish who became the prototype frontiersmen. The men dressed in buckskins, moccasins, and caps of untreated animal pelts, rifles or muskets in hand, girdled about with belts into which were thrust powder horns, axes, and knives. The barefoot womenfolk in short linsey-woolsey gowns and petticoats grew prematurely leathery with work and suffering. Fighting hard, scrabbling for a living without respite, they moved through the forests like human scythes. Some did not move but became isolated in mountainous pockets, where they more or less gave up the struggle to get ahead and became the ancestors of the hill folk who would be discovered by ballad collectors and urban humorists in later generations. But most struggled to achieve something better than a "hog and hominy" existence for themselves and their children, and some succeeded. At worst there was always respite from the grimness of life in the hunt, and in militia muster days, court days, election days, and other occa-

sions for drinking, boxing, wrestling, and matching horses and men in races.

Ultimately the Scotch-Irish of the frontier fell into violent quarrels with the settlers in the older, coastal regions of the colonies—over the lack of protection against Indians, the sad state of back-country roads and bridges, and the tendency to underrepresent frontier counties in the colonial and later in the state legislatures. A tradition of polemical political discourse, laced with Scriptural zeal and rigidity, was maintained by a distinguished corps of descendants of the original Scotch-Irish settlers, among them men like Andrew Jackson, John C. Calhoun, James K. Polk, and countless others. By Revolutionary times, the Scotch-Irish were an inseparable part of the social fabric. Twice transplanted in a century and a half after 1600, they had found a home, a mission, and a style in America.

For the western world's perennial strangers, the Jews, eighteenth-century America offered both a haven and a challenge. In Europe, the devastating pressure of restriction compacted the mass of Israel into self-sustaining ghetto communities. In the English colonies, however—particularly in liberal Pennsylvania and Rhode Island—Jewish cohesiveness and dedication to tradition had to stand the test of voluntary action. The use of adversity was not available to religious leadership; Jews could more or less blend into the larger social pattern, with some reservations, taking with them as much of their heritage, of their identity's core, as they thought to be consistent with success in the "outside" world. This is still the basic ground for understanding American Jewry. In the 1700s, as individual Jews in America began to taste the subtle mixtures of emancipation and traditionalism, assimilation and separation, they changed the quality of their lives and that of their Christian neighbors as well.

"Back in the old country," as the historian Jacob R. Marcus has observed, "the pious Jew, whatever his occupation, studied rabbinic literature, . . . prayed for the Messiah, and exulted in the martyrs who had died for the glorification of the Ineffable Name. Here, in colonial towns, in the dark forest, on the high seas, the man who had to flee from pirates, face the Indians, and dare the hazards of frontier life was surely not the same man who rocked back and forth, intoning the Talmud, in a German or Polish ghetto academy." He was not, indeed. Moreover, the "colonial town" to which he brought wine, furs, or cloth—and in which he built himself a synagogue—was not quite the same town.

The first group of Jews to land on North American soil were twenty-three who were set down in New Amsterdam in 1654. An unconfirmed and possibly romantic

As in Britain, Presbyterian ministers in the American colonies presented a small lead disc to each member of the congregation who had completed his formal religious instruction known as the rite of catechism. The discs, left, were given out at the service following catechism, and had to be shown before the parishioner could receive Communion.

The German-born Jew, Moses Levy, left, became a successful merchant in New York. His daughter Rachel, center, was married to Isaac Seixas, of another great Jewish clan, and the union produced the first American-born rabbi, Gershom Mendes Seixas, right.

legend says that they came on a French privateer, which had liberated them from a Spanish vessel that had in turn taken them from another ship. One thing is certain: they came from what had been a successful Jewish colony in Pernambuco (now Recife), a Brazilian city taken by the Dutch in 1630. The liberality of the Dutch had made their cities, both in Europe and in their colonies, havens for religious refugees of all kinds, including English Separatists (like the Pilgrims), French Huguenots, and Hispanic Jews. The latter were descendants of a once flourishing Iberian community of scholars, professional men, and traders. Persecution by the Spanish Inquisition, which was established in 1478, had forced Spain's Jews to become either Christians or marranos—converts who secretly continued whatever Jewish practices they could—or to flee. Many of the exiles had established themselves as brokers, bankers, and shippers, in parts of South America and the West Indies that were not under Spanish control.

Pernambuco's Jews were from this background. The recapture of the city by the Portuguese in 1654 was a catastrophe for them. They dispersed, many bound for the homes of friends and relatives in French and English Caribbean colonies, where restriction was relatively light, and some to other Dutch outposts, including New Amsterdam.

Governor Peter Stuyvesant was no model of toleration. Under pressure from the Dutch West India Company, he gave "these people" the right to "travel and trade to and in New Netherland and live and remain there, provided the poor among them shall . . . be supported by their own nation." Stuyvesant was determined to withstand the pressure of the Jews, who were anything but backward in measuring the extent of Dutch liberty. In 1655 he refused to permit Salvador Dandrada, Jacob Cohen, and several other Jews to trade at Fort Orange and along the Delaware River on identical terms with Gentile merchants. Next he refused Dandrada's application for the right to purchase a home in the city. But New Amsterdam's Jewish community had friends in old Amsterdam, and orders arrived the next year commanding Stuyvesant to allow the Jews to trade and buy real estate (but not to open retail shops, become craftsmen, or hold public worship). Next, Asher Levy and Jacob Barsimson claimed and won the right to serve in the local militia, instead of paying a tax in lieu of enlistment as they had been compelled to do. Finally, they got full rights of citizenship, though Stuyvesant argued that "Giving them liberty, we cannot refuse the Lutherans and Papists."

The Dutch went, the English came, and the Jewish community grew. Most were Sephardim—Jews of Iberian origin—and a few were Ashkenazic, or German Jews. (The great subsequent Ashkenazic migration from Russia, Poland, and the Balkans was centuries in the future.) One by one, individual families began the process of succeeding in America. Success had a different meaning for each individual who experienced the process, but the case of Abraham de Lucena is illustrative if not typical. He imported Madeira wine and exported grain to Europe, bacon to Jamaica, and flour to Canada. He married one of his daughters to a man named Mordecai Gomez, a member of a New York Jewish mercantile clan with strategically placed representatives in Old World and West Indian trading and banking centers. It was a common thing among eighteenth-century mercantile families to create relationships in Amsterdam, London, Hamburg, or Lisbon, either by dispatching a son or nephew abroad or by strategic marriage.

Outside New York, Jews also won places for themselves as individuals and in groups. The keen interest of New England's Puritan founders and their descendants in the Old Testament was a source of closeness between some Yankee preachers and their Israelite neighbors. A famous friendship of the colonial period sprouted between the Reverend Ezra Stiles of Newport, Rhode Island, and Rabbi Haim Isaac Carigal, of the Jewish congregation in that city. They were drawn into contact by Stiles' interest in Hebrew and rabbinic lore, and corresponded throughout the rabbi's lifetime in Hebrew, Spanish, and English. Stiles eventually became president of Yale College, and once remarked to some students who objected to studying the Hebrew psalms that they "would be the first we should hear sung in heaven, and that he would be ashamed that any one of his pupils should be entirely ignorant of that holy language."

In a curious way, the Huguenots of colonial America were somewhat like the Jews. They formed a small group with what contemporary sociology would call high status, income and skill levels, and social cohesiveness. They were French Protestants, the majority of whom were expelled from France in 1685, when King Louis XIV revoked the Edict of Nantes, under which toleration had been granted to them a century before. Within two years of that date, 150 Huguenot families had come to Massachusetts, and there were other settlements in Rhode Island and Maine. Many of the refugees had been workers in silk and glass, silver and gold, wood and leather, and other fine crafts. The capital accumulated among Huguenot families enabled some to go into trade, and they made their deepest impress in the cities of Boston, New York, Philadelphia, and Charleston, where their family links to the trading ports of the Atlantic community (like those of the Jews) were invaluable. The honor roll of Huguenot names is long and not always recognizable, because their assimilation was so complete that it often involved transformation of old family titles into something American. Apollos De Rivoire is hard to recognize as the father of Paul Revere, and the Bowdoins of Maine and Massachusetts are descendants of a Pierre Baudouin. John Greenleaf Whittier got his middle name from a Huguenot mother whose original family title was Feuillevert. The Faneuils of Boston, the Bayards and De Lanceys of New York, the Dupres and Ravenels and Legarés of Charleston and other South Carolina cities, attest how

firmly the Huguenots became, in a short time, part of the colonial aristocracy of talent and property. If their impress on customs and religion was light, their weight in the economy was palpable—and a further evidence of growing colonial cosmopolitanism.

In a sense, one of the most fateful waves of immigration began in August of 1619, when, as John Rolfe recalled, a Dutch "man-of-Warre" landed at Jamestown bringing, presumably for sale, "twenty Negars." It was the start of a trade that went on for another 189 years (until 1808) with the law's sanction, and then, furtively, for fifty-two more, as naval patrols pursued "blackbirding" vessels, which sometimes escaped to land their forbidden cargoes in Chesapeake Bay or Gulf inlets. It is estimated that in the three hundred and fifty years from the sixteenth to the mid-nineteenth century, some fifteen to twenty million Africans crossed the Atlantic against their will.

Not all of them went to the United States. They also flowed to the West Indies and Latin America, mingling with Indian and Spaniard to form entire new population types. Their labor raised the great staple commodities—sugar, cocoa, coffee, cotton, tobacco, rice, and indigo—on which Western Europe prospered. In their millions, they exercised a tremendous transformative influence on North and South America alike. In the United States, from the start, their presence affected life in profound and intricate fashions. The exodus from Africa, in chains, was a haunted migration, whose ghosts have not yet been laid to rest.

To begin the story of immigration from Africa it is

Neue Reading Kalendar, 1819, NYPL, RARE BOOK DIVISION

The wide variety of German pious sects that gravitated to Pennsylvania were welcomed by the Quakers, who shared their strong religious and moral opposition to slavery. As in Pastorius' protest of 1688, this antislavery sentiment was frequently expressed in sermons and tracts; an illustration from one of these, dated 1819, is shown above. At left, Nathaniel Jocelyn conveyed the stoic determination of the slave Cinqué, who led a successful mutiny in July, 1839, on the slave ship Amistad.

necessary to cut through thickets of mythology, grown in the soil of racial stereotypes. In Europe the causes that drove men to America were depression, war, and religious persecution arising out of the creation of modern states. In Africa, the decline of sub-Saharan federated empires set the stage. A contemporary generation accustomed to visualizing Africa as the "dark continent"—a Victorian image still suggesting fearful infinities of jungle, peopled by Stone Age blacks—will find it hard to believe that when Europe was in its "Dark Ages," around A.D. 900, a Central African empire of Ghana, known only to the Arab world, was at its height. In 1067 Al Bakri, a scholar living in Moorish Spain, wrote a description of the empire based on the records of traders and the tales of adventurers who for centuries had crossed the Sahara in search of Ghana's gold and salt. The rulers of the empire, wrote Al Bakri, could put "two hundred thousand warriors in the field, more than forty thousand of them being armed with bow and arrow." The major city of Aoudaghast was full of "fine houses and solid buildings," and when royalty gave an audience to the public, it was held in a pavilion crowded with pages holding gold-mounted swords, horses draped in cloth of gold, and princes "splendidly clad and with gold plaited into their hair."

By the middle of the thirteenth century, Ghana was superseded by Mali, whose leaders had long been converts to Islam. In 1324 Mali's greatest King, Mansa Kankan Musa, made the pilgrimage to Mecca. According to Al-Umari, a contemporary writer, he left on his

journey with five hundred slaves, each carrying a staff of gold weighing six pounds, and with eighty to one hundred camel loads of gold, each weighing about three hundred pounds. Mansa Musa administered great cities—Timbuktu, Djenné, Walata—the "Milans and Nurembergs of the medieval Sudan," according to the historian Basil Davidson, into which caravans came "in stumbling thirst out of the northern desert with loads of copper and salt, Venetian beads, the sword blades of Europe and Damascus." But it was not until 1339, two years after Mansa Musa's death, that Mali first appeared on a map in Europe. Domestic and foreign wars and the greed of its rulers led to Mali's decline by the beginning of the fifteenth century. It was soon displaced in importance by the Songhai Empire, which had not reached its greatest heights when the Portuguese came to Africa late in the fifteenth century.

But the Songhai state was the last of a disappearing pattern. Raids by Moors from the north and by tribesmen from the African south were breaking up the old centralized empires. Meanwhile tiny West African "kingdoms" were emerging—Dahomey, Kongo, Benin —with whose princelings the Europeans dealt for ivory, pepper, gold, and slaves. And the "civilized" men who came in great ships from the north not only gave tools and other "trade goods" to the Africans but also firearms for them to use against one another. The various peoples of the West African coast—Mandingos, Fulani, Krumen, Ashanti, Fanti, Yoruba, Ibo— already separated by language and customs, did not unite against the invading slavers but remained isolated and vulnerable. "It was easy for slavers to set one group against another," a historian of the trade has written. "It was as though an invading force had arrived in Europe during the Dark Ages and had exploited the continent by pitting each feudal lord against his neighbors."

The European discovery of West Africa came just when the opening of the New World was creating a voracious demand for labor in mine and plantation. It did not have to be black labor necessarily. But Indians and white convicts, also available for forced work, proved difficult to manage for a variety of reasons. The Negroes native to the region extending from Senegal to Gabon suited the colonizers' needs far better —not because they were particularly docile or servile, but because they adapted easily to an agricultural way of life. They were themselves mostly farmers, not food gatherers or hunters, and they were acclimatized to hot latitudes. And they were already available as slaves.

Those who as early as 1540 were brought by the tens of thousands to Mexico, the West Indies, and other parts of Latin America were prisoners even in Africa.

The Ewes, Yorubas, and other tribesmen who dwelt in the primary American slave-producing area along the Ivory and Gold Coasts were first made captives and then sold by other black men. Actually, slavery in an African kingdom might mean something different than it did on a Carolina rice plantation. Often it involved no change of home, tribe, or even status—merely the ownership by another of all the products of one's labor. Africans enslaved to other Africans were sometimes paying for crimes and sometimes taken in war. During hard times some actually sold themselves or their families into bondage to escape starvation. Some were kidnapped by slave catchers and traders; these predators usually were non-Europeans, for white men seldom ventured inland. Whatever the method of enslavement, the victims were a negotiable asset, sometimes sold by their own chiefs. It was a barbarous custom in European eyes, but one which very conveniently excused the slave trade and which Spaniard, Dutchman, and Englishman readily turned to profit. It may be remembered that in Europe this was an era when jurisprudence still kept the rack and thumbscrew in its armamentarium, and exacted executions for petty crimes. Cruelty has no exclusive native land.

The lot of the African slave changed harshly once he was marked for sale to Europeans. Long coffles, sometimes made up of hundreds of slaves tied neck to neck by bark thongs, were marched down to such coastal ports as Popo, Lagos, Bonny, or Calabar, and collected in barracoons, or pens, to be bargained over. The collectors who served as middlemen between native slave-owners and slave-ship captains gathering a cargo were of varied backgrounds. Sometimes they were agents, or "factors," of great companies formed expressly for the trade, such as England's Royal African Company, founded in 1663 under the patronage of the Duke of York himself to furnish three thousand slaves annually to the colonies. Sometimes they were half-caste adventurers, free-lance agents of imperialism, trying to make their fortunes while struggling to preserve their own personalities against the rot of boredom, drunkenness, disease, insects, and the temptations of too easily available power and sex. It was with these men—the dregs of white society—whom the captain made arrangements to have his vessel "slaved."

Once the purchases were completed, the horror began. Few slave ports had wharfage, so ships stood offshore while huge canoes fought their way through the surf, laden with sixty to eighty terrified bound and branded Africans. The slaves were then packed into the holds as tightly as flesh could endure and more. Profit hunger inexorably dictated overcrowding; five and six

hundred manacled blacks would be crammed into spaces as small for each as sixteen inches wide, two and a half feet high, and six feet long. Frequently they could neither sit upright nor even turn unless their neighbors turned too, spoon fashion.

In good weather they might be brought up on deck to stretch their legs twice a day and to be fed gruelly mixtures of yams, rice, corn meal, and manioc. But when storms arose, they were sealed below for weeks at a time in air so foul that crewmen fainted when opening the hatches. (Slave ships were distinguishable for miles by their stench.) In the darkness the miserable "passengers" had to wallow in pools of their own excrement, urine, vomit, and bloody mucus from ever-present dysentery. Disease might kill a quarter or more of a "cargo" in the six- or eight-week passage. Some conscientious captains, eager to preserve the merchandise, did attempt rudimentary sanitation measures, and it was remarked in defense of slave-trade skippers that they often took care of the Negroes better than the masters of immigrant ships looked after their "free" passengers, from whom money had already been collected and whose fate was therefore a matter of indifference. Whether or not that was true, the miserable German or Irishman on the high seas had at least the consolation of thinking that in the long run he would be sweetening his lot in life. The terrified, uncomprehending African had no similar solace. Occasionally, in deep depression or stubborn resistance, slaves would throw themselves overboard if not watched carefully, or attempt suicide by refusing food. In the latter case they were flogged, or their lips were blistered with hot irons, or a cruel device called a speculum oris was hammered between their teeth to pry their mouths open, whereupon they were fed through funnels.

So, in dumb agony, the migration to America took place for the ancestors of almost all black Americans. The trade, at first only a trickle, swelled steadily under the twin stimuli of the Southern plantations' need for muscle and the enterprise of New England and middle-colony merchants who fitted out the slave ships. As many as a thousand Negroes were imported into the Southern colonies each year at the beginning of the eighteenth century, and the total increased as new lands were opened to cultivation. In 1714 there were some 59,000 slaves in the North American colonies of Great Britain. Forty years later the number was 298,000. In 1790 the first United States census would count 697,681 slaves. Most of them were below the Mason-Dixon line, and in many areas of the South they far outnumbered the whites. A new social pattern had taken shape in less than a hundred years.

This allegory, entitled The Voyage of the Sable Venus from Angola
to the West Indies, *was the work of a British artist, Thomas Stothard.
It used as its reference Botticelli's famous* Birth of Venus *and attempted to make palatable the harsher truths of the commerce in slaves.*

From the outset, the fate of the blacks was separate
and inferior. No slave codes existed in the colonies early
in the 1600s, and some historians have even speculated
that when Negroes first arrived, it was not taken for
granted that they would all be slaves. In fact, some
Negroes were employed under ordinary contracts of
indentured service. The English, however, knew from
the start that the Spanish and Portuguese used Negroes
as slaves, and a work of 1623, published in London,
explicitly referred to the "blacke people" whom the
Spaniard carried "into the West Indies, to remaine as
slaves, either in their Mines or in any other servile
uses. . . ." Racial prejudice, ignorance, and fear, evidenced in a variety of ways, soon created the basis for
a different, harsher treatment of Negro "servants" than
of white. In Maryland, an act of 1639 spoke of the

rights of "all Christian inhabitants (slaves excepted)";
nine years later, a ban was imposed on allowing "any
Pagan" to carry guns. In a typical court case of 1640,
three runaway servants were punished. Two had their
terms of indenture extended by four years, but one,
"being a Negro named John Punch," was to "serve his
said master . . . for the time of his natural Life."
Twelve years later another legal document recorded the
sale of a Negro girl "with her Issue and produce . . .
and their services forever." And in a historic departure
from the practice in other slaveholding countries, Virginia in 1662 provided that the child of a slave mother
and a white father should follow the status of the
mother. In the future, there would be thousands of
slaves to whom a mixture of "white blood" in their ancestry—superior though that blood was said to be—

did not bring liberation or even any lightening of their burdens.

By 1700 the manacles had been fastened firmly on the African. And yet even at the beginning, somehow, the self-justifying myth that the "pagan" black could only grub and hoe under the lash was shredded by fact. The plantation was almost an isolated little society. Not only did it demand hands to prune and plant and dig; it also needed men to build and to repair the machinery of a primitive, self-contained economic enterprise. If the master had to make himself an amateur practitioner of law, medicine, and pedagogy, the slave likewise had to learn unaccustomed skills. As early as 1649, a description of the estate of a Captain Matthews of Virginia referred to his possession of "forty Negroe servants," whom he "brings . . . up to Trades in his house." Various documents listing deceased masters' assets showed that Negroes in colonial Virginia and the Carolinas were coopers, carpenters, blacksmiths, and "mechanics"—a catchall name for artisans. Advertisements in eighteenth-century South Carolina newspapers showed Negro slaves practicing many trades—as shipwrights, cabinetmakers, wheelwrights, tanners, shoemakers, spinners, brickmakers, plasterers, painters, and glaziers, among others.

Artisanship was a pathway out of the most binding rigidities of slave control. A man with a manual talent could not be treated quite like livestock. Moreover, many plantation owners discovered that they could hire out their skilled slaves by the month or the year, much as one would rent tools to a neighbor. But "hiring out" involved, very often, permission for slaves to travel and to discharge tasks without supervision. In 1768 a Charleston man proudly offered to sell two or three Negro shoemakers who had "done all my business for nine years past." Another advertised the merits of a black man who "has been intrusted with the Care of a Shoemaker's Shop, without any Assistance from a White Man, for several years." Such facts, brought repeatedly to public attention, were poor props to the theory of the Negro's helpless dependence upon white leadership for his very survival. If further evidence of black potential was needed, it was to be found in the Northern colonies, where slaves were fewer in number but much more likely to be trusted with responsibilities as craftsmen's assistants and house servants than they were to be put to work in the fields. Some masters were even beginning to allow hired-out slaves to save their earnings and buy their freedom. Others were occasionally providing for the emancipation of slaves in their wills. The nucleus of a free black population was present and growing by Revolutionary times.

It was only a small beginning, however, and the trend of white attitudes was against any real upward steps for the African newcomers. Churchmen in the South occasionally made efforts to "Christianize" the slaves, but it was difficult to achieve this without introducing them to concepts of spiritual equality and freedom, and possibly to literacy as well. That was dangerous; a Bible-reading Negro might be made restless by passages that related to such matters as the departure from Egypt. Training Negroes in craftsmanship undoubtedly held the same perils. The black carpenter who learned enough arithmetic to measure his work was less likely to regard numbers as powerful and inaccessible white men's magic. It is hard to keep a little independence from expanding.

Law and custom among whites, especially in the South, militated against much work in educating the children of Africa; the feeling was summed up in a statement of Virginia's House of Burgesses in 1699, objecting to any massive efforts to convert the slaves as unprofitable because of the "Gros . . . Barbarity and rudeness of their Manners, the variety and Strangeness of their Language and the weakness and shallowness of their Minds." So ignorance was allowed to remain, and to become the excuse for further deprivation and continued ignorance. By 1776 a clergyman could say of the Negroes of South Carolina that with few exceptions they "are to this day as great strangers to Christianity, and as much under the influence of Pagan darkness, idolatry and superstition, as they were at their first arrival from Africa."

It was probably a somewhat comforting rationalization for the continuance of slavery. But slave or free, the black presence in America was palpable. Each year, Southern whites became more deeply involved in the consequences of the slave trade. With each new black arrival or the birth of new black children, the habits, patterns, language, customs, fears, and unconscious beliefs of white Americans were being more surely molded by the biracial community's existence—even in terms of black subjugation.

The blacks, in short, had done what the voluntary migrants had done. They had become part of a new society. All of them—the peasants from the Rhineland, Sephardic Jews, Ulstermen, Irish Catholics, and Huguenots—all these, like the powerless blacks, were being fused into a people. That was the development Crèvecoeur observed when he looked at "the American, this new man." It was a long-range development, on which the political revolution that began with the fighting at Lexington and Concord in the spring of 1775 merely superimposed a new form of government.

Unwilling Immigrants

MUSÉE DES BEAUX ARTS NANTES

On the Bottom Rung

In many respects, the earlier the immigrant's arrival, the better; there has always been a special prestige attached to the First Families of Virginia and the descendants of the passengers on the *Mayflower*. But even Americans able to trace their ancestries back more than a generation or two in the new country have qualified as "old" Americans. When a new wave of foreigners reached the wharf, they formed a new bottom rung on the American ladder, and the earlier bottom rung graduated. Each of the bottom rungs seemed to be established on national as much as on class lines: in the eyes of already settled inhabitants, the lowliest English debtor, German peasant, or Irish indentured servant was imbued with the qualities of his nation as a whole, not just his old position in it; he tended to rise and be

accepted as American when the next wave swept in behind him. The pattern, however, did not completely apply to all newcomers. Among America's first immigrants were twenty individuals who came ashore from a Dutch ship at Jamestown in 1619—a year before the *Mayflower* dropped anchor at Plymouth. These twenty were never considered First Family, their descendants never "old" Americans. They were Negroes. West Africans were of various nationalities; like Europeans they had lived in class societies and came from various social ranks. They were lumped together in a single category, but it was continental and racial rather than national. True, experience taught that different black nationalities were useful for different kinds of work; but that was the extent of recognition. They were African slaves—"inferior to the whites in the endowments both of body and mind," according to Thomas Jefferson, whose slave Isaac is shown above. The Negro was stereotyped as naïve, ignorant, outlandish of feature, foolish of look; the image bore little resemblance to the ways in which the black man saw himself at home—as demonstrated by the dignity of the bronze head at the left. Slave traders on occasion excused their occupation on humanitarian grounds: slavery would lead the "savage" blacks to civilization. But one slave trader described a West African town where he saw the people "weave cotton, work in leather, fabricate iron from the bar, engage diligently in agriculture, and, whenever not laboriously employed, devote themselves to reading and writing, of which they are excessively fond." The myth of savagery resulted in part from gaps in African culture, which, while advanced in farming, metallurgy, art, economics, and law, was fragmented by its many languages and its lack of written traditions: the writing of native languages, while not completely unknown, was very rare in sub-Saharan Africa. Further, Europeans saw the blacks as different from themselves, and thus, though "noble savages," not quite so noble as the conquering white man. And white Americans, in a remarkable tour de force, managed to mold a good many of their slaves to conform to the conveniently unflattering stereotype.

The fine bronze, left, was cast in the sixteenth century at the court of the kingdom of Benin, in what is today Nigeria.

REMARKS

ON THE

METHODS OF PROCURING SLAVES

WITH A SHORT ACCOUNT OF THEIR

TREATMENT IN THE WEST-INDIES, &c.

THE reſpectable and increaſing numbers of thoſe, who, from motives of Humanity, have concurred in rejecting the produce of Weſt-Indian Slaves, cannot but afford a ſubject of the ſincereſt joy to every friend of mankind. Even thoſe who from motives of Intereſt ſtill favor or engage in the Trade, have been obliged to be ſilent upon the injuſtice of firſt procuring the Negroes, and have not had the hardineſs to excuſe or palliate the horrors of the MIDDLE PASSAGE: but ſtill they aſſert that the treatment the Slaves meet with in the Weſt-Indies amply counterbalances their previous ſufferings; they have not ſcrupled to extol a ſtate of ſervitude as a happy Aſylum from African Deſpotiſm, and calmly maintain that the condition of the labouring poor in England, is much harder than that of the Negroes in the Weſt-India Iſlands. Upon this ground the oppoſers of ſlavery are willing to meet its advocates, and the deſign of the following Extracts is to enable the public to form an impartial and deciſive judgement upon the ſubject.

When a Ship arrives at the port in the Weſt-Indies the Slaves are expoſed to ſale, (except thoſe who are very ill, they being left in the yard to periſh by diſeaſe or hunger) The healthy are diſpoſed of by public auction, the ſickly by ſcramble. The ſale by ſcramble is thus deſcribed; the ſhip being darkened by ſails, the purchaſers are admitted, who, ruſhing forward with the ferocity of brutes, ſeize as many Slaves as they have occaſion for. In none of the ſales is any care taken to prevent the ſeparation of relatives or friends, but Huſbands and Wives, Parents and Children, fig. 5, are parted with as much unconcern as Sheep and Lambs by the Butcher. Abſtract of the Evidence page 46 and 47.

With reſpect to the GENERAL treatment of the Slaves, Mr. Woolrich ſays, that he never knew the BEST maſter in the Weſt-Indies uſe his Slaves ſo well as the WORST maſter his ſervants in England. Abſtract of the Evidence ſee page 53.

To come to a more PARTICULAR deſcription of their treatment it will be proper to divide them into different claſſes: the firſt conſiſting of thoſe bought for the uſe of the PLANTATION: the ſecond of the IN and OUT-DOOR Slaves.

The Field Slaves are called out by day light to their work: if they are not there in time they are flogged. When put to their work they perform it in rows, and without exception under the whip of Drivers; a certain number of whom are allotted to each gang. Such is the MODE of their labour: as to the TIME of it they begin at Day-light, and continue with two intermiſſions (one for half an hour in the morning, the other for two hours at noon) till ſun ſet. Beſides this they are expected to range about and pick graſs for the cattle, either during their two hours REST at noon, or after the fatigues of the day.

SIR G. YONGE adds, that women were in general conſidered to miſcarry from the cruel treatment they met with; and Captain Hall ſays that he has ſeen a woman ſeated to give ſuck to her Child, rouſed from that ſituation by a ſevere blow from the cart-whip. Abſtract of the Evidence ſee page 53, 54, 55.

THE above account of their labour is confined to that ſeaſon of the year which is termed OUT OF CROP. In the crop ſeaſon the labour is of much longer duration. Mr. Dalrymple ſays, they are obliged to work as long as they can, that is as long as they can keep awake or ſtand. Sometimes through exceſs of fatigue they fall aſleep, when it has happened to thoſe who feed the Mills, that their arms have been caught therein and torn off. Mr. Cook on the ſame ſubject ſtates, that they work in general eighteen hours out of the twenty-four; he knew a Girl loſe her hand by the Mill while feeding it, being overcome with ſleep ſhe dropped againſt the rollers. Abſtract of the Evidence p. 55, 56.

To this account of their labour, it ſhould be added, that it appears that on ſome eſtates the Slaves have Sunday and Saturday afternoon to themſelves, on others Sunday only, and on others only Sunday in part. It appears again that IN CROP on no eſtates have they more than Sunday for the cultivation of their own lands. Abſtract of the Evidence page 56.

THE point next to be conſidered is the FOOD of the Slaves, which appears to be ſubject to no rule: on ſome eſtates they are allowed land, on others proviſions, and others are allowed proviſions and land jointly. The beſt allowance is at Barbadoes, of which the following is the account. The Slaves in general, ſays Gen. Tottenham, appeared to be ill fed: each Slave had one pint of grain for twenty-four hours and ſometimes half a rotten Herring. When the Herrings were UNFIT FOR THE WHITES, they were bought up FOR THE SLAVES. Nine pints of corn, and one pound of ſalt-fiſh a week, is in general the utmoſt allowance. As a proof that ſome have not food enough, Mr Cook ſays that he has known both Africans and Creoles eat the putrid carcaſſes of animals THROUGH WANT. Abſtract of the Evidence page 57 and 58.

As to the accuſation of their being THIEVES, all the Evidences maintain that it was on account of their being HALF STARVED. Abſt. of the Evidence page 58.

CONCERNING the PROPERTY of the field-ſlaves, all the Evidences agree in aſſerting that they never heard of a field-ſlave amaſſing ſuch a ſum as enabled him to purchaſe his freedom. Abſtract of the Evidence page 60.

HAVING now deſcribed the ſtate of the plantation, it will be proper to ſay a few words on that of the IN and OUT-DOOR Slaves.

THE IN-DOOR Slaves are allowed to be better clothed, and fed, and leſs worked, than the plantation; on account however of being conſtantly expoſed to the cruelty and caprice of their Maſters and Miſtreſſes, their lives are rendered ſo wretched, that they not unfrequently wiſh to be ſent to the field: the OUT-DOOR Slaves are porters, coopers, &c. who are obliged to bring to their Maſters a certain ſum every day.

THE ordinary puniſhments of the Slaves are inflicted by the Whip and Cow-ſkin. This, ſays Mr. Woolrich, is generally made of plaited Cow-ſkin, with a thick ſtrong laſh, it is ſo formidable an inſtrument that ſome of the overſeers can by means of it take the ſkin off a horſe's back, he has ſeen them lay the marks of it into a deal board: the inciſions (according to Dr. Harriſon and the Dean of Middleham) are ſometimes ſo deep, that you may lay your finger into the wounds, and are ſuch as no time can eraſe. As a farther proof of the SEVERITY of the puniſhments, the following facts are adduced. Mr. Fitzmaurice has known pregnant women ſo ſeverely whipped as to have miſcarried in conſequence of it. Davidſon knew a Negro Girl die of a mortification of her wounds two days after whipping. Dr. Jackſon recollects a Negro dying under the laſh or ſoon after. Abſtract of the Evidence ſee page 66 and 67.

WE now proceed to the EXTRAORDINARY puniſhments, in the infliction of which, malice, fury, and all the worſt paſſions of the human mind, rage with unbridled licence. Benevolence recoils at the dreadful perſpective, and can ſcarce collect compoſure to diſcloſe the Bloody Catalogue.

CAPTAIN RAP has known Slaves ſeverely puniſhed, then put into the Stocks, a cattle chain of ſixty or ſeventy pounds weight put on them, and a large collar round their necks, and a weight of fifty-ſix pounds faſtened to the chain, when they were driven afield: the collars are formed with two, three, or four projections, which hinder them from lying down to ſleep. See fig. 7 and 8.

A NEGRO man in Jamaica (ſays Dr. Harriſon) was put on the picket ſo long, as to cauſe a mortification of his foot and hand, on ſuſpicion of robbing his maſter, a public officer, of a ſum of money, which it afterwards appeared THE MASTER HAD TAKEN HIMSELF. Yet the Maſter was privy to the puniſhment and the Slave had no compenſation. Abſtract of the Evidence page 69.

MR. FITZMAURICE mentions the practice of dropping hot lead upon the Slaves, which he ſaw performed by a Planter of the name of Ruſhie in Jamaica, this ſame man in three years deſtroyed by ſeverity FORTY NEGROES OUT OF SIXTY. The reſt of the conduct of this planter was ſuppreſſed by the Houſe of Commons, as containing circumſtances TOO HORRIBLE TO BE GIVEN TO THE WORLD.

AN overſeer on the Eſtate where Mr. J. Turry was, in Grenada, threw a Slave INTO THE BOILING CANE JUICE who died in four days.

CAPTAIN COOK relates that he ſaw a woman named Rachel Lauder, beat a Slave moſt unmercifully, and would have murdered her had ſhe not been prevented. the girl's crime was, the not bringing money enough from on board of ſhip, WHITHER SHE HAD BEEN SENT BY HER MISTRESS, FOR THE PURPOSE OF PROSTITUTION.

LIEUTENANT DAVISON relates, that the wife of the Clergyman at Port Royal, uſed to drop hot ſealing wax on her Negroes after flogging—he was ſent for as Surgeon to one of them whoſe breaſt was terribly burnt.

IF it ſhould be aſked for what offences the puniſhments recited have taken place, the following anſwer may be given.

UNDER the head of ORDINARY puniſhments, the Slaves appear to have ſuffered for not coming to the field in time, not picking a ſufficient quantity of graſs, for ſtaying too long of an errand, and Theft, to which they were often driven by Hunger.

UNDER the Head of EXTRAORDINARY puniſhments the following have been alledged as reaſons; for running away, for breaking a plate, or to extort confeſſion, in the moments of paſſion, and one on a diabolical pretence which the maſter held out to the world to conceal HIS OWN VILLAINY, AND WHICH HE KNEW TO BE FALSE. WOMEN puniſh their Slaves, for being found pregnant, for not bringing home the FULL WAGES OF PROSTITUTION, and others, without EVEN THE ALLEGATION OF A FAULT.

ALL the facts that have been now adduced are of unqueſtionable authority, having been extracted from the Evidence laid before the Houſe of Commons by eye-witneſſes of the facts. Let now every honeſt man lay his hand on his breaſt, and ſeriouſly reflect whether he is juſtifiable in countenancing ſuch barbarities; or whether he ought not to reject with horror, the ſmalleſt participation in ſuch infernal tranſactions. To the weaker ſex, whoſe amicable characteriſtic it is, to be "tremblingly alive" to every tale of woe, the friends of the Abolition return their warmeſt acknowledgements, for the zeal with which many of them have eſpouſed the cauſe of humanity, and for the noble example they have ſhewn, in rejecting the produce of Slavery and Miſery.

FIG. I.

Repreſents the manner of Yoking the Slaves by the Mundingoes, or African Slave Merchants, who uſually march annually in eight or ten parties, from the River Gambia to Bambarra; each party having from one hundred to one hundred and fifty Slaves.

FIG. II.

Theſe Log-Yokes are made of the roots of trees—and ſo heavy as to make it extremely difficult for the perſon who wears it to walk, much more to eſcape or run away.

FIG. III.

Where the roads lay through woods, the captive inhabitants are made to travel ſeveral hundred miles with a log hung as here deſcribed.

FIG. IV.

A view of the leg bolts or ſhackles, as put upon the legs of the Slaves on ſhip board, in the middle paſſage.

FIG. V.

The Huſband and Wife, after being ſold to different purchaſers, violently ſeparated—probably never to ſee each other more!

FIG. VI.

When Slaves are purchaſed by the dealers they are generally marked on the breaſt with a red hot iron.

FIG. VII.

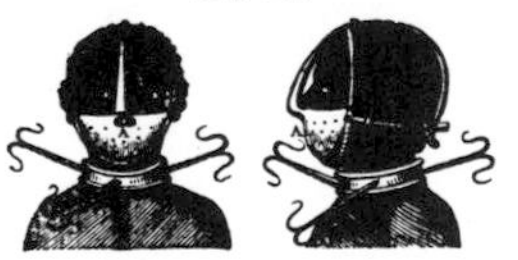

A front and profile view of an African's head with the mouth piece and necklace, the hooks round which, are placed as a preventative to an eſcape when purſued in the woods, or, to procuring of reſt by laying the head down.

N.B. At A is a piece of flat iron which goes into the mouth—and ſo effectually keeps down the tongue, that nothing can be ſwallowed, not even the ſaliva, a paſſage for which is made through holes in the mouth plate.

FIG. VIII.

A repreſentation of a Slave at work as cruelly accoutered—with a head frame and mouth piece to prevent his eating—with boots and ſpurs (as they are called) round his legs, and an half hundred weight chained to his body to prevent his abſconding.

FIG. IX.

An enlarged view of the mouth piece—which when long worn—becomes ſo heated as frequently to bring off the ſkin along with it.

N.B. A late reſpectable tradeſman in London, had an order for a great number of theſe and other ſuch like inſtruments—but after they were made, finding the uſes they were intended for, he declined ſending them.

FIG. X.

An enlarged view of the Boots and Spurs, as ſeen uſed on ſome plantations in Antigua.

FIG. XI.

The manner in which ſome Slaves are placed to be flogged.

FIG. XII.

Another method of fixing the poor victims on a ladder to be flogged, which is alſo occaſionally laid flat on the ground for ſeverer puniſhments.

LONDON: PRINTED BY AND FOR DARTON AND HARVEY, N°. 55, GRACECHURCH-STREET. MDCCXCIII.

[PRICE THREE PENCE.]

Methods of Procuring Slaves, 1793, NYPL

ABOVE: *An English brochure commented on the slave trade, illustrating methods of manacling and flogging slaves.*
RIGHT: *This ivory carving was done by a Yoruba artist; many members of his nation went as slaves to America.*

The terra-cotta head above, probably done before 1300, exemplifies the best in Ife art.

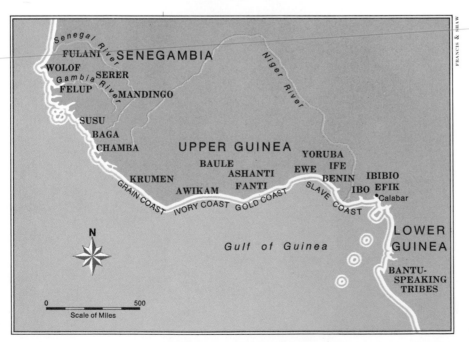

SENEGAMBIA

Senegal River

FULANI

WOLOF

SERER

Gambia River

FELUP

MANDINGO

Niger River

SUSU

BAGA

CHAMBA

UPPER GUINEA

BAULE

YORUBA

IFE

KRUMEN

ASHANTI

EWE

BENIN

IBIBIO

AWIKAM

FANTI

IBO

EFIK

GRAIN COAST

IVORY COAST

GOLD COAST

SLAVE COAST

•Calabar

N

Gulf of Guinea

LOWER
GUINEA

BANTU-
SPEAKING
TRIBES

0   500
Scale of Miles

*The detail of a wood sculpture, right, testifies to the fine work in that medium done
for centuries, as a part of ancestor worship, by the Baule people in West Africa.*

From Many, One

The blacks who came in chains to the New World were as varied in appearance and cultures as the men who enslaved them; the sculptures shown here indicate some of that diversity. Most had lived on or near the West African coast (see map). From the north, Senegambia, came light-skinned Fulani—Moslems, many highly literate in Arabic; the dark, powerful Wolof; Mandingo, themselves slaveholding planters and merchants; Serer and Felup. Senegambians were thought too "genteel and courteous" for hard labor but "cleanliest and fittest for house servants." Down the bulge, between the Gambia River and the Grain Coast, lived the Baga, Susu, and Chamba. From the Grain, Ivory, and Gold Coasts came marvelous boatmen, the Krumen, and the Awikam, Ashanti, and Fanti; Gold Coast blacks were prized highly, though their instincts for leadership made them "troublesome," as in their frequent instigations of slave mutinies. Eastward, along the Gulf of Guinea, lived the Ewe and Yoruba, rugged farmers, and the Benin, Ibo, Ibibio, and Efik. From south of Calabar, along fifteen hundred miles of the Lower Guinea coast, came Bantu-speaking peoples. Whatever their differences, in America most were classed as one group—slaves—and were dismissed, with increasing frequency, as "all alike."

"Wilful and Loth to Leave"

The Africans' reaction to the white invader is not well documented; there are few firsthand accounts of their impressions, since not many captured Africans ever learned to write English. One record, however, was left by the son of a Benin village elder. Olaudah Equiano and his sister were kidnapped while playing near their home and sold to different traders two days later. The boy was carried, terrified, aboard the slave ship: "I was immediately handled and tossed up to see if I were sound by some of the crew and I was now persuaded that . . . they were going to kill me." He remembered that he "would have freely . . . exchanged my condition with that of the meanest slave in my own country," and that the sight of a mass of black people chained together in utter dejection moved him to ask "if we were to be eaten by these white men with horrible looks, red faces, and long hair." This fear was widespread among West African peoples, who looked on the intruders as a barbarous tribe of man-eating savages. Even before they reached the ships, a number of the selected blacks had succumbed to panic. After each of them had been branded on the chest to denote the nationality of the purchasing company, the slaves were herded down to the shore. As they approached, with the surf out of sight and crashing thunderously, many of them who had never seen the ocean believed that the sound they heard was the voice of a monster. Then they saw the sea. Some threw themselves on the beach, "clutching handfuls of sand," as one writer put it, "in a desperate effort to remain in Africa." Others tried to commit suicide by throttling themselves with their shackles. "The Negroes are so wilful and loth to leave their own country," wrote a slaver, "that they have often leap'd out of the canoos, boat and ship, into the sea, and kept under until they were drowned. . . ." Still others followed a different course to the same end: in deep melancholy at finding themselves separated from family and tribe and their intricately organized relationships, customs, ceremonies, and taboos, and facing the rumored horrors of "the land where the slaves are sold," they starved themselves to death during the long ocean voyage.

The bronze figure of a musketeer, right, made by a Benin artist, reflected the West African's image of the European intruders, whose firearms enabled them brutally to exploit the region. Perhaps some whites appreciated the skillfulness of such art and might have been fascinated by the mysteries hidden behind secret-society masks like the Ibo example opposite. But few of them had any interest in the old cultures that they were disrupting.

The World They Left

Save for his acquaintance with Egypt and North Africa, the white man has known little of what happened in the African continent before his own arrival there. Historical inquiry has been hampered by the lack of written records and documents, but discoveries by twentieth-century archaeologists and the use of radiocarbon dating are bringing to light some of the missing pieces of the African past. It has long been known that after the tenth century A.D. powerful kingdoms, with widespread commerce and trade, rose and fell in the homelands of the people who were brought to America as slaves. But recent archaeological discoveries now indicate that a much older culture, the Nok, going back to perhaps nine hundred years before Christ, flourished in northern Nigeria. The Nok figures, writes Basil Davidson, show "a rare sensitivity" and "a sophistication of style that seems extraordinary for the times in which they were made." Still, archaeology has not yet answered all the questions about Africa's past. The Yoruba mask above, adorned with snakes (a symbol of the supernatural in ancient Egypt), has led some students of Africa to look to the north for the key to the origins of the sub-Saharan people, while others now believe that "Egypt owed more to Negro Africa than the other way around."

Though considered by most whites to be primitive in all things, the blacks who were wrenched from Africa as slaves actually left behind them a rich cultural heritage and a complex commercial network. Trade across the Sahara existed as early as 2000 B.C., but it was not until the introduction of the camel into North Africa (probably in the first century after Christ) that trans-Saharan trade was made relatively easy. By the ninth century, Ghana was already known to the Arab world as "a country where gold grows like plants." Besides natural resources, West Africa was rich in the art produced by native craftsmen. The mask shown at bottom, opposite, was carved by a Guro tribesman of the Ivory Coast, and on the Gold Coast the Ashanti made brass figurines, such as the hunter at the left, which they used in the weighing of gold.

Humanity Forgotten

The unreality in the situation drew stereotyped reactions from all quarters, as typified by the saccharine woodcut at left, depicting a slave couple about to be separated by sale. Slave masters were all brutes (or noble benefactors); slaves were all miserable (or playful and content). Arguments could not often be debated because they were infuriating; too much depended on the outcome—wealth, social structure, political power. And everyone's humanity seemed to be forgotten, especially that of blacks like the man at the right—the last slave to be freed in New York State.

The black man proved to be a particularly hardy strain of immigrant and was responsible for much of the nation's agricultural growth. But his presence was also upsetting: in a land of free men, he was bound. The slave could not marry; he was denied education, could not testify against a white in Southern courts, and, for purposes of state representation, was counted as—that ultimate in insults—three-fifths of a man. Much of this was done simply to maintain the institution of slavery, but attitudes toward slaves spilled over on freed blacks, too. To justify the treatment, white Americans easily developed a rationale: the Negro was inherently inferior and could not exist above a savage level outside slavery. And then this character was forced on the Negro. Treated as a child, and safest when he so responded, the slave helped the white man by behaving, to some degree, like a child.

Near this spot on the Concord River, by such a "rude bridge," Americans fired the shots that signaled Revolution.

A QUESTION OF LOYALTIES

AMONG THE IMMIGRANTS who reached American shores in 1774 was a thirty-seven-year-old Englishman named Thomas Paine, a loner whose principal occupation in life seemed to be to fail at things. He was separated from his wife, he belonged to no church, and he had successively proved unable to earn a living as a sailor, grocer, tobacconist, corsetmaker, and tax collector. His only assets on arrival were some letters of introduction from Benjamin Franklin, one of which he presented to Philadelphia's Dr. Benjamin Rush, a distinguished physician and political figure. Franklin had met Paine in London while the latter was attempting to persuade Parliament to improve the working conditions and salaries of his fellow excisemen. Franklin found Paine's political views, and the language in which he delivered them, unorthodox and interesting. So did Dr. Rush, particularly when the newcomer ardently pressed his conviction that the colonies should go beyond seeking better treatment from Britain and strike out without equivocation for total independence.

Dr. Rush had entertained similar notions himself, but he was not quite ready to risk "the popular odium" that conservative Philadelphia might heap upon the author of such a radical proposal. Paine, in contrast, had no roots in Penn's city and little to lose, so Dr. Rush encouraged him to write a pamphlet on the subject. When it appeared in January, 1776, under the title *Common Sense*, a small-scale miracle ensued; as many as 120,000 copies were sold in three months, according to one estimate—a total far in excess of any reasonable expectation. It was as if Americans had been waiting for Paine's thudding sentences to jar them into confronting the implications of their own rebellion.

For page after page Paine hammered away at the sanctities of generations: monarchy, hereditary succession, loyalty to the mother country, government itself. As he warmed to his subject, his field of vision widened. All the world had a stake in the battles between redcoats and patriot militiamen. "'Tis not the affair of a City, a Country, a Province, or a Kingdom; but of a Continent—of at least one eighth part of the habitable Globe. 'Tis not the concern of a day, a year, or an age; posterity are virtually involved in the contest, and will be more or less affected even to the end of time, by the proceedings now." Paine the wanderer, the defeated European, had grasped the continental and historical dimension of the American struggle, and flung it in the face of all humanity as a challenge:

O! ye that love mankind! Ye that dare oppose not only the tyranny but the tyrant, stand forth! Every spot of the old world is overrun with oppression. Freedom hath been hunted round the Globe. Asia and Africa have long expelled her. Europe regards her like a stranger, and England hath given her warning to depart. O! receive the fugitive, and prepare in time an asylum for mankind.

An asylum for mankind! The phrase codified something already inherent in America, and made it a reason to fight; it far exceeded a demand for a voice in taxation or a fairer share in the profits of imperial trade. The United States came into being not merely as an emancipated colony but with certain commitments to that "candid world" which was to be addressed by the Declaration of Independence. In the eyes of at least some Americans in every later generation, their country would have a solemn obligation to serve as a model of

Humbly dedicated to the Jacobine Clubs of France & England! by Common Sense
"These are your Gods, O Israel."

Pub. May 28th 1791. by H. Humphrey
No. 18, old Bond Street

"THE RIGHTS OF MAN; or TOMMY PAINE, the little American Taylor, taking the Measure of the CROWN, for a new Pair of Revolution-Breeches.

Common Sense *was credited with having converted thousands of colonials to the cause of American independence. Its author, Thomas Paine (shown above in a miniature portrait painted by John Trumbull), turned his attention to his native England after the success of the American and French Revolutions. "My country is the world," he once said, "and my religion is to do good." In 1791 and 1792 he published* The Rights of Man, *a treatise that supported the French radicals and called for a republican revolution in England. "Moderation in principle is always a vice," Paine believed. But his lack of moderation evoked such reactions as the cartoon at left, which presented him as a not very bright "American Taylor" trying to fashion a suit of democratic clothes for the British government. British officialdom, not taking kindly to* The Rights of Man, *suppressed the book and shut its author out of the country.*

what liberty could achieve in a commonwealth and also as a haven to those elsewhere to whom liberty was denied. Behind this faith was an awareness of how many men of "foreign" blood had helped to fuse provincial loyalties into American nationalism in the War for Independence.

The long crisis of empire that ended in revolt in 1775 was a time of special testing for those colonists not of English stock. In what ways would they respond to quarrels between London and provincial capitals over the "rights of Englishmen"? Would they remain aloof? Would they follow the tug of old-country loyalties and line up on one side or the other in solid phalanxes of Dutchmen for King George or Irish behind the Continental Congress? Or would they divide among themselves along lines of cleavage scored by geography, economic interests, local feuds, class ties, clan habits —just as other American crown subjects were doing?

In the blaze of gunfire it was this last pattern that leaped into clarity. Members of the immigrant groups split into opposed factions, and in so doing demonstrated—even when they took the Tory side—the overwhelming Americanizing effect of the environment. Had they stood in monolithic blocs, they would have been loyal aliens, under whatever banner they chose. But when families, communities, and congregations of the foreign-born broke apart as "rebels" and "loyalists," they shared to the full the pain of national birth.

The Scotch-Irish, for example, followed their traditionally pugnacious leadership in divergent paths. In Pennsylvania, so many of them bore arms in the homegrown force known as the Pennsylvania Line that General "Light Horse Harry" Lee called it "the line of Ireland." Yet in Philadelphia in 1778, the commanding general of the British occupation forces was able to raise a regiment made up almost exclusively of "Volunteers of Ireland"—men from all parts of the Emerald Isle, who had little in common but a desire to polish off Washington's half-starved army at nearby Valley Forge. What turned the Ulstermen toward British or American recruiting camps was often enough their reaction to the provincial leadership and their estimate of what would best overcome it. In Pennsylvania, those who fought on the side of independence hoped that collapsing royal authority would drag down with it the Quaker oligarchy whose pacifism and stinginess had left the frontier vulnerable to Indian raids

In the Carolinas, however, the Scotch-Irish of the back country nursed long-standing grudges against the tidewater planters, whom they saw as land-grabbing, power-hungry, haughty aristocrats, battening on God's poor. There, indeed, resentment ran so deep that when the planters chose the side of resistance, thousands of Scotch-Irishmen fought for the King, hoping that when the war ended His victorious Majesty would render justice by dividing the "rebel" landholdings among the faithful. Yet not quite all of the Carolina frontier's Scotch-Irish families took that road. In the district known as the Waxhaws, on the border between North and South Carolina, a British officer reported the populace to be "universally Irish and universally disaffected." Among the disaffected was the son of a Carrickfergus farmer, who joined a militia company of dragoons in 1780 when he was thirteen years old, was captured by the redcoats the next year, and had his scalp laid open by a saber when he refused a British officer's peremptory demand to clean his boots. His sixteen-year-old brother died of smallpox contracted in British detention, and his mother of typhus caught while nursing still other prisoners. His name was Andrew Jackson.

In New Hampshire, the outbreak of war stirred forty-six-year-old John Stark, whose father had come from Ulster in 1720, into instant action. A tight-lipped man of medium height, with strong features and keen eyes, he was a veteran of Rogers' Rangers, a hard-fighting frontier outfit of French and Indian War fame. Forsaking his farm, he rode to Cambridge, Massachusetts, and offered his services to the American army. For nearly two years he fought gallantly, but he *was* an Irishman, and no man to brook an insult, real or imagined. When Congress promoted several junior officers over his head, Stark resigned his commission in March, 1777, and went home. But only four months later General John Burgoyne's army, slashing down from Canada toward Albany, raised the alarm in western New England. On July 18, New Hampshire commissioned Stark brigadier general and authorized him

to raise a force and speed to the aid of Vermont. In twenty days he assembled more than fourteen hundred men, armed them, and hustled them through the mountains to Manchester, Vermont. A little more than a week later, he fell upon a British force at Bennington and devastated it, capturing nearly seven hundred men and killing their Hessian commander, Colonel Friedrich Baum. Stark made his way into the history books by allegedly crying out to his men: "There, my boys, are your enemies, the red-coats and tories; you must beat them or my wife sleeps a widow tonight."

The history books fail to add a significant minor note in the story. A year previously, at the Battle of Long Island, Stark's brother William had been killed in action at the head of a regiment—of loyalists.

Although the lessons of history are drawn from the behavior of aggregates, history itself is lived by individuals. The records of two German and two Huguenot families give human dimension to the story of how immigrants and their sons became participants in a war that would decide the fate of a continent. The names of these four illustrative and illustrious families are Mühlenberg (which soon jettisoned the umlaut), Herkimer, Laurens, and De Lancey.

The Muhlenbergs form what one author, Stephen Hess, has called an American political dynasty, whose achievement was to transport the colonial Germans—"speaking a different language, following different customs, suspicious of outsiders, prone to stand apart" into full participation in national life via the avenue of politics. The patriarch was Heinrich (Henry) Melchior Mühlenberg, who arrived in Pennsylvania in 1742 to answer the cry of the colony's growing number of Lutherans for trained leadership. Mühlenberg was steeped in the profundities of classical theological disputation as taught at the universities of Göttingen and Halle. He was also a zealous organizer, and within six years of landing in Philadelphia had created the first Lutheran synod in America. Inside of ten years he had linked twenty congregations together at a price that included the wrenching of his own bones in endless, jouncing trips across the middle Atlantic and Southern colonies. In 1745 he united two branches of German immigration by marrying John Conrad Weiser's daughter. Weiser's family had come to New York's Schoharie Valley as part of the Palatinate settlement of the early part of the century. Weiser himself became spectacularly Americanized. He ran away from home, living with the Mohawks and learning their tongue (they bestowed on him the name of Tarachiawagon, "he who holds the heavens"). As a result he became a crack Indian trader, and an agent in dealing with the red men.

Some of the wild Weiser strain passed to Heinrich Melchoir's sons Peter and Frederick. Both followed their father's wish in becoming ministers (though Peter, the elder, did not complete the studies for which he was sent to Germany). But there obedience reached its high-water mark. Old Heinrich Melchior did not burn with revolutionary zeal. Instead he followed a German tradition in effect since the brutal Thirty Years' War, under which each prince set the religious style of his domain. Thus civil and religious authorities were partners. It was natural that the founding father of American Lutheranism saw George III as a sponsor of his efforts and shrank from challenges to royal authority. But Peter, off to take a Virginia pastorate in 1772 when he was twenty-six, drank of the intoxicating waters of protest. The German community he served elected him to the House of Burgesses, where he was influenced by the ideas of firebrands like Patrick Henry. Peter Muhlenberg became chairman of Dunmore County's pro-Revolutionary Committee of Public Safety in 1774. In January of 1776, if there is truth in a local legend, he ascended to the pulpit one Sunday, gazed firmly at his parishioners, and announced his text as Ecclesiastes 3:1: "For every thing there is a season, and a time to every purpose under heaven." He then went on to review the history of British oppression and build his argument. There had been a time to petition, and there was now a time to resist. There was a time to pray, and a time to fight. As the services ended, Pastor Muhlenberg impatiently ripped away at the ties of his gown, shrugged it back off his shoulders, and stood revealed in the uniform of colonel of the Continental Army. Simultaneously, the regimental recruiting sergeants, gathered by prearrangement outside the church door, launched into a clamorous, irresistible drum roll.

Transformed from pastor to warrior, Muhlenberg went on to carve out a distinguished combat record. He earned the nickname of "Devil Pete" in the course of several hard-fought engagements, and was in on the last act of the drama at Yorktown. On October 24, 1781, by now a brigadier general, Muhlenberg led an attack against one of two strong points anchoring the British lines. (At the head of his advance party was another immigrant, from the West Indies, named Alexander Hamilton.) At the end of the war, the former minister, now a hero to Pennsylvania's Germans second only to Washington, reaped his reward. He became a member of Pennsylvania's Supreme Executive Council, then its vice-president (under an early constitution), then a member of the First, Third, and Sixth Federal Congresses, and finally a Senator.

Frederick, the younger son, was of little more comfort to Heinrich Melchior. He had a congregation in New York, but he too immersed himself in radical politics—to such an extent that when the British occupied the city he was forced to flee to Philadelphia, where in 1779 he was elected to the Continental Congress. Less colorful than his brother Peter, he nonetheless was more influential politically than anyone in his family. After serving in the Pennsylvania convention that ratified the Constitution, he was elected to the First Congress—as was Peter—and was chosen first Speaker of the House of Representatives. He was then not quite thirty-nine, and his family had been in America for fewer than fifty years. The Congressmen who voted for him had, knowingly or not, made a powerful statement about the "asylum for mankind" that they were preparing to govern.

Heinrich Melchior Mühlenberg, who died in 1787, did not witness this particular family triumph, but he lived long enough to see his two older sons' rise in the "hurle burle" of politics, and possibly even to hope that the openness of American society would allow his many descendants distinguished careers. These they did achieve, in law, medicine, science, religion, and education, providing a fresh level of meaning for the Revolution that the patriarch resisted and his heirs embraced.

Unlike Heinrich Mühlenberg, Nicholas Herkimer found the choice between resistance and rebellion neither painful nor unclear. New York's Mohawk Valley is a fruitful and gentle country of glacial soils pushed up into softly swelling ridges. In 1725, when John Herchheimer arrived in the valley, later known as Tryon County, it was thickly wooded and was controlled by the Iroquois. Patiently Herchheimer and his fellow Rhinelanders hacked away at the forest, planted flax, wheat, oats, corn, and rye in their seasons, built cabins and barns, and dreamed of a safe future for the children, such as young Nicholas Herchheimer, born in 1728. But by the time Nicholas had become a young man with the Anglicized name Herkimer, it was clear that security was still at least a generation away. Indian attacks periodically scorched the settlements. And there were other enemies, too, in the valley's great landholding families, including those headed by Sir John Butler and Sir William Johnson. Their wealth, their control of trade with the Indians and with importers of European goods, their political connections, and their ability to hire and allocate the services of vitally needed artisans like millwrights and wheelwrights, all added up to something resembling feudal power. The German (as well as some of the Dutch, Irish, and Yankee) pioneers of Tryon County resented that resemblance. They turned to leaders of their own, like Herkimer, whose

As quickly as Mühlenberg was Anglicized, the Muhlenbergs were Americanized. Heinrich Melchior (bottom right), German-born founder of Lutheranism in the colonies, did not share the Revolutionary ideals of his sons Frederick (bottom left) and Peter (top). Both left the ministry for politics and served in the new United States Congress.

steady worldly efforts had enabled him to build a brick house—an impressive symbol on the relatively undeveloped frontier. They elected him a lieutenant of militia during the French and Indian War, then colonel, then chairman of the local Committee of Safety. In America, that could happen to the son of an untitled "Dutchman" easily—if he had the right qualities.

The Revolution tore the valley wide open. Many of the settlers believed that their best hope of safety lay in alliance with the powerful Tory families who had the crown's seeming protection. The Butlers and the Johnsons intended to convince everyone of the wholesomeness of that policy. They led raiding parties of white and Indian followers in savage strikes against nests of suspected revolutionaries. Herkimer had not hesitated for a moment to cast his lot with the enemies of royal rule. As a militia leader, he had his hands full defending settlements like German Flats and Stone Arabia against despoilment. Then, in the summer of 1776, he faced a new and more formidable enemy.

Late in July, a British colonel, Barry St. Leger, moved out from Oswego at the head of a force of five hundred British and Hessian troops, five hundred Tory rangers, and about a thousand Indians. His objective was to reach the Mohawk River and follow it down to Albany to join Burgoyne's main force there for the final thrust against the rebels. A week's march brought him to Fort Stanwix (renamed Fort Schuyler by the Americans) on the site of today's Rome, New York. There seven hundred and fifty colonials under two Dutch-

descended officers, Marinus Willett and Peter Gansevoort, held him off. St. Leger threw siege lines around the earthen walls and log palisades of the fort, and Gansevoort and Willett sent messengers slipping stealthily out along forest trails for reinforcements.

Up from the southeast came the Tryon County militia, eight hundred strong, under the thickset, pipe-puffing Herkimer—"Old Honikol" to his troopers, who were also his neighbors. At Oriskany, eight miles from the fort, an ambush party was waiting for him. On August 6, they pounced from the woods in an explosion of hatred. It was Indian against Indian (St. Leger's Mohawks against some friendly Oneidas recruited by Herkimer), settler against settler, possibly even German against German. There were no flags and no trumpets—only the screams of dying men, many stabbed repeatedly after they fell and scalped while they were still conscious. Two hundred militiamen were killed and as many more wounded or captured. Herkimer's knee was smashed by a bullet, but, propped against a tree, he pulled his shattered troops together on high ground, where they held out against repeated assaults. Then rain fell, soaking gunpowder and men alike and halting combat. Later that day, the Tryon County militia retreated, carrying Old Honikol on a litter.

It was not complete defeat. While the fighting was at its height, Marinus Willett led a sortie into a British camp and destroyed or seized everything portable—including fifty brass kettles and a hundred blankets intended as gifts for the Indians—without losing a man. This discouraged the red men mightily; they had little other motive but material gain for sacrificing braves in quarrels between the whites. Later, in the face of rumors that a huge American relief column was on the way, they abandoned St. Leger entirely, forcing him to retreat to Oswego. But Herkimer did not live to see this. Back at his brick house, a surgeon had crudely amputated his leg. Resultant complications proved too much for even his toughened constitution. He died ten days later, reputedly reading a Bible verse: "My wounds stink and are corrupt because of my foolishness." The settlers, who thought more kindly of his contribution than he, later named an upstate town and county in his honor.

Sometime after Louis XIV revoked the Edict of Nantes in 1685, two French Protestant gentlemen, probably unknown to each other, arrived in New York. They were Stephen De Lancey and André Laurens. What befell them and their grandsons superbly condenses two varieties of American experience. Stephen De Lancey remained in New York and married Anne Van Cortlandt, a daughter of a rich Dutch family. In

1703, their first son, James, was born. James went neither to France nor Holland, his parents' ancestral homes, for his education, but, as was proper for an aristocrat in the British colonies, he was sent to Cambridge to acquire the accomplishments of an English gentleman, then to the Inner Temple to read law and to make friendships of future utility. Back in New York in 1725, he soon married Anne Heathcote, whose father was receiver-general of customs of North America. With this connection, James De Lancey was able to rise to the office of chief justice of the colony, where he earned the rather clouded distinction of presiding at the trial of the printer John Peter Zenger, a German immigrant, for seditious libel. In 1753 De Lancey became lieutenant governor, vigorously carried on feuds with such other great families as the Clintons and the Livingstons, in 1754 became a signer of the charter of King's College (later Columbia), and died in 1760.

His son, also named James, was sent to Eton and Cambridge, and entered the army on completing his studies. He took part in the French and Indian War, and indulged a country gentleman's passion for horseflesh. Soon after his father died, Captain James imported the first English thoroughbreds ever brought to New York. He divided his time between caring for them, looking after real-estate investments on what is now New York's lower East Side, guiding the family's mercantile ventures, and managing the affairs of the "De Lancey interest," in effect a political party. From time to time he joined in objections to crown policies that adversely affected the family businesses. But essentially, James De Lancey had become an upper-class Englishman. When the fighting came, he sold out his stud and racing stable and moved with his family to England. The Revolutionary New York legislature, by acts of 1777 and 1779, confiscated all the De Lancey estates, ending the dynasty's participation in American economic life.

This seizure, of course, depended for its effectiveness on the triumph of the American cause, which two other De Lanceys were striving mightily to prevent. Captain James had a cousin, also named James—the son of Peter, old Stephen De Lancey's second son. This James, known as Colonel James, loved horseflesh not merely on the track but amid the thunder of the cannons and the heat of battle. After the British occupied New York in 1776, he organized a band of fifty mounted guerrillas who harassed the rebels in Westchester County. De Lancey's Horse was no plumed troop fighting a Walter Scott war. They plundered, they burned, and they specialized in raiding the herds of cattle that Westchester farmers had annually driven down to Manhattan mar-

kets. The patriots called them the Cowboys, a term that did not then have the meaning it was later to take on in the American West. De Lancey unrepentantly enjoyed such nicknames, and added his own to the string: "Colonel, Westchester Refugees," for one, and "The Outlaw of the Bronx" for another. But he had chosen the wrong side. At the end of the war he had to move to Nova Scotia, with many other Loyalists.

Both cousins had a dashing model in their Uncle Oliver, youngest of Stephen's sons, born in 1718 (only fourteen years older than Captain James, he was a good twenty-eight years senior to the Bronx Outlaw). Although a merchant like his brothers, Oliver was no model for the mercantile class; he was vigorous in contests and violent in language, a remorseless individualist who shocked two families by eloping with the wealthy Jewish heiress Phila Franks. He brawled his way through political service as an alderman, assemblyman, and member of the provincial Council, the legislative upper house. At the outbreak of the war, he raised a brigade of fifteen hundred Tories. As a brigadier general, De Lancey occupied the highest military position of any colonial loyalist in the British Army. (Patriots gave his exalted status an ironic official recognition when they sacked his mansion at Bloomingdale in 1777.) The De Lancey battalions fought well but vainly. Oliver went into exile in the 1780s with his nephews and other kin.

André Laurens had spent an indefinite period of time in New York in the 1680s and possibly later, but had moved to Charleston shortly before 1715. The requirements of business life in America led his son Jean, a maker and supplier of saddles, to change his name to John. John's eldest son, Henry, born in 1724, was not sent to an English university, like the De Lancey youngsters, but he got the best education that tutors in

South Carolina, hired by his prosperous father, could impart to him. He later went to London, to be sure, but only to make business contacts. In 1747, when John Laurens died, Henry returned to Charleston and soon entered an import-export partnership.

For some years Laurens shipped Carolina rice, indigo, and deer hides to ports in England, Holland, Portugal, Spain, and the West Indies, and in return received wine and slaves. As he prospered, he followed a Southern pattern of investing his profits in plantations, which brought a gentlemanly status that the countinghouse simply could not confer. Then the quarrel with England engaged him. Gouty, sensitive, and sarcastic, he made a tough and self-righteous adversary in a debate with British customs officials or with supporters of the governor in the provincial assembly, where he served almost uninterruptedly from 1757 to 1771. He then went to England for three years to supervise the education of his own sons, John and Henry. By then, whatever loyalty he had felt for English ways was cooling; outraged at what he thought was the corruption of the English ruling classes, he sent the boys away to school in Geneva and returned to Charleston.

In January of 1777 he was elected to the Continental Congress, and in November of the same year he was chosen president of that body, an office he held until December of 1778, when he was succeeded by John Jay, another Huguenot descendant. In August of 1780, Laurens set out from Philadelphia on the brigantine *Mercury* on a mission to Holland. His job was to interest practical Dutch bankers in advancing ten million dollars to the Americans and to negotiate a treaty of amity and commerce. Three weeks out of port, the *Mercury* was spotted and captured by a British warship. Laurens was taken to England. There he was treated as a state prisoner suspected of high treason. Louis XIV of France had expelled Laurens' grandfather as a disloyal subject who put faith above king. England's George III imprisoned Laurens as a renegade who put his home province above the throne. For fourteen months Laurens languished in the Tower of London, not seriously mistreated but in circumstances hardly healthful for a man of fifty-seven. Finally he was released in time to join the American peace commission in Paris, some months after his son John, who had returned home to join Washington's staff in 1777, was killed in action in one of the last skirmishes of the war in the Carolinas. In 1792, Laurens himself retired to one of his plantations, where he died after a long illness. (He had been elected to the Constitutional Convention but could not attend.)

The most surprising transformation from newcomer into patriot in the whole era, however, may have been that of Phillis Wheatley. In 1761, at about eight years of age, she was brought to Boston on a slave ship. A kindly merchant, John Wheatley, saw the little African girl standing terrified and nearly naked on the auction block, took a fancy to her, and brought her home to his wife. Taught to read, she developed into a poet whose work was primarily cast in neoclassic couplets, not quite adequately imitative of Alexander Pope's verses. Whatever their aesthetic deficiencies may have been, her verses found a publisher—a rather astonishing thing for any woman, white or black, at the time. Moreover, when Phillis, as ardent as any Boston follower of Sam Adams or John Hancock, sent a congratulatory poem to George Washington on his appointment as commander in chief, the Virginian wrote back: "Thank you most sincerely for your polite notice of me, in the elegant lines you enclosed . . . the style and manner exhibited a striking proof of your poetical talents. . . ."

Blacks participated in the Revolution in many ways, and this may have slightly sped emancipation in the North, though it is not easy to demonstrate the connection. There is a firmer possible link, however, between the role of the foreign-born on the ramparts and the pressures in the Constitutional Convention to allow immigrants quick access to equal political rights with native Americans. On the 8th, 9th, and 10th of August, 1787, and again on the 13th, the perspiring framers grappled with the question of the term of citizenship required for eligibility for election to the House or Senate.

George Mason of Virginia proposed a period of at least seven years for a Representative, arguing that he was for "opening a wide door for emigrants; but did not chuse to let foreigners and adventurers make laws for us & govern us." Three years (the original proposal on the floor), Mason held, was "not enough for ensuring that local knowledge which ought to be possessed by the Representatives." Yet when the question of the proper seasoning in Americanism for a Senator came up, Mason, though he argued for a fourteen-year requirement, confessed that he would ordinarily have contested for restricting the Senate to the native-born, "were it not that many not natives of this Country had acquired great merit during the revolution. . . ." It was a view that must have had some support in the group, though the only other delegate to be recorded explicitly on the subject was James Wilson of Pennsylvania, who noted that "almost all the General officers of the Pennsylvania line of the late army were foreigners. And no complaint had ever been made against their fidelity or merit." Wilson spoke with particular zeal. He himself was a Scottish immigrant, and it galled him to think that if "some gentlemen" had their way, he would be denied the right to hold an office under the Constitution which he "had shared in the trust of making." Moreover, his state, Pennsylvania, a colonial melting pot, had generously granted foreigners "all the rights whatsoever of citizens" after only two years' residence, and Wilson proudly pointed out that, possibly as a result of its encouragement of immigration, even though it was "perhaps the youngest settlement [except Georgia] on the Atlantic; yet it was at least among the foremost in population and prosperity."

The whole debate on the liberal proposals submitted by the Committee of Detail—three years' citizenship for a Representative, and four for a Senator—brought attitudes on immigrants and immigration into sharp focus. Charles Pinckney of South Carolina was fearful of permitting Senators, who had so much power in foreign affairs, to be drawn from non-native ranks. He reminded his classically learned colleagues of the Athenians' policy of making it death for any stranger "to intrude his voice into their Legislative proceedings." But James Madison, who yielded to none in his respect for ancient models, nevertheless denounced rules that would give "a tincture of illiberality" to the emerging national charter. "Great numbers of respectable Europeans," he remarked, "men who love liberty and wish to partake its blessings, will be ready to transfer their fortunes hither. All such would feel the mortification of being marked with suspicious incapacitations though they should not covet the public honors."

Pierce Butler responded with a defense of his South Carolina colleague's misgivings. Foreigners "without a long residence in the Country" (which the foreign-born Butler himself happened to enjoy) brought with them attachments to other countries, and "ideas of Government so distinct from ours that in every point of view they are dangerous." It was an idea picked up later on by Elbridge Gerry of Massachusetts, who was to make a long career out of distrust of Frenchmen, democrats, Southerners, the unpropertied, and strangers. Only the native-born, he declaimed, should serve in Congress, or else "persons having foreign attachments will be sent among us & insinuated into our councils, in order to be made instruments for their purposes." The "vast sums laid out in Europe for secret services," Gerry insisted, were a matter of common knowledge.

The aged Benjamin Franklin pleaded for the doctrine of asylum. He saw things from a cosmopolitan viewpoint; the people in Europe were friendly to the United States, and in the Revolution not only had many "strangers" (presumably men like Lafayette, Kosciusko, and von Steuben) served the rebel cause faithfully, but some had even taken part against their own countries: "When foreigners after looking about for some other Country in which they can obtain more happiness, give a preference to ours it is a proof of attachment which ought to excite our confidence and affection." He joined Madison in crying out against "illiberality."

That provoked a humorous speech from another Pennsylvania delegate. Tall, fleshy, and with a wooden leg, Gouverneur Morris was described by a colleague as one who "winds through all the mazes of rhetoric, and throws around him such a glare that he charms, captivates, and leads away the senses of all who hear him." His remarks, as recorded by Madison, began with a rebuttal to the charge of illiberality:

What is the language of Reason on this subject? That we should not be polite at the expence of prudence. There was a moderation in all things. It is said that some tribes of Indians carried their hospitality so far as to offer to strangers their wives and daughters. Was this a proper model for us? He would admit them to his house, he would invite them to his table, would provide for them comfortable lodgings; but would not carry the complaisance so far as, to bed them with his wife. He would let them worship at the same altar, but did not choose to make Priests of them. . . . He owned he did not wish to see any of them in our public Councils. He would not trust them. The men who can shake off their attachments to their own Country can never love any other. These attachments are the wholesome prejudices which uphold all Governments. Admit a Frenchman into your Senate, and he will study to increase the commerce of France: an Englishman, and he will feel an equal biass in favor of that of England.

In the end, the convention's decision was something of a retreat from the liberality of the first draft. No person could be a Representative who had not been seven years a citizen, and to become a Senator required nine. Yet the atmosphere created by the new state and national governments was, in the main, hospitable enough to continue to lure the disaffected of Europe, and it is estimated that 250,000 white aliens arrived in American ports between 1783 and 1815, most of them before the outbreak of the Napoleonic Wars. They came in search of the asylum that Thomas Paine had envisioned, and also, as always, in quest of less abstract advantages: work, cheap land, the chance to become shopowners, burghers, founders of thriving families.

They came largely from the same sources as the prewar migration. The Scotch-Irish and the Germans continued to furnish large numbers of indentured servants. (It was not until the early nineteenth century that the end came for that trade, which the British helped wipe out; they limited the number of passengers per ship, making it unprofitable for captains to pack the hold with nonpaying passengers who could be "sold" for their fare and costs on arrival in America—and restricted the emigration of skilled craftsmen, the kinds of servants most in demand. Moreover, the turmoil of war in Europe made recruitment of emigrants difficult and ocean transport a risky business. Finally in 1819, the United States itself, by the Passenger Act, forbade the importation of indentured labor in order to remedy the horrible abuses which made hell ships of the vessels carrying redemptioners.)

The German contingent also included several thousand Hessian prisoners, who remained in America instead of returning to the liege lords who had sold them like so many oxen. Besides these, some French, English, Scottish, and other settlers were enticed by agents of speculative companies that bought huge tracts of Western lands and desperately needed purchasers. One example was the Scioto Land Company, a syndicate with vast virgin acreages in Ohio. It employed Joel Barlow, a talented poet, ex-army chaplain, linguist, businessman, and radical pamphleteer, to enlist a company of Frenchmen who would bring Gallic civilization to the West. Barlow rounded up his culture bearers, who duly made their way to the banks of the Ohio River and founded Gallipolis in 1790. There they stayed until they found that their titles were defective and that their brave new world abounded in Indians, mosquitoes, malaria, violence, and ignorance, whereupon they abandoned the scene and their plans for producing wine, silk, and virtue in an undespoiled land.

As early as 1790, the first census takers enumerated a white population that modern scholars—using admittedly crude tests—estimate to be approximately 60 per cent English, 9.5 per cent Irish (both Ulster and

John Singleton Copley, who reversed the immigrant trend and left his native America for England, painted this portrait of Henry Laurens, Revolutionary leader and diplomat, in 1782.

southern), 8.6 per cent German, 8.1 per cent Scotch, 3.1 per cent Dutch, 2.3 per cent French, 0.7 per cent Swedish, 0.8 per cent Spanish, and 6.8 per cent unclassified. The pattern was already so variously hued that Crèvecoeur could invoke "the American, this new man." And a German observer could describe America as housing a "promiscuous crowd of almost all nations in Europe." He predicted that such a mixture would "require a long fermentation before it will contain the spirit, the feelings, and the imprint of a united people." Yet the fermentation was already in process; French, Swedish, Welsh, Dutch, and German began to wane as languages used in church services and newspapers. De Witt Clinton, the mayor of New York, somewhat complacently but accurately reported in 1814 that "the triumph and adoption of the English language have been the principal means of melting us down." (It is intriguing to find the practical politician Clinton using that particular verb some ninety-five years before the

The Boston an immigrant saw in the tense 1760s stood close upon its harbor. This engraving is the work of Paul Revere, whose

To the Earl of Hillsborough. His Majest's Sec'ry of State for America. THIS VIEW of the only well Plan'd EXPEDITION, formed for supporting y' dignity of BRITAIN & chastising y' insolence of AMERICA, is humy Inscrib'd

immigrant father, Apollos De Rivoire, changed the family name, he said, so that "the Bumpkins should pronounce it easier."

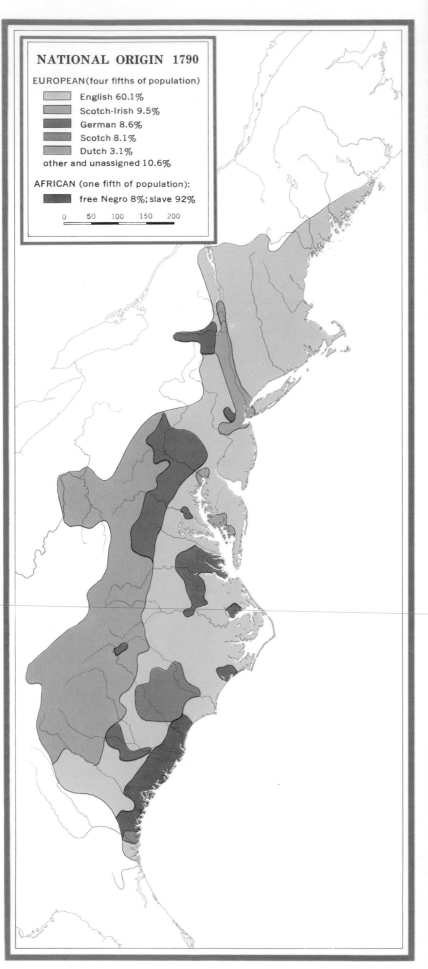

NATIONAL ORIGIN 1790

EUROPEAN (four fifths of population)

- English 60.1%
- Scotch-Irish 9.5%
- German 8.6%
- Scotch 8.1%
- Dutch 3.1%

other and unassigned 10.6%

AFRICAN (one fifth of population):

- free Negro 8%; slave 92%

0 50 100 150 200

The map at the left shows the ethnic diversity of the United States at the time when the framers of the Constitution coped with the question of naturalization requirements. Three of the men involved in the argument were Charles C. Pinckney (top), George Mason (center), and Gouverneur Morris; all were of British stock.

playwright Israel Zangwill, an English Jew, used the phrase "the Melting-Pot" to describe the United States.

The new nation appeared to be embarked on a path of peaceful assimilation of whatever fortune seekers and fugitives made their way into its extended arms. Yet from the start, as the remarks of men like Gerry at Philadelphia in 1787 portended, there was a dark underside to the welcome mat. KEEP OUT was written on it, in letters of pitch. In times of stress, there has always been a struggle to turn that side uppermost. The late 1790s were the first of such times. The question of immigration became entangled with European wars and revolutions, and with the development of the two-party system in American politics. An outburst of xenophobia splashed the closing years of the decade with hostility, which expressed itself in the passage of the Alien Acts—measures of firm rejection to all those who were in quest of Thomas Paine's asylum, or indeed thought in any way like Tom Paine on any subject.

When the First Congress enacted a "uniform Rule of Naturalization," as authorized in the Constitution, it provided that application for citizenship could be made after only two years of residence in the country. But almost immediately thereafter, events pushed the nation away from this generous policy. In 1792 the French Republic was established and war broke out in Europe —to continue, with only short intervals of peace, for twenty-three years. The policies of the Jacobin rulers of France drove thousands of their opponents into flight for their lives. Meanwhile, the monarchies of Europe trembled at the genuine threat that the virus of revolution might spread. In their attempts to effect quarantines, they vigorously harassed reformers of every kind. Political imprisonment and escape became increasingly visible features of public life. The Poles, the Irish, the Italians all stirred restlessly under Russian, British, and Austrian masters. In Haiti and Santo Domingo the blacks rose against their plantation masters, killed (and were killed) in thousands, and provoked a panicked dispersement of white settlers.

It was a time like the middle years of the twentieth century, an era of exile. And then, too, it affected immigration to America. As one historian, James Morton Smith, sums it up: "The neutral United States immediately became the haven of refugees. To its shores came discontented Englishmen, aristocratic Frenchmen, German Pietists fleeing forced military service, French planters escaping from West Indian uprisings led by Toussaint L'Ouverture, and Irishmen in flight from British repression."

These castaways from the shipwreck of the old order arrived in the period when the United States was ad-

ministered by the inherently conservative Federalists. Men like John Adams and Alexander Hamilton deplored democratic "excesses," especially in France. To exacerbate matters, the French, in their warfare with England, persistently seized or destroyed American ships trading with their enemy. The British did the same (thereby bringing about war finally in 1812), but in 1798 it was the French "spoliations" that were most abrasive. The infant United States Navy was actually in a state of undeclared war against France. Furthermore, three American envoys sent to Paris to seek a settlement had been treated with disdain, visited by three unofficial envoys (referred to in the publicly released account of the mission simply as X, Y, and Z), and told that they would have to bribe the French government with nearly a quarter of a million dollars before even hoping for satisfaction. The release of news of this "XYZ Affair" in April set off a wave of Francophobia in the United States. It was against this background that the Alien and Sedition Acts were passed.

The prelude was a stiffening of the naturalization law. It had already been modified once, in 1795, raising the residence requirement from two to five years. Now, three years later, the Federalist-dominated House Committee for the Protection of Commerce and the Defense of the Country brought in a measure for further amendment: this time to make the minimum residence before naturalization a full fourteen years, and to insist as well that five years elapse between a declaration of intention to be naturalized and the final award of citizenship. Some Federalists found the new proposal too mild, and hoped to exclude the foreign-born from voting and officeholding altogether. Among them was Harrison Gray Otis, a young Representative from Boston and the bright hope of Harvard's first post-Revolutionary graduating class. In 1797 Otis had declared: "I do not wish to invite hordes of wild Irishmen, nor the turbulent and disorderly of all parts of the world, to come here with a view to disturb our tranquility. . . ." He thus sounded a battle cry long to reverberate in Boston. (An Irish newspaper writer, taking up the challenge, metrically retorted with a threat that would actually be executed: "Young man, we would have you remember/While we in this country can tarry,/ The '*Wild Irish*' will choose a new member/And will ne'er vote again for *young Harry*.")

Otis did not prevail, any more than Republican opponents who could only succeed in making the bill nonretroactive, allowing aliens who had entered the United States before 1795 to apply for naturalization under the old law. But holding back for fourteen years a suspected future surge of naturalized voters was not enough to appease Federalist fears. President John Adams was informed that Frenchmen in Philadelphia were planning on May 9, 1798, to destroy the city by fire and massacre its inhabitants. A Federalist cleric, Jedidiah Morse, warned his congregation that the American "Jacobins"—that is to say, Jefferson's followers—were agents of a secret society called the Illuminati, which was dedicated to the destruction of all churches and governments.

To forestall such calamities, Congressional leaders drafted two bills. One, the Alien Enemies Act, providing for wartime restraint of noncitizens, was passed with little argument and formed the foundation of later American policy in this area. The other, the so-called Alien Friends Act, bore all the earmarks of a full-fledged witch hunt. As proposed by a Senate committee, it allowed the President to expel any foreigner on the mere suspicion of treasonable machinations. If the alien so deported returned and was detected, he could be imprisoned without trial at hard labor for life. Even those aliens not suspected and expelled could remain in the country only by securing a special Presidential permit, and would thereafter—even in peacetime—be subjected to surveillance. Moreover, any citizen who wished to "harbour, entertain or conceal any alien" had first to give written notice to a Federal court.

Jefferson warned that the measure was "worthy of the 8th or 9th century," and Madison commented that it was "a monster that must forever disgrace its parents." A letter writer to one newspaper wrote that he had seen, in a museum, an "American medal" inscribed with the motto "An asylum for the oppressed of all nations." "The gilding of this coin," he wrote, "is a little worn off and evidently shows base metal beneath." Another sardonically advised Irish refugees from British bayonets and nooses not to come to the United States, but to seek instead some country where "hatred to tryanny will not subject you to transportation without a trial by jury." The coast of Africa was suggested. Unlike Federalist Americans, it was implied, "the Hottentots are a hospitable people."

Before the President signed it on June 25, 1798, the bill was somewhat modified. The alien was given notice of a specific time within which he had to leave. If found in the United States after the deadline, he could stand trial, facing a maximum sentence of three years' imprisonment. During the grace period before his required departure, he could also present evidence in his favor, and might even receive a Presidential permit to remain in a specified place. If he was deported but returned and was found, he was entitled to a trial. If convicted, he could be jailed for as long as the President

Phillis Wheatley, "snatch'd from *Afric's* fancy'd happy seat" *as a child, was well known when she sent this poem to George Washington to celebrate his appointment as commander in chief.*

SIR,

I Have taken the freedom to addrefs your Excellency in the enclofed poem, and entreat your acceptance, though I am not infenfible of its inaccuracies. Your being appointed by the Grand Continental Congrefs to be Generaliffimo of the armies of North America, together with the fame of your virtues, excite fenfations not eafy to fupprefs. Your generofity, therefore, I prefume, will pardon the attempt. Wifhing your Excellency all poffible fuccefs in the great caufe you are fo generoufly engaged in. I am,

Your Excellency's moft obedient humble fervant,

Providence, Oct. 26, 1775. PHILLIS WHEATLEY.
His Excellency Gen. Wafhington.

CElestial choir! enthron'd in realms of light,
Columbia's fcenes of glorious toils I write.
While freedom's caufe her anxious breaft alarms,
She flafhes dreadful in refulgent arms.
See mother earth her offspring's fate bemoan,
And nations gaze at fcenes before unknown!
See the bright beams of heaven's revolving light
Involved in forrows and the veil of night!
The goddefs comes, fhe moves divinely fair,
Olive and laurel binds her golden hair:
Wherever fhines this native of the fkies,
Unnumber'd charms and recent graces rife.
Mufe! bow propitious while my pen relates
How pour her armies through a thoufand gates:
As when Eolus heaven's fair face deforms,
Enwrapp'd in tempeft and a night of ftorms;
Aftonifh'd ocean feels the wild uproar,
The refluent furges beat the founding fhore;
Or thick as leaves in Autumn's golden reign,
Such, and fo many, moves the warrior's train.
In bright array they feek the work of war,
Where high unfurl'd the enfign waves in air.
Shall I to Wafhington their praife recite?
Enough thou know'ft them in the fields of fight.
Thee, firft in place and honours,—we demand
The grace and glory of thy martial band.
Fam'd for thy valour, for thy virtues more,
Hear every tongue thy guardian aid implore!
One century fcarce perform'd its deftin'd round,
When Gallic powers Columbia's fury found;
And fo may you, whoever dares difgrace
The land of freedom's heaven-defended race!
Fix'd are the eyes of nations on the fcales,
For in their hopes Columbia's arm prevails.
Anon Britannia droops the penfive head,
While round increafe the rifing hills of dead.
Ah! cruel blindnefs to Columbia's ftate!
Lament thy thirft of boundlefs power too late.
Proceed, great chief, with virtue on thy fide,
Thy ev'ry action let the goddefs guide.
A crown, a manfion, and a throne that fhine,
With gold unfading, WASHINGTON! be thine.

deemed necessary to the "public safety." While the amended act was an improvement on the draft, it was still a severely repressive measure, coupled in historical infamy with the almost simultaneous Sedition Act, which allowed for the jailing of those who in speech or writing brought the government "into contempt or disrepute." The best thing about the Alien Friends Act was that it was considered merely an emergency measure to be revoked after two years.

Happily, the actual enforcement of the act was haphazard. President Adams was loath to enforce it. He had long been a defender of the principle of asylum, and he was now compelled to eat his own words, explaining that while he believed in America as a refuge "for virtue in distress and for innocent industry, it behoves us to beware, that under this pretext it is not made a receptacle of malevolence and turbulence, for the outcasts of the universe." Some of the more conspicuous "agitators" who were the objects of Federalist suspicion solved the Presidential dilemma by leaving before proceedings were instituted against them—among them the historian Médéric Moreau de Saint-Méry, then a bookstore proprietor in Philadelphia, and Constantin Volney, a writer and former French National Assembly member. Both represented the colony of radical refugee intellectuals who were particularly irksome to certain patriotic Yankees. A blank warrant was issued for the arrest of the French economist Pierre Samuel Du Pont de Nemours, who was supposedly due to arrive in the country with a French delegation of visiting experts, but he delayed his landing until the act had expired. Otherwise, a distinguished industrial dynasty in America might have had a convict in its past.

The kind of fumbling application that unwittingly tempered the execution of the act is revealed in the story of the efforts to evict a French general, Victor Collot. Collot had been governor of the French island of Guadeloupe, which was captured by the British in 1794. Since Collot suspected that the Paris authorities might decide to punish him for his lack of revolutionary zeal, he asked his captors to allow him to go to the United States and remain there as a paroled prisoner of war, to which they agreed. While in America, Collot aroused American (and Spanish) anxieties by a long, leisurely trip along the Ohio and Mississippi Rivers, from Pittsburgh to New Orleans. It appeared to some that he was laying the groundwork for a possible French-organized "uprising" to seize Louisiana, then Spanish-owned. As a consequence, the American government had him kept under surveillance.

In October of 1798, Secretary of State Timothy Pickering, who was responsible for the execution of the Alien Friends Act, asked the President for blank warrants authorizing the arrest of Collot, Du Pont, and an associate of Collot's named Sweitzer. Then further deeds of heroism suggested themselves to him. He had heard from informants that another French general, Jean Serurier, was also in the United States, in disguise, and might attempt to contact Collot. So, in the fashion of police officials in a thousand melodramas, Pickering decided not to arrest Collot, hoping that he might lure additional game—Serurier—into his bag.

Affairs dragged on inconclusively until June of 1799, when it was reported that Collot was on the verge of leaving the country. Collot had in fact decided earlier that the new government in Paris would be in a forgiving mood, and had asked the British authorities for a passport to return to France. Pickering, then hoping to catch Serurier, had actually asked the British not to grant the request, and they had obliged him.

Now, however, Pickering was apparently ready to give up. Collot must be got rid of, Serurier or no Serurier. But he was reluctant to use the Alien Law, which he already considered a dead letter. President Adams, on the other hand, was eager to test it against the "pernicious and malicious intriguer." While they debated the issue, Collot moved to Newark, where he resided incognito. A Federalist judge, Elisha Boudinot, darkly reported to Pickering a series of "facts" and rumors of the kind that have always delighted superpatriots. Collot subscribed to a violently Republican newspaper, the Philadelphia *Aurora*—and under an alias! He had an "intriguing spirit." He had criticized the government in conversation with a Frenchman named Boisobier, who had obligingly reported the fact to Boudinot. He had asked many questions about Frenchmen living in his neighborhood. And he had allegedly threatened that if war should break out between France and the United States, he would revenge himself on some of his local enemies.

Despite Boudinot's urgings, Adams and Pickering somehow failed to take action against Collot. The "intriguer"—if he was such—finally left under a British passport in August of 1800, and was allowed to come home by his government. An arbitrary law, tempered with doubt, inefficiency, and overreaching, had proved endurable for at least one alien.

The dawn of the nineteenth century brought a new administration to Washington, and the uncontested expiration of the Alien and Sedition Acts. The first fever of nativism had passed, and in the bustle of the Jeffersonian revolution, the issue was not raised again. The young republic entered a new era with a fresh set of attitudes toward the stranger at the gate.

Cities burgeoned, absorbing many immigrants before the Civil War; above, Chicago in 1858.

REFUGEES, REBELS, AND ROMANTICS

ON BOTH SIDES OF THE ATLANTIC, the year 1815 marked a major turning point—perhaps the real beginning of the modern age. In Europe, the soldiers who had survived nearly twenty years of Napoleonic battles exchanged their swords for plowshares and beggars' cups, and a century of almost uninterrupted peace among the major powers began. Internal revolutions would work their effects on European life, but the destructive potential of international war would not be fully realized for another hundred years. In the United States, the momentum of the westward movement accelerated apace as the American people turned toward the immense, unprobed domain of forest, prairie, and mountain stretching to the Pacific, and began to settle it with a rush that carried them to California and Oregon within the span of a generation.

The pace of the era was set by the steam engine, an eighteenth-century creation that came into its own in the nineteenth. Powering paddle wheels and propellers, chuffing along tracks on land, it became the conqueror of oceans and of interior continental spaces. Before it, the forest melted and the mountains leveled, and the aboriginal life that hitherto had been hidden from modernity—of buffalo and Sioux, of zebra and Zulu—was doomed to subordination. Steam-operated machinery was the driving force behind a new world of goods—goods mass-produced with the prodigality of a god multiplying universes. And as all this new energy was released, all humanity stirred.

It was in such energized circumstances that an expanding global population began to move in mighty tides. Immigration to the United States is only part of the unfolding story of human development in our time. Between the census years 1820 and 1860, more than five million individuals came to American shores—a number greater than the nation's population in 1790. But other millions went to Australia, Latin America, Canada, and to European settlements in coastal North and South Africa. Still others severed their ancestral roots while remaining within Europe itself—Irishmen going to England in search of jobs, and Germans seeking better lands in Russia, to take just two examples. On a shrinking earth that they did not yet think of as a crowded spaceship, men swarmed across the artificial lines drawn by political geographers.

European emigration to the United States grew each decade. In the 1820s there were 151,000 arrivals; 573,000 in the 1830s; 1,479,000 in the 1840s; and, in the last decade before the Civil War, when the country's total population passed the thirty-million mark, more than 3,000,000. Most of these immigrants—a point which would be labored at the end of the century but which attracted little notice before 1860—were from Northern and Western Europe. Some two million Irishmen took part in the 1815–60 migration, and a million and a half Germans, while around three quarters of a million came from England, Scotland, and Wales, along with smaller contingents from Switzerland, Scandinavia, and the Netherlands. During the same period there were also more than 112,000 known entrants from Canada and Newfoundland, many of whom undoubtedly were European-born. In addition, there was always a literally unchecked current of immigrants who went from Canada into the United States by walking across an unpatrolled border.

The forces that propelled dissatisfied Europeans to-

Scenes like this—the firing of Waldenburg Castle—occurred often during the 1848 revolutions.

ward Hamburg, Liverpool, Le Havre, and other popular embarkation points were many. Some were created by transient upheavals—political revolutions such as those in Poland, France, and Belgium in 1830, and in France, Germany, Italy, Austria, and Hungary in 1848. Each of them—and many abortive attempts to bring them off earlier—begot political exiles. Bad harvests and epidemics, religious schisms, and restrictive laws aimed at certain groups and classes impelled men to depart. The classic combination of many such factors was the Irish potato famines of the 1840s. The Irish already were politically helpless, punished in a variety of ways for their continued Catholicism, and desperately poor. Many who had not already fled their native soil were now chased out by starvation. But behind these crises were other, long-range developments.

One was a steady increase in the world's population, which aroused the gloomy apprehensions of the English economist Thomas R. Malthus. His *Essay on the Principle of Population*, published in 1798, attempted to prove that the populace would always outrun the food supply; thus war, famine, and plague were salutary checks. Besides furnishing somewhat specious arguments to a generation of economists who preached that wages had to remain at near-starvation levels,

Malthusianism helped bring about a change of heart on the part of statesmen regarding emigration. Formerly, a nation's people were thought of as an economic resource to be husbanded, so that emigration, especially of skilled workers, was discouraged. But in the light of the population explosion, departing citizens were looked upon merely as fewer mouths to feed. Great Britain repealed most of its laws restricting exit by 1827; within twenty years Sweden, the Netherlands, and the German states had done likewise.

Ironically, an even greater impetus to migration came from industrialization, which helped to sustain the population increase. The same amount of labor could produce sustenance for far greater numbers of human beings in need of food, clothing, and shelter. But factory production and scientific agriculture were ruthless dislocators. Machines rendered hand skills obsolete, and suddenly weavers and shoemakers and metalsmiths, who once were proud guildsmen, found themselves displaced wanderers, trudging the world's roads in search of new work to do. Villages decayed as handicrafts that had once supported their menfolk were destroyed by factory competition. Improvements in the cultivation of the soil—new chemical fertilizers, selective breeding of herds, deep plowing, irrigation, and the like—made possible such miracles as the feeding of great multitudes by a relative handful of farmers, but they destroyed ancient security. Planned crop rotation, pest control, and the fencing that would maintain breeding conditions productive of the woolliest sheep, the meatiest steers, the most productive milk cows—all these innovations meant the end of common fields for grazing a whole town's livestock, of tiny plots laid out in patchwork patterns, of forests left standing to furnish firewood to all comers. And so the peasants who had eked existences from fragments of soil while following the customs of centuries were now driven to seek new lives wherever they could find them. Well-managed estates and eviction seemed to go hand in hand, and the more modern a country became, the greater were its swarms of likely emigrants.

Those who were ready to move were lured toward the United States by new enticements. Now the call came not only from promoters who walked the streets of German villages chinking money in their pockets but also from the "America letters" of men like Samuel Crabtree, who in 1818 averred in print that around Wheeling he saw "more peaches and apples rotting on the ground than would sink the British fleet," hogs without number, and an abundance of "tea, coffee, beef, fowls, pies, eggs, pickles, good bread" on the tables of the poorest families. Now the printed allurements of the broadsides struck off in seventeenth-century London or Amsterdam, replete with broken type and crude woodcuts of leaping Indians, were replaced by sophisticated handbooks citing land prices and travel routes. Some were issued by immigration bureaus, set up in the 1850s and afterward by population-hungry Midwestern states, and some by railways with land grants for new settlers. Michigan had an office for the promotion of immigration as early as 1848, and its first commissioner was instructed to spend half his time in New York and half in Stuttgart. Wisconsin, which created the post of Commissioner of Immigration in 1851, eventually found itself publishing pamphlets in seven languages and buying advertising space in such journals as the *Leipziger Allgemeine Zeitung* and the Tipperary *Free Press*.

Other, practical inducements beckoned toward America. Cheap passages were made possible by the booming trade in grain, cotton, and timber between Europe, Canada, and the United States. Passengers made up an attractive source of income for lightly laden westbound ships. The fare from Liverpool to New York dropped from twelve pounds to just over three between 1816 and 1846; that between Le Havre and New Orleans, from about 400 francs to as low as 120. Once one was

in the Promised Land, reaching the interior was not expensive. To go from New York to Detroit in 1840, for example, by way of the Hudson River, the Erie Canal, and the Great Lakes, a traveler paid as little as eight dollars. An additional $6.50 got him as far as Chicago or Milwaukee. Rail transportation cost more but was still not prohibitive, although the accommodations for a two- or three-day trip on an "emigrant train" were apt to be Spartan—boxcars with benches but without any other amenities whatever, not even drinking water. Immigrants who ventured on the river steamers plying the Mississippi, Ohio, and Missouri Rivers also paid little but endured overcrowding, sickness, and the chronic risk of fires and exploding boilers. Still, in the long run, for thousands of foreigners the promises were more potent than the risks.

Immigration became a wholesale shifting of peoples among nations pulled into ever-closer contact by transportation improvements. Inevitably, governments came to measure and control the flow by modernizing their pre-nineteenth-century statutes on the subject. The United States was no exception. The Federal government passed an act prescribing certain minimum standards for sea-borne passenger accommodations as early as 1819. Massachusetts (in a legal move later declared unconstitutional as an interference with Federal control of commerce) began collecting fees from immigrant

In a series of riots that took place during the Great Famine, desperate Irish peasants looted Galway's potato stores.
RADIO TIMES HULTON PICTURE LIBRARY

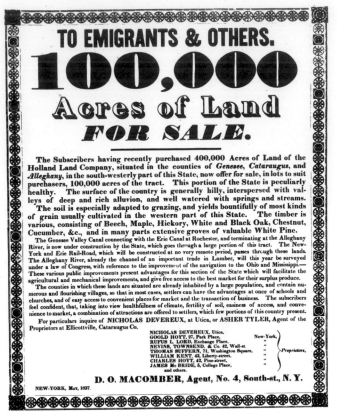

This 1837 broadside glowingly described the high quality of timber, grain, and grazing land available in western New York.

passengers in the 1840s to pay the costs of administering a hospital for those who arrived ill. New York State required reports of immigrant arrivals, and in 1847 it set up a Board of Commissioners of Emigration to devise orderly procedures for receiving immigrants, registering them, assisting them where necessary, and protecting them from swarms of swindlers and pitchmen—representing boardinghouses, employers, and transportation companies—who previously had pounced upon them as they came down the gangplanks. In 1855 the board bought the building known as Castle Garden, at Manhattan Island's southern tip, and turned it into an immigrant reception station. It served that function until it was replaced by Ellis Island, under Federal jurisdiction, in 1892.

In the world-wide stream of migration, the supposedly "isolated" and "unsophisticated" United States stood with open doors. In 1860, states that led in recent immigrant populations were leaders in industrialization: New York and Pennsylvania, followed by Ohio, Illinois, Wisconsin, and Massachusetts. The states on the farthest frontier and the fifteen slave states attracted fewer newcomers from abroad. The South was particularly unattractive to them. Even for those who

condoned slavery, the plantation system offered no industrial employment, while blacks pre-empted the chores often performed in the North by immigrant maids, cooks, teamsters, barbers, stevedores, janitors, and the like. Of the 4,138,697 foreign-born who lived in the United States in 1860, only some thirteen per cent were found in the South—most of them concentrated in St. Louis, Baltimore, and New Orleans, where urbanization widened their opportunities.

The cities were a major lodestone for the new arrivals. Then as now, the streets were sensitive reflectors of social change. In 1860 an observer in the cities could see the homogeneous nature of America's population being altered. St. Louis had a foreign-born contingent of sixty per cent, and New York, Chicago, Cincinnati, Milwaukee, Detroit, and San Francisco were nearly half foreign-born. In New Orleans, Boston, and Baltimore, the proportion of immigrants was more than a third. The Irish and the Germans were particularly urbanized. There were exceptional groups, to be sure, such as the Norwegians, almost all of whom were cultivating prairie soil in Wisconsin, Minnesota, and Iowa. But the lure of the cities was evident.

The patterns of deployment were drawn by experience and the availability of jobs and land. The Scandinavians were attracted mainly to the prairies of the Midwest and to the North Central timberlands, which were much like the terrain they had known at home. Miners from Wales and Cornwall went to dig coal from the hills of Pennsylvania, or lead and iron from the earth of Wisconsin, Michigan, and Illinois. Germans farmed the Midwestern states—where bargains in already developed farmland were available as older American families pulled up stakes and moved farther west—or practiced such familiar skills as brewing in the cities. The Irish, however, rejected their peasant past and clung to the cities or fanned out along the lines formed by the canals and railroads then under construction, which offered work to unskilled hands.

Even before the fateful year of 1845, the lot of the rural Irishman was squalor, with frustration for anyone who was ambitious. The genial qualities of the Irish are a tribute to good nature's triumph over bitter reality. Irish farmlands were fertile, but Irish eggs, butter, bacon, and flour were exported to pay rent to absentee landlords. The peasants relied for their own sustenance on what they could coax out of tiny plots that sometimes would have been barely adequate as urban back yards. Forty-five per cent of all landholdings in Ireland in 1845 were less than five acres in extent, and more than ninety-three per cent of all farms comprised fewer than thirty acres. Even these

In Samuel Waugh's 1855 painting, Irish immigrants disembark in New York; the setting includes Castle Garden and a Chinese junk.

were subdivided as the population rose mysteriously—in a land largely without towns, industries, or medical care—to more than eight million in 1841, making Ireland the most densely populated country in Europe.

There was little that an Irish child could expect to attain beyond a tiny patch of sod. Catholics were forbidden to hold public office, purchase land, or attain rank in the army, the navy, or at the bar. There were no upper or middle classes into which talented youths could rise. Parents had to divide their poor lands among their sons or condemn them to starvation. It was only natural that thousands of youthful Irishmen should escape by emigration as fares were lowered and opportunities abroad beckoned. Even before 1845, an annual Irish movement to Canada and the United States was reaching occasional heights of 65,000 emigrants and rarely dipping below 30,000.

The great majority, however, stayed where they were, living lives that shaped the national character into patterns that would later remain largely the same in New World surroundings. Denied an open religious life that might change with the times, the Irish clung all the more stubbornly to the authority of their priests. Denied education, they grew more rooted in supersti-

tion. Outsiders so far as the law was concerned, they were often attracted to secret terrorist societies as the only means of dispensing popular justice against the informer, the exploitative landlord's agent, or the supplanter of an evicted tenant. Conspiracy was part of the very tissue of life; drinking, storytelling, and fighting were the alleviations of a frustrating existence. So despite all a vital spark was maintained, and its great supporter in the early decades of the nineteenth century was the potato, which could be cultivated with almost no skill or tools on the tiniest of plots. An acre and a half in potatoes could feed a family of five or six for a year. Any surplus could be converted to cash, which was then put by toward the purchase of a pig, and even perhaps a cow and some fowl. Peat was freely available to keep roaring fires going in windowless earthen cabins throughout the long cold and wet seasons. The housekeeping might be primitive, but the means of self-support were within reach of almost anyone.

It all rested, however, on the potato, which fed livestock and people alike. "What hope is there," an English official once cried, "for a nation that lives on potatoes!" None whatever if the crop was stricken, and in the autumn of 1845 that calamity fell upon Ire-

117

land. A blighting fungus, *Phytophthora infestans*, spreading rapidly, turned the leaves and roots of the plant black, pulpy, foul-smelling, and totally inedible. Not all the crop was affected at first, but in the winter of 1845–46, whatever had been harvested successfully was consumed or sold. The 1846 and 1847 crops failed completely, and those of 1848 and 1849 were but little better. Ordinarily during the growing cycle, Ireland lived on last year's harvest. Without that, Ireland starved.

The precise number of victims of starvation and epidemic disease is not known, but there certainly were hundreds of thousands and the total may have reached seven figures. Horrible scenes were enacted, like that described by a British ship captain who in 1846 saw thousands of persons writhing in the torments of diarrhea. In one hut he gazed at four adults and three children crouching, vacant-eyed and wordless around a fire, while a man and a woman lay dying in the next room. In cabin after cabin the living lay paralyzed, surrounded by their dead. Bodies were buried without coffins by exhausted relatives, only a few inches below the soil, soon to be unearthed by dogs and rats. Soup kitchens and public-works projects, relief ships, and donations of food (including large quantities from the United States) barely touched the edges of the misery.

The only hope offered was flight. Passage brokers who sent agents into the Irish countryside to sell space on chartered vessels found ready customers among those who could somehow scrape together the necessary pounds. "All with means are emigrating," noted one official; "only the utterly destitute are left behind and enfeebled labourers." The British government attempted to entice settlers to Canada with specially arranged low fares. The Irish, however, even in desperation, had doubts about going to a British colony—"a second edition of Ireland with more room." Thousands of them took advantage of the cheap rates for passage to the mouth of the St. Lawrence and free transportation upriver to Quebec, then set out to walk into the United States. It is estimated that the majority of the Irish who reached Canada made it only a way station.

The flood had begun. In New York, in the single eight-month period between May 5, 1847 (when the Commissioners of Emigration began to keep records), and the year's end, there were 52,946 Irish arrivals. The ailing were unloaded at Staten Island, where three hospitals and a workhouse for the destitute awaited them; the rest battled their way ashore through crowds of runners for boardinghouses (some of which were dens of thieves where the immigrant's little baggage and money was stolen from him and where he was fed and lodged in "a state of misery and wretchedness not to be

Contemporary cartoons echoed the Irishman's expectations of America —the chance to make a quick leap from poverty to comfort. The tattered Dubliner looking at poster billings of packet ships to America, above, could, after a few years in New York, become prosperous enough to consider returning to the old sod (above, opposite). Right, the luck of the Irish comes to the rescue in Gold Rush days. "O'Flannigan Among the Sharps in California" is doing well with his three aces, to the great dissatisfaction of attending players and kibitzers.

D–n your Irish luck!

borne or countenanced by any civilized community").

In Boston, during the same year of 1847, some 25,000 emigrants—three quarters of them Irish—arrived by sea and some 12,500 by land. But whereas New York was a city of more than 370,000, Boston's 1845 population had been only 114,366, which was increased virtually overnight by an impoverished, dependent third. Suddenly Boston was confronted by the problem of the slum, a full generation before it was to become a national issue. And because the problem was inseparably connected with the newly arrived Irish, a cruelly unfair association between degradation and Hibernian origins developed in the minds of some Americans. Confronted with alien poverty, they made the common error of blaming the victim for the disease.

It was inevitable that the Irish of Boston and New York should become the urban poor in short order. Penniless for the most part, they were unable to move westward and take up vacant farmland, even where the prices were rock-bottom—and even if they had not been thoroughly disillusioned with farming as a way of life. Single men could join work gangs bound for construction projects in the interior, but those who had families they chose not to abandon picked up the lowest kind of unskilled jobs: yard, street, and stable work for the men; and for the women, whose extra earnings were indispensable to survival, domestic service. Like other female migrants after them (black women coming to Northern cities from Mississippi farms in the twentieth century, for example), the mothers and homemakers of Ireland "went off," in the words of Oscar Handlin, "to serve at the table of strangers and bring home the bitter bread of banishment."

The scanty returns from such labor forced the Irish to live in places normally considered unfit for human habitation. Slumlords, the scavengers of every urban society, rapidly bought up cellars, stables, and sheds in alleys and yards, and rented them to the immigrants at gold-rush prices. A Boston Committee on Internal Health found that there were three-story houses into which as many as a hundred inhabitants were jammed; that a single room might house nine people; that thousands of Irish lived in cellars without windows or privies or a water supply—"in many cases huddled together like brutes, without regard to age or sex or sense of decency." In such an environment, it was noted, "intemperance and utter degradation reign supreme." So did cholera, which broke out in the city in 1849.

And so did the crime rate, which rose rapidly in the years immediately following 1843—particularly attempts to kill (up 1,700 per cent), assaults on police officers (up 400 per cent), and aggravated assaults with

119

With such come-ons as "no night changes" and "no ferrying," American railroads attracted immigrants into the westbound cars.

knives, dirks, pistols, slingshots, razors, pokers, hot irons, clubs, iron weights, flatirons, bricks, and stones (up 465 per cent). Proper Bostonians reacted with predictable concern as to whether people who lived in such style could ever be redeemed for equal citizenship. Many of them nursed the idea that somehow the Irish freely chose their social position in the lower depths—a conception verbalized in the report of the New York Association for Improving the Condition of the Poor, which held that the Irish were "content to live together in filth and disorder with a bare sustenance, provided they can drink and smoke and gossip, and enjoy their balls and wakes and frolics without molestation."

German migration moved to a different rhythm from that of the hunger-harried Irish. The potato blight struck in the German states, too, but the growers were not completely dependent on the ravaged plant. Its impact, however, did jar a goodly number of farmers already hard pressed by bad harvests, taxes, falling prices, and disadvantageous changes in land-tenure systems. Thousands of them could be seen making their way to the emigration ports in the 1840s, in carts piled high with their belongings and pulled, according to a French journalist, by "starved, drooping beasts."

Emigrants such as these, patiently enduring salt fish, potatoes, and soup on the six- or eight-week trip from Hamburg and then fanning out into the interior, were much like their eighteenth-century forerunners who had Germanized Pennsylvania. The new century, however, saw a new kind of exile from the fatherland—the skilled craftsman seeking an American fortune (perhaps even with the idea of eventually returning home), and the member of the educated middle class who had been caught up in the new liberalism at home and had fallen afoul of the police and the courts, which were still on the side of absolutism. Not many of the German-born residents of America by 1860 were intellectuals, revolutionaries, businessmen, or bankers in either their former or their adopted land, but those who were gave a flavor to their communities and to American life as a whole that was not to be lost until the time of the First World War. The essence of it was idealism, organization, love of culture, and a strong sense of communal solidarity. Its occasional austerities and rigors (especially felt by the children of German-American households) were softened somewhat by music and lager beer.

The romantic figure in the history of immigration is the lone pilgrim coming down the gangplank with his worldly goods on his back. From the time of the first colonial plantings, however, group settlements have been a persistent experience, and nineteenth-century Germans made their contributions to this tradition.

Some of these communities collapsed under the divisive pressures of the competitive American environment. Others laid the foundations for prosperous townships.

In 1833, for example, a committee was formed in the university town of Giessen to plan an exodus to America. Its sponsors were children of the age of liberal nationalism. They included such men as Paul Follen and Friedrich Münch, alive with the faith that national consciousness bound men together in ethnic families, whose mutual trust and love would pave the way to universal brotherhood. It was an exciting idea, but the foundation for a united Germany could not be laid at a time when the great powers of Europe—especially Austria—preferred to see the German people divided among a cluster of small, relatively weak states. The Giessen planners hoped that in the interior reaches of America, far from the powerful Foreign Minister Prince Metternich's agents, they could create a community that would operate under American law but that would be "German from its foundations up" and a "model state for the whole commonwealth of man."

To this end, a shipload was gathered and dispatched to New Orleans in the spring of 1834. They were substantial citizens, able to finance their own passage and the cost of locating and purchasing a site. Soon after their arrival in Louisiana, reality began to erode the vision. There were quarrels over whether the settlement should be in Arkansas, Missouri, or Illinois. A decision was reached to go upriver to St. Louis, there to await a second shipload of migrants before choosing a final destination. But the steamer that was chartered proved incapable of the trip up the Mississippi's shallows and tricky channels. By the time two others were hired in its place, faith in the wisdom of the directors was waning fast among the settlers. Moreover, the milk and honey of the Promised Land was beginning to look most accessible to those who went it alone. One by one, families broke away to take up individual occupations and farms. A tiny remnant settled near St. Charles, Missouri, and some members of the second contingent from Germany joined them there. But most of the family heads in the new shipload also followed the example of the Israelites in the days of the judges: each did what was right in his own eyes.

During its nine years of independence, from 1836 to 1845, Texas attracted many German colonizers who were particularly fascinated with its low-priced land. The Texans were eager to populate their prairie stretches, and hard-working "Dutch" farmers promised just the kind of social and economic stability that a young "nation" seemed to need. In the early 1840s, settlements of Germans had been planted on the Colo-

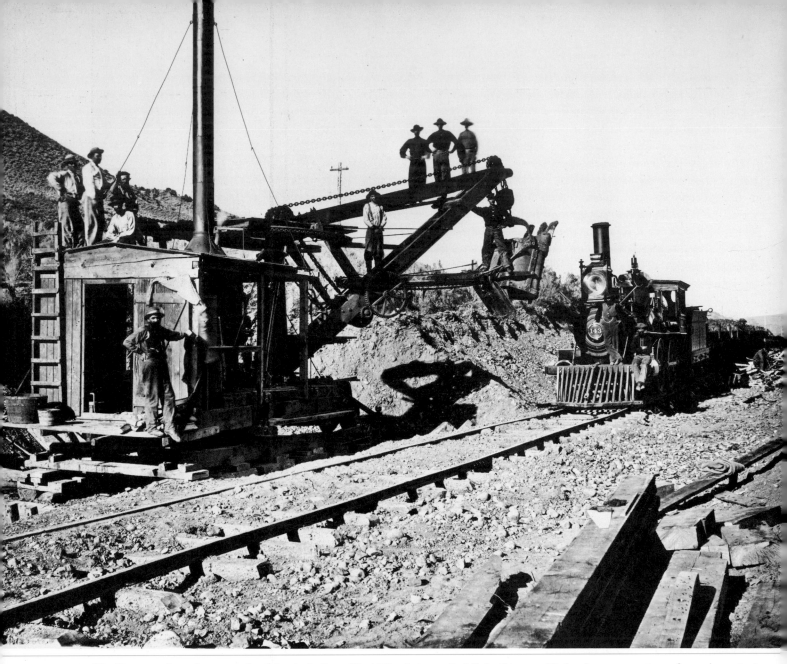

Machinery such as the steam shovel in A. J. Russell's 1869 photograph of Echo Canyon, Utah, above, was not nearly as important to the laying down of America's great railroad lines as was the muscle and sweat of the thousands of Irish construction laborers.

rado River by a nobleman from Holland, Felipe Enrique Neri, Baron de Bastrop, and near San Antonio by a French entrepreneur, Henri Castro. In 1842 a group of Hessian noblemen who called themselves the Mainzer Adelsverein contracted to buy a large tract on the San Saba. Prince Carl of Solms-Braunfels was involved in this undertaking, and in May, 1844, he headed for the American Southwest to arrange things for an expected ten thousand colonists who would follow. In March, 1845, after selecting and buying a new site, he founded the town of New Braunfels. Shortly, however, it was discovered that feudal honor was not impeccable. The prince had embezzled funds in his trust, and was removed. His successor, Ottfried Hans, Baron von Meusebach, signed a treaty with the Comanches, bought

an additional tract on the Pedernales River, and carried the work forward.

By 1857 the Germans in Texas numbered thirty-five thousand. A local commentator believed that the colonies at Bastrop, Castroville, New Braunfels, and elsewhere would "remain German, with all their good points and all their bad ones, with all their wiseheads and their dunces, their fanatics and their philistines—they will remain German until, well, they are Americanized. History knows nothing of fusion, it witnesses only victory and defeat." But the landscape architect Frederick Law Olmsted, reporting in *A Journey Through Texas* (1857), found a pattern that suggested a blending of frontier and fatherland: "You are welcomed by a figure in blue flannel shirt and pendant beard, quoting

Tacitus, having in one hand a long pipe, in the other a butcher's knife; Madonnas upon log-walls; coffee in tin cups upon Dresden saucers; barrels for seats, to hear a Beethoven's symphony on the grand piano; . . . a book case half filled with classics, half with sweet potatoes."

Far to the north of Texas, another German model town rose at New Ulm, Minnesota, in the 1850s. It too derived its special character from the fact that in a time when Western development was largely in the hands of free-swinging promoters, land sharks, squatters, would-be magnates in rails, lumber, transportation and milling, and other wholly individualistic operators, it grew by plan. New Ulm was the product of German settlers who were already in the New World but who were looking for fresh opportunities—the German Land Association of Chicago and the Turner Society of Cincinnati. (Turner societies were the Anglicized version of the *Turnvereine*, associations of Germans ostensibly dedicated to the promotion of physical culture but really concerned with social and political planning.) New Ulm was situated on a six-thousand-acre site, and around the town itself 494 neat little four-acre plots were laid out for vegetable gardens. (Francis Pastorius had supervised the same kind of harmonious design for Germantown in the 1680s.) Parties of settlers arrived on the *Frank Steele*, a Cincinnati-built steamer plying the Minnesota River, and took up their assigned acreages. It was a far cry from Daniel Boone's day, but fully as significant in its power to implant civilization in the interior of North America.

Along with regularity, the German spirit was noted for pedagogy (and pedantry), diligence, and national pride. Many of the upper-class migrants of the 1820–50 era filled the bill as "model Germans." Often they were scholars who could have enjoyed careers in the expanding bureaucracy of the slowly modernizing German states, especially Prussia. But they had chosen to identify themselves with the drive for elected assemblies, written constitutions, national unification, the glorification of folk culture, and other goals of liberalism. Inevitably, frustration and failure turned them into refugees. Germany was without a major revolution until 1848. Then there was a rising in many of the constituent states, the summoning of an all-German parliament, and a roseate dawn of hope for a free, united, and progressive Germany. But the potential leader of the movement, the King of Prussia, lost his nerve. Before 1848 was over, reaction set in. Newspapers and magazines were suppressed, liberals jailed, the German National Assembly at Frankfurt fell apart, and those who chose resistance were dealt with by the bayonet. A final wave of refugees—"Forty-Eighters"—joined those who

had gone into exile before the dramatic year. Many of them chose America.

The early arrivals from this group included editors, scholars, and professional men. Somewhat like the German refugees of the 1930s, they found their educational attainments an actual burden in the hurly-burly of American life. Success and status in the New World seemed to go to men of action and to accumulators. Learning that could not be applied in the market place had little effect in advancing a man's fortunes. Some Germans (in both centuries) reacted to this discovery with contempt for American boorishness and refused to compromise with Yankee practicality. Others turned their hands to whatever they could and swam with the current, happily or otherwise. Not a few became successful and enthusiastic Americans.

Friedrich Münch, for example, one of the original members of the Giessen Society, tried agriculture in Missouri for a time. Americans had a name for this kind of *émigré* who trod furrows while ruminating upon metaphysical mysteries—"Latin farmers." Numbers of them were supplied to the frontier by the German colonization societies, both in Europe and in such American cities as Pittsburgh, Chicago, and Cincinnati, which bought land and sped the wanderers onward. Münch eventually graduated from the Latin-farmer ranks into journalism and literature. Fellow intellectuals likewise found themselves appropriate niches, if lucky.

Francis Lieber enjoyed a distinguished career in academic groves. Lieber was a firebrand when he came to the United States in 1827, having already fought in the Waterloo campaign (at the age of fifteen) and in the Greek War of Independence. He was the guiding spirit of the first *Encyclopaedia Americana* (1829–33), and from 1835 to 1856 he taught history and political economy at South Carolina College, now the University of South Carolina. When his liberal opinions finally proved too much for the conservative slaveholding establishment, he moved to New York and Columbia University, where he became a political theorist and teacher.

Whereas government in the abstract engaged the mental energies of Lieber, Gustav Philipp Koerner found the day-to-day life of bread-and-butter politics to his taste. Koerner, born in 1809 to a Frankfurt am Main bookseller, matriculated at the University of Jena in 1828. He subsequently studied at Munich and Heidelberg, and at each place kept up his contacts with the vigorous student movement for German unification. Such a course leads to trouble as the sparks fly upward; inevitably, when there was a brief uprising against the government in Frankfurt in 1833, young Koerner was involved. When it failed, he went into exile. After a look at St. Louis, Koerner decided to try his luck elsewhere. He may have found the city on the Missouri all too Germanified for his taste, as he was an outspoken opponent of those who were trying to create islands of German separatism in America. He settled in Belleville, Illinois, and engaged in the practice of law—the great avenue to professional, social, and economic advancement in nineteenth-century America. Koerner soon drifted into politics and campaigned for the Democrats in 1840 and 1844. He was then made a justice of the Illinois Supreme Court. Finally, in 1852, he was elected lieutenant governor.

Koerner's career is a smaller-scale version of the life and times of the man who may be the quintessential German-American, Carl Schurz. Schurz has been described by one recent writer as "a man so laden with statesman-like virtues"—honesty, clarity, independence—"that it would be almost comforting to find a flaw or two in his character." He began his political life as an idealist swimming against the current in Germany, and he ended it as combatively as ever, denouncing his fellow Americans for their indecent imperialism in subjugating the Philippines. Skinny, bespectacled, bearded in later life, he looked more the schoolmaster than the man of action, but his record belied his image.

Schurz was a university student in Bonn when the revolution of 1848 broke out. He was an enraptured follower of Professor Gottfried Kinkel, poet and prophet of the New Germany; a nineteen-year-old spirit coiled to spring at a touch. The right moment came one day when he was bent over his desk working on a dramatic treatment of the life of Ulrich von Hutten, a noble Renaissance writer, scholar, and controversialist. A friend dashed in with the news that the French had just ousted King Louis Philippe. Schurz flung down his pen and rushed out to join in the rejoicings of his liberal brethren. "That was the end of *Ulrich von Hutten*," he recalled later. "I never touched it again."

The following spring found Schurz in a situation calculated to take the romance out of revolution. With other troops of the temporary government set up by liberals in the Rhenish provinces, he was shut up under Prussian siege in the fortress of Rastatt. When the garrison commander decided to surrender, Schurz escaped through a sewer that led under the walls to the fields outside. After a near-drowning, near-starvation, and concealment in a farmer's loft with soldiers scarcely inches away, he crossed the border into France and eventually joined a large group of German refugees in Zurich. But he was not finished with the Prussians. Professor Kinkel was being held in the prison at Spandau, and Schurz rescued him in what appears to modern eyes to be a scenario for an adventure film.

Under an assumed name, Schurz traveled to Berlin. There, posing as a doctor, he made contacts that finally put him in touch with a bribable officer of the guard. On a November night in 1850, Schurz waited outside the prison while the professor came sliding down a rope that had been smuggled into his cell. Then he and Schurz hustled into a waiting getaway carriage. If the American environment was one that yielded its gifts most freely to the man who could improvise courageously, Schurz passed his citizenship test that night.

He did not go to the United States directly. First there were a few months of journalism in Paris. Then, following his expulsion from France in the spring of 1851 by the police of President Louis Napoleon, he lived in England for more than a year, meeting many other liberal exiles but finding the country unchangeably foreign. Despairing of liberalism on the Continent in the foreseeable future, Schurz set his course for America and landed in New York in September, 1852. Moving to Philadelphia with his bride, he set about learning English by diligently reading Thackeray, Shakespeare, Macaulay, and the Philadelphia *Ledger*—never skipping a paragraph, and never failing to consult the dictionary when a word was doubtful. In 1856 he moved on to Watertown, Wisconsin, and plunged into the study of Blackstone (the starting point of a nineteenth-century legal education)—and into the management of an insurance company, the nurture of the weekly newspaper *Deutsch Volks-Zeitung*, service as an alderman and Commissioner of Public Improvements in Watertown, partnership in a Milwaukee law firm, and campaigning for the newly founded Republican Party. By 1860 he was to the German Republicans of Wisconsin what Joseph was to Potiphar: whatsoever was done in that house, he was the doer of it. Abraham Lincoln's reward for Schurz's efforts in securing the Wisconsin vote for him was to appoint Schurz Minister to Spain.

Schurz's subsequent career defies summary. Eager to be part of the crusade against slavery, in 1862 he resigned from his post in Madrid and was commissioned a brigadier general of volunteers. He served diligently and bravely, though not always successfully. After the war he returned to journalism and eventually moved to Missouri, whose legislature elected him to the United States Senate in 1869. Schurz became increasingly disenchanted with what he thought of as boodling and vengefulness in the Republican Party during Reconstruction. In 1872 he was one of the leaders of a Liberal Republican insurrection that attempted to deny renomination to President Grant. It failed to make a dent in the victorious totals of the hero of Appomattox,

but when Rutherford B. Hayes became President in 1877, he appointed Schurz his Secretary of the Interior.

From this vantage point Schurz conducted a vigorous war on the patronage system of filling government jobs. Though his enemies denounced him as a sinister foreigner, trying to substitute Prussian bureaucracy for the time-hallowed spoils system, he saw his principles triumph in the creation of the Civil Service Commission in 1883. In 1884 he abandoned the regulars again to support Grover Cleveland, as a protest against the Republicans' nomination of James G. Blaine, about whom clung the aroma of too many favors done for railroads and other corporations. In 1896 Schurz was a Republican once more, defending the "sound dollar" against the crusade of William Jennings Bryan for unlimited coinage of silver. And in 1900 he was denouncing William McKinley's conversion of Americans into empire builders. During and between these various campaigns he had done duty as an editor of the New York *Evening Post* and *Harper's Weekly.*

Schurz had the incorruptibility and the pugnacious honesty of an Adams. The stereotype of the German in our century is that of a man whose tongue may speak of liberty while his soul is always ready to click heels to authority. But Schurz wrote from Spain during his diplomatic service there: "I cannot endure people who abase themselves as they do here; and I am embarrassed when all manner of honors and reverences are hurled at my head. Nowhere can I feel right save in a country where the people stand erect in their

"The first German settlers we saw, we knew at once. They lived in little log cabins. . . . simple and cheap habitations, but there were many little conveniences about them, and a care to secure comfort in small ways evident, that was very agreeable to notice." Frederick Law Olmsted's words from A Journey Through Texas *in 1857 could have described Julius Meyenberg's green and peaceful farm in Fayette County, Texas, the subject of a watercolor (circa 1864), above, by Louis Hoppe. Other Germans who gravitated west helped to turn rough mining villages into tidy towns. The procession below, which took place in 1860, was part of a German May Day festival in Weaverville, California.*

boots." In his fifty-four American years, Schurz neither bent a knee nor allowed his heels to emit the ghost of a click.

By mid-century it was already a commonplace of American life that Cincinnati, St. Louis, and Milwaukee were heavily Teutonized. In 1840 the Germans of Cincinnati owned five thousand houses and cast a third of the city's votes. In the following decade, the German language was given parity with English in the local schools. Milwaukee was often called the German Athens. Forty thousand Germans contributed to the rise of Wisconsin's population from 3,600 in 1830 to 300,000 in 1850, and many settled in the lakeside city, where they brought German newspapers, choral groups, *Turnvereine*, coleslaw, and pumpernickel, and introduced the names Schlitz, Pabst, Blatz, and Miller to the Ameri-

Robert Owen, left, a British saddler's son who made a fortune in textile manufacturing and wrote numerous expositions of his principles of educational philanthropy, himself received a formal education only until he was nine years old. His elaborate plan for New Harmony, Indiana, below, drawn up by an architect, envisioned a great quadrangle with gardens and exercise grounds surrounded by public buildings, workers' houses, and schools.

can scene. St. Louis' German population made the city an island of free-soil sentiment in a slaveholding state. In other cities, too, the German influence was abundantly evident. It is not surprising to learn that New York had 100,000 Germans in 1860, supporting not only a congeries of beer gardens but also twenty churches, fifty German-language schools, ten bookstores, five printing establishments, and a theater; nor that the Germans of Philadelphia were sufficiently strong in voice and number to hold a choral festival, or *Sängerfest*, as early as 1846. Two years later, in New York, the Germania Orchestra, a pioneer American symphony organization, was launched. And it may be somewhat disconcerting to those who believe that the pre-1860 South was a homogeneous land of English-descended "natives" to find that Germans flourished there. In Richmond as early as 1840, the local German population held a festival in honor of Gutenberg. Seventeen years later, the unveiling of a bust of Baron von Steuben was attended by a German rifle company, a German singing group, a Schiller Society, a *Turnverein*, and a German dramatic club. In 1860 more than one of every six people in the future capital of the Confederacy was of German origin. Louisville had three German newspapers in the 1850s. Nashville, Mobile, and Natchez all had German social clubs and professional men. Charleston, deeply marked as it was by the culture of planters who followed eighteenth-century French and English Caribbean models, nevertheless counted 1,200 Germans in 1842. New Orleans had many German inhabitants, and, as we have seen, Texas had sev-

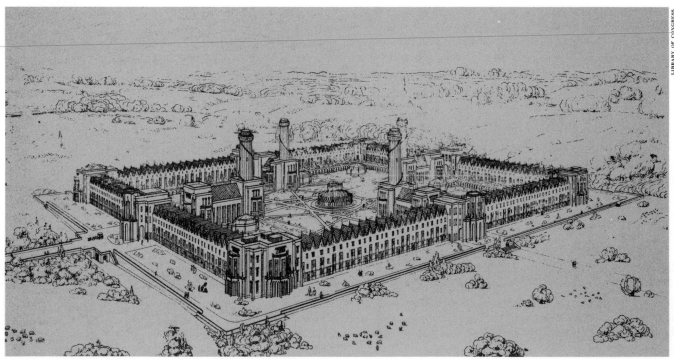

eral colonies of Germans even before it became a state.

Wherever the Germans were able to take hold on something like their own terms, their impact was palpable. It was something that could be measured in dollars when German skills raised and operated breweries, glass factories, binderies, packing plants, sawmills, and machine shops in the valleys of the Ohio, the Mississippi, the Missouri, and their tributaries—those streams which not long before had flowed through wildernesses. It was something that left names on the land and pictures in the mind, too.

Thus the Germans of the nineteenth-century migration and the people-hungry American economy and society met and altered each other. And as with the Germans, so with the Swiss, the Dutch, the Scandinavians, and the other new arrivals. Each group found ways of interweaving its characteristic styles with the needs of a young country. Each group tended to respond to some mood of the American moment, and help it to expression in reality—whether it was the quest for a perfect society, or westward expansion, or the liberation of technology to create a triumphant capitalist order. There were always foreign faces in whatever caravans moved, physically or intellectually or through politics or investment, toward new horizons.

Among the most colorful of the European promotions of the young century were the vest-pocket Utopias that were conceived in the Old World to be realized (or, more often than not, unrealized) in the New. Native Americans themselves were fertile in devising models of the good society. It was natural. America had no past to speak of to enchain its nobler aspirations, but it had an almost empty continent as a stage on which to act out dramas of social invention. Revivalism fed the fires of millennial hope. Scarcely a county lacked its evangels of an American Zion. But it was not only religious frenzy that begot perfectionist fantasies. The lingering spirit of the French Revolution led some rationalist dreamers to meditate the creation of the perfect state, deep in the wilderness, minus priests and kings—the shrine of reason, unprofaned by bayonets. George Rapp and Robert Owen are two faces on opposite sides of the coin of Utopianism. One was deeply and mystically religious, the other totally opposed to any vision not supported by rationally considered pragmatic evidence. Yet each essayed an American projection of his dream of the good society, and by coincidence their creations occupied the same piece of ground.

"Father" Rapp was born Johann Georg Rapp in 1757 in Württemberg and grew to be one of those solid Pietists whose records checker German religious history. Somehow, engaged in farming and in raising a son and a daughter, he acquired the dangerous habit of reading and deeply pondering on philosophy and theology. Soon he began to feel that the forms of church worship interfered with the true communication between believers and the Holy Spirit. The preaching of that doctrine got his followers jailed and earned him the opposition of the state church. So, like English Puritans a century and a half before him, he became a Separatist (after his fashion), and then, thanks to his patriarchal qualities, a Separatist with a following of about 830 persons. In 1803 he journeyed to America to seek a suitable haven, and most of his flock joined him there the next year.

Pooling their resources, the Rappites bought five thousand acres of wild land some twenty-five miles north of Pittsburgh, on which they established the Harmony Society. Its principles were plain: wants to be supplied from a common store, dress to be simple, social distinctions to fade in the interest of common purpose. In two years of hard work they built more than fifty houses, a church, a schoolhouse, sawmill, gristmill, tannery, barns, workshops, and a distillery that produced excellent whiskey. In 1807 a portentous new revelation came to Rapp: celibacy was the true and sanctioned path for the faithful. Those who could not accept this tenet quietly withdrew from the community. Those who could but were already married remained together and practiced restraint. Those still chaste went on as before—or so, at least, they claimed. Asked many years later if there were safeguards built against temptation, an elder replied: "None at all. It would be of no use. If you have to watch people, you had better give them up." A subsequent ordinance enjoined the sacrifice of tobacco, too—and a somewhat jocose commentator later remarked that this was "a deprivation which these Germans must have felt almost as severely as the abandonment of conjugal joys."

In 1814, a series of agricultural setbacks convinced Father Rapp that the Pennsylvania locality was less than ideal. The Rappites then sold the original site for $100,000 and bought thirty thousand acres on the Wabash River in Indiana. There they built the town of Harmony, once more went through the process of raising homes, shops, and buildings, and bringing smiling prosperity to the rude creek bottoms. Success followed virtue nicely. They even recruited new members and rose to a strength of something between seven and eight hundred community members. Unfortunately, however, the swamp mosquito was no respecter of faith. Agues and fevers beset the community. Moreover, Father Rapp had a practical eye for such worldly factors as the slow development of southern Indiana, which kept the settlement inconveniently far from good markets.

The neighbors were unfriendly and showed little prospect of becoming sources of future profit. And last, the Harmonists themselves grew restless; a move would reassert their unity. For all these reasons, Rapp put Harmony on the market in 1824, and a buyer was almost immediately found in a Briton, Robert Owen, who paid $150,000 for the land, buildings, and all other assets. The Rappites, it should be recorded, moved out to build Economy, near Pittsburgh, which flourished for years. Visitors found the paterfamilias Rapp holding court in a fine brick house, bands serenading crowds in the orderly streets on Sundays and summer evenings, and factories distinguished by the presence of vases of flowers on each worker's machine. The tempter finally entered into Eden in 1831, in the form of a newcomer who styled himself Count Maxmilian de Leon and who eventually led a secession that ruined the old colony.

Back at the renamed New Harmony, Robert Owen was undertaking some remarkable alterations in the world. He was himself an inordinately successful self-made textile manufacturer, whose model Scottish factory town of New Lanark was the wonder of social reformers in that era of industrial cruelty. He had deliberately created a planned and paternalistic laboring community because of a profound belief in environmentalism—or what would one day be called behaviorism. It was Owen's credo, as explained in numerous pamphlets and speeches, that the infant responded totally to his nurture. Owen would tell fascinated audiences of middle-class Englishmen and Americans that if they had been brought up at the foot of the Rocky Mountains by Indians, they would be redskins to the core, or, if exposed from infancy to the culture of China, they would be mandarins and coolies in all but pigmentation. This apparently rigid doctrine led in the direction of great expectations. The evil that men did came from wrong or outmoded ideas and from irrational religion. Replace an environment of error with one of truth, and man would leap into his natural state of virtue. Owen hoped to try nothing less at New Harmony. "I am come to this country," he announced in April, 1825, "to introduce an entire new system of society; to change it from an ignorant, selfish system to an enlightened social system which shall gradually unite all interests into one, and remove all causes for contests between individuals." Then he returned to Great Britain, leaving affairs in the hands of deputies, among whom were his sons.

Theoretically, New Harmony was to rework the old Rappist surroundings to conform to various ideas of Owen's. There were to be four main buildings arranged around a central square. Kitchens, laundries, and refectories were to be communal. Schoolrooms, laboratories, concert halls, and ballrooms would be placed with geometric precision at corners and in the centers of the buildings. Rooms for married couples would occupy the lower floors; the upper would be reserved for single persons and for children—who, at the age of two, were to be removed from the confusing influences of their parents and educated by the community. Education, in the first American coeducational system, would include music, history, drawing, astronomy, geography, botany, and agriculture. The community as a whole would hold property in common, recognize the equal rights of all, and devote its nonworking hours to moral lectures, dancing, singing, and military drill. (How the last would be reconciled with perfect equality seems not to have been specified.) Owen, like most perfectionists, was suspicious of individualism; one of his cherished ideas was that all the communitarians should wear uniforms—pantaloons and collarless jackets for the men; pantalets tied at the ankles with short slips over them for the women.

The history of New Harmony need not be spelled out in detail. A gathering of intellectuals made its collective way down the Ohio and up the Wabash to partake of the feast of reform. It included a distinguished geologist, a chemist, an artist, assorted European pedagogues, the zoologist and entomologist Thomas Say, who had been curator of the American Philosophical Society, and others whose conjoined abilities led someone to dub the keelboat that brought them on a January day in 1826 "a boatload of knowledge." They worked under an elegantly drawn-up constitution, called the Community of Equality, that divided productive labor into neat categories (agriculture, manufactures and mechanics, science and education, literature, domestic economy, general economy, and commerce) and contained a kind of declaration of community objectives calling for co-operation, sincerity, kindness, courtesy, order, health, and learning. These high objectives notwithstanding, Owen's Utopians were all so hopelessly impractical that the original community fragmented and then failed in a very short time.

Many equivalents of Harmony and New Harmony were founded by visitors and settlers from Europe. In their quest for the impossible, the European projectors of ideal communities were demonstrating once more the deep connections between American and European experience in the modern age. It was an age of men set on edge by the possibilities of their ever more powerful technology. Especially in a new land, nothing seemed impossible to the god-men who made, and still believed they controlled, the machine.

Germany Transplanted

STATE HISTORICAL SOCIETY OF WISCONSIN

A Sense of Identity

"The Germans live here as in their old Germany. They are *gemüthlich*, drink beer, practise music, and still ponder here 'über die Weltgeschichte [over world history]. . . .'" So one traveler described Cincinnati in the 1850s—a city typical of many across America that felt the impact of the German migration.

Immigrants tended to settle in areas that reminded them of the homes they had left behind. In Cincinnati in 1850, some 49,000 Germans congregated in a section across a canal, known as "Over the Rhine," where "the front steps of each of the brick row houses were whitewashed every Saturday, there were potted plants in the windows and tiny garden plots in the rear . . ." and four German newspapers kept the residents informed.

"He who leaves Europe permanently must bid farewell to all museums, galleries, Gothic monuments, gardens and theatres . . . ," Gustav Koerner warned in his *Memoirs*, "and must console himself with the thought that he must forever content himself with substitutes for these, with the green of thick forests and the flowering of the wide prairies." But for the German in America, prairies were not enough. He was determined at all costs to preserve his *Kultur*. "It was a German world in which we lived, . . ." author Hermann Hagedorn wrote of his boyhood in Brooklyn. "The girls and I generally talked English with Mother, but, when Father was around, and especially at the dinner table, the language was German." When his father first came to America, he worked for a German firm. "The boarding-house in Brooklyn where he found lodging was run by a [German] woman. . . . When Father went out for a meal with his new friends they went to German restaurants; when they went to church they went to a German church; when they wanted to be entertained, they went to the Irving Place Theatre and saw the latest German comedy or some Schiller drama or a Shakespeare play, in German."

Partly because of their educational background in Germany, partly as an effort to preserve the German language, and partly because they believed the American cultural level to be so low, Germans took a special interest in the American educational system. Not only the kindergarten but also the state-endowed vocational institution has German roots. And in the individual German family, Hagedorn related, education was a matter of great pride. "Failure to be promoted from one grade to the next brought a stigma. . . . 'Have you heard? Hans Schmidt is stuck in the third grade.' The whole family felt itself socially downgraded."

Cincinnati in the 1830s looked like a port on the Rhine.

Organized Fellowship

The old Roman maxim *"mens sana in corpore sano"* has probably been more enthusiastically endorsed by Germans than by any other group of people. Taking the saying for his motto, patriot Friedrich Ludwig Jahn in 1811 established his first *Turnplatz* (open-air gymnasium) in Berlin, dedicated to creating sound bodies that could fight for a unified Germany, and sound minds to champion freedom and liberty. Although the movement was suppressed and Jahn imprisoned, a number of his followers later came as political refugees to America, where they carried on the Turner tradition. *Turnvereine* sprang up across the country. They began as athletic clubs, but soon they also filled many philosophical, social, and political needs of the immigrants. As a result, they became centers of German neighborhoods.

Mrs. Elizabeth Wasser Ritchie's confirmation certificate

The lithograph above shows the members of the German Gymnastic Society in Cincinnati in 1850.

Mrs. Ritchie, a German Swiss who arrived in 1831, lived thirty-eight years in America without learning English.

Industrious and Inventive

Just as the German farmer was admired for his hard labor and inventiveness, so too the city worker. Well before technical schools existed in the United States, such institutions had reached a high level in Germany—one reason, perhaps, for the German domination of such fields as electrical engineering and the manufacture of scientific and musical instruments. Henry Steinway, who began his famous piano company in a small New York factory in 1853, was originally Heinrich Steinweg, born in Brunswick. Lazarus Straus, who developed both Macy's and Abraham & Straus, came from Bavaria; John Wanamaker and the Studebakers, from Pennsylvania-German families. Food industries also particularly attracted those of German background—among them Henry John Heinz, a second-generation American. German culinary contributions to America included wieners (wienerwurst), hamburgers, frankfurters, hasenpfeffer, cole slaw, and dill pickles—and these seemed to mix happily in the American stomach with good Kentucky bourbon (see left).

At left, the German impact on the corner of Cincinnati's Fifth and Vine Streets about 1890. Above, Cincinnati pork packing in the 1830s.

"The Strongest in Us"

For many Germans—scholars, journalists, and professional people, refugees of the revolutions in Germany—finding new roots in America was a wrenching experience. Lawyers, teachers, and writers were forced to accept work as bartenders, house painters, and laborers; men who could read the classics in Latin and Greek toiled the fields, and were dubbed by their American neighbors "Latin farmers." Refusing to relinquish "the intellectual achievements of a thousand years in the old world for the culture of the primeval forest," they dedicated themselves to creating in America a "New Germany." Countless others found the greatest expression of their ideals in the words of Carl Schurz (left), who vowed unwavering loyalty to his adopted country. He urged his fellow countrymen not to forget that "we as Germans are not called upon here to form a separate nationality but rather to contribute to the American nationality the strongest there is in us, and in place of our weakness to substitute the strength wherein our fellow-Americans excel us, and blend it with our wisdom."

In cities and towns, German-Americans found an outlet for their gregarious instincts and a way to perpetuate the life they had known at home by creating a wide range of organizations. These included fraternal and benevolent associations, militia companies, Humboldt societies devoted to lectures and discussion, study groups, workingmen's associations, and lodges such as the Masons and Odd Fellows. And there were innumerable social clubs—sharpshooters', bowlers', and luncheon (the members of one such club in Cincinnati pose with pipes, above, in the 1880s). With the promise that "Milwaukee is practically a German city," one promoter, William Wehner, lured to that city in the 1880s a whole colony of German artists (right) to paint panoramas of United States history.

OVERLEAF: A German band stands in front of the Cincinnati Music Hall.

Little German bands, like the one at right, consisting of five to ten tolerably proficient musicians, were an important part of every German community, where they played on street corners, at holiday festivities, or on Sundays in the parks, places "of pavilions and picnics, of long open-air tables and benches where lusty Männerchor roared drinking songs between rounds of steins, and children frolicked on the carousel." In pursuit of culture, Milwaukee Germans flocked to the German-language dramas at the Pabst Theatre, or in Cincinnati to concerts at Highland House, whose program cover appears below.

SUMMER EVENING

CONCERTS.

Street Bands and Music Halls

Wherever Germans settled, choral societies and bands were formed to rehearse the folk songs and music of the fatherland. On Monday nights in Milwaukee, German boys practiced with the Männerchor, whose director one young singer described as "a choleric man with a bristling black dyed moustache . . . [who] works himself and his family furiously. He directs three singing societies, including our Orpheus, for very little pay . . . [as well as] two orchestras and a string quartet. . . ." The first *Sängerfest* was held in Cincinnati in 1849, and by 1857 this competition in Philadelphia had attracted fifty-nine singing societies—nearly fifteen hundred voices. Mid-century saw the arrival of a number of traveling orchestras, the most famous of which was the Germania. During the half-dozen years of its existence, the Germania gave some eight hundred concerts, a remarkable achievement, as Carl Wittke points out, considering that "at the beginning of the last century bands which tried to play a Haydn symphony in New York were pelted with eggs and vegetables as crowds shouted for 'Yankee Doodle.'"

"It is not proper to miss it," opined one Milwaukee German on the subject of Sunday concerts at the Turnerhalle. *"Besides it costs only fifteen cents on a season ticket, and the music fits in with the slumbrous Sabbath feeling that follows a dinner of Knoedel and Sauerbraten. . . . Also, the setting is meant for relaxation. There are tables and chairs . . . and when we come in the hall is already misty with cigar smoke. . . . waiters [come] laden with steins . . . waitresses bring trays of coffee and cakes . . ."*—an excellent description of Turnverein festivities (program right) and the Cincinnati Music Hall (below).

Turnverein „Milwaukee"

Eröffnungs Feier der
NEUEN TURN HALLE.

Tanz-Programm zum

Ball

Montag, den 22. Januar, 1883.

The German beer saloon was a respectable place, "as family oriented," said one writer, "as the corner grocery." So too were the Lustgarten (beer gardens), where Germans gathered for refreshments, music, and conversation. In the 1860s, New York City's Bowery area was particularly well known for the number of its "better class" beer gardens, "patronized chiefly by the German element of the city. These are immense buildings, fitted up in imitation of a garden. . . . They will accommodate from four hundred to twelve hundred guests. Germans carry their families there to spend a day, or an evening." Beer was also served in theaters and concert halls. And many of the most respected men in a German community were the brewers. During the panic of 1857, in fact, many Germans transferred their savings from banks and placed them in the brewers' safes. The lithograph at right, by the Monsch Brothers, features the Beer Brewers of Cincinnati. Although the beer gardens came into some conflict with Sunday closing laws, they were generally condoned as preferable to the "dancing parlours." "To the influence of the German immigrants in particular, . . ." wrote John F. Kennedy, "we owe the mellowing of the austere Puritan imprint on our daily lives."

142

Mellowing the Puritan

". . . There remained neither taverne, beer house, nor place of re-liefe," early settler Thomas Studley complained when the ship that had brought him to Jamestown headed back to England. And al-though the English and Scots eventually began to produce ale in some American cities, it was not until Civil War taxes on hard liquor coincided with the heavy immigration of beer-loving Ger-mans that breweries became big businesses in America. Even among non-Germans there was a growing demand for the less heavy, or "lager," variety of German beer, which could be drunk by a factory worker during the day without impairing his effi-ciency. Beerhouses sprang up. "The commencement of one of these establishments appears to be very simple," wrote an editor in 1853. "A German obtains a cellar, a cask of beer, a cheese, a loaf of bread, and some pretzels—puts out a sign and the business is started." Made from a special malt, the lager beer aged through the winter and was just right in the spring. And on Easter Sunday morning in St. Louis, children carrying buckets ran to the saloons for the first of the popular dark bock beer; during the short bock season, an exhilarating mood prevailed. "We knew," recalled a woman who spent her childhood in St. Louis, "that while bock beer lasted the *Eltern* [elders] would be gayer, kinder. . . . From after supper until dark we might follow a Little German Band from beer saloon to beer saloon . . . , listen to the singing, reap pretzels . . . we attended charivaris, pinochle and *klatsch* fests . . . and never did we see our beds before nine, even ten, o'clock."

Germans maintained a monopoly of Amer-ica's beer manufacture throughout the nine-teenth century. By 1880 Cincinnati had twenty-five breweries, one of the largest of which was the Christian Moerlein company, shown at right, founded in 1841. Pabst, Schlitz, Blatz, Miller, and other beers gave renown to Milwaukee. The cartoon, left, suggests the German aspects of that city—a sightseeing charabanc fueled by a keg of Pabst, with dispensers offering pumper-nickel, frankfurters, sauerkraut, and cheese.

OVERLEAF: *The quality of the German-Amer-ican mixture is typified in the photograph, taken in 1911, of the Hedlund family in Min-nesota celebrating American independence.*

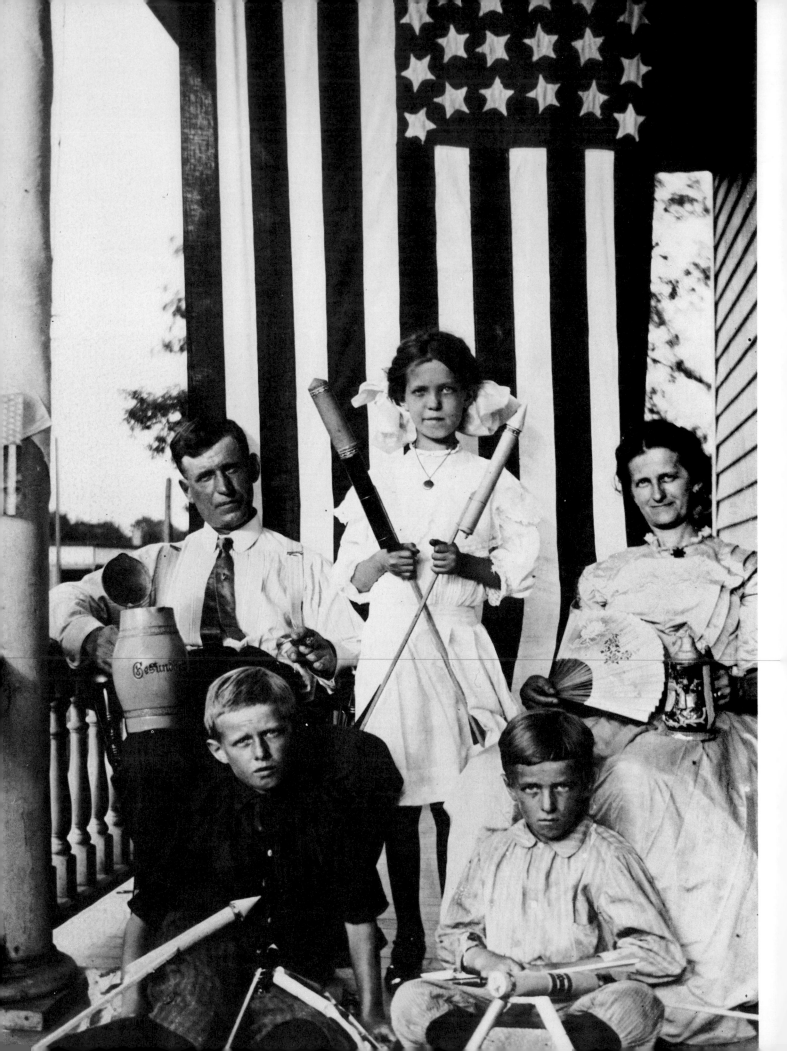

To People a Continent

IN THEIR WORDS

American independence, economic growth, and the beginnings of industrialization gave nineteenth-century immigration a new flavor. The immigrants were needed, and sometimes were welcomed, to build the railroads, mine the coal, operate the machines, and cultivate the fields for a growing population. And so they came in increasing numbers (Castle Garden, below), now from other countries than England—skilled mechanics from a European industrialism that had a head start on America, and unskilled workers as well. The Irish were the forerunners of this new group. Poverty, land shortage, urban filth, and finally—after the potato blight had struck in the 1840s—starvation sent them streaming across the Atlantic. Many took jobs building canals and railroads, but they collected mainly in the cities. The tide of German immigration overlapped the Irish, reaching its peak in the middle of the nineteenth century and carrying its settlers to the cities and rich farm lands of Ohio, Missouri, Minnesota, and Wisconsin. With them came the Scandinavians who populated the prairies and forests of the Midwest and West. These new immigrants were men in a hurry, full of a sense of immediacy and promise, and ready to surmount all obstacles in their struggle to succeed. As the following selections indicate, the obstacles were many: a lengthy sea voyage that ended in a confused and often frenetic arrival, a difficult journey across country or a struggle to make a home in an American city—and, most important of all, a search for a place in the American economy.

Disastrous Voyage

Until steam power was in general use in ocean-going vessels, most ships carrying immigrants in the nineteenth century were little better than those that had beat their way across the sea two hundred years before. Steerage quarters, lined with double bunks, were usually only five feet high and poorly ventilated, even when the hatches were open. The passengers were expected to provide—and cook—their own food. Seasickness, starvation, fever, even madness lay in wait for them on the voyage. "Now would I give a thousand furlongs of sea for an acre of barren ground; long heath, brown furze, any thing," cried Shakespeare's tempest-tost Gonzalo. Many immigrants would have agreed.

William Smith wrote a particularly detailed account—entitled An Emigrant's Narrative; or a Voice from the Steerage *—about his eight-week trip from Liverpool to New York in the winter of 1847–48.*

I engaged passage in the steerage of the ship India, belonging to H———n & Co. The day advertised for sailing was the 12th of [November], but in consequence of not having got in the cargo, which consisted of pig iron and earthen-ware, we were detained ten days for that purpose, and one day to stop a leak, which sprung as the ship was leaving the dock; the immigrants being thus detained eleven days, and as they were of the very poorest class, and most of them having families, with only a small stock of provisions, and that too of the coarsest description, most of them having left Ireland a week, some a fortnight, before the day fixed for sailing, this detention of eleven days was severely felt by those poor creatures, many of them having consumed half of their provisions, without the means of obtaining more. Under these circumstances, the immigrants applied at the office of H———n for the sum of eleven shillings, which was due to each adult immigrant, as the law allowed one shilling per day to each adult passenger from the day advertised to sail to the day of sailing; but as they refused to comply with the request, the immigrants selected six persons to go and state their case to the Government agent. . . . he came with us to the office of H———n, and ordered them to obey the law by paying the amount due to

each person. They promised him that they would do so. He then left us, telling us to call upon him again if we did not receive the sum already stated. The ship owners ordered us to go immediately on board, where we would be paid the amount due us. Believing that they would do so, we all went on board the India, when we were paid two shillings, and two pounds of sea-biscuit. No sooner had we received this trifle, than a steamboat towed us down the river, in order to prevent us from again complaining to the agent of their base conduct. There we remained two days, anchored, during which time there was great confusion and uproar on board, from the above cause. On the next morning, Friday, November 26, 1847, we set sail. . . .

The day on which [the] storm commenced it rained so heavily the whole day we could not make a fire on deck to cook our victuals with. About three o'clock in the afternoon, the rain began to fall in torrents, the clouds were black, and moved rapidly, and the wind gradually increased in force till eight o'clock, when the roaring of the tempest was truly appalling. I heard the mate order the hatchways to be fastened down, (an order indispensably necessary to the safety of the ship.) The order was quickly obeyed, and from that time commenced our sufferings. The increasing violence of the storm, the moaning and creaking of the ship, the howling of the wind, and the roaring of the waves, was horrible to those not accustomed to such scenes . . .

About midnight, a number of boxes and barrels broke loose and rolled from side to side, according to the motion of the ship, breaking the water cans and destroying everything capable of being destroyed by them; to fasten them was almost impossible, for we could not keep ourselves from sliding down without grasping something. In a few minutes the boxes and barrels broke to atoms, scattering the contents in all directions —tea, coffee, sugar, potatoes, pork, shirts, trowsers, vests, coats, handkerchiefs, &c., &c., were mingled in one confused mass. The cries of the women and children was heart-rending; some praying, others weeping bitterly, as they saw their provisions and clothes (the only property they possessed) destroyed. The passengers being sea-sick, were vomiting in all parts of the vessel; the heat became intense in consequence of the hatchways being closed down, and the passengers, 300 in number, being thus kept below, we were unable to breathe the pure air or see the light of heaven but a few hours at a time. The scent arising from the matter vomited up, and from other causes, became intolerable. Things continued in this way until the fourth day, when the storm abated, and the hatchways were opened. Most of the passengers were so eager to get on deck that they pushed each other off the ladder; several were severely hurt . . .

We had been at sea four weeks . . . I felt sure . . . that however good the motives were which induced the captain to take a southerly passage, that that dreadful scourge, the ship fever, (which was already on board our ship) would be increased by it; an opinion which facts soon verified by the number of cases and deaths increasing. . . .

Most of those who died of ship-fever were delirious, some a day, others only a few hours previous to death. One day there were three men walking about the ship raving mad; one fancied himself a priest, and told the passengers they would all die and go to hell, unless they permitted him to make the sign of the cross and baptize them; at daylight, next morning, he was found dead in his berth. The second one . . . ran up on deck, and before any one was aware of his intentions, threw himself into the sea and was drowned. . . . The other lunatic having attempted to stab his wife, had to be tied down to his berth. . . .

. . . when we had been a month at sea, the steward discovered that four hogsheads [for water], by oversight or neglect, had not been [filled]. On the following morning, by Captain Thompson's order, our water was reduced from two quarts to one quart per day for an adult and one pint for a child. The week following, the captain died. Mr. Connor upon succeeding him, showed us the necessity of his reducing our allowance of water from a quart to a pint per day. My health, which had hitherto been good, notwithstanding all the hardships I had suffered, began to fail me. My

provisions were consumed, and I had nothing but ship allowance to subsist upon, which was scarcely sufficient to keep us from perishing, being only a pound of sea biscuit (full of maggots) and a pint of [foul] water . . . I began to get so weak that if I walked upon deck for a short time, I was compelled to sit down from fatigue. . . . I felt as though I had no life in me. . . . I had been in this state two days, when I was seized with the ship-fever; at first I was so dizzy that I could not walk without danger of falling. I was suffering much from a violent pain in my head, my brains felt as if they were on fire, my tongue clove to the roof of my mouth and my lips were parched with excessive thirst. . . . I . . . became so sick that I could neither sit nor stand, and was therefore compelled to keep to my berth . . . Every day I felt weaker, and became exhausted upon the least exertion, and, as if to increase my misery, another storm arose and continued three nights and three days. I had to use all the little strength I had to prevent being thrown out of bed . . .

Captain Connor came down among us for the last time, leaning upon the shoulders of two seamen. He visited every sick person—a task that usually took him two hours to perform, having so many sick, as he had to stay a few moments with each person to ask questions and give medicine to them. He

had not been able for a few days past to leave the cabin, and his visiting us the moment he was able, although still so weak that he could not walk without assistance, proved, if proof was needed, his determination to save as many of the lives of the passengers as lay in his power, if there was anything on board that he thought would be instrumental in doing so. . . . pale, thin and exhausted, he had to rest many times before he could visit all the sick. Like myself, he was suffering from a violent dysentery as well as the ship-fever. When he reached my berth, he seemed somewhat surprised, and exclaimed, "What, Smith! you alive yet!" "Yes, sir," said I, "thank God, I am, but I don't think I can live many days longer." "Don't be down-hearted about that," said he, "for I expect a pilot on board to-morrow, and you will soon be in Staten Island Hospital, where you will have good doctors to attend to you. I see the fever has left you, and if you live to land you will get cured of the dysentery, and perhaps outlive me." These were the last words he spoke to me, and alas, they proved too prophetic. I never saw him more . . .

About nine o'clock next morning, the pilot came on board amid the huzzas of those who were able to shout for joy. Early in the afternoon, the exciting cry of "Land!" "Land!" "Land!" ran through the ship like wild fire. A number of passengers came down from the deck to tell their sick relatives and friends that they had seen it . . . Some fell upon their knees and thanked God for his mercy to them, some wept for joy, others capered about, exhibiting extravagant demonstrations of joy. In a short time the anchor was let down, and we were visited by the Health Officer from Quarantine, who ordered all the sick to be brought into the hospital as quick as possible.

Thus was this disastrous voyage at an end, after an absence of exactly eight weeks from the shores of my native land, (the day we arrived at Staten Island being Friday, the 21st of January, 1848). My whole lifetime did not seem so long as the last two months appeared to me. . . .

Mealtime between decks on an immigrant ship in the 1870s

Welcome to America

America might be the Promised Land for some immigrants. But for many it also proved at first to be terrifying and disillusioning. Finding a place to stay was difficult; it was particularly so if one knew no English. Runners for various hotels fought furiously over the debarking newcomers, promising decent and inexpensive accommodations. Other solicitous greeters—some of whom were countrymen of the immigrants—sold them train tickets to the interior, or land, or homes. But most of this "helpfulness" was simply swindling: the touted goods and services turned out to be shoddy or bogus; the purpose was to separate the bewildered strangers in the land from all their movable possessions.

When his ship arrived at an American port, the immigrant usually found himself dazed, confused, and quite unprepared to face the immediate challenges of his new environment. To one Scotsman, Richard Weston, who came to America in 1833, New York was hardly a welcoming harbor.

At about half-past five we arrived at the custom-house wharf on Staten Island. Here we had to stand under a broiling sun, each man opposite his own travelling trunk, the lid of which was kept open, awaiting the examination of the custom-house officers. They were not long in performing this duty; indeed they scarcely removed any of our articles, and no seizures were made. Perceiving our exhausted situation, they sent a person to bring us water; and I believe he came and returned with a fresh supply twenty times before we were all satisfied, though the water was any thing but tempting. Our travelling articles being again stowed on board the lighter, at sun-down we made sail for New York. The wind chopt round right a-head of us; we had to beat, but the tide was with us; the spray broke incessantly over us, and the rain began to descend. It was half-past ten before we arrived at the quay. Here we were landed in the dark, the rain pouring upon us, and our luggage strewed all around. The shops, if there were any at hand, were all shut, and we had no one to direct us where to proceed. We had therefore no other alternative than to pass the night where we were in the open air. As the spray was occasionally dashing over the wharf, I constructed a barricade of the trunks belonging to myself and two fellow-passengers, man and wife, whose births [sic] had been next my own, over which I put some deals [boards] which were lying on the wharf. Under the lee of this shed we placed the female passenger, who was ill of a fever; and having procured a pitcher, I proceeded into the town in search of water, and some wine for the woman. This I procured from a shop which I found still open, together with a bottle of brandy, and some bread and cheese. . . .

Here then were we, one hundred and sixteen souls, landed with our luggage in a wet, cold, and stormy night, on a wooden quay in New York, where we had to bivouack under the canopy of heaven. This was our first sample of American hospitality, freedom, and liberty. No person came near us to give us any instructions; indeed we got a cold reception—yet we had each paid five shillings as hospital money, and God knows such a night as this was sufficient to have fitted one and all of us for the benefits of that institution. In fact two of our party only survived a few days. . . .

The rain was still falling, not in showers, but absolutely in torrents, the wind blowing a stiff northwester, the spray breaking over the quay, and thereby wetting with salt water us who were already drenched with rain. But this was really an advantage to us, for a person is not so apt to catch cold by being wet with salt water as with fresh.

After having recruited ourselves by eating bread and cheese and drinking some spirits and water, which latter was very brackish, despairing of getting any assistance till next morning, we creeped under the lee of our barricade of chests and trunks, and endeavoured to compose ourselves to rest, for to sleep was out of the question. Though neither Old Countrymen nor Americans came to visit us, we had myriads of the American rats squeaking and frisking over us, as if sporting at our wretchedness; and they took the usual license practised towards strangers, by robbing us of the remains of our supper. We longed much for day light, which seemed to tarry longer than usual. About 3 A.M. the rain ceased, and the wind lulled considerably. At length day broke . . .

I requested the family who were next to me to look after my luggage while I went into the town and enquired for a furnished room, which they promised to do. On going along the quay, I observed many holes in it large enough to allow a person, or even a chest, to fall through; and as there were no lamps on the quay, I wondered that no accident had befallen some of us on the previous night. One of these chasms was near where I bivouacked. I passed two other encampments of emigrants in Washington street; some of them were lying huddled together under carts, some within the recesses of doors, and some on the bare pavement. I enquired at a good looking elderly woman who was lying on the pavement—her head bare, and her long grey hair fluttering in the breeze—how long it was since she landed; and she answered in German that it was six nights, and that her party had lain all that time on the streets.

William Brown arrived in New York from England in the 1840s. Later he vividly described the typical debarkation scene.

. . . the varieties of strange objects you see in sailing up to New York almost bewilder the mind of a stranger: to look around him and see on his right the castellated islands of the bay; on his left, the noble river Hudson; and fair in front the splendid looking city of New York, the steeples of numerous churches, which are glittering in the sun like gold and silver; while not a cloud of smoke issues from or around any of the high towers. Indeed, from the appearance, you would think that not a single pipe of tobacco was being smoked in the whole city. The wharves extending on both sides as far as the eye can reach, and the forests of masts lying along them, are a sight which can only be exceeded in London and Liverpool. The weary traveller, coming for the first time to this sumptuous looking city, thinks that really, if a paradise exists in this sublunary world, it is here to be found; he is in perfect ecstasy of delight at his prospects. The vessel he is in approaches the wharves, and a helping-hand catches the rope, and the vessel is safe moored. Then all these illusions vanish at once, and the sad reality strikes you with the more force from the contrast. A gang of 300 or 400 ruffians, calling themselves runners, jump on board, begin, very much in the style of plunderers or pirates, seizing hold of the passengers' baggage, and endeavouring to persuade them to go to some inn or lodging-house which they represent, and where each avers accommodation can be had at such and such prices; another comes and states that the person who has just left you is the greatest scoundrel living, and that you will certainly be robbed and perhaps have your throat cut, if you entrust yourself and baggage into his hands. Then the swearing and fighting of these runners, the

shouts of the passengers, the crying of the women and children, makes as great a confusion as ever was heard at Babel. I certainly heard more swearing and more horrid oaths before I had been four hours in that city than I had before heard in the whole course of my life.

The appearance of these men is the most disgusting possible; they are without coats, without cravats, with shirt necks flying open, a large roll of tobacco in each cheek, the juice from which exuding down the corners of their mouths adds to the unsightliness of their cadaverous aspect. They principally seem of a mongrel breed, half Indian and half Irish. Their physiognomy has some resemblance to that of the English gypsies. These men live partly by alluring travellers to the lodging-houses and grog shops, and receive a York shilling, or 6½ per head, and make up the remainder of their living by stealing trunks from passengers, which they call *playing at Trunk loo.* . . .

The steerage passengers by our vessel lost about twenty-seven trunks by these gentry, and some of these trunks contained all the money they had in the world; and the losers were forced to sell what odd things they had left for subsistence till they could get some employment. When passengers are going West they will find plenty of runners, who promise to take them to their destination: their offices are upon the wharves, and they will book you and take your money, and give you tickets to any place you wish to go to; but beware that you pay no money beforehand, as in thousands of cases the captains of canal-boats will make you pay over again, saying you have not paid *them*; and they will seize your trunks till you pay the fare they choose to charge, which you cannot resist, as the evidence which you can bring is perhaps 400 or 500 miles off, and you have no option but to pay the passage over again, or be left without baggage.

During the voyage there was a young Scotch lad aboard, who had neither provisions nor bed. We took the young chap into our service, and he boiled water for us and did other jobs, for which we gave him some cushions and

blankets to lie upon, and as much meat as he could eat. A relative of this young man met us in the harbour, and when the boy informed him how we had behaved to him, he returned us his very best thanks, and brought a landlord with him whom he introduced to us as having good accommodation for passengers in South street; and, as this person seemed a decent Welshman, we agreed to go to his house on the terms proposed. In the hurry and labour which we had in the lifting and carrying of baggage, we were all thoroughly tired, and we enjoyed our tea with a zest which they only can know who have earned it as we had done. Our landlord wished us, as a favour, that we would all sleep in one room, as they had not more accommodation at that time vacant. We agreed to it; but next morning we were in a most woful state; the beds were full of bugs, which bit some of us severely. We had also a legacy of great grey lice; and worse than all, the musquitoes sung all the night, and bit every one of us upon every part which was exposed. That night was indeed a torment, and thousands of times we wished the Scotch boy's uncle was doomed to sleep in the same beds for a month, as a small punishment for his treachery in recommending us to such a house.

Purse-picking (right) at Castle Garden

Journey to the Interior

Immigrants often passed quickly through the port city and headed inland, although, observed a contemporary, many had "scarce an idea of what they are going about." To be sure, some had purchased land before they came, or else went to places where friends and relatives were already established. But the choice of destination was just as likely to be dictated by chance—a ship's schedule or a suggestion by a new acquaintance. Because overland routes were slow, dangerous, and expensive, most immigrants preferred to travel by steamboat or, whenever possible, by the less expensive canalboats. But even then the journey could be arduous and filled with unexpected complications.

Bavarian-born Jacob Schramm was one immigrant who carefully planned his trip to the United States. In 1830, he gave a friend and business associate, to whom he referred as George H——, a sum of 2,000 thaler (about $1,400) and sent him across to buy land and establish a farm that they would share. Five years later Schramm sailed for America with his pregnant wife, his little daughter, his father-in-law, a maid, and two companions, Karl and Gottlob. Below, in letters to in-laws in Saxony, Herr Schramm described the journey to their new home in Hancock County, Indiana, in the autumn of 1835.

Our affairs at last in order, we embarked on the steamboat at 6 o'clock Friday morning, and went up the Hudson to . . . Albany. This is a distance of 160 English miles, or 33 German ones, but at 5 o'clock that same evening we arrived. You can thus get some idea of the rapid journey upstream. . . . One is free to move about . . . for the deck is not separated into classes. The captain has a little office on deck, where everyone gets a ticket and pays his passage money. Later all the tickets are taken up, and anyone who has none must pay. While this is going on no one can move about, lest the captain become confused. It is the same with meals. Whoever wishes to eat in the cabin, first goes to the captain and buys a ticket for half a dollar. . . .

Karl met us as we came off the boat, and we went to a German inn. Everywhere in America, the German inns are the poorest, and that was the case here.

Everywhere one looked there was dirt; the beds were miserable, and furthermore we had a bag stolen during the night with some dry goods and waistcoats. There were also some letters which we had been given to deliver, and which thus cannot reach the right place.

With the help of a New Yorker who traveled with us to Albany and could speak some German we arranged for the trip to Buffalo in a canalboat: sleeping quarters, and meals with the captain, 8 dollars each. . . .

We had scarcely gone aboard when I became very unwell, for gradually I was feeling the change in my way of living and in the water, as usual when I am in a new climate. I had a miserable pain in the stomach. Since we could not talk to the captain or anyone else, at my wife's insistence I lay down without any further ado on one of the beds in the women's cabin, there being no other couch visible on the ship, and the day being sharp and cold. Since we had not been able to learn the rules and regulations of the boat for want of understanding the language, we were guilty of all sorts of blunders. . . . I had scarcely lain down when the captain came, threw me out, and showed me by pantomime that in America it was a great misdemeanor, because the women, and everything about them, are looked upon as something sacred. . . .

As we traveled along, people were constantly coming on board and leaving again at their destinations and their homes. Among them I found a man whose parents had immigrated from Germany, and who consequently spoke pretty good German. He and his wife had been on a visit to Albany . . . We were delighted with him. We talked about everything, especially with the captain; among other matters, as to why I had lain down to sleep in the ladies' cabin, and why he threw me out. This explanation furnished much cause for laughter. We all took pains to learn a little English, and before long we could name and ask for this thing or that. . . .

When we reached Buffalo, we met Karl and Gottlob at once, and went with them immediately to their inn. . . .

I intended to start early Monday by a Lake Erie steamboat to Cleveland. The agent told us, however, that if I would wait until Tuesday morning, when their own boat was going, and would then go along with my goods, I wouldn't have to pay any storage. This was satisfactory to me; the next morning, however, when I paid the charges and was about to put my goods into the vessel, I was required to pay $7 for two nights' storage. Our landlord called the agent a liar to his face, but the proprietor insisted the man had no right to make us any promise. We took our goods by a horsecart, such as is found in every city, to the boat, which left Tuesday evening. . . . As we got out into the lake, a brisk wind came up, and almost everyone was seasick except those who had crossed the ocean . . .

The steamer made frequent landings, people and goods were put off, and new ones taken on, each according to his destination. Once when we were turning in a cove, the ship grounded. Due to the construction of the boats, this is not particularly dangerous. When the ship sticks fast, the wheels, one at each side of the boat . . . , spin like a mill wheel in the water without moving the boat, and no damage is done. But passengers and crew, some 50 men, under orders of the captain, have to keep rushing full tilt on the deck of the boat from one side to the other, until the boat is moved, and can be got afloat with the help of the machinery. This maneuvering took about 2 hours before the ship got afloat.

A circumstance no less funny, and about which we still laugh, concerned grandfather. He would not learn English, and in spite of every opportunity, did not speak one word of it. One night when we were going to bed in the cabin, we pulled off our boots and left them at the foot of the bed. Grandfather, waking first next morning, found some small boots there instead of our big ones. Much disturbed, he waked me. He was sure the little boots belonged to a couple of boys who had slept in the cabin; perhaps they had landed during the night, and had exchanged boots with us. I was of the same opinion. But what could be done under the circumstances? Should we put on our other boots? This was almost impossible, for the box containing them was heaven knew where among the other boxes and bales. Were we to run around barefoot? This would bring all kinds of ridicule down on us. In this dilemma, grandfather tried more than once to thrust his feet into the little boots, and when that was not successful, he suddenly opened his mouth and cried out wretchedly: "Where are our 'Buts'? . . . Our 'Buts' are gone." This plaintive cry finally brought a young man to us, who, when he made out the situation, gave us to understand by pantomime that our "Buts" were on deck being cleaned. I slipped on a pair of bedroom slippers which the young man pointed out, and brought back our polished boots—to the joy of grandfather, who, on this occasion, for the first time had disclosed any knowledge of English. . . .

As we came into Cincinnati at night, we saw many steamboats lying there in

German immigrants prepare to board a train for Colorado in 1870.

the moonlight; we were happy, for we had finally done our last traveling by water. . . .

Here we were then, but we didn't know what to do next. I wanted to take a carriage and drive out to my farm with my family, but no liveryman or cab driver would listen to such a thing. They would not start out for any price for they said the road was too bad to use. Twice a week there was a mail to Indianapolis, but none for several days. In the meantime, George H_____ might come with horses and wagon, and save us the fare. We decided finally that my family and Gottlob should stay meanwhile at the inn at Cincinnati; that Karl and I should start out on foot, and if we met George H_____, return with him. . . .

We walked about 10 English miles and stayed overnight at an inn. At first we had a turnpike; then there began an exceedingly miserable road. . . . We made what use we could of our small store of English, and already fared much better than when we landed in New York. By this time we could inquire about the way, ask for meals, knew how much they were, could ask for our bill, etc. The next morning, when we had gone a few miles further, I saw George H_____ at a distance, coming along with a wagon and two horses.

My joy at this sight was so great that

I cannot describe it. I hurried to him and embraced him. . . .

I now engaged teamsters, whom I paid $1.50 per 100 pounds, to take my family and the greater share of my goods to my farm. It had rained without stopping for three days, and the road, which was never good, became indescribably bad. . . .

After we had forged our way along this terrible road, which was nevertheless a highway between Cincinnati and Indianapolis, until we were about 12 English miles from the latter place, George said suddenly: "Now the road turns to the right, into the wilderness." We began to laugh, thinking that was impossible—there was no road. But he cried "Go on, I tell you! That is the right road." So we plunged into it, and the wagons had to work their way in and out and round about among the trees. It was dreadful. . . .

When we finally reached my farm, we found two little three-room log cabins, in which, in spite of the best fire that can be built in the fireplaces, one may be half frozen in the winter. Fortunately we had bought an iron stove before winter set in, and brought it back with us on our second trip from Cincinnati. We set this up in one of the rooms, and every day we burned a quarter of a cord of wood without being bothered by the warmth (I won't say heat). . . .

Settling In

Each newcomer set out along a personal road toward making himself at home. For many it was a struggle. An Irishman wrote in 1852: ". . . I am now in a fair way bettering myself, but I will tell you . . . that I have suffered more than I thought I could endure, in a strange Country far from a friend . . . [The experience] may serve me the remainder of my life." Difficult or easy, the process had common denominators. One had to live, so one found work to do—if it was possible, in a place that suited him—and built or found a roof for shelter; one discovered new friends, new things to enjoy, perhaps even new knowledge of himself—and each at his own pace.

The chief clerk of a town in Norway departed for America in 1851, his journey paid for by his friends. From San Francisco he wrote home to Drammen, and his letter was published in the local paper.

What could I write about that would be new from a country the newspapers have described? About the gold mines? I have not been there. About the appearance of the country? Of this I am just as ignorant as you are, for I have not yet been outside the city limits of San Francisco. About social conditions? I do not think I am qualified to do that. About what then? I only want to write you a few lines about very ordinary things and about myself.

Having arrived here on September 9 last year, I stayed in San Francisco to look around for a job, as I did not feel like going to the mines. At first I had to endure some hardships to get ahead. I had to take a job as a dishwasher and developed a leg ailment because of long hours of standing. For a man not accustomed to it will find it hard work to stand from four o'clock in the morning to nine in the evening without a chance to sit down. Cured of this leg ailment, I was lucky enough, to get a job as a clerk in a lawyer's office at a monthly salary of $100, which is considered rather poor here, as board and lodging cost $10 a week in the cheap places and twice as much in fashionable hotels.

I have now been in this position since November 15 last year and have managed to save a couple of hundred dollars, with which I have bought a fourth of a share in a house on which at the present time I take in $40 a month—an interest that we are not accustomed to at home. But because of fire hazards, rents are very high here.

Since I have learned a little Spanish so that I may start translating Spanish documents, I expect a raise in salary of at least $30, and I hope thus to be able to save $100 a month, which is not bad. It is not easy for those who have no trade or skill or who are not accustomed to hard work to save money. To qualify for office jobs you must be an accomplished linguist, that is to say you must be able to speak Spanish, German, and French, apart, of course, from having a good command of English; but even so it is very difficult to be successful in this field because there are so many applicants for such jobs. . . .

From an 1856 ABC for Germans in California

Like thousands of others, Jacob Saul Lanzit arrived with some education, a little nest egg, and few salable skills. He soon discovered that making his way would be far more difficult than he had expected. In his diary for 1858–59 he recorded the hope, despair, determination, and joy of his first year in America.

Tues., September 21, 1858, nine-thirty o'clock. Rockets in the air. Gun fired. Ten-twenty-five o'clock: anchored in the channel. Passengers checked until Wed. 22 at eight o'clock . . . by steamboat to Castel Garden . . .

New York is altogether too big to find anyone. This noise, this tumult, rattling traffic, drove me out of my mind. I bought a ticket on Septem. 24 in order to take the morning train on the twenty-seventh to Chicago. . . .

[In Chicago] I had myself taken to a German hotel, Hotel Meisner, [run by] a very decent man. Oh, how the blood stopped in my veins, not having spoken a word to anyone during the whole journey! I realized that I lack the English language. However, immediately upon my arrival I agreed with the hotelkeeper on $4 per week and ran to town to look for something. I could not be very demanding. I am in Americka, 3,200 miles from Europe, and in Chicago, too, which is 1,200 miles from New York.

Thurs., the thirtieth. I went, recommended by an offis, to an innkeeper who needs a porter, who is supposed to pay board and $2 per week. I, for one, would be satisfied, but he believes that I am too good for this kind of work. He said, however, I should inquire tomorrow again. However, Thursday passed, too, and Friday.

Octob. 1. No chance of getting a job with the innkeeper. I went to several tobacco dealers; perhaps they can use me in the factories. One of them proposed to hire me for three years: first year $25, second year $50, third year $100, plus board and laundry. . . .

Saturday, October 2nd. As I see, there is nothing to this either. I went from store to store and offered my services. No one would give me even an indefinite answer; they all said everything was taken.

Serious, bad, very bad. To be sure, I still have enough to live for ten to twelve months, but the question is, what then, perhaps use my pistols? As I thus went in desperation once more to the cigar dealer, he offered me a small business, and if it should be the will of God, I can at least earn my board in it. May the Lord only give me success and health, and this little business that is to come to life on Tuesday, Octo. 5, will get started. . . .

Tues., 5. Opened the business at six in the evening. It consists of a cigar stand at the restaurant of . . . August Redig. I have to pay him a monthly rent of $10 and have to help out a little at the bar and the tables, and for that I receive free board. I hope, if I cannot make any profit, at least to pass the winter without expenses. . . .

Tues., 12, six o'clock. After closing the books of my business, had a profit of $3.05 after deducting rent of $2.50. Great God, I thank thee. Give me only health and success and life, for thou art the Almighty.

Thurs., 15. The little business is improving. I am working hard in the saloon and act as baarkeper; thereby I learn the business. Time passes; business gets worse. . . .

Decem. Lost in the cigar business; lost in the beer business.

Wednesday, Decem. 9. Bought in Chicago a ticket on the Central Railroad.

Thurs. Departed at 8:00 P.M.

Friday. Boarded a wrong train in Dunkirk [New York], by mistake, 100

miles and back, then once more on the emigrant train. Stayed in Dunkirk until Monday. . . .

Monday. To Boofalo. There with a pedlar, Adolf Mejer. He advised me to peddle in New York. . . .

Tues. In Albany, and the same day, four o'clock, in New York. How I got here, I do not know myself. I managed to get into the Sackspaer [Shakespeare] Hotel.

Decem. 20. Days go by; still no work. Now I have to take hold of whatever there is. I decided to peddle stationery. . . . And now I have been going around for two weeks already, and there was

Cigar peddler

no day when I made my expenses. . . .

On January 5 [1859]. I decided to learn a profession; that is, to learn either to make cigars or to sew on Singer's machine. I decided for the latter and began to learn in earnest. Tuition $3. I will probably have to learn for five or six weeks. However, I can make a living. It is hard work, to be sure, but I am now in America; that means working. By chance I got into a factory after ten days' training, though for small wages.

1859, January 29. But the way I manage, I still save money. The Enlisch tong is becoming easier and easier for me.

February 20. Still in the same factory

with higher wages. By the end of February our factory closed down. I went around for three weeks without work. My money was partly used up. I bought a machine for $40 and went without eating. Finally I came to a Mr. Amer, where I received $7 a week and stayed one month. Now idle for a few days.

All at once I advertised in the paper and was hired by a lining maker for $9 a week. That was too hard. On May 18 a factory opened on William St. Many machines. I came there as an operator for $7 a week and with God's help, I will be able to stay there for some time. . . .

July and August. I worked industriously all the time. Finally I saved something, and on August 1, I deposited $20 in the bank, and on the same day I [met] a girl named M[is]s Rachel Max. That was on Monday. The following Sunday I went out with her for the first time, to Central Parc. We love each other to a most extraordinary degree.

Sunday, August 14. I bought a Singer's machine and traded in my machine, and Monday, August 15, I entered into partnership with a certain Liwey and, God willing, we will do well.

My Roschen [Rachel] loves me; she now works for me. On the sixteenth I spoke with her mother. Hardly had the business begun when I learned the art of being involved with mean people. Whenever I want to visualize a mean character, I can only use the word tailor, and after six weeks of hard work I gave up my partner and remained without a cent. I even owed for board, and I still owed $17 on the machine. What could I do? I decided, therefore, [to make] linings on my own account.

September, 1859. My beloved Rosa helped me with everything possible, not only with her hands but even with money, and within two weeks' time all my debts were paid. My . . . former partner named Liwei, a red-haired creature (may God damn him in all eternity), insisted that I marry his cousin, who has a few hundred dollars, to be sure, but I love Rosa and therefore did not want the other girl. But he, the mean scoundrel, whose blood would not cool my anger, constantly stirred up quarrels and arguments between me and my

Rosa, so that one day there almost was a knife battle between us and the redhead.

I moved out on October 4, and rented a small room on the same street, $4 rent. However, a terrible lack of work caused me at that time great financial embarrassment, and my Rosa gave me the ring off her finger to pawn. Finally I got work. I was at odds with Rosa's father and made up, whereupon he bought a stove [stovepipe hat?] and silk clothes [presumably for Lanzit]. I rented a larger apartment on [Essex] Street (rent $6.50), and began to have a lot of work. I am doing good business.

Stephen Watson settled with his family at Albany, New York. Below are selections from a letter one of his young daughters wrote to her grandparents in England.

Albany,
October 27th, 1825.

My Dear Grandparents,

Partly in compliance with your requests to know about America, and partly for my paternal solicitude for you, I again resume the pen. We are all well in health, and we hope you are enjoying the same blessing. It would be very agreeable for me to see my English friends, but I don't wish to return to England again. I like America much the best: it is a very plentiful country. A person may get a very good living here if they are industrious. My father is doing very well, and is very well satisfied to stay in this country. He has got a cow of his own, and nine hogs. . . . I have been very fortunate; I have got good clothes, and I can dress as well as any lady in Sedlescomb. I can enjoy a silk and white frock, and crape frock and crape veil and Morocco shoes, without a parish grumbling . . . If you are not dressed well here, you are not respected. The girls here that go out to doing housework, dress as well as any lady in Sedlescomb. I don't think of going to Meeting with leather shoes on: we wear Morocco and Prunella. Altogether Leghorn hats are worn here very much; straw bonnets are very fine and handsome: I have got one cost about twenty-four shillings. . . . We have wrote

to uncle John, but have received no answer: father wants you to write us word whether he has written to you since you received our letter. We want uncle William to come over to America very much; and if he comes, to bring some ferrets with him, for they have none here. . . . Dear uncle, you must be sure and come, and bring all your working tools with you. . . . Don't be discouraged now because some come back. Don't do as Mr. Roof did, step on shore, and before you know any thing about the place, go right back again. . . . Father has had a very good summer's work, a sawing; he is now at work in the malt-house for this winter. We have got a very good house to live in, and well furnished; better than we had it in England. Please to excuse this writing, as I am a new beginner: it is a great pleasure for me to write to you; for the anticipation of ever seeing you again is totally relinquished from my mind. I have nothing more at present to say to you in particular. Adieu. Adieu.

I am, with particular respect,
Dear Grandparents,
Your very affectionate grand-
daughter,
MARY JANE WATSON.

A dealer in secondhand goods

The Reverend Olof Olsson, who came with his wife to Kansas in 1869, in a group of Swedish immigrants, took a realistic attitude toward settling in on the prairie.

Salina, Saline Cy., Kansas, North
America, via Hamburg,
September 11, 1869.
Brother C. W. Weinberg! . . .

You should see our settlement out here. It is a beautiful sight. Prairie and still more prairie. Here and there a line of green trees on both sides of the winding Smoky Hill River or in the small valleys where the water seeks an outlet. The view of the prairie is at the outset dismal. Many who come, overwhelmed by this dreary prairie, do not take time to dig a hole in order to observe the rich soil, which nourishes the luxuriant grass. They turn back immediately, or devote themselves to idle sorrow. The only thing they do is to write long lamentations to Sweden. Others, with greater maturity, stay over night where best they can, secure later a spade, dig a cave, cover it as well as they can, secure some food for the family, leave them in the dugout, and go in search of work. If only they keep well, it goes forward one year after the other. It has been wonderful this summer to see the large seeded fields, which a few years ago belonged to the buffalo and Indians. The crop in Kansas has really been excellent this year, although our settlement has not profited much from it, since all of us have just arrived.

We are using Winter wheat here for the first time. Plowing and harrowing are going on with all strength. Maize, which some planted in the Spring on newly plowed soil, is wonderfully beautiful. I stood one day and examined the soil, which my brother is now plowing for the second time . . . It looks like a well-worked and fine garden plot. . . . We do not dig gold with pocket knives, we do not expect to become bountifully rich in a few days or in a few years, but what we aim at is to own our own homes, where each one has his own property, which with God's blessings will provide him with the sustenance which he and his family need. We are like the old Swedish yeoman in our freedom and

154

The Kansas home of a settler from Sweden, in a linoleum cut by Birger Sandzen, an immigrant

Dearly esteemed Friend! . . .

We now have a new house built for us. Our former house was cold and unpleasant, so we could not live there since it was so poorly built. The congregation realized this and offered to build a better house at their own expense. We now live in the new one and it was finished a year ago. There are warmer and more pleasant rooms in this house. . . . You should come here soon and call on us and see something here in America. I mean it seriously! You would not regret it!!

This year it has rained much, so that everything which grows has been very beautiful, the grass is very tall this year, but not so tall as the first Summer. All the farmers here in Kansas have received an abundant harvest of rye and wheat, and the maize . . . is very beautiful. I used to say I did not know why I was in America before this year but now has the Lord blessed our crops and animals in all ways so I do not have great troubles as mistress of the household. You will surely not make fun of me if I in all simplicity speak of how we have it here. We now have 3 milk cows (3 of our best milk cows died 3 years ago when we lost 6 cattle from . . . sickness) but the 3 we now have milk easily, 3 pigs for butchering, and 4 small ones, 3 dozen hens, so we got a score of eggs a day for a long time and sometimes more but now we get only 10–12 a day. We now have 47 chickens but we have had many more which have died, but I have the luck to get many roosters. I want us to get so many that we can butcher the year around since it is so cheap to feed chickens here. Last year we pressed 52 gallons . . . of molasses . . . out of sugar cane so we do not plan to press any this year. You should come here sometime and see how sugar-cane grows. I had a few of several kinds of vegetables. Next year I think we will have peaches. . . . Our fruit trees have grown quite beautifully.

The Lord guide us by His spirit in all truth to His heavenly kingdom. Hearty greetings from Olle.

ANNA

independence . . . The advantage which America offers is not to make everyone rich at once without toil and trouble, but the advantage is that the poor, who will and are able to work, secure a large piece of good land almost without cost, that they can work up little by little. . . .

A few days later that fruitful summer, Pastor Olsson wrote to Mrs. Weinberg.

Salina, Kansas. September, 15, 1869.
Mrs. Ulrika Weinberg

Hearty thanks for the letter to Anna. Anna planned to write, but early this morning the Lord sent us a little, healthy girl, which development hinders Anna from writing. Through the Lord's wonderful mercy everything went especially well at the delivery, and Anna is very well under the circumstances. Anna thrives especially well here. We live for the time being in a two room stone house . . . Meanwhile, we have now begun to build our own stone house with three rooms and so high that we can have a gable room. The kitchen is always built here next to the house proper, since the heat in the summer makes a fire inside . . . unbearable. . . .

I have seen many farmers with such extensive fields and such large herds of cattle that one should be ready to say: "Here must be a Count's estate," but

when one looks for the castle, one finds a house that Mrs. Weinberg would look upon at her farm as suitable for a pigsty at best. One might think that swinish men lived in such swine houses, but that is not the situation. There one meets often men with knowledge and refinement so that they hold a position in the State's legislative assembly. People in Sweden look upon the Americans as a crowd of wild men and barbarians. This is an error. True, barbarians are found here, bandits of the first class, but I have already met many Americans, for whom I hold the highest respect as men. Although the real American is in his manner forward and unceremonious, so is he nevertheless pleasant and friendly in his associations. I have already enjoyed with many an obliging hospitality which has astonished me. Always when I ask Americans how they like it when so many other nationalities come to their country, they answer in such a manner, that even in this situation they wish to acknowledge the principle of equality. . . .

Pastor Olsson told the Weinbergs that his wife liked the house they were in. Possibly that was ascribable to masculine wishful thinking. At any rate, her settling in seems to have taken longer than his did. Four years later she wrote:

The Dark Side

Often the challenges were too great. Those who could afford it might go home again. But there were others who were too poor, or in whom the shock of change had produced too deep a numbness. They stayed. They might eke out of the soil a meager living. Some ran away from families and vanished. Some went mad. Many holed up in the city slums; those who did not die of disease or violence might scrape along dispiritedly on part-time work and peddling and, if the children were still under control, send them into the streets to gather firewood, find work, or beg. But America's promise, on the darkest side, often meant children without homes at all and adults with no purpose.

This material, from the New-York Daily Times *for June 23, 1853, was headlined "WALKS AMONG THE NEW-YORK POOR. Emigrants and Emigrants' Children." The author was evidently involved in rescue work with many slum children.*

If you would see, for a moment, one of the streams in the great current which is always pouring through New-York, go down a Summer afternoon to the North River wharves. A German emigrant ship has just made fast. The long wharf is crowded full of trucks and carts, and drays, waiting for the passengers. As you approach the end you come upon a noisy crowd of strange faces and stranger costumes. Moustached peasants in Tyrolese hats are arguing in unintelligible English with truck-drivers; runners from the German hotels are pulling the confused women hither and thither; peasant girls with bare heads, and the rich-flushed, nut brown faces you never see here, are carrying huge bundles to the heaps of baggage; children in doublets and hose, and queer little caps, are mounted on the trunks, or swung off amid the laughter of the crowd with ropes from the ship's sides. Some are just welcoming an old face, so dear in the strange land, some are letting down the huge trunks, some swearing in very genuine low Dutch, at the endless noise and distractions. They bear the plain marks of the Old World. Healthy, stout frames, and low, degraded faces with many; stamps of inferiority, dependence, servitude on them; little graces of costume, too—a colored head-dress or a fringed coat—which never could have originated here; and now and then a sweet face, with the rich bloom and the dancing blue eye, that seem to reflect the very glow and beauty of the vine hills of the Rhine.

It is a new world to them—oppression, bitter poverty behind—here, hope, freedom, and a chance for work, and food to the laboring man. They may have the vaguest ideas of it all—still, to the dullest some thoughts come of the New Free World.

Every one in the great City, who can make a living from the freshly arrived immigrant, is here. Runners, sharpers, peddlers, agents of boarding-houses, of forwarding-offices, and worst of all, of the houses where many a simple emigrant girl, far from friends and home, comes to a sad end. Very many of these, who are now arriving, will start to-morrow at once for the far West. Some will hang about the German boarding-houses in Greenwich-street, each day loosing

In a New York City tenement

their money, their children getting out of their control, until they at last seek a refuge in Ward's Island, or settle down in the Eleventh Ward, to add to the great mass of foreign poverty and misery there gathered. From there, you shall see their children sallying out these summer mornings, as soon as light, to do the *petty work* of the City, rag-picking, bone-gathering, selling chips, peddling, by the thousands, radishes, strawberries and fruit through every street.

We have now a German gentleman, the Rev. Mr. BOGEN, employed in visiting in that quarter, and he reports that not one family in a hundred ever send their children to school. They were forced to school them in Germany; here they want the pleasure of having their own way. The boys, some of them, do well—though very many fall in with the multitude of young thieves and vagrants of that Ward. The girls, in the great proportion of cases, as soon as they mature, are more or less dissolute in morals. The filthy habits of their parents, and the open street-life which they must pursue, seem of necessity to degrade the morals.

Yet, the children themselves long to do better. In visiting for the Girls Industrial School, in Avenue D., the difficulty to all has always been with the parents, not the girls. They jump at the chance of learning something beyond what their parents have known; and, as that school shows, only want the opportunity to make great progress. Who, that knows this School, will forget a dirty, ragged girl, found first dragging her huge bag of shavings, bare-headed, through the muddy streets, now the neatest, quickest, bright-eyed little thing—the pet and pride of the kind ladies who have rescued her?

It is a fact worth noticing, that of all the many children who came under our operations, very seldom, indeed, is ever one an American or a Protestant. The Irish emigrants are generally more degraded, even, than the German. They rise more slowly, and are cursed with that scourge of their race—Intemperance.

I visited lately one of their lodging-houses for the newly-arrived—a den such as I had no idea existed in New-York. It was in the neighborhood of Water-street—a high, respectable-looking brick house on the outside. A number of ragged children were playing at the door; within, the hall was dark and reeking with the worst filth. I climbed the dirty stairway, knocked at the door, and entered a little room where some women were cooking; in the room adjoining, a little closet of a place, half-a-dozen Irish girls were sitting, making coarse straw bags, "for a cent a-piece," as I was afterwards informed. I told my object to a sharp-looking man in charge. He said there were no children there, and directed me up stairs. The girls looked overdone [exhausted], and were probably freshly arrived, and not in the best hands. I wanted to have a few words with them, but it seemed hardly advisable, and I went up stairs. A knock again, and this time, a little room, five feet by fifteen; two women sitting and another, younger, on a bed. "Have you any children here you would like to get work for in the country?" "No, Sir, we haven't—yes, though—there's NELLY!" said one; "and what is the work, plase?" I told them, and said a little of the dangers for a poor man's children in a great city. They allowed it: "Oh, NELLY, Sir,—she's not my child; but then I love her as mine; and, plase God, I never meant to lave her. But, then, you see, Sir, we can't take care of her. She's only fourteen, and she's away and in the streets so much, and I'd rather have her dead than in some places."

The fate of "many a simple emigrant girl"

"*It's ruin here!* I've lived it all! I know it," said the young woman on the bed. I turned, and saw for the first time, how care-worn and wretched her face was.

"But could you get a respectable situation, Sir, for NELLY?" I told her what we could do, and NELLY is to come up to the office.

The upper part of the house was filled with little narrow rooms, each one having five or six occupants; all very filthy. The people seemed very poor, honest Irish, not long here, and without work, usually. Women and men, evidently not of the same family, were herded in the same rooms, as one sees them in peasants' cabins in Ireland. They all looked depressed, worn, degraded. "Oh, yes, Sir," said an old woman, as I asked her, "I do want my boy out of the City. I can't do nothin' with him. He sleeps out nights, now, and he gets in with the bad boys. It's all thrue what ye say, Sir, and I fear ivry day to have bad news of him amang the Police."

In an attic room, a young woman with a black eye and bloody face was making a fire of shavings, and a child was beside her. "Children?" she said, wildly, hardly looking at me—"No, thank God! I have none but her. Why would I have children? It was *he* bate me—he strikes me. They say the childer here all is ruined—I know it;" and, turning abruptly to me, "Yes, Sir, there be paple down below that set their ain children to stale cotton, I've seen it— I know it, Sir. They *makes* 'em thieves.

But what does *he* care, wid his liquor?" She spoke of her husband, who was lying on the floor in the corner—"It is he who is a murthering us!"

I was glad to leave as soon as possible. There were other rooms in the same way, filled with these poor, half-brutalized men and women. The girls and the boys left to themselves in the street— not a family sent children to school.

The whole was very depressing. It seemed like the worst part of old Europe transplanted. There was not even intelligence about their sensuality. You felt hopeless of ever reforming such natures—and, under all common probabilities, the children must be beggars, and prostitutes, and thieves.

You appreciated the dangers if many such colonies were scattered about in our cities.

As I went out, a man, maudlin with drink, asked me to see a child he had and do something for her. I followed him to a similar boarding-house. The child was at the door—a sweet, blue-eyed little Irish girl, though looking sadly neglected. She was an orphan, the man said, in his charge, and he would do nothing about her without a drink. I demurred, and at last left him, until I could see him again sober.

Our work with this immense class of poor children is often very discouraging.

The suspicions and prejudices of their parents, brought with them from another society—the aspect it gives of the crushing temptations to evil over all the poor and friendless in our great cities —the difficulty of arousing even good men from their old accustomed ways, to help in new channels—and the sad contrast of the unresting activity of Society, when those whom they once neglected are to be hunted and punished. Almost every week there is the gloomy knell of some new execution through the land—generally of young men, once the street boys, the poor or neglected children of our great cities.

The papers are full of the conviction of young offenders. One cannot but think how easy, a few years ago, a cure might have been. We could have made a useful man of the vagrant lad then— now, we can only hang him.

Southern Cosmopolis

New Orleans' most noticeable flavor was always that of its founders, the French. But the Spanish added their own savories. And then, between 1830 and 1860, the city's population more than trebled. Ships carrying cotton to Liverpool offered special passenger fares for the return voyage, and the Irish in particular took advantage of this, pouring into the city to form its largest immigrant group. Low fares from the Continent, too, attracted Germans and more Frenchmen; the ocean trade added a sprinkling from many nations, and the Mississippi River brought other newcomers from the north. Perhaps more than any American city in mid-century, New Orleans was cosmopolitan.

The New Orleans waterfront in 1873

In an 1860 work of fiction, The Sunny South, *Maine-born Joseph H. Ingraham used the form of a letter from a Northern governess to present a picture of the city.*

As we approached . . . [by train] through a level landscape, level as a lake, we flew past now a garden on this side, now a Spanish-looking little villa on that, the gardens richly foliaged with lemon and banana trees, and far over-stretching verandahs shut in by curtains to keep out the sun from the piazzas. Such gardens and villas one after another in great numbers we passed for a mile or so, when the houses grew more numerous, the gardens narrower and narrower, and shops and small tenements were crowding together . . . Side-walks of brick, as we darted forward, now took the place of green way-side paths by walls and fences, and stone pavements were substituted for natural dirt roads.

People began to grow more numerous on the walks, carts laden with brick and lumber, carts laden with vegetables and butcher's meat, bread carts, and ice carts, and omnibuses (those unsightly vehicular monstrosities) rolled, galloped, rattled, thundered, raced, and rumbled past, and cross-street wise, making it impossible almost to hear one's self speak for the noise. Onward our car wheels bore us, deeper and deeper into the living heart of the city. Nothing but small shops were now to be seen on either hand, with purchasing throngs going in and coming out of them, while myriads of children seemed to swarm about the doors, crawl along the curb-stones, paddle in the gutters, and yell miscellaneously everywhere. I never saw so many children in my life. Some were black, some not so black, some yellow, some golden skinned, some tawny, some delicate milk and gamboge

color, and some pure white, at least, such spots of their faces as the dirt suffered to be visible, seemed to promise an Anglo-saxon complexion underneath. The major part, however, were olive brown, and plainly of French extraction; and I could hear the bright black-eyed little urchins jabbering French, to a marvel of correct pronunciation that would have amazed a school girl.

At length the houses grew more stately, the streets more genteel, the crowds more elegantly attired, and the cars stopped, and we were in New Orleans!

In an instant we were besieged by a very great number of polite gentlemen with whips in their hands and eager visages thrust up to the window.

"Fiacre, madame!" "Hack, sir!" "Carriage, ma'am." "Will yer ladyship's bright eyes jist look at my iligant haack?" insinuated a snub-nosed son of

Green Erin, with an old fur cap cocked on his head, the visor behind, giving him a superlatively impudent look.

Seeing me apparently hesitate, he added with an eloquent intonation in his rich brogue. "It is vilvit kushioned, m'im, and glass windies intirely, Miss, and I've got the naatest tame dat'll take ye where ye wist in no time at all, at all!"

At this juncture Isidore came to conduct me to a carriage with the rest of our party. As we descended the steps of the car, a Chinese, in his small tea-cup of a blue cap, presented to my irresistible temptation, as he thought, some beautiful kites made of blue, yellow, green, and crimson tissue paper in the shape of superb butterflies. They were two feet across the wings, and elegantly constructed of light wire bent into the desired shape, and covered with the paper. He asked but twenty-five cents a piece, and they looked so invitingly pretty, that I was half tempted to buy one for myself, recollecting my girlish days, when I used to fly kites, fish, and play ball with my brothers; but before I made up my mind to this speculation, a slender sloe-eyed quadroon girl of sixteen, with a superb smile, offered me a delicious bouquet from a basket filled with them, which she was adroitly balancing on her head. The rival John-China-man interposed one of his handsome kites between my eyes and the bouquet, and while I was bewildered which to choose, a Frenchman thrust nearer my face than all, his forefinger, on which was perched a splendid parrot, with a nose like the Duke of Wellington's.

"Puy de kitee, Meesee! twenty-vive cen'," eagerly urged the Chinese.

"Mussier ne veu' 'pas le bouquet pour mamsel?" softly and musically entreated the girl, of Isidore, in her Creole patois.

"Buy pretty Pollee. Achetez mon joli oiseau!"

"Polly wantee cracker," screamed the parrot in my ear.

Thanks to the carriage-step at hand, . . . I was enabled to secure a flight from the scene; and Isidore laughingly handed me the bouquet, which he had purchased of the quadroon, who thanked him with a brilliant smile.

Having purchased one of the persevering Chinaman's beautiful kites to take North, as a curiosity for Yankee boys, and implored the parrot-man to take his noisy, squalling, crooked-beaked, saucy-eyed, knowing-headed bird out of my sight, the carriage, at length, moved on out of the throng; and after a few minutes' rattling through rough paved streets, narrow and foreign-looking, we reached the St. Louis hotel, an edifice that looks like a superb Parisian palace. . . .

After the Civil War, the journalist Edward King toured the Southern states, and in 1875 he published his impressions in The Great South. *In his description of New Orleans, King paid particular attention to the French quarter of the city.*

Step off from Canal street, that avenue of compromises which separates the French and the American quarters, some bright February morning, and you will at once find yourself in a foreign atmosphere. A walk into the French section enchants you; the characteristics of an American city vanish; this might be Toulouse, or Bordeaux, or Marseilles! The houses are all of stone or brick, stuccoed or painted; the windows of each story descend to the floors, opening, like doors, upon airy, pretty balconies, protected by iron railings; quaint dormer windows peer from the great roofs; the street doors are massive, and large enough to admit carriages into the stone-paved court-yards, from which stairways communicate with the upper apartments. . . .

Turning into a side street leading off from Royal, or Chartres, or Bourgogne, or Dauphin, or Rampart streets, you come upon an odd little shop, where the cobbler sits at his work in the shadow of a grand old Spanish arch; or upon a nest of curly-headed negro babies ensconced on a tailor's bench at the window of a fine ancient mansion . . .

Or you may enter aristocratic restaurants, where the immaculate floors are only surpassed in cleanliness by the spotless linen of the tables; where a solemn dignity, as befits the refined pleasure of dinner, prevails, and where the waiter gives you the names of the dishes in both languages, and bestows on you a napkin large enough to serve you as a shroud, if this strange melange of French and Southern cookery should give you a fatal indigestion. The French families of position usually dine at four, as the theatre begins promptly at seven, both on Sundays and week days. There is the play-bill, in French, of course; and there are the typical Creole ladies, stopping for a moment to glance at it as they wend their way shopward. For it is the shopping hour; from eleven to two the streets of the old quarter are alive with elegantly, yet soberly attired ladies, always in couples, as French etiquette exacts that the unmarried lady shall never promenade without her maid or her mother. . . .

There is no attempt on the part of the French or Spanish families to inaugurate style and fashion in the city; quiet home society, match-making and marrying of daughters, games and dinner parties, church, shopping, and calls in simple and unaffected manner, content them.

The majority of the people in the whole quarter seem to have a total disregard of the outside world, and when one hears them discussing the distracted condition of local politics, one can almost fancy them gossiping on matters entirely foreign to them, instead of on those vitally connected with their lives and property. They live very much among themselves. French by nature and training, they get but a faint reflection of the excitements in these United States. It is also astonishing to see how little the ordinary American citizen of New Orleans knows of his French neighbors; how ill he appreciates them. It is hard for him to talk five minutes about them without saying, "Well, we have a non-progressive element here; it will not be converted." Having said which, he will perhaps paint in glowing colors the virtues and excellences of his French neighbors, though he cannot forgive them for taking so little interest in public affairs.

Ohio Entrepôt

Surrounded by rich soil and accessible by the Ohio River, Cincinnati early developed as a commercial center. But after the introduction of the steamboat there in 1817 it became the "Queen City of the West." The steamboat encouraged old trades and created new ones—in shipyards, foundries, forges, repair shops, and eventually in machine-tool shops. In contrast to such ill-paid, restricted jobs as those in New England's crowded textile mills, Cincinnati offered work to skilled individuals who, with luck, could branch out on their own. The immigrants came not because they were destitute, but because their talents could be applied to particular, specialized jobs.

Frenchman Michael Chevalier spent two years in the United States—from 1833 to 1835. In this passage from his Society, Manners and Politics in the United States, *he observed the opportunities for individual enterprise in Cincinnati.*

Cincinnati contains about 40,000 inhabitants, inclusive of the adjoining villages; although founded 40 years ago, its rapid growth dates only about 30 years back. It seems to be the rendezvous of all nations; the Germans and Irish are very numerous, and there are some Alsacians; I have often heard the harsh accents of the Rhenish French in the street. But the bulk of the population, which gives its tone to all the rest, is of New England origin. What makes the progress of Cincinnati more surprising is, that the city is the daughter of its own works. Other towns, which have sprung up in the United States in the same rapid manner, have been built on shares, so to speak. Lowell, for example, is an enterprise of Boston merchants, who, after having raised the necessary funds, have collected workmen and told them, "Build us a town." Cincinnati has been gradually extended and embellished, almost wholly without foreign aid, by its inhabitants, who have for the most part arrived on the spot poor. The founders of Cincinnati brought with them nothing but sharp-sighted, wakeful, untiring industry, the only patrimony which they inherited from their New England fathers, and the other inhabitants have scrupulously followed their example and adopted their habits. They seem to have chosen Franklin for their patron-saint, and to have adopted Poor Richard's maxims as a fifth gospel.

I have said that Cincinnati was admirably situated; this is true in respect of its geographical position, but, if you follow the courses of the rivers on the map, and consider the natural resources of the district, you will find that there are several points on the long line of the rivers of the West as advantageously placed, both for trade and manufactures, and that there are some which are even more favoured in these respects. . . . Pittsburg was marked out by nature at once for a great manufacturing centre and a great mart of trade. Louisville, built at the falls of the Ohio, at the head of navigation for the largest class of boats, is a natural medium between the commerce of the upper Ohio and that of the Mississippi and its tributaries. In respect to manufacturing resources, Louisville is as well provided as Cincinnati . . .

But the power of men, when they agree in willing anything and in willing it perseveringly, is sufficient to overbear and conquer that of nature. In spite of the superior advantages of Louisville as an *entrepôt*, in spite of the manufacturing resources of Pittsburg, Cincinnati is able to maintain a population twice that of Louisville and half as large again as that of Pittsburg in a state of competence, which equals, if it does not surpass, the average condition of that of each of the others.

. . . with the exception of the pork trade, one is surprised not to see any branch of industry carried on on the great scale of the manufacturing towns of England and France. The Cincinnatians make a variety of household furniture and utensils, agricultural and mechanical implements and machines, wooden clocks, and a thousand objects of daily use and consumption, soap, candles, paper, leather, &c., for which there is an indefinite demand throughout the flourishing and rapidly growing States of the West, and also in the new States of the Southwest, which are wholly devoted to agriculture . . . Most of these articles are of ordinary quality; the furniture, for instance, is rarely such as would be approved by Parisian taste, but it is cheap and neat, just what is wanted in a new country, where, with the exception of a part of the South, there is a general ease and but little wealth, and where plenty and comfort are more generally known than the little luxuries of a more refined society. The prosperity of Cincinnati, therefore, rests upon the sure basis of the prosperity of the West, upon the supply of articles of the first necessity to the bulk of the community. . . .

Cincinnati's city directories once listed trades and birthplaces. At right, top, in 1825, the "O"s fall on page 74, the "Sc"s on page 86, and both show mainly Eastern-state origins; in the 1839–40 directory, at bottom, the corresponding sections fall on pages 309 and 347, and show mostly Irish and German origins.

Nutting Stephen, supervisor of highways, c. Ludlow and Congress Ms.

Nye Stephen, carpenter, Fourth b. Plum and Elm Ms.

O.

OBEAR EBENEZER, shoemaker, 194 Main Me.

Obear Simeon, shoemaker, John b. Longworth and Sixth Me.

Oberdorf Francis J. C. Dr. c. London and John Ger.

O'Bryan Edward, clerk in a store, 93 Main Md.

Odell John, merchant, 60 Lower market N. H.

Oegler Zimon, gardener, Deer creek above Symmes Ger.

Ogan Thomas, brick maker, W. end of Fifth Va.

Ogden James K. potter, Race b. Fourth and Fifth N. J.

Ogden Thomas, drayman, b. John and Smith N. J.

Ogg Reuben, drayman, alley r. Water b. Main and Walnut O.

O'Keeffe Thomas, shoemaker, 25 Main Ire.

Oldfield Samuel, shoemaker, r. Seventh b. Western Row and John Pa.

Oldham Moses, ship carpenter, 2 Columbia Pa.

Oldham Moses, carpenter, Columbia near the water works Md.

Oldham Thomas, carpenter, congress b. Pike and Butler Pa.

Oliver Nathan, grocer, Water b. Elm and Plum, store c. Walnut and Second N. J.

Oliver Robert, tailor, Sixth b. Walnut and Vine Md.

Oliver Thomas T. currier and leather dresser, Lawrence b. E. Front and Congress Eng.

Oliver William, receiver of public monies at Piqua, 57 W. Front Va.

Oneal James, brick maker, Mill b. Front and Third Ky.

Oneal John, cabinet maker, John b. Fifth and Sixth N. J.

Oneill Jesse, shoemaker, 106 Main Con.

Oneal William H. carpenter, Columbia near the woollen factory O.

Schillinger William, cooper, Second b. Main and Sycamore N J

Scholes John, river-trader Front b. Race and Elm Eng.

Schooley Israel, organ builder, Seventh b. Walnut and Vine Va.

Schroeter Jacob, grocer, c. Broadway and Second Ger.

Scofield Elizabeth, grocer Fifth b. Plum and Western Row Eng.

Scott Jane, washer, rear of Water, b. Main and Walnut Ire.

Scott John, accountant, 62 Main Pa.

Scott Michael, house architect, Walnut b. Third and Fourth Ire.

Scott Samuel, merchant, 36 Main

Scowden Theodore, steam engineer, Front b. Smith and Mill Pa.

Scrivner Thankful, boarding house, r. Second b. Elm and Plum Me.

Scudder Clark, carpenter, Seventh b. Vine and Race N. J.

Scudder John, Vine above St. Clair N. J.

Scudder William, mason, Vine b. Seventh and New Market N. J.

Seaman Francis, baker, Sycamore above Court

Seaman Jonas, carpenter, Vine b. Front and Second N. J.

Sear Garret, grocer, Western Row b. Seventh and London N. Y.

Searin Robert, chairmaker, on Front b. Vine and Race N. J.

Sedge Jessee, carpenter, Plum b. Water and the river Con

Sedgwick Thomas, laborer, Kemble b. Western Row and John Pa.

See Peter, tailor, western Row b. Richmond and Catharine Del.

See William, tailor, 159 Main Del.

Sefton John, weaver and Methodist minister Fifth b. Main and Sycamore Ire.

Seldon Douglas A. merchant, Walnut b. Fifth and Sixth N. Y.

Seldon Roger, merchant, Sixth b. Main and Walnut Con.

Selleth Anthony, c. Ludlow and Third Ger.

O'C	O'D	O'H	O'K	O'L	O'M	O'N	O'R	O'S

O'Connor, Michael (Ire) Soap-boiler, res, Wes R near Clinton.

O'Connor, James (Ire) Drayman, bds at M O'Connor's.

O'Donnell, Jas (Ire) Labr at C & J Bates', res, 10 b Wal & Vi.

O'Hara, Marcus (N Y) Brass-fdr at J W Coffin's, res, Arch st.

O'Hara, Michael (Ire) Labr, res, E s Mill b 3d and 4th.

O'Hara, John (Ire) Brick-layer, bds at Richard Shay's.

O'Hara, Wm (Ire) Clerk at Franklin Bank, res, cor John and Elizabeth.

O'Keoffe, Thomas (Ire) Shoe-mkr at J H O'Connor's.

O'Leary, Bernard (Ire) Physician and Surgeon, bds at Pl st H.

O'Meara, Jas (Ire) Bdg-h, Syc bet Yeatman and Front.

O'Neale, Jas (Md) Shoe-mkr at J Dennis', bds E s Syc n Front.

O'Neil, Hugh (O) Black-smith at Powell's Foundry, res, corner Friendsnip and Butler.

O'Neil, Wm (O) Follows the River, res, Col b Syc and Bdy.

O'Neil, David (Ire) Tailor, bds at P Easley's, Wat b Wal & Vi.

O'Neil, Jeremiah (Ire) Labr at G H Bates', res, F b Wal & Vi.

O'Neil, Daniel (Ire) Cooper, res, corner Columbia and Syc.

O'Neil, John (Ire) Cooper at Richards' on 8th street.

O'Neil, Peter (Ire) Clerk at Thomas Salters'.

O'Neill, Wm (Ire) Clerk at the Chronicle office.

O'Neill, Jesse (N Y) Constable, res, cor 8th and Elm.

O'Neill, Mrs Mary (Ire) Seamstress, res, Wes R b F and Wat.

O'Neill, Henry (Ire) Labr, res, 7th bet Wes Row and John.

O'Reilly, Mrs Mary Ann (Pa) [O'Reilly's Brewery,] res, N s Congress, bet Lawrence and Pike.

O'Reilly, Wm (O) at the Brewery, bds M A O'Reilly's.

O'Riley, Thos (Ire) Clothing-store, res, E F b Bdy and Ludlow.

O'Riley, John (Ire) Tailor at T O'Riley's.

O'Rourke, Timothy (Ire) Coachman at Wm Neff's.

O'Shaughnessy, Thos (Ire) [Withers & O'S] res, Syc b 5 & 6.

Schreifer, Henry (Ger) Shoe-mkr, at B Waltkamp's.

Schriefer, Frank (Ger) Machinist, at Harkness', res, Congress b Lawrence and Pike.

Schriber, Mrs Elizabeth (N Y) res, Broadway near Franklin.

Schroeder, Christopher (Ger) Black-smith, res, 7th and Syc.

Schroeder, Bernhardt (Ger) Blk-smith, res, near Bdy Hotel.

Schroeder, Henry (Ger) Carpr, res, Abigail b Main and Syc.

Schroeder, Henry (Ger) Clerk at A B Rohmaan's, res, 6th bet Race and Elm.

Schroer, Henry (Pruss) Black-smith, at Geo C. Miller's.

Schroder, S. B. (Ger) Lock-mkr, N s 3d b Main and Walnut.

Schroder, Christopher H. (Ger) Lock-mkr, res, cor 7th and Syc.

Schror, Daniel (Ger) Labr, res, Broadway b Front and Col.

Schroze, Gerhardt G. (Ger) Labr, res, cor 7th and Lodges st.

Schu, Joseph (Ger) Fruit-seller, res, Friendship street.

Schuck, Jacob (Ger) Shoe-mkr, cor Walnut and 13th.

Schule, Adam (Ger) Labr, res, N s 6th b John and Smith.

Schuler, George (Fr) Sawyer, res, Cherry alley.

Schulte, Gerhardt (Ger) Shoe-mkr, res, Water b Wal and Vi.

Schulte, Henry (Ger) Carpr, bds at P Kock's.

Schulter, Gasper (Ger) Cabt-mkr, at Jones & Rammelsberg's, res, 7th b Sycamore and Broadway.

Schultz, Wm (N Y) Block and Pump-mkr, at J Walls'.

Schultz, C & Co, Washington Brewery, E Frt E of Wat Wks.

Schultz, Charles (Pa) [C S & Co] bds at Broadway Hotel.

Schultz, Henry (Md) M D [C S & Co] res, opp W Brewery.

Schultz, Gasper (Switz) Dry-goods Store, W s Main b 9 & Crt.

Schultz, Andrew (Ger) Tailor, res, in Church alley.

Schultz, Anthony (Ger) Labr, res, do.

Schuster, John (Ger) Labr, res, Allison b Wal and Vine.

Schuter, Arnold (Ger) Shoe-mkr, res, Wdwd b Main and Syc.

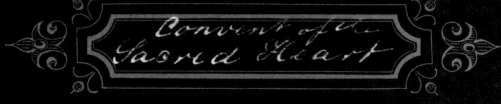

The Convent of the Sacred Heart, a Catholic church near Philadelphia, was one of many churches serving newcomers.

ENTERING THE PARTNERSHIP

WHEN THE ISRAELITES FOUND THEIR WAY into the Promised Land, their program for dealing with the local inhabitants was simple and approved by God. They slew the natives or drove them from the choicest spots. The European settlers in America applied something of the same human-relations technique to the "inferior" Indians, but when they dealt with white predecessors they did not consider that they had such an option—at least, not often. In general, native American and newcomer had to adjust to each other somehow, and that process of mutual adaptation was one of the great shaping forces of life in America.

Historical tradition sketches the process as a one-way street: the immigrant was "Americanized" as a result of his contacts with "old stock" Americans, of different blood from his. Reality supplies a more labyrinthine map of interplay. New immigrant arrivals mingled with a "native" population that also included their own countrymen who had arrived earlier and those countrymen's offspring, who had grown up sharing two cultures. Successful sons of Irish Catholic settlers looked warily on post-famine shanty dwellers fresh from the old sod. "German Latin" farmers and "Forty-Eighters" —freethinking and worldly—found themselves sharing community institutions with Germans who had migrated for religious reasons and were still bound to the pieties of their past. Frenchmen whose forebears had helped to settle Louisiana met with refugees from revolutionary upheavals in the French West Indies, and found that they had little except language in common, and less than language with Frenchmen from Canada.

Moreover, the different immigrant groups seeking styles of their own while conforming to American life were actually redefining the term "American" by their participation. The process was fluid and continuous, and left indelible marks on the national character.

In the so called immigrant churches, for example, an interesting drama was played out. The first act saw planted in the wilderness a largely ethnic church—one whose members were drawn heavily from a single nationality. The second act revealed a relaxation of doctrine and practice, as a new generation grew up in an American setting. In the third, fresh arrivals from the same immigrant stock burst on the stage, outraged at the old church's falling away from orthodoxy, and often brought on a turbulent scene of heresy charges and secession. The prototypal script was written in the churches of New England—planted by Puritan "saints," then broadened to accommodate the less zealous children of the founders (who were not as sure of their salvation), then scourged by revivalists.

German Lutheranism is another model case. Not all German settlers worshiped in the Lutheran fellowship, but those who did, especially in the eighteenth century, clung zealously to Old World formulas, rituals of faith, and even language. "Since it has pleased Thee," said a liturgical statement of the German churches in Pennsylvania in 1786, addressing the Almighty, "by means of the Germans, to transform this state into a blooming garden, . . . help us not to deny our nation, but to endeavor that our youth may be so educated that German schools and churches may not only be sustained but may attain a still more flourishing condition." Yet God had other designs. Following the pattern set by "Americanizers" like the Muhlenbergs, German Lutheran pastors in the United States drifted away from a concentration on doctrine into the currents of good works. They joined in associations to promote worthwhile causes, exchanged pulpits now and again with non-Lutheran shepherds, took sides on political questions, and seemed unmoved while English steadily displaced German as the language of worship. In the 1840s, a voice was raised in prophetlike anger to chastise them. It belonged to C. F. W. Walther, sometimes known as the "Lutheran Pope of the West." Himself a relatively new arrival, Walther scorned both the secularism of the German intellectuals who had become prosperous in the new country and the apostasy of German churchmen who allowed themselves and their congregations to become involved in such crusades as abolitionism. What had such things to do with "the ancient true Church of Christ on earth"? From a base in St. Louis, Walther harried the liberals and eventually organized the Missouri Synod, a bastion of "old" Lutheranism to this day. This schism was not the only one to rend the Lutherans; ultimately they split into Northern and Southern branches, just as did the Presbyterians, Baptists, and Methodists.

In effect, American freedom and space and social conflicts had imposed themselves on Lutheranism and broken it along certain lines that were not so much religious as political and cultural. The subdivision would probably not have taken place without continued immigration and the stresses it created. At the same time, the existence of more than one kind of Lutheran "denomination" among which German-Americans (and non-Germans, too) could choose served to strengthen the American religious pattern of variety and diversity.

Patriarchs of immigrant churches flourished in American soil in the 1800s. T. N. Hasselquist, a farmer's son in his native Sweden, was trained as a pastor, crossed the sea, and began a ministry in 1852 among scattered Scandinavian farmers in Illinois. Often he held services in such makeshift surroundings as barns. But adversity stimulated him. Soon he had established the *Hemlandet* newspaper, a society of Swedish Lutheran missionaries, a seminary, a printing press. He sought out parishioners with the zeal of a born fisher of men who knew his America. The Illinois Central Railroad wanted purchasers for lands granted to it by the national government. Hasselquist promoted himself to the railroad as an agent, wrote tirelessly to friends, ministers, and editors in the Northeast and in Sweden, and sent emissaries as far as Quebec and Montreal, where they met Scandinavian newcomers and told honeyed tales of rich acres and Lutheran neighbors awaiting them in Illinois. Hasselquist's Scandinavian Evangelical Lutheran Augustana Synod waxed prosperous on such efforts, and,

Carl Ferdinand Wilhelm Walther, the Lutheran clergyman from Saxony, is pictured above in 1885, two years before his death.

except for the departure of a number of dissident Norwegians in 1870, remained untroubled by secessions.

The process by which religious traditions were given new shapes in the multinational American setting also touched the ancient faith of the Jews. Reform Judaism came to the United States as an import from Germany. Its Moses was Isaac Mayer Wise, born in Bohemia in 1819, educated in a rabbinical school and at the Universities of Vienna and Prague. Wise grew up in heady times for Jews in German-speaking countries. During intermittent periods of liberalism, they were allowed, if they chose, to emerge from the ghettos, attend public schools, and participate in professional and political life more freely than ever before. Yet it was difficult for them to reconcile this liberation with the rituals by which the Orthodox Jew testified to his chosenness—the distinctive dress, diet, holidays, prohibitions, and prayers that every waking moment demanded. Thousands of German Jews found an answer in a new idea, namely that the ethical and historical content of their religion could be separated from such trappings as beards and side curls, forbidden Sabbath fires, prohibited pork, and the swaying, incomprehensible, rapid-fire Hebrew chanting of liturgical poetry. They made this belief the foundation of a new kind of religious life, which enabled them to move less distinctively and thus more comfortably among their non-Jewish brethren, and to build temples where such novelties as or-

John Ireland, who came to America in 1849, was a chaplain in the Union Army and Archbishop of St. Paul, Minnesota.

gans, choirs, and preaching in German were permitted.

Those Jews of the new persuasion who migrated to America from German states naturally brought their views with them. Isaac Mayer Wise did more. He joined his Germanic Reform Judaism to American religious liberalism, in a kind of second assimilation of a faith already assimilated. He became a devoted reader of the works of Unitarian and Transcendentalist thinkers such as New England's William Ellery Channing and Theodore Parker. Channing and Parker believed that God was a God of reason, and that mankind was essentially virtuous but was sometimes betrayed into error by compounds of ignorance and superstition. The university-trained Wise agreed; he privately lamented "the disappearance of Judaism in . . . Polish-cabalistic rabbinism and supernaturalism," and raged that "poor Hebrew reading and indecorum were as necessary an accompaniment of Jewish orthodoxy as was dog Latin of Catholic orthodoxy, and the poorest imaginable translation of the Psalms of Scotch Presbyterianism."

From a post as the rabbi of Congregation B'nai Jeshurun in Cincinnati, Wise directed the campaign for an American Judaism worthy of the best that nineteenth-century idealism had to offer. He led in creating a rabbinical training school (Hebrew Union College), an organization of rabbis (the Central Conference of American Rabbis), and a congregational association (the Union of American Hebrew Congregations) that would work together to perpetuate Reform Judaism when its German-speaking founders had passed from the scene. Yet by the time this work was completed, in the 1880s, a new wave of European Jews was washing over American cities. They were from the *shtetls*—the tiny villages of Russian Poland and western Russia; they had been restricted to that region and to the most humble occupations by the edict of the Czar. They were lower-class, uneducated in anything non-Jewish, mystical, superstitious, suspicious of the entire Gentile world, crabbily argumentative—in short, the reverse of everything that Wise, the apostle of reason and the enemy of parochialism, stood for. Yet by sheer numbers they made American Reform Jews a minority elite—one more example of mass migration's power to disrupt well-established patterns in the nation's life.

The most fascinating story of the relationship between American immigration and American religious life, however, is unfolded in the records of the Catholic Church. Its founding fathers in the thirteen colonies were Englishmen; Frenchmen and Germans, in their turn, became its most visible supporters. Finally the Irish arrived, and they came to conquer. Though they were followed in the parishes by Italians, Poles, and Latin Americans, the ethnic flavor of the Church of Rome in the United States is still largely that of corned beef and cabbage. By the end of the nineteenth century, the Irish had created the situation in which St. Patrick's Day was in part a Catholic, in part an Irish, and in part an American holiday.

The political and spiritual center of the church that the Irish found in the 1840s was Maryland, where the Calverts had placed it two centuries earlier. The first American archbishop, John Carroll, was a distant cousin of the Charles Carroll who signed the Declaration of Independence. The then Father Carroll was chosen Prefect-Apostolic in America in 1784, and he built an organization sturdy enough to withstand and absorb heavy inflows of newcomers in succeeding decades. Frenchmen swarmed into the fold, thanks to the Louisiana Purchase of 1803 and to slave uprisings in the West Indies that drove large numbers of refugees into American havens. Early German migrations included numbers of Catholics, and by the 1820s the infiltration of still other nationalities had confronted the church fathers with an unprecedented situation. One historian has noted that "An Irish Lutheran, a German Episcopalian, a French Methodist, a Swiss Baptist, and an English Mennonite might then have been thought something of an oddity, but no one thought it strange to see men of all five nationalities occupying neighboring pews in a Catholic church of New York, Philadelphia,

This gathering of Norwegian Lutherans was photographed outside a church in Blue Mounds, Wisconsin, about 1875.

or Baltimore. Willy-nilly, the American Church had become catholic in the broadest sense. . . ."

Although they admired its universality, the first Irish on the scene lost no time in asserting their desire to see the church pay attention to particular national prejudices in assigning clergymen. In 1803 a group petitioned Carroll to replace their German priest, Father Helbron, who did not "know how to utter himself in the English tongue," with someone who could understand "the Irish language." If none should prove available, the supplicants added, they would as soon "depend on providence a little longer than get a German priest."

French priests were not considered a notable improvement. The Irish-born Bishop of Charleston, South Carolina, John England, spoke for the majority of his countrymen when he declared in 1835:

The Irish are largely amalgamated with the Americans. Their principles, their dispositions, their politics, their notions of government, their language and their appearance become American very quickly, and they praise and prefer America to their oppressors at home. The French never can become American. Their language, manners, love of *la belle France*, their dress, air, carriage, notions, and mode of speaking of their religion, all, all are foreign. . . . The French clergy are

generally good men and love Religion, but they make the Catholic Religion thus appear as exotic, and cannot understand why it should be made to appear assimilated to American principles.

The bishop himself was one reason for Irish success in church leadership. He was the firebrand offspring of a Cork tobacconist and had supped on hostility to the British from his childhood. After studying for the priesthood, he was assigned as a chaplain to prisoners awaiting transportation to exile in Australia. Immediately he became a vigorous spokesman for better treatment of these prisoners. In the Cork *Mercantile Chronicle*, he damned the British in ways that made church officials, wincing, set him down as one who "lacks sacerdotal meekness, and prudence." There was a place for hotheaded young clergymen: in 1820, he was ordered to Charleston, in the wilds of America. He plunged into the currents of Americanization without a backward look. He applied for citizenship almost before he had recovered his land legs, and was soon off to Washington to meet and admire such American worthies as President James Monroe and Secretary of State John Quincy Adams. In 1826 he was well enough known in the capital to be invited to address the House of Representatives—the first priest so honored.

It was Bishop England's belief, in 1831, that before half a century had elapsed, Catholicism would "extensively flourish" in the "land of steady habits." And it did, thanks to the dedication of thousands of Irishmen. They streamed into America faster than the church could train pastors or build tabernacles for them, and so, like others before them, they held services conducted by laymen (a "dry Mass," they called it) or by missionary priests in whatever place might be available—basements, stables, haylofts, billiard parlors, firehouses, storage rooms, and even saloons, with the bar hidden by blankets. As fast as pennies could be collected, houses of worship rose. "Hundreds of churches have been erected in a few years," wrote one priest in 1850, "and the country studded from Maine to Key West and from N. York to Minnesota with convents, hospitals, schools and colleges, erected mainly in the cities, by Catholic servant girls living at six dollars a month, and in the country by Catholic laborers working on the railroads and canals, at a dollar or a dollar and a quarter a day." The supposedly shiftless Irish contributed their savings and their sons alike to the faith. In Brooklyn in 1826, there was a small Irish community; the men, mostly navy-yard workers, organized themselves into the Erin Fraternal Association. One of them, Patrick McCloskey, was the father of a boy, John, who became the first American cardinal. George McCloskey, a milkman, had two sons who also entered the church; one was made the Bishop of Kentucky, and the other the first head of the American College in Rome.

It was no wonder that the Irish came somehow to identify opportunity, the church, and the United States as elements in a kind of social trinity. "In Ireland," said one pastor, "a father often wept to think that his children would grow up, and never be able to rise above the conditions in which they were born. Here there is no honor, no station, no eminence they may not aspire to." Hence, a faithful Irish Catholic immigrant would no more think of avoiding naturalization than of skipping Mass. Girls were advised by the priests to look for piety, sobriety, and citizenship in their suitors.

The Americanization of the Irish church, or the conversion of Catholicism in America to something Irish—it is difficult to say which description is more accurate—went on at a rapid pace. The most notable leaders in the American hierarchy in the latter part of the century were authentic sons of St. Patrick. New York's Archbishop John Joseph Hughes was from County Tyrone. The first American cardinal, as noted, was John McCloskey; the second, James Gibbons, was born to Irish parents in Baltimore. Archbishop John Ireland, of St. Paul, Minnesota, had a singularly appropriate name and was Kilkenny-born.

Archbishop Ireland sounded a proud boast at the Third Plenary Council of the American church in 1884:

There is no conflict between the Catholic Church and America. I could not utter one syllable that would belie, however remotely, either the Church or the Republic, and when I assert, as I now solemnly do, that the principles of the Church are in thorough harmony with the interests of the Republic, I know in the depths of my soul that I speak the truth.

Archbishop Ireland's faith in America was so complete that he was known to utter views that bordered on the heretical. "An honest ballot," he once said, "and social decorum will do more for God's glory and the salvation of souls than midnight flagellations or Compestellan pilgrimages." So zealous was he in quest of assimilation that he was among those indirectly rebuked in a letter issued by Pope Leo XIII in 1899, *Testem benevolentiae*, wherein so-called "Americanizers" were warned that too much adaptation of doctrine to local and modern conditions led to falsehood and error.

With the Irish in the ascendancy, the 1890s found many German Catholics in the United States beseeching the church for priests who spoke their own language, just as the Irish themselves had once done. It was even suggested by a German Catholic layman, Peter Cahensly, secretary of the Archangel Raphael Society, that the church would grow faster in America if parishes, schools, and bishops were clearly separated and assigned by nationality.

Rome never accepted this idea. "Cahenslyism" was antithetical to the unity of the believers in the true faith. But this kind of controversy contributed to ethnic discord in the United States. When two suffragan bishops were appointed for the heavily German Catholic church in Minnesota in 1889 and both proved to be Irishmen, Archbishop Ireland exulted: "Thank God, we've dished the Dutch!" The Vatican, of course, would not have seen the matter in that light, and Ireland himself was not so much anti-German as he was intensely committed to the idea expressed by a New York priest in 1851: "Is it not clear and evident that the children of Ireland coming hither in such numbers are the great element of Catholicity in this country?" There could be no doubt that Irish immigration had profoundly affected the course of Catholic history in the United States, and accordingly the destinies of a major segment of the people called Americans.

To a church, pride of nationality was a two-edged sword. It could hold congregations tightly together, and it could also turn away potential converts of other tongues and customs. But the political organizer usually had no such dilemma to face: the party was roomy enough for everyone, and a vote for the right ticket in any language was welcome. The road to advancement for thousands of immigrants lay through the precinct clubhouse, where their accents were a positive advantage. Prior to the Civil War, it was the Germans and the Irish who profited most by the nation's discovery of the ethnic vote. In the major cities entire blocks and election districts were composed of families who spoke in a brogue or in gutturals. Here, clan loyalties could create compact followings for leaders who stood out, and such "armies" of friends were the negotiable currency of politics in the age of universal suffrage.

The major impact of the Germans was on the state and national elections in Illinois, Wisconsin, and Missouri, as shown by careers such as those of Schurz and Koerner. In St. Louis and Cincinnati, among other cities, they also cast a long shadow over local government. Yet the Germans do not furnish the perfect illustration of ethnic politics at work on the street corners. Their clannishness was not usually intensified by the enmity of their neighbors. And when they lined up to vote in phalanx it was apt to be temporarily and over a specific issue: in resistance to temperance laws that would deny them Sunday pleasures in the beer

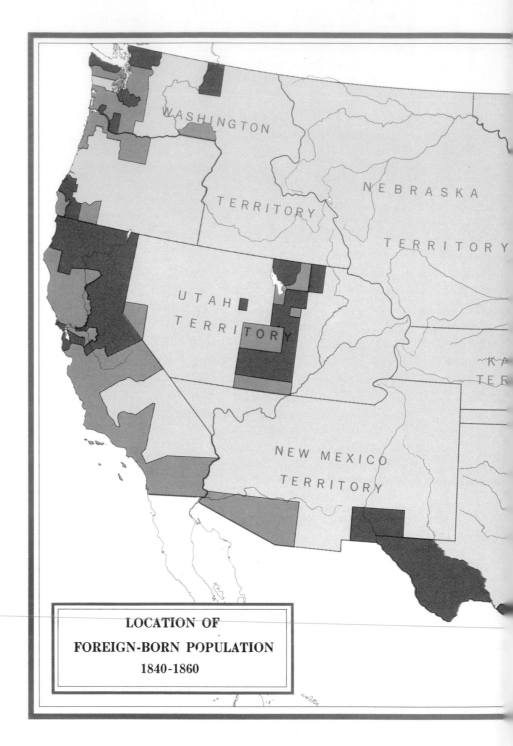

FOR PRESIDENT
MILLARD FILLMORE.
FOR VICE PRESIDENT
ANDREW J. DONELSON.

Immigration was at one of its peaks in the mid-nineteenth century, and the economic and social threat united a variety of Americans in antiforeigner organizations. In the Presidential campaign of 1856, the Know-Nothing party, a political extension of the anti-Catholic, xenophobic Order of the Star-Spangled Banner, nominated Millard Fillmore. The campaign ribbon above was worn by toughs, called plug-uglies, who bullied anti-Fillmore voters at the polls in Maryland, the only state that the former President carried.

LOCATION OF
FOREIGN-BORN POPULATION
1840-1860

gardens, for example. Or if, in some rural areas, they voted against land speculators and mortgage holders along with their Scandinavian or Scottish or Canadian friends, the binding force was their interest as farmers rather than as foreigners.

With the Irish it was different. Their political machines were sometimes built in advance of the issues that put them in motion, and displayed a cunning architecture that rose out of the very nature of the Irish urban experience. For one thing, the hostility of the old-stock Protestant community caused the Irish to cling together. The neighborhood was their world; the leader who was faithful to friends and family, generous with help to the unfortunate, and much in evidence at neighborly functions like wakes, was a man to be admired, trusted, and followed. The judgment of outsiders on him was unimportant. If he was in politics, what he said did not matter; he earned votes simply by what he was.

For the opportunistic young Irishman, politics, in one

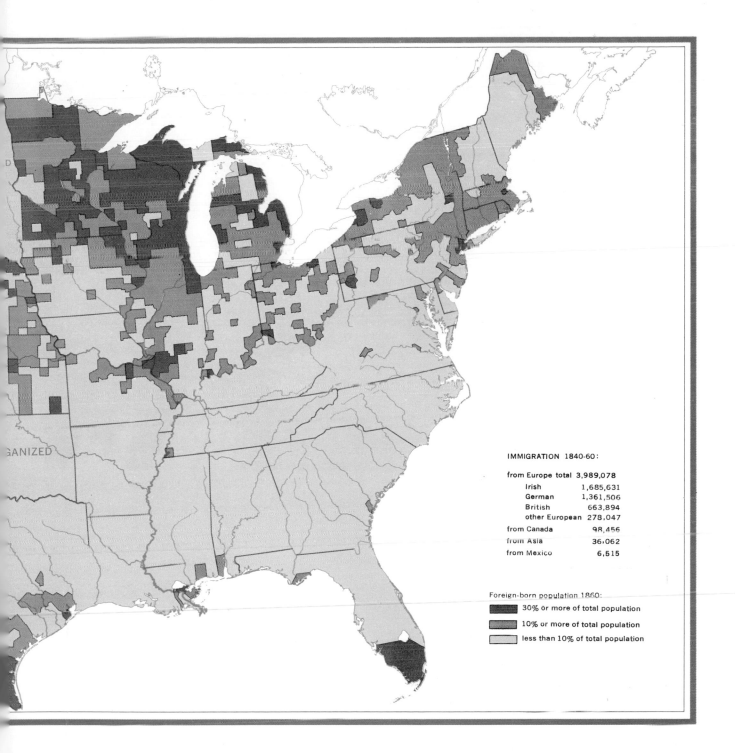

IMMIGRATION 1840-60:

from Europe total	3,989,078
Irish	1,685,631
German	1,361,506
British	663,894
other European	278,047
from Canada	98,456
from Asia	36,062
from Mexico	6,515

Foreign-born population 1860:

- 30% or more of total population
- 10% or more of total population
- less than 10% of total population

writer's words, "like baseball, prizefighting, and the Church, was a career open to talents. . . . Like every other profession, it was expected to reward its practitioners with money, prestige and, if possible, security." This point of view did not automatically predispose Irish politicians to dishonesty, but it clashed ringingly with the "genteel" conception that government should be high-minded, disinterested, and inexpensive, in order to spare the taxpayers from too many exactions on their working capital. The "proper" Americans who became

political reformers thought that expertise and a willingness to leave economic problems to solve themselves were the twin hallmarks of the worthiest candidate in an election, and they were willing to scuttle party loyalties to vote for a man who had those virtues. To a good practical politician, be he Irish or any other kind of nationality, such blackhearted ingratitude appeared far more scandalous than spoilsmanship. The exiles from Erin did not invent a political style tailored to man's unconquerable self-interest, but they were at home with

On April 27, 1875, at St. Patrick's Cathedral, John McCloskey was invested as the first American cardinal and received the red biretta.

it. New York's ward-heeling George Washington Plunkitt was a good example; he told a reporter around 1905, "There's only one way to hold a district; you must study human nature and act accordin'."

New York City became a cultural and political mecca for the Irish—as it would be for many other immigrant groups—early in its modern history. The Irish on the scene around 1800 drifted naturally into an alliance with Jefferson's followers. Republicans, being supporters of France, were foes of Great Britain—a sure guarantee of popularity with wearers of the green. One prop of the Jeffersonian organization in New York was the Society of St. Tammany, founded by old-stock Americans in 1789 for fraternal purposes. By 1817 it was a potent political club, already known after its meeting place, Tammany Hall. In that year, one of its gatherings to nominate a candidate for a Congressional seat was broken up by a group of Irishmen who demanded the honor for someone from their ranks. The effort was unavailing; even two years later the society was noted for a streak of antiforeign feeling. But in 1821 a new New York State constitution removed the requirement that voters be property holders. That was, perhaps, the beginning of Irish power. Its emergence

coincided with the political revolution that brought Andrew Jackson to the fore as the symbol of the common man's yearnings. The Irish were natural Jacksonians. The Whig Party, which opposed Jackson's Democrats, was itself broadly based, but its backbone was composed of the successful: manufacturers, land speculators, bankers, transportation-company owners; it had strong appeal for clergymen, teachers, doctors, and other professionals. These were the people whose kitchens the Irish swept and whose horses they drove, and the opportunity to equalize things a bit at the polls was irresistible. In a local election in 1827, it was alleged, two hundred Irishmen under the protection of a pistol-packing party leader deposited three ballots apiece for a candidate favorable to Old Hickory. In 1834, Irish toughs in the Sixth Ward (known as "the bloody ould Sixth") battled Whig legions in the streets fronting both parties' headquarters for three days. It took the arrival of militia with bayoneted muskets to cool things down. A Whig paper commented sarcastically that voting was, after all, "an affair of Americans" and that "foreigners must needs work themselves into a fury, and attempt to settle the question by club law."

Nonetheless the New York Irish were on their way,

and they were sped along the path of electoral influence by a Whig governor, William H. Seward, who raised an issue involving the perennially sensitive question of who should control and pay for the city's schools. In 1840, New York City's public-education bills were paid by a private organization, the Public School Society, run by benevolent upper-class citizens who collected money from both public and private sources for the purpose. They steadfastly refused to provide funds for any Catholic parochial schools. Seward was from upstate Auburn, and as solid a member of the white Protestant establishment as could be found, but he was appalled to learn that about half of New York City's Catholic children were receiving no schooling at all. Firm in the nineteenth-century progressive belief that the classroom was a useful agency of social betterment, he proposed to the legislature that the Public School Society be ordered to finance the parochial schools on a pro rata basis. "I desire to see the children of Catholics educated as well as those of Protestants," he said, "not because I want them Catholics, but because I want them to become good citizens."

The legislature refused to act on his request, and the Public School Society and the city's Common Council both resisted the Irish demands, which Seward had inspired, for a share of the school fund. The issue was fought with the usual heat on both the Catholic and "secular" (i.e., Protestant) sides, and in the struggle the Irish organized with a new sense of purpose. In the autumn of 1841 a new legislature was to be chosen. Both the Whig and Democratic Parties rebuffed the Irish vote, and named pro-School Society candidates in New York City. Thereupon the then Bishop Hughes summoned a mass meeting four days before the election and got a parochial-school slate nominated. It took enough Irishmen away from their Democratic allegiance to give the Whigs a thin edge, showing that the church could hurt the party in a contest of allegiances.

Although the new state legislature created a public school system, it expressly forbade making payments to schools teaching "sectarian doctrine." The church in New York then went to work laying the foundations of a privately supported network of schools, which in the long run served its purposes better. Another important result was that Tammany accepted the lesson that the Irishman's ballot could not be taken for granted. They began to pass out to their "Paddy" constituents what one writer nicely styles "a host of petty jobs, which it was their small ambition to hold: marshals, street inspectors, health wardens, lamplighters, firewardens, dock masters, weighers, clerks . . . each vested with that official authority, no matter how small . . . by

virtue of which they were raised to the white-collar class." Nor was private employment neglected. "I know every big employer in the district," Plunkitt was to say in defense of his profession, "and in the whole city, for that matter, and they ain't in the habit of sayin' no to me when I ask them for a job."

As the Irish poured in they were naturalized and marshaled in Tammany ranks. Their enemies writhed; in his diary former Mayor Philip Hone made the angry observation in 1843 that Bishop Hughes deserved "a cardinal's hat at least for what he has done in placing Irish Catholics upon the necks of native New Yorkers." In 1868 the New York *Tribune* sneeringly wrote: "It is rumored that Judge McCunn [who owed his election to Tammany] has issued an order naturalizing all the lower counties of Ireland, beginning at Tipperary and running down to Cork." The wave would not recede. Tammany leaders seized on the Irishman's natural gregariousness; they helped in the formation of glee clubs, baseball teams, benevolent societies, and militia units, and then reaped the harvest of loyalty.

By the end of the Civil War, Tammany had become for all intents and purposes totally Irish. At that time its boss was William Marcy Tweed, who sprang from Protestant Scottish, not Irish, roots but had grown up with Irish cronies. Tweed's ring having bilked the city of an estimated thirty million dollars in six years, he was finally unhorsed by newspaper exposures. He was convicted on 120 counts, ranging from grand larceny to conspiracy, and died in jail. Among the members of his ring were Peter Sweeny and "Slippery Dick" Connolly, Irish to the tips of their sticky fingers. The Tammany reins then passed to "Honest John" Kelly, a brother-in-law of Cardinal McCloskey. In 1886 the role of boss was bestowed on Richard Croker. Like Tweed, Croker came from Protestant stock, though at least he was Irish-born, and he joined and remained in the Catholic Church throughout his life. He discreetly betook himself out of the country after a series of threatening investigations, and he laid his bones in Irish earth in 1922, leaving five million dollars behind him. His successor as Tammany's top sachem was Charles Murphy, who carried into the modern era the Irish banner that flew over the Hall. By then there was truth in one writer's remark: "Ask an Irishman, and he will probably tell you that St. Tammany was a younger brother of St. Patrick who emigrated to America for the purpose of taking a city contract to drive all Republican reptiles out of New York."

Religion and politics, then, were two areas in which the catalytic mutual impact of "new" immigrants, "old" immigrants, and "natives" worked upon each other to create a particularly American style. It was inevitable that hostility should be a part of this formula. The United States was self-consciously the land of refuge for the homeless and tempest-tossed. But at every stage there were those crying aloud that the native-born in America constituted a family with unique hereditary gifts for self-government—and that to admit outsiders into the home as equals would dilute and corrupt those precious qualities. This belief was shared both by aristocratic old families, guarding their view of America like a precious jewel, and by violent men at the bottom of the social ladder who saw in every newcomer from abroad a competitor for jobs. The hostility was particularly strong in times of national stress.

So, just as xenophobia had surfaced when Federalism and Antifederalism were being codified in political parties, it emerged again in the 1830s, 1840s, and 1850s, when partisan passions were high and there were many anxieties about the course that the ship of state was sailing. The first shots in the nativist campaign were directed at Catholics in particular. This was not surprising; the Pope was a foreign prince, and in innumerable Puritan sermons, dating back to the beginnings of New England, he had been denounced as the Antichrist. Hatred of Rome was a tradition. In 1830, in New York, the Reverend George Bourne founded a newspaper, entitled *The Protestant*, to fight "Romish corruptions"; in the same city the Protestant Association was formed the following year; and in Boston, the Reverend Lyman Beecher used his middle-class pulpit to loose the fateful lightnings of his oratory against a suspected Catholic design to subvert America.

Angry words led to action, and action blazed— literally—in Boston, where Irish homes were occasionally set on fire under the goad of oratory like Beecher's. One climax came on the night of August 11, 1834. On a hill in rural Charlestown stood a convent of Ursuline nuns, who operated a school to which a number of wealthy Bostonians—most of them Unitarians— sent their daughters. This made it doubly provocative to mobs: it was run by Papists and utilized by the rich. Late in July a very upset young nun had left the convent. Then she returned. Rumors circulated to the effect that she had run away, had been forced to go back, and was even then a prisoner in a dungeon. Shortly a crowd gathered at night, roaring and gesticulating in the light of a pillar of fire created by igniting a pile of tar barrels in a nearby field. Then the rioters broke into the convent, drove out screaming pupils and white-faced nuns, set the building ablaze, and watched it burn to the ground.

Another milestone in the march of bigotry came in 1836 with the publication of two books by Maria Monk: *Awful Disclosures of the Hôtel Dieu Nunnery of Montreal* and *Further Disclosures*. The prurient mind is especially grateful for sensations that come packaged as instruction, and the young Canadian woman's work was a rich diet for those who savored sex in print. She told of how she had become a nun, and learned that her duty was to "obey the priests in all things," including "criminal intercourse." The babies born as a result of such liaisons, she wrote, were immediately baptized, killed, and buried under the convent floor. Many tales of abduction, seduction, secret passages from priests' bedchambers to nuns' cells, and similar Gothic devices filled the books' pages. Though the author was probably demented, and the books were soon shown to be frauds, true believers in Papist perfidy were readily convinced.

In 1844, rioting scarred the streets of the City of Brotherly Love. Early in May, a Protestant society called a meeting in Kensington, an Irish working-class area, to protest a school-board ruling that permitted Catholic children to use their own Douay version of the Bible in school. As the upholders of the King James translation crowded into a meeting hall near an Irish volunteer fire company, shots rang out and at least one Protestant fell to the ground, mortally wounded. It was a signal for turmoil. Before dawn streaked the sky over Kensington's chimneys, the windows of many an Irish home had been shattered by rocks. That day and evening the crowd returned to the attack, this time firing private houses. Soon whole blocks in the Irish district were crackling and blazing; pitched street battles were fought amid choking clouds of smoke, while a nativist newspaper shrieked: "Another St. Bartholomew's Day is begun in the streets of Philadelphia. The bloody hand of the Pope has stretched itself forth to our destruction." A special police force was finally formed to restore order, but fresh fighting broke out early in July, escalating to a confrontation in front of the Church of St. Philip de Neri in which both the crowd and the defending militia had—and used—cannon; thirteen people died and fifty were wounded.

In the 1850s anti-Catholic feelings blended with a general assault on foreigners. A tumultuous decade, it opened with the Southern states threatening secession and closed with the threat near validation. It witnessed bloodshed in Kansas and at Harpers Ferry, riots as fugitive slaves were captured in Northern towns and then rescued by abolitionists, the collapse of the Whig Party, the birth of the Republican organization, a boom in railroad and factory building, threats of war in Central America, the "opening" of Japan, even literary explosions—*The Scarlet Letter, Leaves of Grass,*

THE AMERICAN RIVER GANGES.

In an indictment of the Tweed ring's concessions to the church, cartoonist Thomas Nast portrayed children being fed to invading bishops wearing miters with crocodile teeth, as a public school crumbled in sight of a Tammany-controlled Roman Catholic school.

Moby Dick. The times were fluid and fearful; much of the fear was focused on the more than three million immigrants who entered the gates.

The litany of charges was familiar. The aliens dwelt in slums, loved wickedness, drank to excess, sold their votes. "They bring the grog shops like the frogs of Egypt upon us." "America has become the sewer into which the pollutions of European jails are emptied." Elections had been turned "into an unmeaning mockery where the rights of native born citizens are voted away by those who blindly follow their mercenary and selfish leaders." What was novel in the 1850s was the emergence of influential national organizations to bind together those who scorned the aliens, and the launching from those platforms of a temporarily successful political movement.

The founding fathers of nativist clubs had imaginations that were richly romantic; Tom Sawyer was no more giddy with the incantatory power of ritual than the officers of the Order of the Star-Spangled Banner, founded in 1849. To enter its ranks a new member had, first, to swear that he was born of Protestants in the United States, was not married to a Catholic, and would support only native-born citizens for all offices of honor, trust, or profit. Then he had to remember secret passwords, mysterious grips, and strange devices for carrying on the great work. Meetings, for example, were announced by the clandestine distribution of heart-shaped pieces of paper to the members—white for routine occasions, red if danger threatened. There was a "cry of distress" to bring help from other members, much like the "Hey, Rube!" of the carnival. There were secret gestures like a baseball coach's signals; as an instance, if two people in the order were with strangers and one began to speak too freely, the other reminded him of security precautions by drawing the thumb and forefinger across the eyes. Since all of the initiates were supposed to disclaim any knowledge of the order's very existence, they soon acquired the name of Know-Nothings. Presumably this secrecy was to protect members from reprisals. But in the political climate of 1854, it was inevitable that the Know-

Nothings should forsake their protective cover in order to enter candidates' names in elections.

The organization of the order, providing for local, state, and national councils, paralleled the committee structure of the parties; and the apparatus of newspapers and speakers that united partisans of the Whigs and the Democrats was not hard to duplicate in those simpler times. The Know-Nothings came out fighting, and astonished themselves and the country. Their candidates in 1854 won control of the governments of Massachusetts (where they swept every state office and nearly all the seats in the legislature) and Delaware. In Pennsylvania a coalition of Whigs and Know-Nothings won the election. The next year the Know-Nothings conducted successful campaigns in Rhode Island, New Hampshire, Connecticut, Maryland, and Kentucky; they came close to victory in Virginia, Alabama, Georgia, Mississippi, and Louisiana, and they ran well in New York and Pennsylvania. They were probably helped in 1855 by the growth of another nativist league, the Order of United Americans.

However, despite the nature and origins of the movement, the Know-Nothing victories did not signal a sudden, massive revulsion against immigration. Local issues had much to do with the election results. In the border states and in the South, many voters were eager to dodge the slavery question. They disliked abolitionists and slavocrats with equal intensity; the Know-Nothings had taken no national position on the question and provided a fine refuge for neutrals. The Democratic Party was splitting into Northern and Southern factions, and many Democrats sulked in Know-Nothing tents or used them as halfway houses on the road to turning Republican. Whigs found in Know-Nothingism a life raft as their party broke up and sank.

For all these reasons, therefore, the motley collection of politicians elected as Know-Nothings (under such party labels as Americans or Native Americans) never united on a program dear to anti-alien hearts. Some in the Congress of the United States submitted a bill requiring a twenty-one-year residence period prior to naturalization, but it died in that dungeon of much other legislation, the Judiciary Committee. The "Americans" could not even secure passage of legislation to forbid the admission of paupers, criminals, idiots, lunatics, and blind people to the country. In the states the record was little more impressive; even in Massachusetts, where the government was nearly all Know-Nothing for a year, the most they could achieve was a pair of laws confining officeholding to the native-born and voting to those who had resided in the land for twenty-one years and were naturalized. Both acts were repealed by succeeding legislatures. The Massachusetts Know-Nothings hastened their own extinction by creating a "Nunnery Committee" to investigate convents, schools, and seminaries, and to see if indeed they harbored helpless white slaves of the Vatican. The body of legislators chosen behaved so grossly and consumed such huge quantities of food and drink at public expense that the chairman was expelled from office. In Massachusetts, the nativist enterprise went down to the sound of laughter. And when the American Party ran the ex-Whig Millard Fillmore for the Presidency in 1856, he floundered to defeat, receiving only Maryland's electoral votes.

Nativism and its political offspring had transiently electrified groups of voters, but the American people seemed to agree with Abraham Lincoln, who in 1855 gave a classic reply to the question whether he was sympathetic to Know-Nothingism:

How could I be? How can any one who abhors the oppression of negroes, be in favor of degrading classes of white people? Our progress in degeneracy appears to me to be pretty rapid. As a nation, we began by declaring that "*all men are created equal.*" We now practically read it, "all men are created equal, *except negroes.*" When the Know-Nothings get control, it will read, "all men are created equal, except negroes, *and foreigners and catholics.*" When it comes to this I should prefer emigrating to some country where they make no pretence of loving liberty—to Russia, for instance, where despotism can be taken pure, and without the base alloy of hypocrasy.

Then, in 1861, a new sound was heard in the land that aroused foreign-born and native population alike —the gunfire of civil war. The immigrants and their offspring reacted to the emergency with promptness and generosity—sometimes stimulated by the offer of bounties, certainly, but primarily in what was once more a proof of what had already been proved, namely, that the majority of immigrants considered the United States to be genuinely their country, and its trials their trials. It has been estimated that the two most numerous groups of "foreigners," the Irish and the Germans, between them contributed at least 370,000 troops to the armies of the Union. Some of these warriors were integrated into ordinary army units, but others were grouped in special companies, regiments, and even larger formations. Early in the war it was a common practice to raise volunteer forces composed entirely of men from a particular locality or occupation or nationality. For their part, the Irish formed units bearing such names as the Irish Rifles and the Mulligan Regiment, and sometimes even marched into battle with a

Whatever their attitudes toward blacks, secession, and states' rights, Irishmen in the North seemed generally agreed after Fort Sumter fell that the Constitution must be supported. Many did riot against the draft, and others who went to war insisted they were not fighting a "nigger war" or befriending those who had called them "Papists" and "Paddies." Still, Irishmen by the thousands responded to such calls as that of the Boston Pilot: "Stand by the Union; fight for the Union; die for the Union." In the litho graph above, the 69th Regiment marches out on April 23, 1861, from "Irish headquarters around St. Patrick's Cathedral" in New York. Despite such evidence, many Americans held to the view of the cartoon at right, that the one unmixable element in the national pot was the Irish.

Puck, JUNE 26, 1889

175

flag of green carried next to the national colors. There were ten regiments made up wholly of Germans in New York, six in Ohio, six in Missouri, five in Pennsylvania, four in Wisconsin, and three in Illinois. One German romantic hero of the war was Brigadier General Ludwig Blenker—sometime jeweler's apprentice, medical student, volunteer in the revolutionary armies in Germany, and now a merchant in America and a lover of good things. In his mess tent, champagne and beer flowed as if the Virginia wilderness were the Black Forest and were populated by Teutonic knights—an illusion strengthened by the ringing German commands of the officers in his brigade. Compared to Blenker, political generals of German extraction like Carl Schurz or professionals of German descent like Godfrey Weitzel were prosaic.

Some military organizations, rather than being ethnically exclusive, were spectacularly mixed. While the 23rd Wisconsin could count companies of Swedes, Irish, and Germans, New York's Garibaldi Guards boasted a Hungarian colonel, an Italian lieutenant colonel, a German surgeon, and companies designated as "hussars" and "carabinieri." The Adjutant General's muster rolls unimaginatively listed this miniature Foreign Legion as the 39th New York, but on parade it carried with dash a set of regimental colors (the same as those in the Hungarian flag) presented by Garibaldi himself. A New York cavalry regiment was for a time commanded by a genuine Italian count, Luigi Palma de Cesnola (who later became director of the Metropolitan Museum of Art in New York), and another unit from New York, the Gardes Lafayettes, had French, German, Italian, and Spanish names on its roster.

The Confederacy had exotic soldiery, too, especially from Louisiana. Almost from the first days of New Orleans, the city had been an international port and a mingling ground for adventurers from Latin America, Europe, and the Mississippi Valley. The 1st Louisiana Regiment claimed to have representatives of thirty-seven nationalities in its ranks; a single company of the 10th Louisiana listed soldiers from Austria, Corsica, England, France, Germany, Greece, Ireland, Italy, Martinique, Portugal, Scotland, Sicily, Spain, and Switzerland. When the 13th Louisiana marched through New Orleans, the home of many of its volunteers, cries arose from the crowd: "Oh, Captain, for the love of God, let Patrick go home with me. I have a good dinner cooked for him. . . ." And "Mon Dieu, Lieutenant! let my lil' Garçon, Jules, go my 'ouse. His petite sis-ter seek." At the top levels of command, Jefferson Davis had five generals born in Ireland, including one, Patrick Cleburne, whose brother served in the Union Army.

There were, of course, foreigners who stayed home on both sides of the fighting lines—who profiteered and evaded taxes, sowed discontent among the troops, pretended that the whole conflict did not exist, or denounced the war. Less than two weeks after Irish troops had fought brilliantly at Gettysburg in July of 1863, thousands of Irishmen in New York City staged a draft riot that lasted for four destruction-filled days. They were outraged at a conscription act that allowed the rich to buy exemptions from army service but forced the poor—themselves—to fight a war for "niggers," who might some day claim a share of the unskilled jobs that were their sustenance.

Yet by and large the immigrant communities bore their share of the burden of the terrible war, which Lincoln, in the Second Inaugural Address, suggested might be God's punishment for the sin of two and a half centuries of black enslavement. Thus the newcomers participated in the nation's guilt and expiation. In 1858 Lincoln had noted that Fourth of July celebrations honored the brave grandfathers and great-grandfathers of his audience for establishing a nation that was prosperous and free. Then he added:

We have besides these men—descended by blood from our ancestors—among us perhaps half our people who are not descendants at all of these men, they are men who have come from Europe—German, Irish, French and Scandinavian—men that have come from Europe themselves, or whose ancestors have come hither and settled here, finding themselves our equals in all things. If they look back through this history to trace their connection with those days by blood, they find they have none, they cannot carry themselves back into that glorious epoch and make themselves feel that they are part of us, but when they look through that old Declaration of Independence they find that those old men say that "We hold these truths to be self-evident, that all men are created equal," and then they feel that that moral sentiment taught in that day evidences their relation to those men, that it is the father of all moral principle in them, and that they have a right to claim it as though they were blood of the blood, and flesh of the flesh of the men who wrote that Declaration [loud and long continued applause], and so they are. That is the electric cord in that Declaration that links the hearts of patriotic and liberty-loving men together, that will link those patriotic hearts as long as the love of freedom exists in the minds of men throughout the world. [Applause.]

The men of foreign birth and extraction who died on the nation's Civil War battlefields, to save or to break a Union their ancestors had not made, were in a sense validating Lincoln's faith that the Declaration of Independence had made all of them "native Americans."

The First Hurrah

When a mayoralty election in 1865 resulted in victory for a candidate of Tammany's Irish politicians, Tammany's Grand Sachem, William Marcy Tweed (left) and his followers—"the Tweed Ring"—took over New York and developed a kingdom of graft. Throughout the wards, Tammany headquarters issued red tickets, printed "Please naturalize the bearer," to be presented by Irish immigrants to Tammany judges. The cornerstone of the new Tammany Hall building was laid in 1867 with a silver trowel (below) on which Irish names were conspicuous. Although Tweed wasn't Irish himself, the New York Irish thought him a Robin Hood. To them, said the Nation, *he was "a friend of the needy who applied the public funds, with as little waste as was possible under the circumstances, to the purposes to which they ought to be applied—and that is to the making of work for the working man." Cartoons, such as the one at right, done by Thomas Nast in 1871, were instrumental in the ring's inevitable downfall.*

"WHAT ARE YOU LAUGHING AT? TO THE VICTOR BELONG THE SPOILS."

An Attraction to Politics

"Let them come, then, as the waves come, and cause the absentee English landlords to mourn over their deserted glebes. It is very easy for every man of them to have a farm which they can soon call their own. . . . If politics are necessary to the existence of Irishmen, they can get plenty of the needful in this country, in some parts of which they vote so soon as they touch the soil. Our Celtic friends are good at voting, they vote early and sometimes often, and as a general thing can be relied upon for the whole Democratic ticket." This cheery greeting appeared in the Boston *Evening Transcript* on March 5, 1880. By then the Irish had for years played a notable part in a rough and rowdy political era.

Irishmen felt somewhat the same attraction to politics as to the neighborhood saloon. With their energy, adaptability, warmth, and predilection for oratory, they were naturals in the atmosphere of an election campaign. Then, too, they came to American politics with certain advantages not shared by most other immigrants: they were familiar with the culture and spoke the English language. Having been serfs to their landlords in Ireland and accustomed to following their religious leaders, Irishmen in America readily accepted a similar role as minions of their political bosses. And the bosses played on Irish nationalism to produce desired results at the polls. Since the newly arrived immigrants were more likely to vote for one of their own than for a native American, politics was an excellent career for the individual Irishman— one of the very few professions in which being an immigrant actually proved an asset. Not prepossessed by the Brahmin concept of politics as "public service," the Irish regarded it like any business, expecting it to offer the same financial and emotional rewards. As Irish populations grew in major cities, Irish politicians began to take over and, to some degree, redesign urban Democratic machines, such as Tammany Hall.

In the Days of Honest John

Before the collapse of the Tweed Ring in 1871, Tammany Hall had become, to most conscientious citizens, a byword for corruption. Now shorn of its power, the Tammany Society still had its charter and its rank and file; to speed recovery it needed a new image. Two men stepped in to pick up the pieces—"Honest John" Kelly (above) and John Morrissey (in a *Harper's Weekly* caricature, opposite, left). Kelly, whose parents had emigrated from County Tyrone, grew up in one of New York's toughest districts, where he divided his time between stonecutting and neighborhood fights. He became a Congressman controlling most of the city's Federal patronage, and then served as sheriff under Tweed. But, fortunately, at the time of the Tweed scandal Kelly was touring the Holy Land; after his return, he affixed an "Honest" before the "John" and set about reforming Tammany Hall. His assistant was John "Old Smoke" Morrissey, a saloon bouncer and professional fighter who earned his nickname when he fell over a stove during a barroom argument and, coattails ablaze, knocked out his opponent. Kelly swept out the last of the Tweed men, systematized a common campaign fund for future candidates, and, to complete the new Tammany image, brought into its inner circle some of the most outspoken Democratic reformers and businessmen, such as Samuel J. Tilden, William C. Whitney, William R. Grace, and August Belmont.

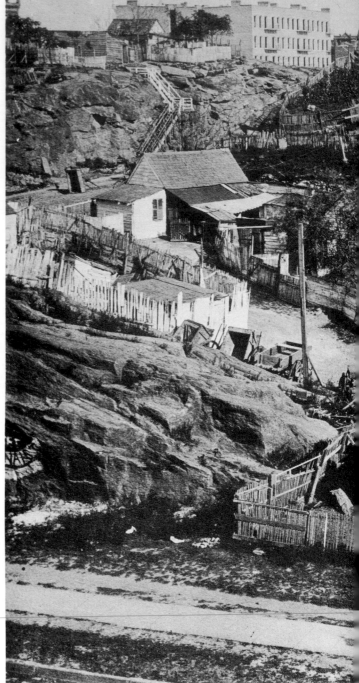

"To Fifty-ninth Street this afternoon, traversing for the first time the newly opened section of Madison Avenue between Fortieth Street and the College [Columbia], a rough and ragged track, as yet, and hardly a thoroughfare, rich in mudholes, goats, pigs, geese, and stramonium [Jimson weed]. Here and there Irish shanties 'come out' (like smallpox pustules), each composed of a dozen rotten boards and a piece of stove-pipe for a chimney." George Templeton Strong's description, in his diary for 1867, still held good for many New York Irish neighborhoods at the turn of the century. The photograph above, taken in 1893, is of the shantytown section on the east side of Fifth Avenue between 116th and 117th Streets in Harlem. For the shanty Irishman, living with filth, poverty, disease, and little hope of change, the career of a politician beckoned enticingly.

John Kelly was unable to satisfy both the conservative business-men he had brought to Tammany Hall and the old-line politi-cians who missed the Tweed carnival and wanted a greater share of the patronage. As evidenced by the Puck cartoon at right, Kelly's firm leadership was not unchallenged. "I think," wrote Mayor William Havemeyer to Kelly after a violent disagreement in 1874, "that you were worse than Tweed. . . . The public knew that Tweed was a bold, reckless man, making no preten-sions to purity. You, on the contrary, were always avowing your honesty and wrapped yourself in the mantle of piety. Men who go about with the prefix of 'honest' to their names are often rogues." Compared to Tweed's stealing, however, Kelly's was on a respectable level; he had an estate, it was re-ported, of only half a million dollars at the time of his death.

181

Kelly's successor, Richard Croker, managed New York's Democratic politics from 1886 to 1901. In 1899, asked by an investigating lawyer, "... you are working for your own pocket, are you not?," Croker snapped, "All the time—the same as you!"

That Fine Word Gratitude

Richard Croker had come to America from Ireland as a child. Raised in a family that moved out of New York slums, he became a railroad car machinist. As a reward for serving as captain of an election-day "repeater" gang for ward leader Jimmy O'Brien, Croker was made a member of the board of aldermen in 1868. After the Tweed Ring collapsed, O'Brien attempted to replace Tammany with an independent faction. The move was opposed by Kelly, and Croker aligned himself with the bigger boss, Kelly. Accused of murder in an election-day shooting in 1874, Croker stood trial and was acquitted, but emerged with considerable loss of reputation and funds. Kelly stood by him, providing minor jobs until Croker regained his alderman's seat. Croker became his deputy, and when Kelly died managed to establish himself as successor. When Croker's fifteen-year reign ended in 1901, he had amassed a fortune of more than eight million dollars. "Gratitude is the finest word I know . . . ," he later said. "All there is in life is loyalty to one's family and friends."

Our Mayor is a puppet of Tammany Hall,
Bourke Cockran will not let him get out of call;
Dick Croker he rings and Grant answers the bell;
But in other respects he is doing quite well.

Because of his inside knowledge of city plans, Croker was able to make "wise" investments in stocks and real estate, and was often the recipient of large blocks of stock donated by friends anxious for his good will. Some of Tammany's protection money—collected from gamblers, prostitutes, and bars—also fell into his hands. Croker had become, as an 1890 Puck *cartoon, above right, implied, a puppeteer of Mayor Hugh J. Grant. In another* Puck *cartoon, below, in 1894, he appeared as Hamlet following the ghost of Tweed across the "Abyss for Smashed Bosses." By then Croker had changed his life style. He owned a Pullman car and an $80,000 house near Fifth Avenue, and had invested $250,000 in a stud farm. He dressed as in the photograph at right (custom suit, top hat, and boutonniere), when, after his retirement to the British Isles, he was pictured with the trainer and the jockey of his horse Orby, winner of the 1907 Derby.*

Born in Ireland in 1827, Hugh O'Brien, top, was a printing-office foreman at fifteen and became Boston's first Irish mayor in 1885. Thomas Taggart, middle, also Irish-born, served as Indianapolis' mayor from 1895 to 1901; and William Grace, bottom, became the first Irish Catholic mayor of New York in 1880. At right, an 1889 Puck *cartoon.*

184

THEY ALL DO

Puck, APRIL 3. 1889

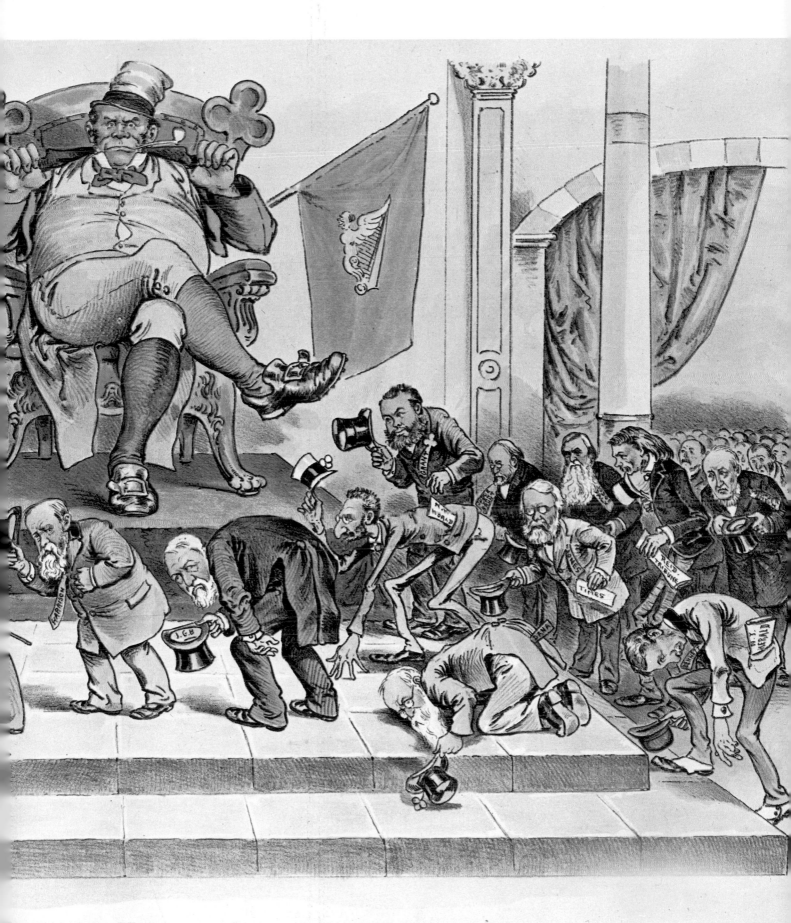

INGING BEFORE THE IRISH VOTE AND SUPPORT.

Honest Graft

A short time after Croker's retirement, Charles Francis Murphy (left) took over the leadership of Tammany Hall, a post he held from 1902 to 1924. Born in New York's lower East Side, the Gashouse District, Murphy became an amateur baseball player, worked in factories, in shipyards, and on horsecars and eventually owned four saloons that functioned as Tammany district headquarters. He was adviser and friend to hundreds of workers. Although Murphy tried to keep the courts, police, and schools untroubled by politics, he was not averse to what some called "honest graft," and by 1903 he too had become a millionaire.

A contemporary of Murphy's was Timothy D. Sullivan. "Big Tim" was also nicknamed "Dry Dollar" Sullivan after he mistook a wet revenue stamp for a dollar and was seen drying it off. A laborer's son, he grew up in an East Side tenement, went to work for Tammany at fifteen, and became expert at managing voting repeaters. Big Tim was well known for such generosity as giving food and clothes to the poor, and when he was run over by a train in 1913, his funeral was attended by twenty-five thousand people.

"Big Tim" Sullivan

"Everybody is talkin' these days about Tammany men growin' rich on graft, but nobody thinks of drawin' the distinction between honest graft and dishonest graft, . . ." said ward heeler George Washington Plunkitt in the early 1900s. "Yes, many of our men have grown rich in politics. I have myself. I've made a big fortune out of the game, and I'm gettin' richer every day, but I've not gone in for dishonest graft—blackmailin' gamblers, saloonkeepers, disorderly people, etc.—and neither has any of the men who have made big fortunes in politics." Murphy and Tim Sullivan operated within the limits that Plunkitt described. In time, Big Tim became half owner of a popular vaudeville circuit and a member first of the state legislature and then of Congress. At the right, his legions collect to honor him at a political dinner.

ALL: BROWN BROTHERS

The Social Aspects

Irishmen, convivial by nature and nurture, were attracted by the social aspects of the political scene. Ward politicians such as George Washington Plunkitt, keenly aware of the need for fraternizing, often provided social outlets for the tenants of their districts, knowing at the same time that they were insuring their political futures. "For instance," said Plunkitt, "here's how I gather in the young men. I hear of a young feller that's proud of his voice, thinks that he can sing fine. I ask him to come around to Washington Hall and join our Glee Club. He comes and sings, and he's a follower of Plunkitt for life. Another young feller gains a reputation as a base-ball player in a vacant lot. I bring him into our base-ball club. That fixes him. You'll find him workin' for my ticket at the polls next election day. Then there's the feller that likes rowin' on the river, the young feller that makes a name as a waltzer on his block, the young feller that's handy with his dukes—I rope them all in by givin' them opportunities to show themselves off. I don't trouble them with political arguments."

The Timothy D. Sullivan Association was particularly conscientious about providing a good time. Against a backdrop of the New York Barrel Co. and John Hennessy's Old Iron Yard (opposite, top), the Sullivan Association standard waves at an outing. Above, possibly at the same outing, men—wearing ribbons featuring Sullivan's picture—shoot dice; at center, in an obstacle race, they crawl through barrels. The boat at left was chartered for an annual excursion. About 1910, William Devery (right) of Tammany gave a barbecue (overleaf) on the New York waterfront.

Smoke billowing from steel-mill smokestacks in this 1909 photograph by Lewis W. Hine meant jobs in Pittsburgh.

RUN, WORK, BEWARE

AFTER THE CIVIL WAR, a flood of immigration washed over the American land. The steam-power revolution continued to add its driving energy to the forces that propelled migrations. Railroads probed deeper into parts of Europe that were until then still locked in medieval patterns, and into areas of North America yet untouched by white civilization. The transatlantic passage shrank to less than two weeks, the train journey across America to about a week. The flow of migrants widened and deepened, and seemed on the verge of engulfing familiar American social landmarks.

The steady increase in the number of newcomers was both an effect and a cause of the explosive industrial growth of the United States. The immigrant ships brought manpower and consumers, critically needed to create and to buy the products of the rising factories. At the same time, each spurt in the nation's productivity created new jobs and new opportunities. The word went back from the "foreigners" who had spent a year or two in America that dollars were waiting to be earned. Along with letters describing the American scene went remittances and steamer tickets. Yesterday's immigrants quickly became the vigorous recruiters of tomorrow's.

The biggest annual migration before the Civil War was 427,833 in 1854. The total was not surpassed until 1873, when 459,803 entered the gates. In 1882 a new record of 788,992 was set. Then came a deluge. Seven times from 1883 through 1903 the yearly total passed half a million, and only twice in that time did it drop below a quarter of a million. The all-time high was reached in 1907—1,285,349 souls—and in the period 1905 through 1914 the million mark was exceeded six

times. (Fiorello La Guardia, who would later be elected mayor of New York, worked as an interpreter at Ellis Island in 1907, and he remembered clearing an average of five thousand immigrants a day in some periods of heavy traffic.)

Between 1860 and 1900, more than thirteen and a half million immigrants arrived. Between 1900 and 1930, another eighteen million landed. In seventy years, the total of entering migrants was greater than that of the entire population of the United States at the time of Lincoln's first election. Such a massive absorption is more than an incident in history: it is, in the words of one scholar, "one of the great outstanding facts of our national life." The marks are still on the nation's economy and psyche.

Moreover, the post-1880 immigration set off more far-reaching reverberations than any ingathering that had preceded it. The foreign-born, in 1910, made up nearly fifteen per cent of the total American population, which was not a substantial increase over the more than thirteen per cent of 1860. But the actual numbers were far greater, and the faces, the accents, and especially the economic roles of the aliens had changed markedly. As the forces of modernization rolled over Southern and Eastern Europe, they drove thousands of uprooted families before them to ports of embarkation. Not all of these exiles chose America as their new homeland, but those who did found, in overwhelming numbers, that their natural environment thenceforth would be the city and the factory. Economic necessity dictated that pattern: the jobs and opportunities were concentrated in cities. But as a result the immigrant became tangled in disturbing complications in American life created by urbanism and industrial upheaval. And to make matters worse, some Americans blamed him for creating the problems in which he was snarled, and pointed the finger of accusation at his strange nationality, religion, or—a vague term—race.

Statistics encompass the facts, if not the emotions, of the big change. In 1870, total immigration to the United States was 387,203. About eighty-five per cent of it—328,626 people—came from Europe, and more than ninety per cent of *them* came from the British Isles, Scandinavia, Germany, Belgium, Switzerland, Holland, and France. Southern and Eastern Europe were hardly in the picture. The sprawling Austro-Hungarian Empire sent only 4,425 immigrants to the United States; Italy fewer than 3,000; Russia a mere 907; and those areas under Ottoman rule or suzerainty, including the present-day Bulgaria and Rumania, yielded all of six. Poland was divided among Russia, Austria-Hungary, and Prussia, but the immigration officials, attempting until 1899 to keep a separate count of incoming Poles, found only 223 of them in 1870. There were fewer than 1,400 arrivals from Greece, Spain, and Portugal together.

A young native American of 1870, therefore, stood an excellent chance of living out his life, even in a city, without ever meeting a foreigner other than a German, an Irishman, or perhaps a Swede. His chances of encountering an Italian, a Pole, a Greek, or one of the Central European peoples with such exotic-sounding names as Magyars, Slavs, Croats, or Slovenes were remote. Nor would alien presences necessarily upset him. Both natives and foreign-born were widely dispersed over a still rural countryside. Nearly three quarters of the total population of some forty million lived in communities of fewer than 2,500 residents. With that much elbow room, differences between peoples were not so noticeable, not so irritating, as they would soon become.

Only thirty-seven years later the same American, in late middle age, would find a wholly different picture. In the peak year of 1907, approximately 1,200,000 Europeans passed through the various checkpoints maintained by immigration authorities (the majority being handled at Ellis Island, which was opened in 1892). But now nearly a million came from the domains of the Czar, the Sultan, and Emperor Franz Josef of Austria-Hungary, and from around the Mediterranean. More than 335,000 came from Central Europe—Bohemians, Serbs, Poles from Galicia, Slovaks, and many more ethnic varieties from a region that was itself an enormous mixing bowl of peoples. Nearly 260,000 came from Russia, a heavy proportion of them Jews. The Italians numbered some 285,000. Rumania, Bul-

In the Puck *cartoon above, expansive Uncle Sam hosts a Christmas dinner where all nationalities join happily in his toast. A Russian-Jewish newcomer who strongly felt the American welcome was Mary Antin, left, who came to America as a young girl and later wrote a book,* The Promised Land, *about her experiences in America.*

garia, and what remained of the Turkish Empire on European soil accounted for 36,510, but there were thousands more from the still Turkish Near East—Syrians, Greeks living on islands under Turkish rule, and Armenians fleeing from severe persecution. And then there were Portuguese, Hispanic-Americans, French-Canadians, and other familiar and unfamiliar faces in the procession, and almost all these new arrivals remained in the increasingly crowded cities.

The balance had shifted at just about the end of the old century. The preponderant share of European immigration now came, and continued to come until 1924,

Fifteen years after he had arrived from Slavic Austria as a fourteen year-old immigrant in 1913, Louis Adamic, right, began a successful writing career in his adopted country. His books about Balkan and American politics and the immigrant's role in America included Dynamite, My America, *and* The Native's Return.

from areas that had sent practically no one to the republic when it was young. The hypothetical American who lived out his adult years between, say, 1870 and 1910 was bewildered, to say the very least, by the sights and sounds and smells of urban neighborhoods full of Lithuanian Jews, Ukrainian Catholics, swarthy Italians, dark-eyed Greeks, heavy-featured Poles and Slovaks. He could not relate them to anything in his own past experience or to the American history that he had read in his schoolbooks. He fell naturally into the habit of calling these strangers "new" immigrants, and he wondered if they would ever really "become

Americans"—if they had the toughness and commitment, the self-improving drives and the political savvy of the "old" immigrants, the Scandinavians and Germans and Irish, whose names were now familiar on tax rolls and on police forces, in legislatures, in advertisements for businesses they owned.

These anxieties, which persisted as the twentieth century unfolded and eventually led to a program of immigration restriction, arose from sources that ran deeper than racial antipathies. The sheer mass of the new immigration was unsettling. It was as if a family took on a cluster of new poor relations every month and had to review its budget and its living arrangements accordingly. Moreover, the period from 1890 to 1917 was one of angry national strife. Lockouts and strikes splattered the industrial scene with violence. Depression haunted the middle and lower classes. Reformers brooded about the vast power concentrated in railroad and industrial combines whose assets were counted in billions. Crusading journalists bared the ugly features of graft and corruption in boss-ridden city and state governments. Many Americans uneasily recalled Thomas Jefferson's gloomy observation that cities were to the body politic what sores were to the human physique. The "new" immigrants—crowded into slums and company towns, working at the lowest levels of skill and reward in the industrial order and carrying all the stigmata of poverty, from poor health to crime and alcoholism—seemed to embody the fulfillment of that warning.

But the concept of an old and a new immigration masked the fact that the newcomers from east and south were not fundamentally different from those who had come before them. Like all pilgrims, they included in their ranks the good and the bad, heroes and opportunists, born leaders and natural failures. Not only would they in time become Americans; they were already Americans when they took ship.

The process must have begun for thousands of Pasquales and Giuseppes with a realistic look at life in southern Italy. The march of progress faltered as it moved down toward the toe of the boot-shaped Italian Peninsula. In Calabria (the toe of the boot), Apulia (the heel), and the island of Sicily, rainfall was uneven: months of drought baked the soil, and the vegetation was as tough as the scrawny goats that tore at it for sustenance. Then came heavy rains, carrying away the earth in great slides—because most of the trees whose roots would have held in the life-giving water had long ago been cut down. Some rainfall remained in swamps, over which the anopheles mosquito whined in ominous triumph. The south Italian peasant fought a constant, losing battle against malaria and nature's whims.

In place of the depleted fields of Italy and Sicily (above), America offered still-rich farmlands and burgeoning urban industries.

Society gave him little help. By the time that national unity was achieved, in 1870, the Italian government had forced the breakup of great church-held estates in the south. But the land fell mainly into the hands of the well-to-do. These landlords rented their estates piecemeal to peasant farmers and abandoned to agents the day-to-day management of the land while they themselves courted the pleasures of Rome and other European cities. Two thirds of all landlords in Sicily in 1900 were absentees; in Calabria the figure was two fifths. The estate managers cheated and bled the tenants as dispassionately as leeches. Life was a daily struggle for a bit of bread soaked in oil and salt; government officials seemed to be merely successors to the conquerors who for many centuries had kept appearing on the scene to take the lion's share of the crop, sleep with the women, and hang the more rebellious men. Priests married the living, buried the dead, and promised heavenly consolations, but greater help than that was seldom available.

In sum, life was what it was in Ireland, for example

—a continuing demonstration that half-starved tenants cultivating worn-out lands could not rise far above an animal existence. There was no escape except in the coffin or the emigrant vessel, and the more ambitious ones of course chose the latter route. Even before 1900, Italians—many from the north, too—had been migrating in large numbers to Latin America, North Africa, and the more industrially developed countries of Europe. After the turn of the century, stories began to spread that jobs were plentiful in the United States. Between 1900 and 1910, more than two million Italians chose to find out for themselves whether that was true.

Not all were poor. Not all were tenant farmers. Among these migrants, for one, was Constantine Panunzio, the offspring of an attorney, who came from Molfetta in Apulia. His father had an abiding faith in the power of the chastising rod to shape a child's life correctly. Young "Costantino" was beaten, tied to a bedpost, and kept on a bread-and-water diet when he seemed to deviate from the course—planned by his grandmother—that would lead him to become first a priest, then a teacher, and finally a statesman. But father and grandmother were fighting a losing battle. Costantino had unwittingly taken his first step on the road to America one day when he wandered down to Molfetta's harbor and saw ocean-going ships riding at anchor. Despite all their rust and scale, to him they looked like proud, venturous galleons. He yearned restlessly for the sea, and in the turbulence of his desire became a schoolboy delinquent: robbing vineyards, playing truant, shirking confession, rattling handfuls of hard candy off girls' windows, setting off firecrackers in public streets. His father used every trick in the jailer's catalogue, from thrashings to compulsory jobs—in a foundry, a soap factory, a blacksmith shop, an electrical-supply plant—hoping that a taste of manual labor would make his boy savor the comforting benefits of a priestly life. It was of no use. In 1897, when Panunzio was thirteen, the paterfamilias gave in to his young rebel and permitted him to join the crew of an Adriatic coasting schooner.

Five years later, Panunzio sailed into Boston on the brig *Francesco*, and promptly jumped ship to escape a tyrannical captain. After five days of sleeping on benches, he was led by a French sailor, whom he met in a park, to Boston's North End Italian colony, where he was allowed to sleep, on credit, in a bed he shared with three men and many bugs. Promptly he found that an Italian beginning a career in the New World could only expect to find work with the "peek and shuvle"—which he said were his first two English words, as he spelled them. Within a few weeks the young firebrand was digging holes for a living. Eventually he would move on to become a logger, farm hand, college student, and social worker. He was one specimen of the "new" immigrant.

Another was Louis Adamic, of Blato, Carniola, in Austria (later part of Yugoslavia). The process began for him, too, when he was a boy. In the village wineshop he heard the returned *Amerikanci*—who wore black derbies, celluloid collars, and loud neckties—boast of their New World achievements. America was a "Golden Country—a sort of Paradise—the Land of Promise," huge beyond imagination, prodigal in surprises, and above all, able to furnish white bread and meat, even on weekdays, to peasants' children. But by the time Adamic was eleven, he had already heard another side of the story. A townsman, Peter Molek, returned from the mines of Pennsylvania with an asthmatic cough, a body twisted by rheumatism, and a warning that America was a jungle that swallowed people unless they were strong and wise enough to save their money and return home. Molek even showed him a book about im-

migrants just like himself and what befell some of them in the New World. It was by a man named Upton Sinclair, and was called, in fact, *The Jungle*.

Yet four years later Peter Molek's health was better, and he was ready to go back to the scramble of American life. Louis Adamic was anxious to go, too. He had spent three years at school in Laibach (later Ljubljana), and he had not lost the America fever. He had eagerly read such books as *Stric Tomova Koča (Uncle Tom's Cabin)* and *Zadnji Mohikanec (The Last of the Mohicans)*, and copies of a Slovenian-American newspaper, *Narodni Glas*, which he borrowed from a classmate, Yanko, who got them from a brother in America.

Yanko and Louis were members of a students' club where Slovenian nationalistic speeches foamed and intoxicated like beer. One afternoon they found themselves in the streets of Laibach as demonstrators for Slovene self-determination—singing, shouting slogans, pulling down German signs from above store windows, and preparing to crown the local statue of Franz Josef with a cuspidor. Suddenly a detachment of Austrian cavalry, with sabers drawn, appeared on the scene. Someone threw a rock; a command ripped out; then there was the heart-stopping rattle of shots. The students scattered pell-mell for the safety of doorways and alleys. But Yanko Radin would never reach sanctuary. He fell with a bullet through his head. Adamic, kneeling over his friend's body in a daze, was arrested. Now he was more than halfway to becoming an American.

He was released from jail after a few days, but he was expelled from the government-run school. The family tried to enter him in the Jesuit seminary in town, but the boy could not face ten years of confinement, prayer, somber clothes, and airless cells. "No more school for me," he decided: "I was going to America." His father was outraged, but his mother interceded. Late in 1913, Louis Adamic sailed for New York on the *Niagara*, out of Le Havre.

The Italian Panunzio and the Slovenian Adamic became Americans via the road of rebellion. For Mary Antin's father, of Polotzk, in the Russian section of Poland, the incitement to emigration was not so romantic. It was simply failure. But then, in a sense, life for a Jew under the Czar was something of a continual exercise in failure. What separated men from each other was the boldness with which they did something about it.

Sentimentality casts a fond aura today around the *shtetls*—the little villages from which the ancestors of millions of American Jews came less than three quarters of a century ago; but all the performances in the world of *Fiddler on the Roof* cannot disguise the fact that the *shtetls* were, in a sense, prison compounds. Russian Jews were required, in the 1890s, to live within the Pale of Settlement, a rigidly limited area. In periods of official liberalism, some exceptions were made for a small number of Jewish intellectuals, businessmen, and factory workers. But the privilege was often arbitrarily revoked; most of the time it could only be sustained by constant, humiliating petitions to an insulting bureaucracy, and also by plenty of bribe money. In the villages of the Pale, Jews confronted a barbed-wire snarl of high taxes, and restrictions on landownership and the choice of professions. As a result, they were forced into competition with each other in the authorized lines of work. An oversupply of tailors, butchers, bakers, peddlers, grocers, barbers, tinsmiths, capmakers, tinkers, harness makers, carpenters, wagon drivers, and other petty tradesmen fought for pittances with a savagery Darwin would have recognized.

Russian Jews took what consolation they could in the intense practice of their religion. Cut off from contacts with a changing world, their faith became increasingly introspective, mystical, superstitious, and parochial. And there was little opportunity to break out, even where there was a will. The great world beyond the synagogue was closed—and threatening. From it came harsh decrees and the hard-fisted tax collector. From it came the dreaded conscription officials who would take Jewish young men away for military service that, prior to 1874, lasted twenty-five years. As soldiers they would be forced to abandon Jewish practices and thus become dead in the eyes of their own community. Far better, then, if one could not bribe the conscriptors, to use the brutal services of the "crippler," who would cut a boy's heel tendon, slash an eyeball, or pierce an eardrum, inflicting hours of pain and terror in youth to spare a lifetime of horror and despair. The outside world, too, was the Gentile peasantry that lived inside as well as beyond the Pale —coarse, uneducated, bibulous men who every now and then, egged on by priests and officials, went on a rampage in the Jewish quarter—burning, beating, knifing, and raping. The pogrom was to Russian Jewry what the lynch mob was to Mississippi blacks: the ultimate threat, the always possible disaster.

Like all Jewish children in Polotzk, Mary Antin learned what helplessness was at an early age. When a tiny neighbor, the boy Vanka, threw mud at her, she ran to her mother and was told resignedly: "How can I help you, my poor child? Vanka is a Gentile. The Gentiles do as they like with us Jews." The second time it happened she did not run to her mother but took shelter, saying to herself, "Vanka is a Gentile." The third time, when he spat on her, she wiped her face

and thought nothing at all. She even learned, when she saw Vanka coming while she was eating an apple, to hold out the core to him with a false smile that made her "feel black inside."

Her father, meanwhile, was practicing the same abasement as he bent and smiled while filling the palms of excise officers and policemen with bribes. He had been a scholarly boy, slated for a life of Talmudic meditation, in which effort he would have been supported by the contributions of less gifted mortals. But when he grew up he found that such piety was not to his taste. The great world called him—at least what little of it was open to a Jew—and so he forsook study and went out to make his living at a series of occupations. He succeeded at none. He got a permit to travel in Russia and was, for a time, assistant superintendent of a distillery. Then he inherited his father-in-law's dry-goods store in Polotzk, and life went very well for a while. But a series of illnesses in the family wiped him out. Candlesticks, furniture, dresses, featherbeds were sold or pawned. There was a brief respite while he worked at another job, as superintendent of a gristmill; then desperation—in the midst of which came an offer from an emigrant-aid society: they would get Antin to America.

He went off penniless, leaving a family on the brink of starvation. His wife kept them from going over the edge by peddling; the children took odd jobs (Mary herself was unhappily and unsuccessfully apprenticed to a milliner); relatives gave their mites. The father continued his restless shifting from venture to venture in Boston, where he had landed, and with undaunted optimism borrowed enough money to send steamer tickets back to Polotzk. The family left town by train, with half the Jews of the village thronging around to cry farewell, to remind them of the perils of the sea, to shout messages for relatives in American towns near Boston such as "Baltimoreh," to wave colored handkerchiefs, and to assist in loading featherbeds and baskets of kosher food aboard. Weeks later, after many miles of rail and steamer travel, delousing, disinfecting, labeling, pigeonholing, and confinement in Hamburg and presumably in Boston too, they all stepped out into the New World.

Panunzio, Adamic, Antin—three names among millions, but each illustrating a pattern of deracination. At first glance, most of the twentieth-century international migrants were an unpromising lot. Even the conscientious and helpful people from the various national immigrant-aid societies and from the settlement houses that sprang up in slum neighborhoods were now and then discouraged when they saw their charges

Photographed above, in 1909, were sleeping accommodations of construction-gang laborers on the New York State Barge Canal.

come down the gangplanks. Most Eastern and Southern European immigrants were uneducated, poorly dressed, easy marks for disease, superstitious, unskilled —and terrified. They *looked* like the wretched refuse of Europe's teeming shore.

Yet they were far from beaten. Like the German redemptioners of the 1750s or the Irish of the 1840s or, for that matter, like the old American families who had yoked up oxen for every new frontier from the Connecticut Valley to Oregon, they may well have been unputdownables, survivors by instinct. A man who responds to failure by seeking out a new challenge in a strange environment is anything but defeated. Even those whose hopes in the New World never were fulfilled, or who returned to the old country or became permanent dependents, had at least had the courage to dice once with destiny.

The newcomers brought with them the fruits of a hard background. Life was a question of pushing and shoving to get one's share. Officials were enemies. Deceit and coercion were sometimes indispensable to keep a roof over the head, a loaf in the pantry. Some genteel Americans might have outgrown such directness,

though their ancestors would not have been shocked— those who had gulled British customs collectors, swindled the Indians out of the choicest lands, duped investors in unsound banks, and used every possible quasi-legal advantage to undermine business competitors. We read Henry Adams lamenting that he, the descendant of Puritans and Presidents, was less fit for modern American life than any "Jacob or Ysaac" from Cracow, who had a keener instinct, a more intense energy, and a freer hand for getting on in the world than he did. While this remark was made in distaste and fear, its import was that the immigrants were contributing a fresh vitality to the land. Henry's equally gloomy brother Brooks thought of the immigrants as the possible equivalent of the barbarians, who overthrew Rome and infused a decayed civilization with new blood—a left-handed compliment if there ever was one.

But the immigrants were not coming to pull down the monuments of American life; they were, in fact, to become deeply involved in building new ones. Whatever cultural and social assets and shortcomings the newcomer brought to the scene, he had an economic

199

role to play. His labor power was vital, particularly in heavy industry.

So much attention has been focused on the immigrant urban laborer that there is danger of overlooking the "foreigner's" role in the final agricultural conquest of the Great Plains. Europeans played a crucial part in that process. Sometimes they came on their own, and sometimes they were recruited by state immigration bureaus or by railroads with land or services to sell. In 1874, for example, the management of the Santa Fe line heard of the imminent arrival of a group of hard-working Russian Mennonites. They were related to the German Mennonites who had come to Pennsylvania in the eighteenth century; but *their* ancestors had elected to go east instead of west, and had accepted generous grants of land from Catherine the Great, who had an interest in seeing southern Russia well populated. Originally, the Russian colony of Mennonites had been exempted from most taxes and all military service, but early in the 1870s Czar Alexander II stopped that. The Mennonites thereupon shopped about for a new place of refuge. By correspondence they learned that some of their American brethren had moved to a treeless but fertile Beulah Land named Kansas. On a September day a first contingent arrived in New York, to be met by agents of the railroad. If the Americans had any impulse to laugh at the Mennonites' styles in beards and clothing, they suppressed it by reminding themselves that the newcomers had brought gold drafts worth two million dollars with them. Eventually the Santa Fe sold the Russians about 100,000 acres of land, but only after sweetening the bargain with such services as chartering a steamer to bring belongings from Russia, hauling building material free for one year, liberally granting passes to Mennonite ministers, and using the corporation's considerable influence in Topeka to get state legislation exempting the Mennonites from any future militia-duty requirements. In return the Mennonites, year after year, sent carloads of good farm produce—primarily hard, red Turkey wheat—rolling to market.

At the turn of the century another railroad mogul, the Great Northern's James J. Hill, also took a hand in the migratory process. A bearded, one-eyed prophet of Far Western development, Hill believed that the northern Great Plains, the Rockies, and the Pacific Northwest might be made to blossom with prosperity (in which his line could share) if it were settled and farmed with techniques suitable to a normally dry area. He sent agents to England, Scotland, Ireland, Wales, Finland, Denmark, Norway, Sweden, Germany, and Russia—agents bearing pictures and pamphlets in the native tongues—and invited all men of spirit to share the banquet of timber, grazing land, and soil that God had spread. By the thousands, Europeans jumped at the bait. Hill had no land to parcel out and sell, but the government was giving away farm land under the 1862 Homestead Act, and he could offer other inducements—fares as low as thirty-three dollars or less from Chicago to any point on the line, and special packages such as the low-price rental of a complete freight car, into which the westward-bound Swede or Bohemian was permitted to put all his household goods and farm machinery, fifty bushels of grain, up to twenty hogs and sheep, as many as ten head of horses, mules, and cattle, feed for the stock in transit, 2,500 feet of lumber, five hundred fence posts, a small portable house, and even trees and shrubbery. Such advantages made it reasonable to try one's luck.

Yet for every homesteader who possessed at least the initial skill and capital to begin a farm, there were dozens of immigrants who arrived with little more than the clothes they had on. Most of them were categorized by the authorities as "unskilled workers." For thousands of Polish, Italian, and Balkan peasants this was an inaccurate statement. They were, in fact, farmers without farms or prospects. Some managed—often with the help of charitable societies—to find their way to the land, either as separate owners or in agricultural colonies scattered from New England to California. And some, after long and grinding years of industrial labor, put aside enough to buy run-down farms in New England, New York, New Jersey, and Pennsylvania, and started to raise fruit, poultry, or vegetables.

The majority of those arriving after 1890, however, underwent a transition common throughout the modern world. They became part of an industrial urban lower class. Hard times, high taxes, poor soils, competition, droughts and floods and earthquakes, had all combined to make life oppressive on the old European farms. Those countries where industry was taking hold needed labor acutely, and the word went out that hands were wanted in mine, mill, loft, logging camp, packing plant, road-building crew and cannery, fishing fleet and freight yard. Two or three dollars, even for a twelve-hour day, sounded like a vast improvement on whatever life had to offer in Zyrardów or Catania. The immigrant went to where the pay dirt could be found. And for a nation such as the United States, in the midst of a long-term boom, he was pay dirt himself.

The pattern of immigrant dispersion tells the story. The foreign-born were drawn into the magnetic field of the country's industrial heartland. As early as the 1890s Chicago, hog-butcher to the world, freight-han-

Rapidly expanding steel mills and coal mines offered large-scale employment to unskilled immigrants. The miners above were photographed in 1910 in Pennsylvania by Lewis W. Hine. Because the supply of immigrants was so vast, mine workers could usually expect a twelve-hour day, a seven-day week, difficult working conditions (right), and minimal standards of health and safety. Serious accidents were common, and in some mines, wages for labor averaged only about $1.60 a day. Often all housing in a mining town was owned by the coal companies, which charged exorbitant rates for flimsy wooden shacks that had no sanitary facilities. The company store was a similar monopoly, where a worker's food and supply bills were charged against his earnings, a system that could reduce his yearly cash wages to as little as one hundred dollars.

The Slavic style of dress pervades Stevens Point, Wisconsin, a center for Polish immigrants, in the photo taken about 1890.

dler, stacker of wheat, and maker of steel, had more Germans than any cities in Germany except Berlin and Hamburg, more Swedes than any place but Stockholm and Göteborg, more Norwegians than any town except Christiania and Bergen. Cleveland, where John D. Rockefeller and Marcus A. Hanna and others made their fortunes in oil and coal and iron and lake shipping and public transit, had 100,000 foreign-born: Detroit, a manufacturing town even before the advent of the automobile, had 80,000. New York, already a center of garment making and other light industries in 1900, numbered 1,260,914 foreign-born—almost a third of the city's total population; by 1910 the number had swelled to nearly two million—Russian Jews comprising the largest single group, followed by the Italians, the Germans, the Irish, and the "Austrians." Twenty years later, when the foreign-born in the nation as a whole totaled greater than fourteen million, fully half of that number were in the heavily urbanized northeastern states; another fourth were in the north central states, concentrated mostly in the industrial sections of Michigan, Ohio, Illinois, Indiana, and Wisconsin.

The post-1900 arrivals naturally tended to cluster where able-bodied males were most in demand. They took up coarse grades of labor, while the earlier immigrants and the native-born workers climbed the occupational ladder. A 1900 tabulation of white male breadwinners showed that among those of German origins, about one in six worked as a nonfarm laborer, or in a mine, mill, or factory; among the Scots, about one in five; of the English and Welsh, approximately one in four; of the Irish, nearly one in three. But almost half the Italians and some sixty-three per cent of the Hungarians fell into the category of laborers. Moreover, there were some spectacular concentrations by area. In Pennsylvania in 1900, nearly fifty-nine per cent of the whites mining bituminous coal were foreign-born. In three anthracite-producing shafts in Lackawanna County, more than seventy-five per cent of the employees were Slavs; not surprisingly, it was reported that "Scores of collieries . . . cannot work when the Slavs observe a religious holiday."

The Italians seemed to find their way to the railroads and to urban construction projects as predominantly as the Slavs went to the mines. There was a natural tendency, once a nationality group had made inroads in a field, for fellow countrymen to gravitate to it. The Italians, too, were fed into the labor market in especially large numbers by the *padrone* system. The *padrone* was an Italian who arranged for passage, greeted new arrivals in their own tongue, got them settled, then sent them out in gangs to various jobs, collecting board money from the immigrants at one end and fees from the employer at the other. Once the *padroni* had established contacts in a particular industry, they tended to funnel their lucrative stream of greenhorns into it until saturation was reached.

"Where do you work-a John? On the Delaware Lackawan'" went the question and answer in a mocking popular song. "John"—or rather, Giovanni—worked on a host of railroads that needed muscle as the network reached its maximum expansion of some 254,000 miles in 1916. A Bureau of Labor study routinely noted that "one of the great lines of railroad reported an increase in its construction and track gangs of 41 per cent in 1906 over 1905," and that "the men employed were all Italian immigrants." In the 1890s the Erie Canal was modernized. Back in the 1820s, when Clinton's Ditch was first being dug, the lowly Paddies grubbed and shoveled their way across New York State, and died of malaria in droves. Of 12,500 laborers engaged in the updating project seventy years later, 10,500 were Italian. The Italians built large sections of the subways of New York, and of the street railways, waterworks, and sewer systems of hundreds of cities that were coping with an explosive growth in the first two decades of the new century. They carried pipe and they poured concrete in Baltimore, Bridgeport and Buffalo, Pittsburgh and Providence, Erie and Hoboken and Jersey City, Schenectady and Springfield and Syracuse—the smoky industrial towns where much of America's wealth was created but little of it was enjoyed. They were also quarrymen, cigar rollers, glassworkers, and employees in clothing factories—where, one Rochester, New York, manufacturer smugly noted, they were "as cheap as children and a little better." Some, like others before them, rose out of ditches and from benches to become foremen, contractors, and suppliers themselves. Some chose to work as waiters, barbers, and shoemakers, or as grocers selling vegetables, olive oil, cheese, salami, zamponi, and pasta to their own countrymen and to other Americans willing to educate their palates.

Those immigrants who were lucky and persevering could expect some reward for their efforts that offered at least a partial fulfillment of the expectations they brought to America. But the way was hard and steep. America's early industrial age was prodigal of resources, and tended to waste human beings as carelessly as it did forest land or pure water. Unskilled workers—and especially recent immigrants—were in a jungle, just as Peter Molek had said to Louis Adamic. They were the prey of the unscrupulous employment agents who collected their money and then loaded them on trains with fake "passes" to nonexistent destinations. They lived in ignorance of what few rights they had against the company-town landlords and storekeepers who bilked them. They were buried and drowned in mine disasters, burned in factory fires, crushed and maimed by unsafe machines in the care of negligent foremen, and they died painfully of lung diseases without the awareness that there might be legal and political avenues of redress. They were forced by the meagerness of their incomes to live in squalid urban tenements, or in migrant labor camps like those characterized by one government inspector as showing "an absolute disregard for comfort, health, morality, and justice." The "new" immigrants learned that the New World's prizes demanded enormous sacrifices and that there was no guarantee of victory for themselves or their posterity, even with unsparing exertion. If their own experience did not tell them, they had only to look around them and see impoverished Anglo-Saxon fifth- and sixth-generation Americans in the coal towns, or in the South, or in pinched but proud rural New England.

Yet there was a chance, provided one did not get discouraged and give up the pursuit, and if one *did* give up certain other things. A guidebook aimed primarily at Jewish immigrants summed it up well. The author appeared to promise eventual success, but with evident misgivings. He told his readers:

Hold fast, this is most necessary in America. Forget your past, your customs, and your ideals. Select a goal and pursue it with all your might. No matter what happens to you, hold on. You will experience a bad time but sooner or later you will achieve your goal. If you are neglectful, beware for the wheel of fortune turns quickly. You will lose your grip and be lost. A bit of advice for you: Do not take a moment's rest. Run, do, work and keep your own good in mind.

Forget the past—forget customs and ideals run, work, beware! This was a new kind of counsel for immigrants. And it was difficult advice to follow, for men of ordinary frailty. Even the enthusiasts whose faith in America was not shaken by sweatshop labor and tenement-house living must have found the prospect of

In Hope of Marriage

The docking in New York of a ship carrying immigrants was seldom newsworthy. But on September 28, 1907, the Times ran this story about a special human cargo, under the head "Shipload of Girls Seek Husbands Here."

When the White Star liner Baltic tied up at the foot of West Eleventh Street yesterday morning 1,002 young women tripped down the gangplank and looked about them for husbands. Some of the young women found those for whom they looked awaiting them on the pier, but there were many left over, and be it said to the shame of Manhattan bachelors that these announced it as their intention to look far inland for their affinities.

Little Gena Jensen, from Christiania, pretty and golden haired, said she hoped none of the men on the pier would try to take possession of her. "Because," she announced, "there is some one waiting for me in a place called Connecticut."

The arrival of the young women had been heralded from abroad when the Baltic sailed. The girls were booked from every country in the north of Europe, the majority of them coming from England, Ireland, Wales, and Scotland.

The State Board of Immigration of Michigan, which had been for some time trying to increase the population around Kalamazoo, immediately wired to the towns in that district, advising that delegates be appointed at once to meet the Baltic. The result was the appointment of a general committee of young farmers of Northern Michigan. They arrived in the city early yesterday, prepared to do their best to persuade the maids that Michigan was the best place in the country to live. The result of the young Michiganders' endeavor will not be known until today, for only a few of the girls were taken off Ellis Island yesterday, after their trip there from the liner's pier.

Most of those who did land were Irish girls, who went back this year to attend the Dublin Exposition, and did not have to go through all the red tape that their fellow-passengers in the steerage will experience. Some interesting and embarrassing incidents attended the arrival of these returning voyagers at the Battery. They were awaited by a large delegation in Battery Park. When the ardent ones greeted them with Sunday-go-to-meeting smiles, a chorus of "Go 'long wid yez" filled the air. The immigration officers finally had to explain to the prospective bridegrooms that there were many young women on the boat who were not looking for husbands and whose wishes in the matter would have to be respected.

Purser H. B. Palmer of the Baltic when asked about his cargo said: "They're here all right. We took on a bunch of them at Liverpool and gathered in over 700 more when we reached Queenstown. You ought to have seen them come up the side of the ship. They did it just as if they expected to find husbands awaiting them on the steerage deck."

The deckhands of the Baltic said that they had the greatest difficulty all the way across in keeping the passageways from the first and second cabins to the decks overlooking the steerage cleared. It was plain that the value and beauty of the cargo were appreciated to the full by those who traveled on the decks above.

The White Star officials could give no explanation of the sudden influx of maids on the Baltic. It is believed, however, that it is due to the fact that the report has been circulated in Europe that wives are scarce here and that those that are to be had demand too much of their would-be mates. It is also undoubtedly true that a certain percentage of the passengers of the Baltic have come with no higher ambition than to work as servants.

LIBRARY OF CONGRESS

Part of the cargo of "marriageables"

Not so with Clara McGee from Roscommon. She admitted that she had never been inside a theatre, but, nevertheless, said that she had decided to be a great actress. Others want to be the wives of railroad engineers, and some decided, after they arrived in the lower bay, that the only men that could win their hands, were the ones who built the skyscrapers. One little blue-eyed girl . . . showed that she was strictly up to date by declaring that "it's a Pittsburg millionaire for me."

Many young immigrants attended schools like New York's West 52nd Street Industrial School, above, photographed by Jacob Riis.

eradication of the past appalling. Surely it was necessary to keep some contact with what had been. And so, despite the advice, the church or the little synagogue in the new American neighborhood was more than a place of worship; it was a center where the old tongue and the familiar faces were everywhere in evidence. The foreign-language newspapers—of which there were about a thousand in 1914, with 140 of them published daily—were also bridges back to the identity formed in another clime, even if what they usually *said* in Italian or Hungarian was that Americanization should be pursued as rapidly as possible. The Polish grocery store, the Greek café, the formal association for preserving the records and culture of the old country (the Polish National Alliance, for example), were all means of easing the shock of stepping out of one's native culture. There were, of course, impatient pilgrims who could not shed old styles fast enough, but most newcomers needed the reassurance of habit, the authority of custom in decision making, the support of the like-minded neighbor.

The creation of many local enclaves of particular "foreigners" in large cities gave them a spectacular heterogeneousness. A New York newspaperman, Jacob

Riis—himself a Danish immigrant—wrote that in 1890 a colored map of New York with a different hue for each block that was dominated by a particular country's sons and daughters would present "more stripes than on the skin of a zebra, and more colors than any rainbow." Not only would there be solid areas for extensive Russian-Jewish, German, Irish, Italian, Negro, and Chinese neighborhoods, but also "dots and dashes of color here and there . . . where the Finnish sailors worship their *djumala*, the Greek pedlars the ancient name of their race, and the Swiss the goddess of thrift." Jane Addams, pathfinding social worker, described the neighborhood surrounding her settlement house in Chicago as the site of "three or four foreign colonies"— Italians (subdivided among Neapolitans, Sicilians, and Calabrians, with an occasional Lombard or Venetian), Germans, Polish and Russian Jews, and a Bohemian settlement "so vast that Chicago ranks as the third Bohemian city in the world." In an industrial town like Lawrence, Massachusetts, workers in the town's dominant industry, textile manufacture, spoke some forty-five languages or dialects and represented twenty-five nationalities. The organizers of a major strike there in 1912 had to be polylingual in their speeches.

Such a variety of human backgrounds in a single community created disturbing problems of adjustment, but it was, in its way, electric. Mass immigration, crossed with the rise of the city, created an urban culture that was distinctive in the modern world. The impact of the almost overnight transformation of whole neighborhoods was registered on a number of widely different institutions. For the political boss, the necessary adjustment might consist of adding *bar mitzvahs*, Pulaski Day parades, or soccer matches to the list of social obligations that already included wakes and communions; and what this meant in turn was that big-city politics not only spawned the ethnically balanced ticket but also developed a special breed of leader, sensitive to cultural diversity.

For the planners of public education, the effect was very likely to emphasize the "progressive" movement: teaching civic and social skills, the practical uses of education, and the routes to personal fulfillment. Confronted with a student body that spoke, ate, squabbled, dressed, played, daydreamed, and thought in half a dozen languages and cultural traditions, a principal could not assume a uniform level of preparation on which to base his academic curriculum. But a row of Chinese, Jewish, Greek, Negro, Italian, Bohemian, and Irish children stood on common ground when they were taught the Pledge of Allegiance, the principles of personal hygiene, and the creative joys of woodworking or dressmaking.

The thrust of the public schools toward Americanization was not merely a patriotic reflex. The schools were in any case only reinforcing what other agencies of popular education, such as the newspapers, were doing in the jingoistic era of Theodore Roosevelt. The schools, however, had a particularly portentous impact, since they caught the immigrants who were young and still malleable. "The public school," Mary Antin said, "has done its best for us foreigners . . . when it has made us into good Americans. . . . You should be glad to hear of it, you born Americans, for it is the story of the growth of your country; of the flocking of your brothers and sisters from the far ends of the earth to the flag you love; of the recruiting of your armies of workers, thinkers, and leaders." It is provocative of wonder that urban schools in 1970 had still not elicited any such responses from black children or been so confident of their own mission and their ability to complete it. The question is, what had changed most in the brief space of sixty years—the children, the teachers, the administrators, the neighborhoods, the expectations, or the society as a whole?

The entire subject of immigrant culture is best ex-amined in the context of what happened to it after its patterns stabilized slightly. That stabilization did not take place until the end of the mass migrations. Only then was it possible for scholars to study institutions without thousands of newcomers arriving almost monthly to disrupt those institutions. Then children and parents confronted each other across the gulf between those molded by Old World traditions and those reared in a crystallized mosaic of traditions. And it was then that the arguments over whether or not the immigrants could or could not be "assimilated," and at what cost, began to be settled (or at least limited) by the practical observation of what was actually happening. Predictions about the fate of the nation's adopted children could be tested against their adult performance. Questions could be asked. Who among the foreigners had genuinely "made it"? Who had not? And why? And, for that matter, who decided the meaning of "making it"?

These puzzlers were formulated during a long period of strife which ended in legislation that shut the open gates. Clamorous public voices arose with the new century, claiming that the United States was—or was not—a "melting pot," that it could—or could not—"melt" whatever material was cast into it, that the net result of unlimited hospitality was—or was not—a national disaster. Statistics of immigrant pauperism and vice, and the records of immigrant achievement, became weapons in legislative battles. Politicians, social workers, teachers, scientists, editors, and ministers joined the combat.

Amid the thunder and the shouting, one fact was underplayed: the argument was almost entirely about the qualities of different clans of white Europeans. In that context, the use of the word "races," and the effort to give meaning to such terms as Nordic, Alpine, Saxon, Teuton, Slav, Celt, and Magyar, was confusing, even ludicrous. But there was one kind of crude racial classification that could be made by almost anyone, educated or not, who had a pair of eyes. That was the difference between those who were "white" and those who were "nonwhite."

The nation could argue, in 1920, about whether a white Pole might be as desirable an immigrant as a white Welshman. But so far as the views of whites about nonwhites were concerned, there was little conflict. A decision had been rendered already. Before the gates even began to swing shut on the "new" immigrants, some very special "old" immigrants—black, yellow, and red—had challenged the traditional American boast of one people out of many, and they had found it full of bitter inconsistency.

Harvesters of the Land

Bountiful, Once Tamed

"What a glorious new Scandinavia might not Minnesota become! Here would the Swede find again his clear, romantic lakes, the plains of Scania rich in corn, and the vallies of Norrland; here would the Norwegian find his rapid rivers, his lofty mountains, for I include the Rocky Mountains and Oregon in the new kingdom; and both nations, their hunting fields and their fisheries. The Danes might here pasture their flocks and herds and lay out their farms on richer and less misty coasts than those of Denmark. . . ." Thus in 1853 did Fredrika Bremer exuberantly describe the attractions of America to her fellow Nordics. For Scandinavians, suffering from low wages, unemployment, and crop failures at home, the Middle West and the Northwest held great promise.

Swedes began to arrive in numbers in the 1840s and '50s and, seeking familiar surroundings, pushed westward to the prairie region, settling mainly in Wisconsin, Illinois, Minnesota, Nebraska, Iowa, and Kansas. Others followed—Danes, Finns, and Norwegians, some of whom chose the Dakotas, Oregon, and Washington. "Those whom I now saw, were wild, rough, almost savage looking men from North Germany, Denmark and Sweden—their faces covered with grizzly beards, and their teeth clenched upon a pipe stem," wrote a Virginian about a Midwestern journey in the 1840s. "They were followed by stout, well-formed, able-bodied wives and healthy children. Neither cold nor storm stopped them in their journey to the promised land."

American railroad and steamship lines and emigrant agents advertised heavily in the Scandinavian press. Such ads as those opposite— at top, a pamphlet for a Swedish line sailing "Direkte" from Göteborg to Chicago; below, a poster promoting Minnesota—encouraged the Nordic exodus. It was furthered by "America letters" and reports of settlers who returned to Scandinavia, often at the expense of steamship lines trying to increase business. Others were enticed by books like the Hand Book for Homeseekers, *published in 1895, for which the photograph at left was taken, although never printed. The neat home at the edge of partially cleared land indicated the kind of work required and the rewards possible in Wisconsin and Minnesota.*

OVERLEAF: *One photograph in the* Hand Book *was this of a farmer with his wife and child standing before a cornucopian display of Wisconsin's fruits of the land.*

Mining as well as lumbering provided an excellent source of income for Scandinavians. The work, as described by one Norwegian in 1849, was arduous. "I start at four o'clock in the morning and keep on till twelve noon. . . . We live in tents; I have not been inside a house since April 1. The ground is our bed and a saddle or something like that our pillow." Above, in an 1889 photograph of Minnesota's first mining camp, Mountain Iron—discovery point of the iron-rich Mesabi Range—the land is raw with stumps and new cabins. Right, horses and oxen haul sledgeloads of logs at a Minnesota lumber camp in 1894; opposite, lumbermen pose in a stand of tall white pine.

The Swedish Fiddle

In a growing country that had a mounting need for new homes, the Swedes were a welcome asset. They brought with them their knowledge of the ax and saw "the Swedish fiddle"—and found work in logging and carpentry. Manning the lumber camps, they felled the virgin trees, and with oxen snaked the timber out to rivers and rode herd on the logs floating downstream to the mills to be sawed. Physically strong, and accustomed by their Scandinavian upbringing to hard weather, they made excellent pioneers. And compared to the tiny farms of their homeland, a homestead of 160 acres in the American landscape seemed worth many a struggle. They built sod shanties, later log cabins, and suffered rigorous winters. "Our house is very small and humble, but it's a shelter. . . . I shall say no more about it," was a typical Scandinavian response, and most seemed to follow the Reverend Gustaf Unionius' philosophy: "I do not expect to 'cut gold with jackknives.' I am prepared to earn my daily bread by the sweat of my brow."

Very Much at Home

Coming from a stratified environment where a huge gulf lay between peasants and persons of quality, Swedish immigrants were charmed by American social equality. "Neither is my cap worn out," wrote one, "from lifting it in the presence of gentlemen." And a Norwegian added: "Here even a tramp can enjoy a chicken dinner once in a while." Not all were so pleased. "We often find," mused one observer, "that he who . . . describes the beautiful carriage he owns, is the owner of a wheelbarrow for which himself serves as the locomotive." Another, who had visited friends near Milwaukee in 1843, complained: "Their home was much poorer than any charcoal hut in Sweden, without floor, almost without roof, and with a few stones in a corner which were supposed to be a stove. Such was the magnificent house which they had written they were building to receive all the Swedes who would come. . . ." And yet the Scandinavians continued to come, and to play an important part in the growth of the United States.

Primarily agriculturalists, Scandinavian settlers often developed prosperous homesteads; opposite, three Norwegian farmers clown for the camera in front of the harvested hay crop, and, right, a family plays croquet in one of their well-kept fields. The sail sleighs below were used on Lake Michigan by the Danish and Norwegian farmers of Washington Island, Wisconsin, when they went ice-fishing for lake trout in the deep water miles offshore.

In a scene photographed around 1912, American flags fly in New York City's Chinatown.

RED, YELLOW, AND BLACK

A PROLONGED NATIONAL DEBATE over immigration began in the 1880s, and it focused sharply on the question of what constituted an American. The country had been constantly redefining itself—by admitting newcomers to the land, by inviting fresh classes to participate in politics, and by spreading out across a continent hospitable to experiments in self-rule. There was a constant mixing of new and old, and no one could say quite what "*the* American" looked like or did for a living, what God he worshiped, or what learning was essential to his life. But there was a basic assumption: the true American was white.

The harshest inconsistency of the 1880s, while the Statue of Liberty was under construction, was that the United States firmly shut the door in the faces of all potential immigrants from China's teeming shore by the Chinese Exclusion Act of 1882. At about the same time, the nation was completing the virtual destruction of its remaining Indian population, killing many, psychologically and socially crippling the rest. And it was also abandoning its post-Civil War guarantees of equality to four million freed slaves.

The first Chinese to enter the United States, writes Betty Lee Sung, a historian of Chinese immigration, were three young men brought over by a missionary. One went on to become, in 1854, a graduate of Yale. Since then there have been many academically distinguished Chinese-Americans, including two Nobel Prize winners. But in his mind's eye, the average American sees the "Chinaman" bent over an ironing board and chattering "No tickee, no shirtee," or pouring tea in a restaurant. Few stereotypes are more crude and unfair. When the "western barbarians" dwelt in

Stygian ignorance, Chinese civilization, far older than Europe's, was full of achievements in art, pure science, philosophy, literature, cuisine, manners, education, and government. But in the nineteenth century, the "barbarians" mastered a technology that was the key to world rule. The Chinese Empire, sometimes referred to as the Celestial Kingdom, was an aloof and isolated realm in 1800. By 1900, Europe's major powers had carved it, like a cadaver in anatomy class, into spheres of influence. Although the empire was still territorially almost intact, its trade and commerce were controlled by privileged foreigners who were protected by their nations' fleets, and China's government was on the verge of collapse. While they walked down this road of humiliation, the Chinese people endured enough wars, uprisings, taxes, and oppressions to make emigration an attractive prospect for millions of them.

That was the situation in the 1850s in the hard-pressed agricultural hinterlands beyond Canton and Hong Kong, when sailors from the Yankee vessels taking on tea and silk there began relating astonishing tales. In a province of their country called California, they said, just across the great sea, were valleys and streams from which one might easily sift nuggets of gold; indeed, the entire region was a virtual mountain of gold. The message had the same meaning to a Chinese as to an American. A few years' work with pick and shovel, and a man could come home rich.

So the Chinese flocked to the ships. By 1852, an estimated 25,000 of them were in the mining camps. All were men; most were married; most, apparently, planned to return to families and farms in China. In their first decade and a half in the Mountain of Gold the Chinese arrivals found plenty of reasons to confirm their plans for early departure, and also a few enticements to remain.

The gold mining did not go well for them. From the beginning the pigtailed strangers were treated with hostility by white miners, who unceremoniously kicked them off the promising claims and forced them into poorer diggings. The California legislature, in the pride of new statehood, also made the Oriental's burden a heavy one. It imposed a miner's tax that somehow was collected only from the Chinese. Together, by 1875, the state of California and the city of San Francisco had also taxed Chinese fishermen, required special payments from shipmasters bringing in Chinese passengers (such payments of course were added to the fare), excluded Chinese from the San Francisco municipal hospital, banned their testimony in court, prohibited their naturalization and exercise of suffrage, and authorized segregated schools for their children. Though some of these measures were declared unconstitutional and others were repealed after a time, their chilly message was clear enough to the growing Chinese community.

But there were positive developments, too. Opportunities to make a living abounded. The Chinese discovered in the 1850s, for example, that the hungry and filthy miners who swarmed into San Francisco between prospecting expeditions were willing to part with cash in return for creature comforts. There were few women around to do the kinds of jobs normally handled in America by women. It was an easy thing to acquire soap and washboards, pots and pans, and Chinese social custom made it no disgrace for males to wash or cook. They began laundry and restaurant businesses and were soon earning some of the gold the white miners had monopolized.

Then another door opened in 1864. Work had begun on the Central Pacific Railroad, the western half of the first transcontinental rail line. As the railhead moved into the steep, forested canyons of the Sierra Nevada, the builders found themselves confronted by an acute labor shortage: hundreds of construction-gang huskies dropped out to try their luck in mining. Charles Crocker, one of the C.P.'s four owners, suggested to his superintendent, J. H. Strobridge, that they recruit some Chinese from San Francisco. Strobridge was skeptical. The Orientals were slender, frail-looking fellows; he thought they would never survive brutal days of grading, blasting, and hauling earth and rock up and down mountainsides. Crocker insisted on a trial run. A covey of Chinese hired hands was brought up to the railhead. On the first day they rose early, put in a grinding twelve-hour day without much hesitation or

emotion, cooked themselves a meal of rice, tea, and dried cuttlefish, and went to bed.

Within months, thousands of Chinese were doggedly carrying basketloads of earth, wrestling and spiking ties and rails into place, clinging to the sides of sheer cliffs as they chipped out roadbeds, and hammering together snowsheds to shield the tracks from blizzards. Crocker got them to work on tunnels and aqueducts, too, and when Strobridge objected that masonry work was beyond the skill of "Chinamen," Crocker pointedly reminded him about the Great Wall of China. The new work force was cleanly, orderly, and perseverant. There were no epidemics, gun fights, or brawls in their camps. Eventually, six thousand of them helped to complete the coast-to-coast link, and then went on to build other Far Western lines.

When the railroad-building boom in the mountain states subsided, Chinese laborers found jobs on other construction projects or on the giant-sized farms that were already a feature of the Far Western economy. In the cities, especially San Francisco, they created the framework of a Chinese community, complete with self-help organizations that grew out of the Chinese family pattern with its strong network of mutual protection, duty, and responsibility. The "invisible government" of the San Francisco Chinese was known as the Six Companies. It served as employment and housing agency, legal-aid society, recreation and gambling center, mutual banking and insurance company, fraternal and burial lodge, lobby and union.

With the life style successfully transplanted, with employment and business prospects reasonably bright, thousands of Chinese were willing to reconsider their original plan of return. Some American public officials, reflecting on the Chinese contribution to the labor pool and to the tax revenues, were warmed with optimism and brotherhood. "Scarcely a ship arrives," wrote a San Francisco editor in 1852, "that does not bring an increase to this worthy integer of our population. The China boys will yet vote at the same polls, study at the same schools and bow at the same altar as our own countrymen." Another newspaperman watched two hundred "Celestials" step along in a Washington's Birthday parade, and beamed at the sight of "our most orderly and industrious citizens."

Such benedictions, however, ran counter to the exclusionary spirit of the latter half of the nineteenth century. In fact, the kindest words for the Chinese tended to come from businessmen to whom Chinese labor was a prime asset. In the depression of the 1870s, jobs became as valuable as pockets of pay dirt had been; once more, white men began to run the Chinese away from

A cartoon exemplifying the fear of unrestricted immigration in the 1880s shows an Irishman and a Chinaman devouring Uncle Sam.

the best claims. In the middle of the decade, when bad harvests, declining yields of gold and silver, and the effects of a nation-wide slump all hit the West Coast, "The Chinese must go!" suddenly became a demand of frightening power in California politics.

The cry was raised by a variety of voices and was sustained by fictions that still stalk ghostlike through the textbooks. One of these fictions was based on the term "coolies," which to white Americans meant slaves, more or less; Chinese contractors were said to be importing workers wholesale and keeping back almost all of their meager earnings. In actuality, "coolie" is a Chinese word meaning to rent muscle or one who hires himself out as an unskilled laborer. Foreigners in nineteenth-century China used the term to describe gangs of Chinese who were sent out under contract for work in Cuba and Latin America. But almost all Chinese emigrants to the United States were individual volunteers. A number, certainly, did sign agreements with the Central Pacific line to borrow passage money and work it out on the railroad within seven months—an echo of the indenture system that had populated colonies in the East and South a century earlier. (The signing of workers to a contract before they arrived in America was finally forbidden by the Foran Act of 1885.)

Another word that lingers in the record of Chinese immigration is "hordes"—as used, for example, by the framers of the California state Democratic platform in 1869. They opposed any move—notably the Fifteenth Amendment to the Constitution, which guaranteed suffrage regardless of race—that would "ruin the white laboring men, by bringing untold hordes of pagan slaves (in all but name) into direct competition." The lurid picture of Chinese swarming ashore by the shipload to take over control of the labor market or of American local governments was hardly verified by what happened in the next ten years. Of the total population of some 865,000 in California in 1880, the Chinese numbered about 75,000, which was well under ten per cent and not even a majority among the foreign-born residents of the state. And as early as 1865, they were contributing about fourteen million dollars annually to the economy, in the form of customs duties, fares, freight charges, taxes, and purchases.

But the Californians were unconcerned with that sort of facts. The state legislature "investigated" Chinese immigration in 1876, and in three hundred unsurprising pages denounced the Chinese as slaves, drug addicts, prostitutes, and heathen who drove honest American laborers from industrial and agrarian occupations. In a summary paragraph, the committee set down its definition of Americanization and its indictment of the Chinese for their failure to measure up:

During their entire settlement in California they have never adapted themselves to our habits, mode of dress, or our educational system, have never learned the sanctity of an oath, never desired to become citizens, or to perform the duties of citizenship, never discovered the difference between right and wrong, never ceased the worship of their idol gods, or ad-

THE PROBLEM SOLVED.

In a continuation of the cartoon on page 219, Uncle Sam is completely eaten and then the Chinaman swallows the Irishman.

vanced a step beyond the traditions of their native hive. Impregnable to all the influences of our Anglo-Saxon life, they remain the same stolid Asiatics that have floated on the rivers and slaved in the fields of China for thirty centuries of time.

Congress, with an eye to the California vote in the 1876 Presidential election, picked up the cue. Its own investigation resulted in twelve hundred pages of testimony and statistics but only a five-page published report, which was like that of California's solons.

While the legislative attacks multiplied, the Chinese had to face the more immediate threats of physical violence. During the depression winter of 1876–77, thousands of jobless workmen gathered in sandy vacant lots in San Francisco to listen to the inflammatory harangues of Denis Kearney, the founding father of California's Workingmen's Party. Kearney was an Irish merchant sailor who had graduated to independence as the middle-class proprietor of a cartage business, and its subsequent failure stung him into hatred of "the interests." He had the Irish gift for translating his wrath into oratory. Night after night he denounced the railroads and other great corporations, which, he declared, monopolized the best land, ground the faces of the poor by conspiring to skyrocket prices, and, worst of all, imported thousands of "filthy coolies" who would work for next to nothing, instead of hiring American laborers who demanded a white man's living wage.

The consequence of a Kearney performance was often a raid on a Chinese neighborhood by stirred-up whites;

they would beat up whatever hapless residents were unlucky enough to be in the streets. In July of 1877, three days of anti-Chinese rioting rocked San Francisco.

Those Chinese who had dispersed from California to other locations in the Far West found no hiding place, either. "Every Saturday night," remembered one old-time mining-camp laundry operator, "we never knew whether we would live to see the light of day." Drunken miners would burst in, trample bundles of laundry, ransack the till and break windows. In 1878 the whole Chinese population of Truckee, California, was driven from town; in 1880 an argument in a Chinese laundry in Denver led to a Walpurgis Night during which every Chinese business and home in the city was destroyed, the militia called out, and the whole Oriental population placed in jail for its own safety; in 1885, twenty-eight Chinese were massacred in Rock Springs, Wyoming. Only in faraway places like the Chinatowns of Chicago and New York and New Orleans was there some relative security of Chinese life and limb.

After the Workingmen's Party proved itself a strong political force in the state election of 1878, California redrafted its constitution to bar Chinese from employment on public and corporate construction. Then Congress in 1879 passed a bill prohibiting any ship from bringing in more than fifteen Chinese passengers. It was vetoed by President Hayes. Whatever else may have underlain his objection, the act was a flat violation of a treaty between the United States and China.

Negotiated in 1868, the Burlingame Treaty stipulated

220

that the citizens of each nation residing in the other's territory should "enjoy the same privileges, immunities and exemptions" as the citizens of "the most favored nation." The Chinese could not give any country's merchants and missionaries better treatment than it gave America's. In turn, Chinese in the United States should be treated as well as nationals of a powerful state like Great Britain. Yet in 1879, with Pacific Coast Congressmen and labor unions breathing down his neck, Secretary of State William M. Evarts suggested to the American Minister at Peking, George Seward, who in turn suggested to the Imperial government, that China might consider restricting emigration to the United States, in view of the widespread opposition to Chinese entry.

The Chinese were willing to make some concessions, but they were understandably indignant. They had, as agreed, opened their gates; the United States was slamming shut its own.

But a righteous cause is no substitute for armed power. The Chinese could do nothing about harassment of their nationals in the United States, and it was clear that the American Congress might soon abrogate the Burlingame Treaty, even if it meant overriding a veto. China settled for what it could salvage by accepting a revision of the treaty in 1880. Under the new terms, whenever the United States government should decide that the entry of Chinese laborers would "endanger the good order of the said country or any locality within the territory thereof," such entry might be regulated, limited, or suspended. The revision did not say "prohibited," small comfort though that was. It also pledged the United States not to pass laws that would subject Chinese to "personal maltreatment or abuse," and to protect the freedom of travel of Chinese teachers, merchants, and tourists.

The ensuing years were a travesty on American good faith. Congress promptly passed the Chinese Exclusion Act of 1882, which suspended the immigration of Chinese laborers for a period of ten years. It was so effective that net Chinese immigration fell from 39,579 in 1882 to 22 in 1885. But in 1888, by the Scott Act, the United States specifically *prohibited* Chinese laborers from entering the country and denied re-entry to those who had left—cutting off thousands of Chinese workers who had gone back home for visits. The Scott Act also redefined "Chinese" to include any member of the race, regardless of nationality. The Geary Act of 1892, besides renewing the exclusion of laborers for another ten years, required all Chinese to secure certificates of eligibility to remain in the United States. Subsequent legislation and treaty modifications between 1894 and 1917

hardened the pattern of rejection. And, in a particularly insulting gesture, after the United States had annexed Hawaii and the Philippines, the various anti-Chinese laws were made applicable in the islands, too.

Even those Chinese intellectuals, businessmen, and statesmen who were granted temporary entry faced harsh conditions. Under the pretext of preventing unscrupulous contractors from smuggling in coolies, immigration officials detained the Chinese in prison-like quarters while their credentials were validated, and subjected the visitors to searches and interrogations as if they were pickpockets haled before night court. The tone is best revealed by a set of instructions propounded for the Chinese exhibiting, by invitation, at the St. Louis World's Fair of 1904. All Chinese delegates were to be photographed and subjected to personal examination by the Bertillon system of identification, used on criminals. Each was to present evidence that he had no intention of remaining in the country, and to post a $500 bond to ensure his departure immediately after the fair closed. They were to proceed by direct and continuous travel from their entry point to the fair and afterward back to the same point, and to depart on the first available ship. None might leave the exposition grounds without a pass from the proper authorities, good for only forty-eight hours. If a Chinese stayed away longer than that, forfeiture of the bond and deportation could follow. No other country's nationals were subjected to the same conditions.

It was difficult to contrive further humiliation. The first-generation Chinese already in America were deprived of the power of political protest, since both judicial precedent and the Act of 1882 denied them naturalization—although their American-born children were automatically citizens. They were forced to accept employment in a limited number of occupations, such as cook, houseboy, and laundryman, and they drew together in Chinatowns where they beckoned tourists into curio shops and spurious "temples," and occasionally regaled reporters with exaggerated tales of tong wars, opium dens, and other images designed to freeze the blood of half-educated readers. Many boosted their children up the ladder of higher education; but the great majority—many of them perpetual bachelors, cut off from the possibility of returning for or importing brides—lived within their cultural enclaves, only voicing among themselves, in their clubs and newspapers, the bitterness they felt.

There was an ironic sequel to the story of the ostracized Chinese. When the closed-door policy cut off the supply of "yellow" farm workers from China, the Japanese took up the slack. By 1900 there were more than

24,000 Japanese in the United States; by 1910 the number had risen above 67,000. Like the Chinese, the Japanese exemplified the Calvinistic virtues that Americans claimed as indispensable to character. They bathed frequently, saved their money, acquired property, and set a high value on schooling, family life, and participation in community affairs. It is sad and almost superfluous to record that their behavior did not protect them in the least from the hostility of most Americans, and especially of Californians. The Golden State, spurred on by such organizations as the Native Sons of the Golden West and the Asiatic Exclusion League, had written into its statute books by 1913 a series of measures that barred "aliens" from landownership, forbade the issuance to the Japanese of licenses for commercial fishing, and in other ways closed avenues of legitimate economic self-improvement to them.

In 1906, the city of San Francisco brought matters to a head by an attempt to segregate Japanese children in separate schools. The Japanese government protested vehemently—and Japan was not, like China, a helpless, dismembered dragon but a major naval power. President Theodore Roosevelt was worried enough to write to his son Kermit, "The infernal fools in California and especially San Francisco insult the Japanese recklessly and in the event of war, it will be the nation as a whole which will bear the consequences." In the end, the Japanese accepted a face-saving device. They concluded with the United States a "Gentleman's Agreement" in 1908, in which Tokyo agreed not to issue passports to laborers, skilled or unskilled, except those who were former residents of the United States and their parents, wives, and children. Japanese immigration thereafter declined. Meanwhile San Francisco, under Federal prodding, dropped its barriers to the entry of Oriental children into "white" schools.

Both the Japanese and Chinese were to endure further insults in 1924. The major immigration restriction act of that year set a top limit on total entries and assigned quotas to various nationalities. No quota at all was allowed to China or Japan.

Nativism had scored its first long-term, palpable victory over the Orientals. The pain of it touched author Robert Louis Stevenson. Describing a transcontinental train journey in his *Across the Plains*, published in 1892, he noted that the whites aboard showed a blind anger at the Chinese and "seemed never to have

Defeated and demoralized, Indians were put on reservations, such as the Sioux' Pine Ridge Reservation in South Dakota, photographed in 1891. Allowed to leave only with passes, they had become prisoners of a country no longer interested in them.

223

3561. Three of Uncle Sam's Pets.
We get rations every 29 days. Our pulse is
good. Expressive medium. We put in 60
minutes each hour in our present attitude.
Photo and copyright by Grabill, '90.

looked at them, listened to them, or thought of them, but hated them *a priori.*" Stevenson mused further:

Awhile ago it was the Irish, now it is the Chinese that must go. Such is the cry. It seems, after all, that no country is bound to submit to immigration any more than to invasion. . . . Yet we may regret the free tradition of the republic, which loved to depict herself with open arms, welcoming all unfortunates. And certainly, as a man who believes that he loves freedom, I may be excused some bitterness when I find her sacred name misused in the contention. . . .

The "sacred name" was not honored when it came to Indians, either. Their fate furnishes another example of how race, culture, and color created limits to the acceptability of particular groups within the basic American fabric. The Chinese came across the sea of their own free will, yet were not welcomed as pioneers. The blacks came involuntarily, but hostility toward them was not mitigated by the consideration that their "offensive" presence was scarcely their own fault. And the Indians were not immigrants at all (unless one counts the prehistoric migration from Siberia) and so were hardly guilty of intrusion. Yet they too were to suffer, and it was especially ironic. For as the original possessors and proprietors of the continent they had a legit-

imate claim to equal participation in the society that was planted on it. As white civilization swept across the remaining open spaces west of the Mississippi after the Civil War, Americans faced a fresh test of how much diversity they would allow. Would the national experiment in mutual accommodation allow for patterns of group living, worship, and expectation different from those of the dominant white culture? If the Indian put aside his implements of war, would there be a place for him, as an Indian and as an equal, in the American tapestry? One eloquent Indian, Chief Joseph of the Nez Perces, asked this of the country in 1879:

If the white man wants to live in peace with the Indian he can live in peace. . . . Treat all men alike. Give them all the same law. Give them all an even chance to live and grow. All men were made by the same Great Spirit Chief. They are all brothers. The earth is the mother of all people, and all people should have equal rights upon it. . . . Let me be a free man— free to travel, free to stop, free to work, free to trade, where I choose, free to choose my own teachers, free to follow the religion of my fathers, free to think and talk and act for myself—and I will obey every law, or submit to the penalty.

Unfortunately, the chief's formula had already been rejected. He spoke at the end of a decade whose keynote, so far as Indian relations were concerned, had

Beginning in the seventeenth century, French-Canadian trappers who pushed westward to the fur country married Indian women from central Canada. Such couples and their descendants were known as métis. These people, who followed the Catholic religion of their French fathers while living a semi nomadic Indian existence, later clashed with Canadian authorities, and many of them, like the Joe Doney family, right, moved across the American border into Montana. The tone of the caption on the picture at left is a bit ambiguous, but white people in the photographer's area of South Dakota were traditionally hostile to Indians.

been sounded by a Wyoming editor in 1870: "The same inscrutable Arbiter that decreed the downfall of Rome, has pronounced the doom of extinction upon the red men of America. To attempt to defer this result by mawkish sentimentalism . . . is unworthy of the age." The Gilded Age was indeed mawkishly sentimental; but then, as always, sentimentality was not incompatible with cruelty. And compassion and restraint in dealing with Indians had never been an American trademark; the Wyoming editor only asked that the nation hew to established patterns and not be "unworthy" of its Indian hating tradition.

In May of 1830, President Andrew Jackson had signed a Removal Bill providing for the "exchange" by Eastern tribes of their ancestral lands in return for "guaranteed" spacious hunting grounds in the West. But even before the Civil War, railroads were tracking out across the Mississippi, and the war had not been over more than a few years before the shining rails had bridged the continent. Suddenly, pioneer ranchers, farmers, miners, lumberjacks, and townspeople were spreading over the prairie and mountain tracts that had been solemnly pledged to the Indians as inviolable refuges. The inexorable process of new agreements and new removals began again, repeated with such frequency that one Sioux chief, Spotted Tail, remarked

bitterly: "Why does not the Great Father put his red children on wheels, so he can move them as he will?" The story of the last Indian wars in the Far West, from the 1862 Sioux uprising in Minnesota and the Dakotas to the massacre of some three hundred Sioux at Wounded Knee, South Dakota, in 1890, is neither pleasant nor absolutely necessary to a full understanding of the American self-image at the time. It is sufficient to say that one by one tribes were forced onto reservations and overwhelmed by firepower when they offered resistance. The Modocs and the Nez Percés, the Cheyennes and the Kiowas, the Navahos and the Apaches, the Utes and the Comanches—one after another were reduced nearly to the condition of the buffalo herds on which they had once depended. At such places as Canyon de Chelly, Arizona, where the Navahos saw their flocks and herds, gardens and orchards, destroyed before their eyes, or at Sand Creek, where Colorado militiamen, under a bloodthirsty Methodist preacher-colonel named John Chivington, slaughtered Cheyenne children with the cry "Nits make lice," American showed the ugliest aspect of its celebrated westward march.

But the slow death on the reservations was almost as bad as outright massacre. Once confined to an area, a tribe depended on the government for the furnishing of rations (to replace the game that was no longer available), for protection of Indian property against marauders, and for assistance, instruction, and support in whatever new activities the tribes undertook for a livelihood. The red man's link to the Great White Father in Washington was the Indian agent—a political appointee and, in all too many cases, a grafter embodying the frontier philosophy that an Indian had no rights a white man was bound to respect. In instance after instance, agents pilfered and sold rations destined for hungry Indians, or permitted whites (in return for generous bribes) to help themselves to Indian land, timber, and minerals. And contracting to provision the Indians was a profitable enterprise for businessmen who persuaded agents—for a consideration—to accept "'steel spades' made of sheet iron; . . . 'best brogans' with paper soles; [and] 'blankets' made of shoddy and glue which came to shreds the first time they were wet. . . ."

Shortly after President Grant took office in 1869, a new policy was inaugurated in response to criticisms of the agency system. This was to apportion the nomination of agents and the direction of Indian "educational" activities among various religious denominations. Inasmuch as the misdeeds of scoundrelly agents often provoked the Indians to resistance, the new dispensation, which was supposed to cure the situation, was referred to as the Peace Policy. But it brought little tranquillity. For one thing, even the worthiest boards of Catholics, Quakers, Episcopalians, Baptists, and Methodists were far removed from the reservations, and many of the agents they chose in good faith turned out to be no better than their less sanctified predecessors; this was at least partly due to the fact that the salaries offered by the government were unattractively low. The religious groups were expected to help the government finance the Indian schools, and both sources persistently skimped on that end of their activities.

But above all, the assumption behind the entire program was that Christianity was the answer to the Indian "problem," and that increasing the missionaries' influence would soothe the savage breast and guide the aboriginal foot in the paths of peace. In general, the Indians were having none of it. They had seen too much Christian charity at places like Sand Creek to be impressed. Moreover, the multiplicity of Christian denominations caused them to doubt the white gospel; if the preachers could not agree among themselves on divinity, what should the Indian believe? As Chief Joseph put it, "They will teach us to quarrel about God as the Catholics and Protestants do on the reservation. . . . We may quarrel with men sometimes about

At right in 1898 are Florida convicts (note the ankle chains); renting out convict labor had long been common. With the Supreme Court ruling in 1896 that separate public facilities for whites and blacks were acceptable, the hope that had dwindled since the 1870s was swamped by a wave of discrimination. But blacks did not give up their aspirations. Above is Robert Stewart, who in the 1890s became Los Angeles' first black policeman.

things on this earth, but we never quarrel about God."

After a short while, the plan of church-guided Indian acculturation was dropped. The Indians still at large were still hunted, and those on the reservations continued to starve, to freeze, and to undergo the slow decay of the spirit that overtakes people when the basis of their culture disintegrates. The clamor of white reformers, however, led to a fresh evaluation in the early 1880s, and to a new avenue of approach. The Indian would never join the mainstream of national life, it was now argued, so long as he clung to his blanket, his tepee, and his chieftains. Progress would come when he was converted into an independent landholder, separated from dependence on the rigid, outmoded patterns of the tribe.

Both those who simply wished to see the Indians canceled as a Federal problem and those who were benignly disposed toward the red men were enthusiastic about the potential of detribalization. It was, after all, America's crowning boast that each man, given education, the means of livelihood, and the ballot, could make himself a lord of creation if he had any ability. Inspired by these visions, the Congress passed, in 1887, the Dawes General Allotment, or Severalty, Act. Under its provisions for "severalty" (separation of land from

common ownership), the government expanded a practice, already begun piecemeal, of assigning individual tracts of up to 160 acres to Indian heads of households. Most of the lands that were then reservations were to be disposed of in this way, or go on the open market. Titles to the individual allotments would be held in trust by the government for twenty-five years, after which the Indians would become the outright owners. Full citizenship accompanied landownership.

President Grover Cleveland, although he signed the act, remarked wryly that the "hunger and thirst of the white man for the Indian's land is almost equal to his hunger and thirst after righteousness." Indeed, white grafters moved in quickly; Indians were persuaded to adopt white "guardians" for their tracts, and these guardians would rob them of the fruits of the land or of the land itself. A modification of the Dawes Act, the Burke Act of 1906, tried, not wholly successfully, to deal with this problem. Moreover, even if making red hunters and warriors into farmers would guarantee them decent treatment (and past Indian experience did not hold out much encouragement there), the process was not a simple one. In the 1880s and 1890s on the Great Plains, well-established white farmers were being driven to economic desperation and political revolt

by droughts, locusts, falling prices, rising interest rates and transportation charges, and an assortment of other calamities. The Indian trying to make a start at agriculture needed long-term credit, tools, stock, seed, and, above all, instruction and sympathetic consideration—absolutely none of which was forthcoming from whites whose major notion of helping the Indian was to take his children into boarding schools where they were taught to cut their hair, sing hymns, and work at trades that were nonexistent on the reservations to which they would return.

The Dawes Act approach was a failure. In 1887 some 138 million acres were held by Indians; by 1932, forty-five years after the act was passed, about ninety million of those acres had found their way into white hands. One Oklahoman casually observed, "If they don't learn the value of property and how to adjust themselves to surroundings, they will be 'grafted' out of it—that is one of the unchangeable laws of God and the constitution of man." In short, they were to be sheep among wolves so long as they clung to their own culture. The concept of America's openness to different kinds of humanity did not extend to the Indians, North America's first arrivals from the Asian mainland, any more than to the Chinese and Japanese, the latest comers from Asia.

Africa's offspring, too, entered modern American life with uprooting and pain; they too encountered the face of irrational hatred; they too were the subjects of debate between white men over their needs and capacities, as if their only function in life was to demonstrate their fitness in eyes other than their own. In a sense, each generation of American blacks became "immigrants." Their forebears had been brought over, a few hundred at a time, year by year, in the nightmarish stink of the slave ships. In 1865, by the grace of the Thirteenth Amendment, blacks became free men and women and were confronted by new responsibilities. The Fourteenth and Fifteenth Amendments, officially adopted in 1868 and 1870, defined them as citizens and forbade states to deny black men the vote on the basis of color. But the weight of color—or rather, of white prejudice against color—was a crushing handicap. The Radical Republican designers of Reconstruction, early in the 1870s, operated under the same theory as the reformers who advocated Indian detribalization in the 1880s. Land, schooling, and the vote would be the materials out of which free, good "colored" citizens were fashioned.

But as it happened, the black freedman was not given land. Extravagant plans, proposed by a passionate hater of slaveholders, Pennsylvania's Thaddeus Stevens, for confiscating rebel estates and redistributing them to freedmen were never implemented. And the ex-slaves had no money to buy the acres that some planters had to put up for sale after the war. In the end they went to work either for their old masters or for those shrewd men, Northern and Southern, who survived war and Reconstruction with profits in their pockets and became planters. Some Negroes worked for wages; most landowners, however, found it more convenient to slice their holdings into small segments, each occupied by a renter who paid his way with a share of the crop he produced. Loan money for stock, tools, seed, and supplies was often raised by pledging the cotton yield of the coming year as security. The system encouraged a maximum of irresponsibility on the part of both tenant and landlord, and a dependence on one crop—cotton—often produced in such a glut that it drove prices far below the cost of production.

Twenty years after freedom, the former slave was apt to be a black peasant, apathetically scratching a crop out of exhausted soil not his own, with scrawny mules and rusted plows and hoes that he had neither the incentive nor the means to improve. He was deeply in debt, lived on a subsistence diet—mainly molasses, cornbread, and hog fat—and gave the name "home" to a decaying cabin that was not much of an improvement, if any, over the slave quarters. And although some poor white "Southrons" were little better off, that did not in the least alleviate certain other major problems of his Negro existence.

In 1877 the North almost completely abandoned the postwar effort to compel Southerners to treat the blacks fairly. Reliance was now placed on the good will and sense of justice of the "best" Southerners, of whom there were simply not enough to carry the burden. White "conservatives," sometimes legitimately, sometimes by fraud, and sometimes by using the Ku Klux Klan and other terrorist gangs to frighten Negroes from the polls, re-established white control. They gave full rein to what one Freedmen's Bureau official referred to as "that pride of race which has marked all distinguished peoples. . . ." In so doing, they shut off one by one the blacks' routes of escape from degradation. The few pioneer factories for making textiles and processing tobacco, established in the South in the 1880s and 1890s in an attempt to create an economic balance, barred black men from all but the most menial jobs. The Yankee schoolteachers who had traveled South after Appomattox to teach the freedmen their ABCs and elementary hygiene were mostly gone; time and social ostracism had swept them away. A few Northern philanthropists had set up funds for financing Negro education, but their resources were in no way equal to the

problem. A handful of Negro academies like Howard, Fisk, Hampton, and Tuskegee, founded between 1866 and 1881, were training blacks for useful vocations and even for the learned professions. But before a stream of potential black lawyers, educators, doctors, ministers, scientists—or even masons and dietitians—could enter their doors, elementary schooling had to be provided. The white governments of the Southern states after Reconstruction were little disposed to finance *any* schools, not to mention those which proposed to try the foolish experiment of giving "niggers" educations which, it was said, they could neither absorb nor put to use, and which would give them impossible hopes of rising above their stations. Most black public schools remained wretched and understandably ill-attended.

In the South, the Negro could as a rule use his ballot only to vote for a choice of Democratic white candidates, and even this choice of an unappetizing menu was taken from him around the turn of the century as the Southern states one after another enacted measures to evade the Fifteenth Amendment, by establishing poll taxes and literacy tests that were enforced against blacks but not whites, and "grandfather clauses" that turned away from the polls those classes of people who had not voted before 1860—to wit, almost all Negroes. "The negro as a political force," wrote Atlanta editor Henry W. Grady in 1889, with satisfaction, "has dropped out of serious consideration." What was more, if Negroes tried, individually or in concert, to raise any protest, they were likely to be whipped, beaten, or arrested on trumped-up charges and almost certainly sent to prison. Jail might well be a steppingstone to a place where Negro labor *was* welcome—a work gang on a road or a railroad, a lumber or turpentine camp in the woods, or a coal or iron mine: the convicted black was liable to be leased out by the state. In such employment, his chances of being starved to death, worked to death, tortured to death, or shot while trying to escape were excellent. And even if the "uppity" black stayed out of jail and escaped all these perils, the threat of rope and burning remained. Between 1882 (when such compilations first were kept) and 1900, the number of recorded lynchings in the South never fell below 100 annually, and reached a high of 235 in 1892. Most victims were Negroes. Some might have been guilty of crimes, but they never came to the trials guaranteed them. And many, there is no doubt, were executed simply for didactic reasons: the strange fruit hanging from Southern trees was intended as a warning to all blacks to remember their condition.

This condition, at the turn of the twentieth century, was accepted as a fate that black Americans either

"The slave of Italy or France could be emancipated or escape to the city and soon all records of his former state would perish," wrote Thomas Dew, a vigorous advocate of slavery, in 1832. *"... But, unfortunately, the emancipated black carries a mark which no time can erase, he forever wears the indelible symbol of his inferior condition;* the Ethiopian cannot change his skin, nor the leopard his spots." *And so it seemed. Despite gains in economic and educational opportunities, long after emancipation most Negroes lived in conditions typified by the shack at left. (A hog killing has just taken place.)*

deserved or could not evade. Majority white opinion viewed racial discrimination as a necessary evil at worst. Reconstruction Congresses had passed the Ku Klux Klan Acts of 1870 and 1871 and a Civil Rights Act of 1875, specifying Federal penalties for forcible denial of equal rights or accommodations to blacks. In a series of decisions from 1876 to 1883, the Supreme Court gutted these measures by interpretations that held the national government not bound to interfere, under the Fourteenth Amendment, when the offensive acts were those of individuals and not of state governments. Then a majority of the justices declared, in *Plessy* v. *Ferguson*, in 1896, that "separate but equal" railroad accommodations on interstate trains did not violate the Fourteenth Amendment either.

In 1890, in an effort to revive the Republican Party in the South, Massachusetts Representative Henry Cabot Lodge introduced a measure providing for Federal supervision of elections when violations of voting rights were evident. This so-called Force Bill was beaten down. In another approach, New Hampshire's Senator Henry Blair had earlier sponsored a measure for Federal aid to education in the states, to be given proportionally on the basis of poverty and illiteracy. Southern states, which stood to get the most money, professed themselves deeply insulted—and saw in the legislation the camel's nose under the tent; if the nation could undertake to improve the educational facilities afforded Southern blacks (even when whites shared in the benefits), it might move on to restore the entire Recon-

struction atmosphere. "If you would allow us to work out our own salvation," Mississippi's Senator James Z. George told his Yankee colleagues, "without your external, and, I might add, infernal intermeddling, we might at last work out something." Itself not committed to racial equality, the North accepted this view. The Blair Bill was defeated. And in 1906, the Yale sociologist William Graham Sumner wrote that in the matter of race relations, it was "evidently impossible for anyone to interfere. We are like spectators at a great natural convulsion. The results will be such as the facts and forces call for. We cannot foresee them. They do not depend on ethical views any more than the volcanic eruption on Martinique contained an ethical element." It was all very laissez-faire and offered very little hope to the blacks.

Intelligent black leaders understood well the import of these events. The court's decisions in the Civil Rights cases made them feel, said one of them, editor T. Thomas Fortune, as if they had been "baptized in ice water."

The question was what redress should be sought, and various voices offered conflicting counsel. In 1879, officials of several black churches encouraged emigration from the South. Some forty thousand Negroes, it is estimated, moved to Kansas and other Western states, but found little improvement in conditions there. There were also efforts at mass departures to Oklahoma in the 1880s and 1890s, which met both Indian and white hostility. Another abortive attempt was made to plant colonies of American Negroes in Mexico in 1895 and again in Hawaii in 1897, but both came to nothing. Not until World War I would Southern Negroes break off in considerable numbers and move, on the currents of job opportunities, to other parts of the country.

In 1895, one of the most interesting of the century's black voices spoke up for a new approach—temporary abandonment of any significant drive for black equality and political rights, in return for vocational and agricultural education, jobs, and assistance in establishing black businesses. Booker T. Washington was born in 1856 and spent his early childhood as a slave on a Virginia plantation. At the end of the Civil War, he was put to work in a salt mine in West Virginia by his freedman stepfather. Ablaze with intelligence and ambition, Washington somehow managed to acquire elementary learning in his few leisure hours. When he was about seventeen years old he walked several hundred miles, broke and hungry, to apply for entrance into Hampton Institute, a school in Virginia that had been founded in 1868. He put himself through the school by working as a janitor, wearing clothes rummaged from barrels of castoffs sent down South by Northern churchgoers. From Hampton's superintendent General Samuel C. Armstrong, the Hawaii-born son of Yankee missionaries, Washington absorbed a complete faith in America's respect for hard work and the dollar.

In 1881, Washington took over the superintendency of Tuskegee Institute, then a school only on paper; it had been authorized by the Alabama state legislature, but was without funds, buildings, or teachers. In less than fifteen years, the driving and energetic Washington had converted it into a model agricultural and technical institute, sustained in good part by Northern capitalists' donations. Tuskegee produced its own electric power, food, clothing, and essential services of all kinds—laundries and kitchens, foundries and animal hospitals. Though critics have since complained that Tuskegee trained its people for skills already obsolete in an industrial society (such as brickmaking by hand and harness repair), its experimental farms and neat shops, all black-run, were marveled at by hundreds of distinguished white visitors, including Presidents of the United States. And at the same time, Washington was busy organizing Negro landowners and small businessmen into mutual self-help societies and turning out a stream of publicity for black self-improvement.

Tuskegee Institute was begun on an abandoned Alabama plantation by a former slave, Booker T. Washington. Its first enrollment in 1881 was seventeen students, but by 1899 the school was educating 1,200 Negroes. Shown here is a student concert in 1903.

Called on to deliver an address at the Cotton States Exposition in Atlanta in 1895, he proposed the "Atlanta Compromise," which offered the white South a faithful and patient labor supply in return for a genuine mobilization of capital for upgrading the rundown cotton economy and an open door to blacks in technical schools, factories, and shops. "In all things that are purely social," he said to whites, "we can be as separate as the fingers, yet one as the hand in all things essential to mutual progress." He also declared that Negroes must begin life at the bottom and not at the top, scorned the idea of Negroes patronizing opera houses, and eschewed "artificial forcing." The white world applauded his speech, made him the most honored black spokesman of his day—and by and large never delivered what he asked for.

Booker Washington has since been condemned as an acquiescent Uncle Tom, selling the black birthright for a mess of pottage—low-grade jobs and proprietorships in a segregated society. Within a few years after the Atlanta address, young black militants—W. E. B. Du-Bois and Monroe Trotter among them—were rejecting his leadership and walking down the road of legal and propaganda combat that led to the founding in 1909 of the National Association for the Advancement of Colored People, of which Washington himself was not a member. Still, the principal of Tuskegee claimed never to have advocated anything but a truce with inequality; in fact, in his last years (he died in 1915), he covertly supported suits contesting disfranchisement and segregation, and he became more outspokenly critical of white failures to render justice to black brothers. The essential premise behind his strategy, however, was that the whites really meant what they said when they protested that the doors of acceptance were opened by achievement, regardless of the achiever's race, national origin, or creed. In his best-selling autobiography, *Up from Slavery*, written mostly as a self-conscious appeal to white intelligence and reason, Washington said:

I believe it is the duty of the Negro—as the greater part of the race is already doing—to deport himself modestly in regard to political claims, depending upon the slow but sure influences that proceed from the possession of property, intelligence, and high character for the full recognition of his political rights.

Washington's mistake may have been in taking this Yankee shibboleth—"property, intelligence, and high character"—too seriously. Frederick Douglass, the fiery black abolitionist (and an ex-slave himself) who was about forty years Washington's senior and who

died in the year of the Atlanta Exposition, would have disagreed with him strenuously. In 1892, Douglass noted that it was precisely the *successful* Negro who provoked jealousy. "The Jew is hated in Russia," said Douglass in a national magazine, "because he is thrifty. The Chinaman is hated in California because he is industrious and successful. The Negro meets no resistance when on a downward course. It is only when he rises in wealth, intelligence, and manly character that he brings upon himself the heavy hand of persecution." No saga of Negro achievement could appease a white Southerner who was capable of averring, as did Mississippi Congressman John Sharp Williams in 1898, that

You could ship-wreck 10,000 illiterate white Americans on a desert island, and in three weeks they would have a fairly good government, conceived and administered upon fairly democratic lines. You could ship-wreck 10,000 negroes, every-one of whom was a graduate of Harvard University, and in less than three years, they would have retrograded governmentally; half of the men would have been killed, and the other half would have two wives apiece.

Such a statement might represent only an extreme position, but on the whole the attitude was not sharply challenged by any significant portion of the elite that formed public opinion—the editors, ministers, professors, and politicians—even outside the South, in the first fifteen years of the twentieth century. That period, which saw the rising tide of Progressivism, has been described in one popular history after another as a testament to refreshed democratic vitality after the sordid materialism of the big industrial boom. But to nonwhites who know their history, such descriptions are an affront. All nonwhites felt the brunt of Social Darwinism (the scientific justification for "Anglo-Saxon" supremacy); all suffered from the arrogance of the light-complexioned. The dominant attitude was well expressed in an 1890 magazine article called "The Race Question in the United States."

By the destruction of the implacable Indian, we have possessed ourselves of his inheritance—the fairest and richest in the world. He would not be a slave, and we drove him out and filled his place with negroes, found in bondage in their native land, and imported as slaves. The patient, thrifty Chinaman was found to be depraved. He was invited to come here . . . When he became the successful rival to our laboring classes . . . we summarily decreed his banishment.

This, the author said, was an illustration of the English-speaking peoples' "unrelenting progress." He could not have chosen a more appropriate adjective.

Guests of the Golden Mountain

Familiar with Hardship

Compared to Europeans, the Chinese were not an emigrating people. Despite the stresses of overpopulation and poverty, normally they were held to their homeland by ties of family and religion, and by repressive Chinese laws that forbade resettlement abroad. But a great many were finally dislodged by economic forces. Most of those who left came from the southern province of Kwangtung, of which Canton is the capital. After several years of floods, famines, and rebellions, many of the peasants had turned to trade in the big cities and nearby ports, where the news arrived that a Mountain of Gold had been discovered in California. A few adventurers set sail and soon sent home packets of gold dust. The scramble was on—and the circulars were promising, if misleading in several respects: "Americans are very rich people. They want the Chinaman to come and will make him welcome. . . . It will not be a strange country." The Chinese took with them a familiarity with hardship and an ability to compensate for primitive conditions and equipment with long, patient labor. By 1860, there were 34,933 Chinese in California—all but 1,784 of them men, and few planning to make it their home. Still, despite white hostility based on race and economics, the Chinese communities in America shortly showed the signs of permanent settlement.

Nankow Pass, above (with the Great Wall in the background), and the burdened peasant, right, only hint at the ruggedness of life in the Celestial Kingdom.

Still working on the Central Pacific in 1877, Chinese in the Sierra Nevada Mountains fill in a trestle with dirt.

Valuable as Gold Themselves

Those who left China for America were called "Gum
Shan Hok"—Guests of the Golden Mountain; at least
half of them were married men who went alone to make
their fortunes, send money home, and eventually return
to China. The Chinese were welcomed mainly as un-
complaining gap-fillers. They cheerfully took on jobs
no white man wanted, finished others that had been left
undone, and seemed to heed the advice proffered by the
chairman of the Six Companies, the Chinese "government" in San Francisco: "We are Chinese in a land of
foreigners. . . . We are accustomed to an orderly society,
but it seems as if the Americans are not bound by any
rules of conduct. It is best, if possible, to avoid any contact with them. . . . Be patient and maintain your
dignity. If you are lucky you may not have to stay here
long." In 1864, the Central Pacific Railroad, in a race
with the Union Pacific to complete the transcontinental
line, made jobs for thousands of Chinese as graders,
track layers, drillers, and masons. Many never lived to
see their Canton hills again. Bitter cold, treacherous
blizzards, and sudden avalanches took their toll: "Not
until months later were the bodies recovered," wrote
one historian; "sometimes groups were found with
shovels or picks still clutched in their frozen hands."
The driving of the Golden Spike in 1869 did not end the
Chinese part in railroad building. But as economic depression set in and fear and prejudice further closed
opportunities to them, they crowded into the cities.

Above right, Chinese and white gold miners beside their flume (used in placer mining) in California in 1851

"Joe," the cook, sits with fan in hand at the John Ming residence in Helena, Montana, in 1893.

Strangers Still

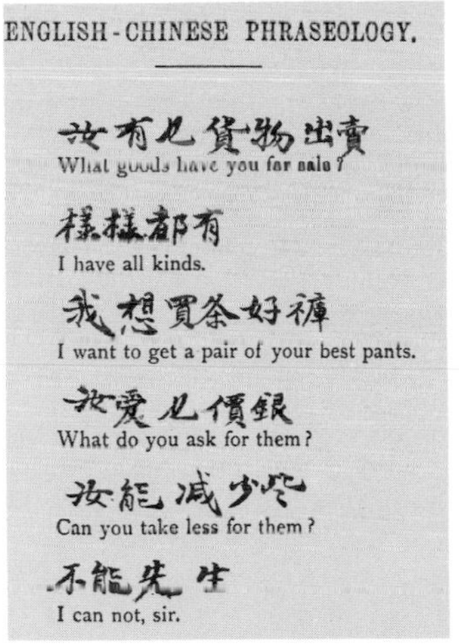

ENGLISH-CHINESE PHRASEOLOGY.

汝有乜貨物出賣
What goods have you for sale?

樣樣都有
I have all kinds.

我想買条好褲
I want to get a pair of your best pants.

汝要乜價銀
What do you ask for them?

汝能減少些
Can you take less for them?

不能先生
I can not, sir.

WELLS FARGO BANK HISTORY ROOM, SAN FRANCISCO

"When I got to San Francisco . . . I was half starved, because I was afraid to eat the provisions of the barbarians, but a few days' living in the Chinese quarter made me happy again. A man got me work as a house servant in an American family, and my start was the same as that of almost all the Chinese in this country." So wrote a Chinese businessman, Lee Chew, in the late nineteenth century. After being a servant for two years, he opened a laundry, an enterprise that was not without its share of unpleasant incidents: ". . . men would come in and claim parcels that did not belong to them, saying they had lost their tickets, and would fight if they did not get what they asked for. . . . So I determined to become a general merchant. . . . I came to New York and opened a shop in the Chinese quarter, keeping silks, teas, porcelain, clothes, shoes, hats and Chinese provisions . . . but do not include rats, because it would be too expensive to import them. The rat which is eaten by the Chinese is a field animal which lives on rice, grain and sugar cane. Its flesh is delicious." Diet, habits of dress, race pride, and traditions contributed to keeping the Chinese integer a separate one in America.

CALIFORNIA HISTORICAL SOCIETY

CALIFORNIA HISTORICAL SOCIETY

LOS ANGELES COUNTY MUSEUM OF NATURAL HISTORY

In nineteenth-century San Francisco and New York, it was possible to visit China without crossing the Pacific. "Some fault is found with us for sticking to our old customs here, especially in the matter of clothes," wrote Lee Chew, "but the reason is that we find American clothes much inferior. . . . Most of us have tried the American clothes, and they make us feel as if we were in the stocks." So the Chinese dressed as at home and re-created their old world. Among other attractions to be found in Chinatown were toy stalls, above; a public letter writer, top; a pick-up-and-delivery laundry service, left; a phrase book, top left.

OVERLEAF: *Eager to preserve his customs and traditions, the Chinese in America continued to eat with chopsticks, to wear his queue, and to celebrate festivals. This Chinese parade was photographed at the turn of the century in Los Angeles.*

LOS ANGELES COUNTY MUSEUM OF NATURAL HISTORY

The Statue of Liberty as it looked in 1890 to the thousands of immigrants.

THE GATES CLOSE

IN OCTOBER OF 1886, workmen wrestled the last huge bronze sections of the Statue of Liberty into place, and New York Harbor was thereafter the proud site of one of the country's most famous landmarks. The statue had been brought to completion by the spirited fund-raising campaign of Joseph Pulitzer's circulation-hungry New York *World*. Pulitzer, a Hungarian immigrant who became a millionaire, undoubtedly thought highly of Emma Lazarus' much-quoted lines, written in 1883 and, twenty years later, inscribed on the pedestal of Liberty:

> . . . Give me your tired, your poor,
> Your huddled masses yearning to breathe free,
> The wretched refuse of your teeming shore.
> Send these, the homeless, tempest-tost to me,
> I lift my lamp beside the golden door.

Like most of his fellow Americans, Pulitzer was not apt to worry over the note of condescension in the welcome. To say that the newcomers riding up the Narrows were "wretched refuse" was not entirely open-hearted: it was something like taking a newspaper advertisement to state that one had kindly volunteered to adopt an illegitimate, crippled, and penniless orphan. Ironically, that was the spirit of a long and generally negative national appraisal of immigration policy, which began at about the same time the Statue of Liberty was dedicated.

The appraisal of the open gate was part of a broad review of the quality and the promises of American life —a review that ultimately would be more or less formalized in the Progressive Era and would take on a liberal coloration. It was a period characterized, for example, by debates about government policy toward railroads, trusts, labor unions, courts, and political machines. There were heated national discussions of such matters as pacifism, progressivism in education, the future of science, the "new" woman, and emancipation of the arts from stifling conventions. In a way, the spirit of the time reached its apex in America's idealistic approach to the World War; and its last gasp might be said to have been Prohibition.

Since it was a time when liberal ideas were popular, it is not surprising that in the argument over immigration, some men were calling for a completely new concept of the nation's character. As stated in a magazine piece by Percy Stickney Grant, pastor of New York's Episcopal Church of the Ascension, it was a summons.

We must construct a new picture of citizenship. If we do . . . we shall welcome the rugged strength of the peasant or the subtle thought of the man in the Ghetto in our reconsidered American ideals. . . . Let us rise to an eminence higher than that occupied by Washington or Lincoln, to a new Americanism which is not afraid of the blending in the western world of races seeking freedom.

Conservative alarm, however, had deepened with every boom period at Ellis Island. This alarm was concisely expressed by Henry Pratt Fairchild in a 1913 volume, which demanded "recognition of the fact that we are by no means prepared to accept the tremendous responsibility of admitting unlimited numbers of aliens whose entire future destiny depends upon the soundness of our political, social, and economic fabric."

Although the Reverend Dr. Grant's clarion call seemed much more in tune with the national chorus of welcome

In the 1898 Puck cartoon below, an Indian attacks Senate Foreign Relations Committee Chairman Henry Cabot Lodge with "An Act to Prevent the Country from Being Overrun by Foreigners." "Where Would WE Be?," asked the caption. "If the Real Americans Had Held Lodge's View of Immigration There Would Be No Lodge Bill Now—Nor Anything Else." But proponents of immigration restriction, such as Stanford University President David Starr Jordan (above, in wing collar), Lodge (above, right), and Missouri Senator James A. Reed, cosponsor of the Johnson-Reed Act (top left), won the fight. When that act took effect in 1924, racially biased restriction of immigration was an accepted notion.

**LOCATION OF
FOREIGN-BORN POPULATION
1900-1920**

Puck, MARCH 30, 1898

to "progress," Fairchild's voice more accurately reflected reality as Congress was to see it. In February, 1917, a law was enacted over a Presidential veto, restricting admission to America to those among the world's people who already knew how to read and write. In the early 1920s the grave of unlimited immigration was dug even deeper: the lawmakers decreed a series of cutbacks in the annual number of newcomers, aiming at an eventual ceiling of about 150,000 a year from outside the Western Hemisphere. Moreover, they applied

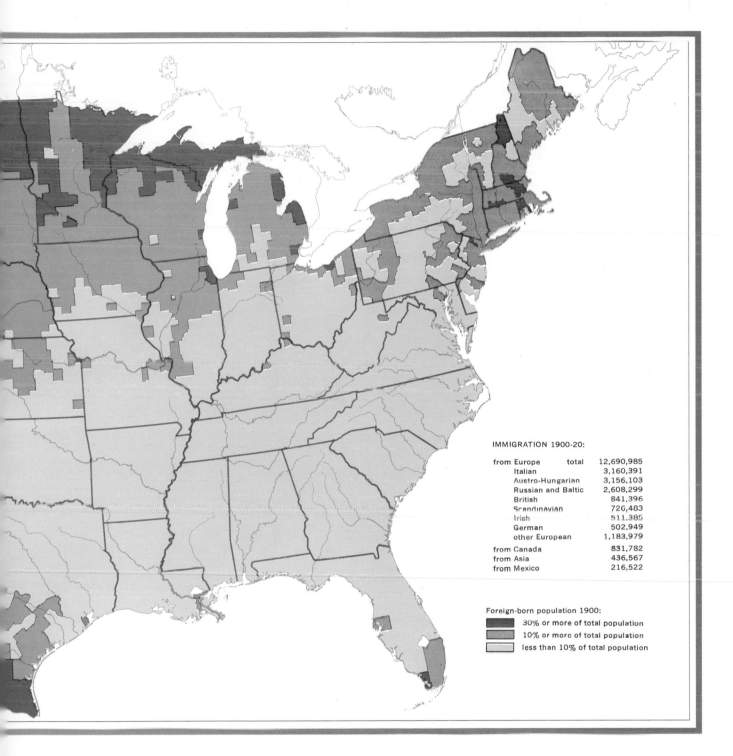

IMMIGRATION 1900-20:

from Europe	total	12,690,985
Italian		3,160,391
Austro-Hungarian		3,156,103
Russian and Baltic		2,608,299
British		841,396
Scandinavian		726,483
Irish		511,385
German		502,949
other European		1,183,979
from Canada		831,782
from Asia		436,567
from Mexico		216,522

Foreign-born population 1900:

- 30% or more of total population
- 10% or more of total population
- less than 10% of total population

to the "new" immigrants of Eastern and Southern Europe the sort of racist attitudes that already held down black and red men and banned Orientals from entry. They created a quota system that froze the proportions of the intake according to the "national origins" of the American people as they were in 1920. The British, who had first come in 1607, had nearly twelve times as many descendants on the census rolls as the Italians, who had been coming in substantial numbers only since the 1880s; thus Britain's share of the annual total was twelve times that of Italy. There was a clear implication that a Briton was also twelve times as desirable a newcomer as an Italian. How the public mind arrived at a state of readiness to accept such a judgment, during a period of American history rich in liberalism, is a remarkable story. It involves labor leaders, intellectuals, patricians and proletarians, city dwellers and farmers, ministers of God and devil's disciples, and a constant interplay between hope and fear.

The story begins with the insecurity of the misnamed

"With the demise of David Kessler the Yiddish stage,—and the entire Yiddish speaking race—has lost one of its foremost disciples," said a newspaper tribute to the actor, left, in 1920. Kessler, a Russian immigrant to America, was considered an innovator in Yiddish theater, stressing a realistic style. Foreign-language theater appealed to the immigrant strain in America; so did productions such as those advertised in the Strobridge lithographs shown below and right.

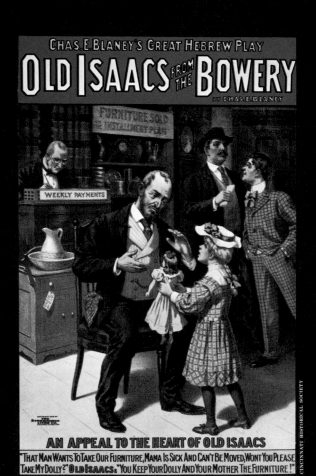

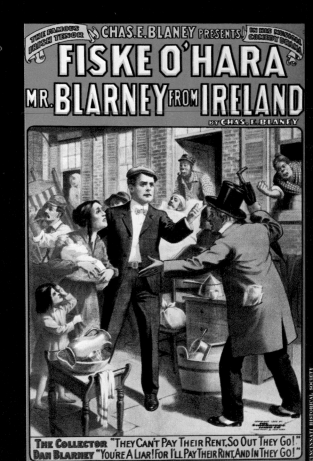

Gay Nineties: 1890 opened a decade that brought tremors of change and unease throughout the land, and before the ten years had passed there were bloody railroad and steel strikes, a brutal depression, a desperate political revolt by farmers that took the name of Populism, and the hotly debated leap into imperial responsibility that sent American young men to fight guerrillas in the Philippine jungles. New social problems seemed insoluble without the destruction of old and cherished values, and people were afraid; this fear attached itself to whatever was "alien"—including the genuine aliens who were entering in an apparently endless procession.

The climate of anxiety was reflected in a curious organization known as the American Protective Association. It was Midwestern in origin, founded in Clinton, Iowa, in 1887 by a Maryland-born lawyer named Henry F. Bowers. Members took an oath to use all their power to "strike the shackles and chains of blind obedience to the Roman Catholic Church" from men's minds, and "promote the interest of all Protestants. . . ." The Pope was the enemy still: papal agents, Irish politicians, were in control of the great cities; papal propagandists demanded tax moneys for parochial schools; the Pope even sent a delegate, Monsignor Satolli, to Washington in 1893 for purposes of secret and sinister intent, concealed behind a diplomatic façade. Thousands of Bowers' countrymen believed such distortions of fact. When the well-known printer and author Elbert Hubbard visited an Illinois friend in 1893, he asked his host if he intended to visit the Chicago World's Fair. The host gazed at him in shock. "Did I not know that the Catholics had been ordered by the Pope to burn the barns and houses of all heretics?" No Protestant dared leave his property untended for a moment.

Thus fantastic night riders—cloaked in papal purple—galloped through the nightmares of rural Protestant mid-America. The American Protective Association grew mainly where the corn grew, and when it affected cities at all, they were often part of the agrarian economic complex—Omaha, Kansas City, Duluth. Exactly how strong the group became is disputed; estimates of membership ranged from 100,000 to 2,500,000 people. In any case, neither major national party endorsed the A.P.A., as both Republicans and Democrats knew the importance of the swelling urban vote—which contained important Catholic elements. The movement faded away soon after 1896.

New England was half a continent away from the heart of A.P.A. territory, but in the 1890s some of her most distinguished sons were gnawed by the same kinds of shadowy suspicion that beset the Middle West. In Boston and nearby Cambridge the enemy was not simply the Catholic but any freshly arrived foreigner of "new stock," and he was a dangerous type, even when not engaged in a plot, simply by virtue of being himself. "Wide open and unguarded stand our gates," warned Thomas Bailey Aldrich in 1892 in the *Atlantic Monthly*,

And through them presses a wild motley throng—
Men from the Volga and the Tartar steppes,
Featureless figures from the Hoang-Ho,
Malayan, Scythian, Teuton, Kelt, and Slav,
Flying the Old World's poverty and scorn;
These bringing with them unknown gods and rites,
Those, tiger passions, here to stretch their claws. . . .

Aldrich had taken considerable poetic license. Migration from the "Hoang-Ho" had already been cut off by the Chinese Exclusion Act, and the Malayan and Scythian components of contemporary immigration, if they existed at all, were invisible to the keepers of records. Yet the sentiment behind Aldrich's imagery was common in the circles in which he moved. The descendants of the Puritan fathers were by and large gloomy, though there were exceptions among them. Politically speaking, they were losing control of—and to a great degree giving up—their inheritance. It was bad enough that the nation no longer looked to the Adams clan when seeking Presidents, and that no Daniel Webster bestrode the Senate like a colossus; but in addition the cities of southern New England were passing into the hands of the Irish. The established middle class was chiefly interested in business, and few "gentlemen" would lower themselves to compete for political power. In 1890, sixty-eight towns and cities in Massachusetts were controlled by Irish politicians. The sons of the wretched Popish peasants who had streamed ashore in the 1840s were making laws for townships laid out by Winthrops and Eliots.

New England's economic hegemony was on the decline, too. In shipping she had long ago lost primacy. Her bankers and investors and insurance companies had prudently put money into Western railroads, mines, and other ventures yielding incomes that tastefully supported the region's old families; but the really big industrial empires were not in New England hands, and the depression of 1893–97 confronted with ruin the thousands of Yankees who lived by clipping coupons. (Henry Adams wrote later that men died like flies under the strain.) New England's farms were largely exhausted. Furthermore, the factories that had produced clocks and sewing machines and guns and textiles, the factories that had made the names of Waterbury and Lowell and Hartford and Nashua and Providence

The shadows of their immigrant origins loom over restrictionist American plutocrats in this watercolor proof for a Puck *cartoon.*

famous, had grown old. Their aging machinery produced goods at smaller and smaller profit. In addition, those factories were worked by a labor force of French-Canadian, Irish, and other immigrant toilers whose social needs would clearly never be supplied by New England frugality.

Confronted by such a cheerless prospect of the present, old-stock New Englanders turned to a nostalgic, almost reverent re-examination of their past. A conviction grew among the elite families, particularly those rich in sons with Harvard degrees, that the institutions created by the English immigrants of the seventeenth and eighteenth centuries were incomparably great and, in fact, *the* essential foundations of American excellence.

This outlook was strengthened by an academic development, the rise of a "scientific" history, which tried to apply Darwin's theories of evolution to social institutions. It was noted, for example, that certain kinds of political behavior had originated among particular "races," who carried them to new environments where they flourished or failed. If they did thrive, it was proof of the biological superiority of the initial stock. New England-born or New England-trained historians, such as Herbert Baxter Adams of Johns Hopkins or Albert

Bushnell Hart of Harvard, taught that self-government had first been practiced among the Teutonic peoples in ancient days. The Saxons, one branch of the family, had taken the democratic passion with them when they invaded Britain at various times before the medieval era. The English settlers in North America, a mixture of "bloods" denominated Anglo-Saxon, had made the instinctive yearning for individual liberty their gift to the future United States. As Herbert Baxter Adams said, the purpose of his Hopkins seminar was "to show the continuity of English institutions in American." To understand the town meeting, one went back to Magna Carta, and beyond that to tribal councils of war in the German forest.

This kind of Anglo-Saxonism was both comical and potentially sinister. Its Germanophilia contrasted oddly with the slighting popular image of the "Dutchman" in America as a beer guzzler with a droll accent; further, its adherents did not explain what had happened to that ingrained Teutonic love of liberty in Kaiser Wilhelm's day. It credited what clearly were acquired social traits to racial instinct. One found the statistician Richmond Mayo-Smith, for instance, insisting that good humor and a concern for the material comfort of the masses were qualities which came naturally *only* to descendants of pre-Revolutionary New England. This attitude of course included a kind of snobbery that was particularly brutal and unbeatable because it judged a man on "scientific grounds."

Since Anglo-Saxon blood was the seed of true Americanism, then the national future was in mortal jeopardy if Anglo-Saxons were becoming a minority in the land, overwhelmed by the descendants of the fecund immigrants. So in 1894 the Immigration Restriction League of Boston was founded, to carry on a vigorous campaign. Restrictionists in other localities quickly followed suit. The League's instruments were the usual ones of lobbyists and propagandists—letters, articles, leaflets, clubs, speeches, and forums. Though relatively few in number, its members were influential. They were soon found throughout the country, and they had ready access to the public ear. Eventually they included such men as Massachusetts Senator Henry Cabot Lodge, the popular author Owen Wister (who wrote *The Virginian*, the prototypal Western novel), and the social worker Robert A. Woods. There were also many academics in the League: historian John Fiske; economists John R. Commons, William Z. Ripley, and Thomas N. Carver; sociologist Edward Alsworth Ross; and university presidents, including Stanford's David Starr Jordan and Francis A. Walker of M.I.T. These men were the turn-of-the-century equivalents of Arthur M. Schlesinger, Jr., Jacques Barzun, Henry A. Kissinger, Eric Goldman, and John Kenneth Galbraith—educators whose words and works made headlines and who were sought out by men of power. When *they* talked about the problem of immigration with the apparent detachment of scientists discussing rock formations, they deployed a formidable power to influence public opinion against immigrants. It was a sign that even in 1901, at the start of immigration's biggest single decade, the concept of the open gate was in serious trouble.

In effect, the Immigration Restriction League purposefully cast suspicion upon the capacity of any immigrants, other than those from Northern Europe, to become Americanized. It was part and parcel of the anxious national argument over what "Americanization" meant.

Well, what did it mean? Was it successfully learning to cope with the problems of a new environment—securing housing, employment, schooling for the young or medicine for the sick and aged, without much dependence on influential outsiders? The immigrants were doing that in great numbers.

A study of Massachusetts in 1914 showed a strong pattern of mutual help among immigrant groups. The Greeks there, for example, did not let their countrymen wander alone through the labyrinth of urban life. Each sizable Greek community had an organization that was quasi-governmental in nature, going so far as to lay a tax of a cent on every loaf of bread sold to Greeks, with the income going toward support of the churches. The national Pan-Hellenic Union, which had twenty branches in Massachusetts, collected dues, paid sick and death benefits, and represented Greek immigrants in conflicts with loan sharks, landlords, and employers. Thirty-one consumer co-operatives in Massachusetts, organized around nationality groups, helped Italians, Finns, Swedes, French-Canadians, Poles, and others to stretch their dollars. Jews adrift in the cities that were like no *shtetl* they ever knew could find directions, counsel, loans, and interpreters at the offices of the Hebrew Immigrant Aid Society. The Lithuanians had sixty mutual benefit societies in the Commonwealth, while Poles had a National Alliance and a Catholic Alliance, as well as a Young Men's Alliance that provided reading rooms, classes in English and civics, and recreational facilities. The language might be that of Pulaski and the national spirit Polish, but the "foreigners" were doing much the same thing that the pious founders of the Y.M.C.A. had undertaken in the 1850s when they provided a haven for American country boys who were in their own way "immigrating" into cities that were strewn with temptations and difficulties.

Curiously enough, many native Americans saw these ethnically based societies as evidence that the foreigners were clannishly resisting incorporation into the main currents of life in the United States. This was an attitude shared even by some immigrants, who made it their business to shed every vestige of "greenhorn" style as fast as possible. But there was another possible perspective. Self-reliance was said to be part of the American strain; so newcomers who divorced themselves as soon as possible from dependence on Anglo-Saxon charity were well on the way to useful citizenship. And for most people, self-reliance demanded a pride in self that was nourished by nationality identification. The Italian who felt despised by old Americans as a "wop" was apt to stand taller when his neighborhood Italian association reminded him that he was an heir of Garibaldi; such self-esteem prepared him for new American responsibilities and obligations. And the foreign-language newspaper, whose presence on the doorstep was taken by some to be a sign of the householder's slowness to give up his old ways, was often more insistent on the superiority of all things American than many an English-language newspaper.

Did Americanization mean succeeding in society by

professional advancement and economic improvement? Of course, thousands of uncelebrated immigrants were quite successful on those terms, working their way up to become foremen and supervisors, independent businessmen, property owners—men who had good reason to say, as did one Italian immigrant, that in the adopted country, "work was rewarded with abundance." Many a grandchild of the great 1900–1914 migration knows men now in their sixties and seventies who began life in America with no more than the clothes they stood up in, and ended it with bank accounts, pleasant homes, college-educated children, and other sweets of life. These stories are deservedly commonplace whenever positive things are said about the promise of America. Then there are the rosters of immigrants who became exceptional figures in business, the arts, science, sport, and entertainment. Entire books have been filled with the doings of such worthies, who range in variety from John Jacob Astor and Andrew Carnegie to Victor Herbert and Charlie Chaplin.

But so much has been made of those who succeeded in this fashion that there is danger of forgetting the contributions of those who did not advance at all. The prism of nostalgia distorts the images of thousands upon thousands of immigrants who contributed their labor to the industrialization of America and received no more than calluses in return. One Slavic immigrant declared, "*My people do not live in America, they live underneath America. America goes on over their heads. America does not begin till a man is a workingman, till he is earning two dollars a day.*" Some never reached that plateau. Restrictionists condemned these "failures" as biological inferiors. Even the ethnic historian, eager to refute the restrictionists by focusing on his group's highest achievements, has ignored them. Yet to ignore them—to suggest that only the economically successful in the United States are truly American—has disturbing implications.

Did Americanization involve bringing up children to embrace American styles of life? In that case, almost all immigrants were Americanized, even if only involuntarily. Except in communities tightly knit by some factor such as religion or racial exclusion (a Chinatown, for example), it was impossible to keep youngsters properly deferential to parental authority and thus bound by old-country traditions. The schoolroom was the first separating force. "It is sad to notice," one commentator wrote, "the patronizing attitude that the child assumes toward his father and mother after a few months in the public school." And a New York district superintendent, Julia Richman, summed up the experience with this observation: "The parents remain foreign; the children become American. There is thus created an almost unbridgeable gulf between the two. Difference in taste, customs and language brings about domestic shipwreck." Half a century before it struck

Goldie Mabovitz Myerson— Golda Meir, later the Prime Minister of Israel—is shown at left playing the part of Liberty in a pageant of Jewish history that was performed in Milwaukee in 1919. Mrs. Meir was brought as a child from Kiev, Russia, eventually taught public school in Milwaukee, and became a member of the labor-oriented Poale Zion Chasidim, which presented the 1919 pageant. She emigrated to Palestine in 1921 to live in a collective-farm village.

upper middle-class American families, the pain of the "generation gap" was an unhappy reality to the once close-knit, patriarchally led immigrant household. All successful parenthood must end in the loss of the child, but immigrant fathers and mothers, who saw their off-spring move into a world of different gods and satisfactions and roles, lost them twice over.

What, then, was the genuine meaning of Americanization? While the newcomers struggled to find it in experience, those who were already "old" Americans ranged widely in their search for the answer.

Some seemed to believe that, whatever the process might have been in the past, it would not work with the post-1900 mass arrivals, because the forces propelling earlier immigrants up the ladder of successful acculturation had burned out.

Men arrived at this conclusion by several routes. Samuel Gompers, president of the American Federation of Labor, came to it as a result of his decision to build a labor movement around skilled workers. The success of the movement, in his eyes, required that there not be a large pool of unskilled workers from which employers could draw replacements when there were showdowns with the unions. And this, in turn, meant keeping out the impoverished new immigrant, an ironic attitude for Gompers, who in his childhood had emigrated from England. Yet his thin turtle mouth uttered speech after speech built around the idea that he expressed typically in a letter to a Congressman: ". . . both the intelligence and the prosperity of our working people are endangered by the present immigration. Cheap labor, ignorant labor, takes our jobs and cuts our wages." Interestingly, converting cheap and ignorant labor to well-paid and trained labor through organization and education was not on Gompers' agenda.

Edward Alsworth Ross thought that immigrants could never take intelligent part in the kind of "rational" politics—concerned with public health, conservation, control of trusts, and protection of the weak —that he and his progressive friends espoused. When he saw a billboard during a 1912 election campaign in Chicago listing candidates named Kelly, Cassidy, Alschuler, Pfaelzer, Romano, and Knitckoff, he did not find it heartening evidence of the flexibility of the American political order. Instead, he despaired of cleaning up corruption in a polyglot community. "The clashings that arise from the presence among us of many voters with medieval minds are sheer waste of energy," he wrote. How could great issues be explored by Cassidys and Romanos who preferred to fight over whose neighborhood would get new playgrounds? Sadly he reflected that the "little homogeneous peoples are forg-

ing ahead of us . . . and learning to look pityingly upon us as a chaos rather than a people."

Even sympathetic social workers among the slum-trapped foreign-born poor sometimes despaired, as one of them revealed to Jacob Riis:

They are down on the scrub level; there you find them and have to put them to such use as you can. They don't know anything else, and that is what makes it so hard to find work for them. Even when they go into a shop to sew, they come out mere machines, able to do only one thing, which is a small part of the whole they do not grasp. And thus, without the slightest training for the responsibilities of life, they marry and transmit their incapacity to another generation that is so much worse to start off with.

Behind even this well-meaning disparagement was the feeling that so large and varied a human swarm as the new immigrants could never be fused into the national whole. And that fusion was assumed to be indispensable to a healthy public life. Richmond Mayo-Smith wrote in 1890 that in order to have the "strength begotten of common national ideals and aspirations" there must be "one language, one political practice, one patriotism and one ideal of social development."

For Mayo-Smith, Ross, and many of their fellow social scientists, the single language had, naturally, to be English, and the single standard of social and political behavior to be "Anglo-Saxon." The immigrant should be "assimilated" into the dominant English-born culture, and if this were impossible, he should be turned away. But had it ever been possible? Anglo-Saxonism seemed to assume that it had been.

At the same time there were enthusiasts of America who thought the amalgamation did take place, but in a different way. In a 1908 play by an English Jew, Israel Zangwill, young David Quixano and his Gentile sweetheart, hand in hand, look out on New York and David says:

There she lies, the great Melting-Pot—listen! Can't you hear the roaring and the bubbling? There gapes her mouth—the harbour where a thousand mammoth feeders come from the ends of the world to pour in their human freight. Ah, what a stirring and a seething! Celt and Latin, Slav and Teuton, Greek and Syrian,—black and yellow—
VERA: Jew and Gentile—
DAVID: Yes, East and West, and North and South, the palm and the pine, the pole and the equator, the crescent and the cross—how the great Alchemist melts and fuses them with his purging flame! Here shall they all unite to build the Republic of Man and the Kingdom of God. . . .

But although the United States has been called a

melting pot again and again by historians justly eager to celebrate American diversity, there has been no time when the nation's peoples have been on the verge of wholly losing their identities as Jew and Gentile, Celt and Teuton, or, most especially, white and red and black and yellow human beings. If the Great Alchemist has made much progress in creating a society blind to color, religion, and national origin, it is a secret to every political boss, every child who has fought in the schoolyard with or against some "minority group," every sociologist scanning an urban neighborhood population map, every employer and union organizer and teacher and social worker and minister who has dealt with large numbers of Americans.

In reality, few people in 1908 wanted a national immigration policy that would encourage such a fusion—any more than, sixty years later, they would support a definition of "integration" that meant a blending of races into indistinguishability. The inability, real or imagined, of immigrants to be amalgamated was simply an excuse not to accept them.

But there were Americans who wished to continue to accept the streams of immigrants, and they developed a concept of Americanization that offered a possibility of mating large-scale immigration with a consistent national character. Perhaps, they seemed to say, it was possible to thrive in a multilingual, multicultural society. Even at Harvard, the nursery of so many restrictionists, there were Yankees who felt disdain for those who wrung their hands over the supposed invasion. Harvard's president, Charles W. Eliot, noted that "the different races already in this country live beside each other, and all produce in time good citizens of the Republic." The philosopher Josiah Royce, commenting on the "scientific" sociology and history of some of his colleagues, wondered "whether a science which mainly devotes itself to proving that we ourselves are the salt of the earth, is after all so exact as it aims to be." William James, distinguished in both philosophy and psychology, privately wished that "the Anglo-Saxon race would drop its sniveling cant" about the white man's burden. A vigorous anti-imperialist, James rejected notions of racial superiority, and he was also impatient of religious bigotry. Once, when a hotel sent him an advertising circular that said that "applications from Hebrews cannot be considered," he fired back a one-line reply: "I propose to return the boycott."

A few young Americans from proper homes, already incubating the revolt against Main Street that would erupt in the 1920s, found the coarse vitality of the "foreign" neighborhoods exhilarating. A man could stand in New York's lower East Side and look around

him at surging life: peddlers bawling the contents of their pushcarts—hot chestnuts, chick-peas, sweet potatoes, pickles, watermelon, and corn; pots, pans, knives, scissors, and can openers; petticoats, shawls, stockings, and scarves. He could hear Salvation Army Sallys wooing the bums home to Jesus with tambourine and trumpet, and Socialist orators lambasting the bourgeoisie in Russian, Italian, Yiddish, and English. On a saint's day, there might be processions winding through the streets, and booths with statuettes and pastries and ribbons for sale lining the sidewalk, and the popping of firecrackers. And on any day there would be children screeching in Chinese, Hungarian, Greek, and Rumanian, dodging wagons, playing hopscotch or jacks or marbles, jumping rope, fishing for coins through sidewalk gratings. The visitor could sample half a dozen cuisines in as many blocks, or, like the writer Hutchins Hapgood, drop into a Yiddish theater and sit down next to "the sweat-shop woman with her baby, the day-laborer, the small . . . shopkeeper, the . . . Ghetto rabbi and scholar, the poet, the journalist."

In 1915, Horace M. Kallen, an educator and philosopher, proposed that rather than a homogeneous culture, there might be a "great and truly democratic commonwealth," whose form was

. . . that of the Federal republic; its substance a democracy of nationalities, co-operating voluntarily and autonomously in the enterprise of self-realization. . . . The common language of the commonwealth, the language of its great political tradition, is English, but each nationality expresses its emotional and voluntary life in its own language, in its own inevitable aesthetic and intellectual forms. . . . an orchestration of mankind.

Four years later, the English-born leader of Chicago's Ethical Society, Horace J. Bridges, put it even more sharply in a book called *On Becoming an American*. Bridges declared that immigrants ought to glory in their own folkways rather than shedding them as they rose in the American economic hierarchy—the same message being beamed at educated young blacks today. There was "yet no fixed or final type" of American, said Bridges, nor could there ever be. Let the newcomers, he wrote,

keep alive Italian and German music and literature, Balkan handicrafts, and the folk-lore and folk dances of the Old World:—not for the sake of the Old World, but as elements contributory to American culture. . . . There is no such thing as humanity-in-general, into which the definite, heterogeneous, living creature can be melted down. . . . The business of America is to get rid of mechanical uniformity.

Adult naturalization classes such as this one made available both daytime and nighttime instruction to future American citizens.

But in 1919 the hour was late. In fact, the nation had already reached the climax of debate and had taken the first steps toward racially biased immigration restriction.

Even before 1900, the government had begun to shut out immigrants who it felt were likely to cause problems. From the beginning it mingled economic, moral, and medical judgments highhandedly. An act of 1891 denied entry to paupers, polygamists, and "persons suffering from loathsome and contagious diseases." In 1903, barriers were raised against epileptics, prostitutes, professional beggars, anarchists, and persons who believed in the overthrow by force of the government of the United States. These last two categories were in part a reaction to the assassination of President McKinley in 1901; though the murderer, Leon Czolgosz, was American, his parents were Polish, and he was an anarchist. In 1907 to the list of undesirables were added "imbeciles," tuberculosis victims, and those who had "committed a crime involving moral turpitude."

Restrictionists meanwhile pressed for a literacy test.

True, it would not satisfy those who feared that the mere presence of too many aliens, literate or not, would water the nation's lifeblood; but it would tend to raise the economic level of incoming immigrants. Bills calling for such a test were introduced in Congress often. Versions were beaten in 1898, 1902, and 1906, presumably out of regard for the ethnic vote. One was passed in 1896 but was vetoed by President Cleveland; another that made its way through Congress in 1913 was vetoed by President Taft. President Wilson also vetoed one in 1915 in a message that got down to basics. Such requirements, he said, were not "tests of quality or of character or of personal fitness, but tests of opportunity. Those who come seeking an opportunity are not to be admitted unless they have already had one of the chief . . . opportunities they seek, the opportunity of education."

In 1906 President Theodore Roosevelt had decided to meet the immigration problem by a device that would simultaneously appease restrictionists, avoid any immediate affront to foreign-born voters and their children, and preserve the theory that his was a progressive administration governing only on the basis of intelligence marshaled by experts. He proposed that Congress create a commission to study the subject exhaustively, as a basis for future legislation. The enabling legislation was passed in 1907, setting up a nine-member body—three each chosen by the House and Senate's presiding officers, and three by the President; supposedly all were to be nonpartisan specialists.

The panel was known as the Dillingham Commission, after its chairman, William Paul Dillingham, a Senator from Vermont. Its impartiality was questionable, to begin with. The chief among its experts, a professor of political economy named Jeremiah Jenks, recalled a time in his life when he and his academic colleagues at Cornell were for the most part "proud . . . of being Anglo-Saxons," and thought that anyone "born in New England must be particularly good." He believed in restriction, and so did the secretary of the commission, Morton E. Crane, whom Theodore Roosevelt had chosen on the recommendation of his old friend Henry Cabot Lodge.

The Dillingham Commission hired a staff of three hundred, spent a million dollars, and labored over statistics and reports for an impressive three years. The end product was two volumes of summary and forty volumes of material, presented to Congress for adoption in 1910. It contained a *Dictionary of Races*, and long analyses of the laws governing migration, of economic conditions in Europe, and of the effects of immigration on literacy, charity, crime, vice, and insanity in the United States. As a document it seemed overpoweringly authoritative—but in its organization and conclusions, the report remorselessly stacked cards.

The *Dictionary of Races*, for example, purported to classify people on the basis of a language, but it deserted its own rules when necessary. On a linguistic basis, Yiddish-speaking Jews might theoretically have been classed with the Germans, since Yiddish is largely a German dialect, but they were not, any more than the English-speaking Irish were classed among the British stocks.

Time after time, data were compared for "old" and "new" immigrants as a whole, in ways that permitted misleading and adverse conclusions about the recent arrivals—conclusions that would have been different had the comparisons been made among specific nationality groups. As an instance, the commission matched arrivals for 1907 and departures for 1908. They found that the countries of the "old," pre-1890s, immigration furnished 22.7 per cent of the 1907 ingathering but only 8.9 per cent of those going back to Europe the following year. Those from the lands of the "new" immigration comprised 77.3 per cent of the 1907 arrivals but a huge 91.1 per cent of 1908's homeward-bound pilgrims. The implication was that the "new" immigrants furnished greater numbers of "birds of passage," who came to the United States to make a lot of money in a hurry and then get out. But when the figures were broken down by national origins, it turned out, of course, that each group was different in this respect. In 1908 the Italians and Croatians had high returnee rates. But more people of English, German, and Scandinavian stock per thousand left the country than was the case with the Armenians, "Hebrews," and Portuguese.

Crime rates were arranged in odd configurations; thus, "frequency of crime by type among different groups" supported the fraudulent notion that hot-blooded Italians committed more assaults than judicious native Americans. Much was made of literacy figures that proved "new" immigrants on the whole to be less literate than Americans; in the main body of the report such illiteracy was blamed on poverty, but in the summary it was blamed on "inherent racial tendencies." The commission found the conditions under which "new" immigrants worked usually deplorable, and asserted that this happened because the newcomers were "as a rule . . . tractable and easily managed." Yet a comparative investigation of the textile workers of the American South would have shown the proud descendants of the warlike Anglo-Saxons, native whites all, grinding away in circumstances as wretched as those in any New York sweatshop. The summary bristled with negative judgments: the Serbo-Croatians had "savage manners," the Poles were "high-strung," the Italians had "not attained distinguished success as farmers."

The commission had, as directed, laid the basis for the immigration policy finally adopted, but its conclusions were not implemented for some ten years after its report was filed. In the interim, the country was increasingly subjected to racist indoctrination. In 1915, *The Birth of a Nation* spread to millions of moviegoers the notion that Negroes in the South during Reconstruction had been gorilla-like despoilers of white women. As if on cue, Colonel William J. Simmons of Atlanta revived the Ku Klux Klan, to battle blacks, Jews, Catholics, and all foreigners who had, as one Klan leader put it, made the "Nordic American . . . a stranger in large parts of the land his fathers gave him." The Klan flourished in the South, the Midwest, and the Far West; it reached a strength of nearly four and a half million by 1924, and shook the Democratic Party as nothing had since the slavery issue.

In 1916 a distinguished New Yorker, Madison Grant,

published an influential work called *The Passing of the Great Race*. Grant was a Yale graduate, an attorney, amateur scientist, secretary of the New York Zoological Society, and a trustee of the Museum of Natural History. Said he: ". . . it has taken us fifty years to learn that speaking English, wearing good clothes, and going to school and to church, does not transform a negro into a white man. . . . We shall have a similar experience with the Polish Jew, whose dwarf stature, peculiar mentality, and ruthless concentration on self-interest are being engrafted upon the stock of the nation." The Jews, Grant declared, "adopt the language of the native American; they wear his clothes; they steal his name; and they are beginning to take his women, but they seldom adopt his religion or understand his ideals."

The whole nation was on the brink of a protracted frenzy. Its entry into the World War made hysteria respectable in a way, especially when it was aimed at foreigners. The logical objects of wartime xenophobia were two "old" immigrant groups, the Germans and the Irish; the latter group because it never developed any collective enthusiasm for the nation's British allies. But the popular fury that was unleashed against such representatives of Evil as dachshunds and band conductors who unwisely programmed Wagner, and against Irish speechmakers who damned King George V, was not fully spent by the effort. Much of it naturally boiled over on other foreigners, especially the "dagos" and "bohunks" who became involved with such left-wing organizations as the antiwar Socialist Party and Industrial Workers of the World. The public mind made persistent connection between foreigners—especially those with names ending in "-ski"—and militant radicalism. This linkage was strengthened enormously by the Russian Revolution, and in 1919 the usually urbane New York *Times* rebuked the Attorney General of the United States for advocating liberal immigration policies. These "ancient and outworn views," the paper said, were "not too pleasant to hear when, all over the country, alien or foreign-born agitators are carrying on in many languages . . . the Bolshevist and IWW propaganda for the overthrow of the Government." If the *Times* was so aroused, it was understandable that a Representative from Tennessee should say just a few years later: "We get the majority of the communists, the I.W.W.s, the dynamiters, and the assassins of public officers from the ranks of the present-day immigrant."

This, then, was the emotional environment: first, the ugly mood of a progressive nation girding itself up and battling for the millennium, then the country's disappointment and frustration in the peace, and the hangover of readjustment. Once the American involvement in the war began, it took only a few years to unhorse the advocates of unlimited asylum.

First came the passage of an act in 1917 that broadened the government's rights to keep out and expel undesirable aliens. The law also created a "barred zone" in the Southwest Pacific area, from which no immigrants could come—a measure to block any Orientals who might otherwise find a way through the existing barbed-wire entanglement of anti-Chinese and anti-Japanese policies. Finally, it required that, with a few

"You can't come in if you have a 'past,'" are the words of the New York City port official scrutinizing a newcomer in this cartoon, which appeared in the London *Daily Express in 1926.*

exceptions, those desiring admission be able to read a short passage in English or some other language. It was the literacy test again, and again Wilson vetoed it. But this time it was repassed over his veto.

The war was scarcely ended when a tide of refugees from the battle-scarred and hungry nations of Europe began to flow westward. Even the literacy test could not keep the numbers significantly down. Between June, 1920, and June, 1921, for example, there were some 805,000 admissions, more than sixty-five per cent of them from Central, Southern, and Eastern Europe; American consuls warned that thousands more would soon be following. In February of 1921 Ellis Island was so jammed that ships had to be diverted to Boston. Meanwhile, since the armistice, the nation had experienced a great Red scare, a brutal steel strike involving a work force that was largely foreign-born, and the start of the Sacco-Vanzetti case.

Congress had begun to react to all these stimuli. In April of 1920 the House Committee on Immigration and Naturalization employed Dr. Harry Laughlin, an expert in the study of human breeding, to dust off the Dillingham Commission report, analyze its data, and advise the country what should be done to protect its future generations. Dr. Laughlin did not render his verdict until late 1922: his tone is reflected in a key sentence, which declared that "making all logical allowances for environmental conditions, which may be unfavorable, . . . the recent immigrants as a whole, present a higher percentage of inborn socially inadequate qualities than do the older stocks."

The Senators and Representatives, however, did not wait those two and a half years before acting. In May, 1921, they passed a law that limited "the number of aliens of any nationality who may be admitted . . . in any fiscal year . . . to 3 per centum of the number of foreign-born persons of such nationality resident in the United States as determined by the . . . census of 1910. . . ." The impact of this first Quota Act was to reduce the allowable figure for immigrants to about 357,000 per year. Originally scheduled to terminate after one year, the law was extended for two more years in the spring of 1922.

Then, in 1924, the temporary measures of 1921 and 1922 were replaced by a long-term plan, the Johnson-Reed Act, which went even further to satisfy the restrictionists. For the next three years, quotas would be cut from three to two per cent, dropping the total permitted admissions to some 164,000: moreover, the base year of calculation would be set back to 1890, when the countries of the "new" immigrants were represented by smaller fractions of the populace than in 1910. After

1927, the law said, total immigration from outside the American continent was to be held to 150,000, with each nation's share proportionate to its representation by birth or descent in the American people of 1920. There was a little leeway: the allowable quota could go higher by as many as one hundred newcomers from each country that had made only a minimal contribution, or none at all, to the American breed before 1920. And no limits were placed on immigration from Canada, Central and South America, and the Caribbean. On the other hand, this generosity did not apply to Orientals. They were shut out completely, without any quotas at all, because by law, unless an Oriental was born in the United States, he was ineligible for citizenship.

The national-origins formula was anything but scientific as a measuring rod. At best, determining the ancestry of fifth- and sixth-generation Americans was chancy. It had to be done by statistical projections, in which guesswork naturally played a major role. There were no firm guidelines for classifying a European forefather's nationality, and the creation of new nations only compounded the problem. Did a grandparent from Galicia —Austro-Hungarian in 1914, Polish in 1920—count with the Poles, the Austrians, or the Hungarians? That, apparently, was up to immigration officials.

Such niceties were not the basic point, however. The point was revealed when the first quotas went into effect in 1929: more than half of all spaces were reserved for residents of the British Isles, whereas only 5,802 Italians and 6,524 Poles could be admitted. And the bureaucracy could use the ambiguities of classification to tighten the valves on various pipelines still further. Restrictionism had won.

Possibly, however, its victory was not so complete as at first it appeared. From Canada, the Caribbean, and Central and South America would come a steady stream of immigrants, many not white, most of them poor, Catholic, and Latin. Nonwhites from various United States territories and possessions would also negotiate the corridors of entry. Total immigration sank only slowly at first—307,255 in 1928, 241,700 in 1930. Then the Great Depression succeeded for a time where the law had failed; in 1933 immigration dropped to a twentieth-century low of 23,068. But after World War II it began to rise again.

Nevertheless, 1924 was a turning point. Not only had a set of laws been written; a chapter of history had been closed, a certain spirit snuffed out. There would be more immigrants, more shiftings and mingling of peoples—spurred on by war, social upheaval, and the special needs of the United States. But after three hundred years, the awesome transoceanic migration was over.

Foreign Labor

IN THEIR WORDS

If many people came to America simply because it was the Land of Liberty, a far greater number came for more mundane reasons: they were impoverished, hungry, out of work. Certainly—the enthusiasts notwithstanding—most of them knew that the streets of America were not paved with gold, but even so an aura of richness brightened the national image and lit the hopes of immigrants. In the United States there would be jobs that paid more than starvation wages. That expectation drew many across the ocean. However, a common immigrant experience had always been that the facts of life in America varied discouragingly from what one heard in Europe—or from what one hoped for despite what one heard. Even as the nation's great industrial expansion was taking place, labor surpluses were common; indeed, it is evident that some major employers took steps that helped to ensure that condition. The material anthologized in the next several pages speaks of jobs that paid better than those in Europe but in an economic context that made the higher pay meaningless. It contains charges that foreigners were glutting the labor market, and it describes appalling working conditions and a general lack of protection given the laboring man; from these circumstances grew leaders —many of them foreign-born or born to immigrants in America—who challenged the system in speeches and strikes. Such things reflected on all immigrants and thus contributed to the movement that closed the national gates.

"You Must Get a Job"

"One morning my friends woke me up at five o'clock and said, 'Now, if you want life, liberty and happiness . . . you must push yourself. You must get a job.'" So wrote a Lithuanian meat packer in Chicago early in the 1900s. But finding employment was hard. Often the job had to be bought with a bribe. At work a man kept his mouth shut; even joining a union might cost him his place. A slumping market brought layoffs and slowdowns, and the laborer had as little defense against such eventualities as he did against the consequences of being hurt on the job. For in that Darwinistic age, the men in charge thought that such vulnerability was good for the worker and the species.

Upton Sinclair's The Jungle *caused an uproar in 1906 as an exposé of unsanitary practices in the meat industry. But it was intended basically to be a novel of protest against the treatment of labor —which is the burden of this selection.*

Grandmother Majauszkiene had come to America with her son at a time when so far as she knew there was only one other Lithuanian family in the district; the workers had all been Germans then —skilled cattle-butchers that the packers had brought from abroad to start the business. Afterward, as cheaper labor had come, these Germans had moved away. The next were the Irish . . . but the most of those who were working in the packing-houses had gone away at the next drop in wages—after the big strike. The Bohemians had come then, and after them the Poles. People said that old man Durham himself was responsible for these immigrations; he had sworn that he would fix the people of Packingtown so that they would never again call a strike on him, and so he had sent his agents into every city and village in Europe to spread the tale of the chances of work and high wages at the stockyards. The people had come in hordes; and old Durham had squeezed them tighter and tighter, speeding them up and grinding them to pieces, and sending for new ones. The Poles, who had come by tens of thousands, had been driven to the wall by the Lithuanians, and now the Lithuanians were giving way to the Slovaks. Who there was poorer and more

miserable than the Slovaks, Grandmother Majauszkiene had no idea, but the packers would find them, never fear. It was easy to bring them, for wages were really much higher, and it was only when it was too late that the poor people found out that everything else was higher too. They were like rats in a trap, that was the truth; and more of them were piling in every day. . . .

The men upon the killing-beds felt also the effects of the slump . . . The big packers did not turn their hands off and close down, . . . but they began to run for shorter and shorter hours. They had always required the men to be on the killing-beds and ready for work at seven o'clock, although there was almost never any work to be done till the buyers out in the yards had gotten to work, and some cattle had come over the chutes. That would often be ten or eleven o'clock, which was bad enough, in all conscience; but now, in the slack season, they would perhaps not have a thing for their men to do till late in the afternoon. And so they would have to loaf around, in a place where the thermometer might be twenty degrees below zero! At first one would see them running about, or skylarking with each other, trying to keep warm; but before the day was over they would become quite chilled through and exhausted, and, when the cattle finally came, so near frozen that to move was an agony. And then suddenly the place would spring into activity, and the merciless "speeding-up" would begin!

There were weeks at a time when

Jurgis went home after such a day as this with not more than two hours' work to his credit—which meant about thirty-five cents. There were many days when the total was less than half an hour, and others when there was none at all. The general average was six hours a day, which meant for Jurgis about six dollars a week; and this six hours of work would be done after standing on the killing-bed till one o'clock, or perhaps even three or four o'clock, in the afternoon. Like as not there would come a rush of cattle at the very end of the day, which the men would have to dispose of before they went home, often working by electric light till nine or ten, or even twelve or one o'clock, and without a single instant for a bite of supper. The men were at the mercy of the cattle. Perhaps the buyers would be holding off for better prices—if they could scare the shippers into thinking that they meant to buy nothing that day, they could get their own terms. . . . Then, too, a number of cars were apt to arrive late in the day, now that the roads were blocked with snow, and the packers would buy their cattle that night, to get them cheaper, and then would come into play their iron-clad rule, that all cattle must be killed the same day they were bought. . . . And so on Christmas Eve Jurgis worked till nearly one o'clock in the morning, and on Christmas Day he was on the killing-bed at seven o'clock.

All this was bad; and yet it was not the worst. For after all the hard work a man did, he was paid for only part of it.

Jurgis had once been among those who scoffed at the idea of these huge concerns cheating; and so now he could appreciate the bitter irony of the fact that it was precisely their size which enabled them to do it with impunity. One of the rules on the killing-beds was that a man who was one minute late was docked an hour; and this was economical, for he was made to work the balance of the hour—he was not allowed to stand round and wait. And on the other hand if he came ahead of time he got no pay for that—though often the bosses would start up the gang ten or fifteen minutes before the whistle. And this same custom they carried over to the end of the day; they did not pay for any fraction of an hour—for "broken time." A man might work full fifty minutes, but if there was no work to fill out the hour, there was no pay for him. Thus the end of every day was a sort of lottery—a struggle, all but breaking out into open war between the bosses and the men, the former trying to rush a job through and the latter trying to stretch it out. Jurgis blamed the bosses for this, though the truth to be told it was not always their fault; for the packers kept them frightened for their lives. . . .

The sweatshop was once practically synonymous with immigrant labor. The text that follows is from an article on "The 'Sweating System' in New York City" by Congressman John De Witt Warner, in Harper's Weekly *for February 9, 1895.*

The materials are cut and "bunched" for each garment by the manufacturer. They are then distributed in large lots to special jobbers, known as "contractors". . . . With this distribution the wholesaler washes his hands of the business, his ignorance of how and where his goods are actually made up being as ideal as intentional.

Not far from one-half of the goods thus distributed are made up in the contractors' factories. As to the other half, the first contractor sublets the work to a "sweater," whose shop is generally one of the two larger rooms of a tenement flat accommodating from six to fifteen or twenty "sweating" employés—men, women, and children. . . . One-fourth of our ready-made and somewhat of our custom-made clothing are thus put together. . . .

Single families, inhabiting one or more rooms, generally having a family as subtenants, or a number of lodgers or boarders, subcontract work from the tenement "sweaters." Thus by tenement "home-workers" are made another one-fourth of our ready-made clothing and a much larger proportion of our children's clothing. . . .

From the wholesale manufacturer, handling each year a product of millions, through the contractor to the "sweater," and so on to the "home-worker," the steps are steadily downward—of decreasing responsibility, comfort, and compensation. The profit of each (except the wretch at the bottom) is "sweated" from the next below him.

The contractors' shops are much like other factories—the large proportion of foreign labor and a tendency toward long hours being their main distinctions. In the tenement "sweat shops" unhealthy and unclean conditions are almost universal, and those of filth and contagion common. The employés are in the main foreign-born and newly-arrived. The proportion of female labor is large, and child labor is largely used. Wages are from a fourth to a third less than in the larger shops. As to hours, there is no limit except the endurance of the employés, the work being paid for by the "task," and the task so adjusted as to drive from the shop any employé who, whenever he is given a bench, will not work to the limit of physical endurance, the hours of labor being rarely less than twelve, generally thirteen or fourteen, frequently from fifteen to eighteen, hours in the twenty-four.

The lot, however, of these "sweatshop" workers is luxury compared to that of those engaged in tenement home work. The home-worker is generally a foreigner just arrived, and frequently a woman whose husband is dead, sick, or worthless, and whose children keep her at home. Of these tenement home workers there are more women than men, and children are as numerous as both. The work is carried on in the one, two, or three rooms occupied by the family, with its subtenants or boarders. No pretense is made of separating shop work from household affairs. The hours observed are those which endurance alone limits. Children are worked to death beside their parents. Contagious diseases are especially prevalent among these people; but even death disturbs from their occupation only the one or two necessary to dispose of the body.

As to the wages in this "tenement home work," there is nothing which can properly be so called. The work is secured by underbidding of tenement sweat shops, and is generally piecework, one process of which may be attended to by the head of the family, and the rest by its other members according to their capacity. Those engaged are so generally compelled to accept rather than to choose their work that it is taken without reference to the possibility of gaining a livelihood therefrom, the miserable workers earning what they can, begging to supplement it, and dying or being supported as paupers when they fail.

Homeworking: a romantic view

The Twelve-Hour Day

A small firm's sole employee could settle questions of wages and hours directly and personally with his boss. The more people an employer hired, the less personal the arrangement became. As large industrial companies multiplied in the nineteenth century, it seemed that everywhere a laborer looked he had to deal with overwhelming power; the power was particularly formidable if he was foreign-born and spoke English poorly. At the same time, the work force grew huge itself, and the opposed masses spawned major issues. One of those issues was work time. The 1919 steel strike was caused in part by the fact that many men were on a twelve-hour day for a seven-day week.

One of the Boston Cabots—Charles M., a stockholder in U.S. Steel—commissioned writer John A. Fitch to prepare a report for other Steel stockholders on the hours of work in the steel industry, which employed thousands of immigrants. Fitch spent eleven months in Pittsburgh in 1907 and 1908, and followed that up with eight months of research in other steel communities in 1910 and 1911. The discussion below is from his pamphlet.

Steel making is a continuous industry. For economical and technical reasons it operates day and night, twenty-four hours every day. In a continuous industry there must be workmen on duty every hour in the twenty-four. . . . there must be all of the time a man for each job. . . .

In addition to being a continuous twenty-four hour industry, steel-making is also, in part, a continuous seven-day industry. Therefore, large numbers of men work not only twelve hours a day, but seven days a week. The Federal Bureau of Labor in a recent report to the United States Senate, on labor conditions in the steel industry, reported that out of 173,000 steel workers in those branches of the industry covered in the investigation about 20 per cent worked twelve hours a day, seven days a week.

Ten hours and twelve hours are terms that indicate a minimum; either is capable of indefinite extension and is often extended from an hour or two on up to incredible lengths. . . .

A twelve-hour man, you would naturally think, would be relieved by a man on the other shift at the end of his twelve hours. He generally is. But I have talked in the last year with twelve-hour steel workers who have been obliged to work thirty-six hours at a stretch because the other men did not relieve them. Such cases occurred not in any emergency, not because of a breakdown, but in the regular routine of events in the running of the mill. It is all very simple. Jones goes to work in the morning and works until night— twelve hours. Smith should take his place at that time, but Smith's wife is sick and he doesn't come out. The mill doesn't stop when Smith's wife is sick. It needs a man in a certain position, and what are the odds whether his name be Smith or Jones? Jones stays and works the night shift. Next morning his own day shift begins again; so he works that, too, before he goes home, making a total of thirty-six hours on duty. . . .

. . . turn to the decision of the Supreme Court of the state of Indiana in the case of Republic Iron and Steel Company *vs.* Ohler. The facts of the case are reviewed in the opinion of the court. Ohler got hurt at four o'clock in the morning of December 20, 1899, while working in a rolling mill at Frankton, Ind., a plant that has since been abandoned. He had begun the shift that ended so disastrously in the morning of December 18, forty-eight hours before. And he had worked, repairing a breakdown, all of these forty-eight hours. At the end of the thirty-sixth hour, he had told the foreman that he didn't believe that he could stand it any longer. The foreman told him that he must stay until the job was finished, as he wanted to start the mill the next morning at six o'clock. Ohler remembered that when, a few months previously he had refused to work on a Sunday, he had been discharged by this same foreman; so he stayed on and worked . . .

Yet these are the exceptional cases. Breakdowns that require several days to repair do not occur with any regularity. Twelve-hour men do not often have to work three shifts consecutively. But these exceptional cases are not so far removed from conditions that some men must meet regularly.

There is a very large class of workmen in the steel industry, many thousands of them throughout the country, who work consecutively either eighteen hours or twenty-four hours regularly every two weeks. This is so because the two shifts alternate working nights, the day shift of one week becoming the night shift of the next and so on. When the plant works only six days, this can be accomplished without difficulty, but in a seven-day plant it is made possible only through the institution known as the "long turn." . . . The [most] general custom . . . is for the day shift to get in line for night work by working a full twenty-four-hour period, Sunday and Sunday night, finishing Monday morning. That puts the night crew on to Monday's day shift and allows them twenty-four hours off duty. Where the change is made every week, each crew works six days in one week and eight in the next. In some plants the change is made only each two weeks. In that case, each man works the long turn once a month. . . .

In October, 1910, I talked with an employe of the Cambria Steel Company, an independent concern, who had one week a ten-hour day and next week a fourteen-hour night, and who every other Saturday night went out and worked through until Sunday night, a twenty-four-hour shift. It took him an hour to get from his home to the mill and another hour to go back. So his actual time away from home was twelve hours on day shift and sixteen hours at night.

"It's pretty hard to get rested in summer when you're on the night turn," he told me, "It's too hot to sleep well daytimes. But in the winter you can drop down and go to sleep anywheres, you're so tired. The day shift isn't so bad—ten hours long—but after you've worked the Sunday long turn, you're used up pretty bad. It takes several days to get over it."

The same month an employe of the Pennsylvania Steel Company, another independent, at Steelton, Penn., who had the same kind of a job, remarked to me: "I never get used to the long turn; it always leaves me nearly dead, and then on the end of it I go onto the night shift for a week—thirteen hours of work every night. I never get a decent rest in the day-time, and I feel miserable all the week. The end of the week on night turn comes Sunday morning. I get twenty-four hours off then, so I try to stay up and have dinner with the family; it's the only time in the week that I have with them—but it's pretty hard. I'm so sleepy all the time. . . ."

There are many company heads and plant managers who are opposed to a twelve-hour schedule, and probably they number many more than I would naturally think, for no individual, not even a president of a company, could change a schedule of hours over night. . . .

But there are steel men, nevertheless, who not only do not apologize for, but actively defend, the existing state of

CULVER PICTURES

A Bessemer converter being operated in a steel mill

affairs. A majority of the managers whom I have met, including representatives of nearly all of the largest steel companies in the United States, have defended the twelve-hour day.

The president of one of the big Steel Corporation subsidiaries, evidently a Darwinian, told me that it did the men good to work long hours. "Good men are developed through hardship," he said, "It is overcoming obstacles that makes men strong. Look at A——, for example"—referring to a vice-president

of a large company—"he worked twelve hours a day in a mill for a good many years and see what it did for him." The company in question employs 20,000 odd men and there are as many as two vice-presidential jobs in the company to which they may aspire. It was this same president who once told a committee of Congress that a twelve-hour day was necessary because the men didn't do their best in the earlier hours of work. It took them until the eighth hour to get their swing.

261

No Stable Anchorage

One of the major organizations that grew out of labor discontent was the Industrial Workers of the World—the I.W.W., the Wobblies; their enemies called them the I-Won't-Works. The Wobblies' goal was what they referred to as the O.B.U., the One Big Union, through which the workers would own the means of production. But although they did organize some laborers in heavy industry and led strikes in the Northeast, their principal strength lay among migratory workers in farming, mining, and lumbering in the West. An industrial-relations specialist, Robert W. Bruere, discussed in an article of 1918 the conditions that made the I.W.W. attractive to migrant laborers.

Bruere's interpretation of the I.W.W. appeared in Harper's Monthly, *July, 1918.*

According to our best information, approximately four-fifths of these migratory workers are men whose family ties have been broken—"womanless, voteless, and jobless men." Competent authorities estimate that about one-half of them are native Americans, and the other half men who have been uprooted by labor-brokers and padrones from their native ethnic and social environments; voluntary or forced immigrants from the agricultural districts of Ireland, from the Welsh and Cornish mines, from the hungry hills of Italy, Serbia, Greece, and Turkish Asia Minor. . . .

The division superintendent of a great Western railroad recently explained to me his reluctant part in the creation of the socially disintegrating conditions out of which the migratory workers and the rebellious propaganda of the I.W.W. have sprung.

"The men down East," he said, "the men who have invested their money in our road, measure our administrative efficiency by money return—by net earnings and dividends. Many of our shareholders have never seen the country our road was built to serve; they get their impression of it and of its people, not from living contact with men, but from the impersonal ticker. They judge us by quotations and the balance-sheet.

"The upshot is that we have to keep expenses cut close as a jailbird's hair. Take such a detail as the maintenance of ways, for example—the upkeep of tracks and road-beds. This work should be going on during the greater part of the year. But to keep costs down, we have crowded it into four months.

"It is impossible to get the number and quality of men we need by the offer of a four months' job. So we publish advertisements broadcast that read something like this:

'MEN WANTED! HIGH WAGES! PERMANENT EMPLOYMENT!'

We know when we put our money into these advertisements that they are—well, part of a pernicious system of sabotage. We know that we are not going to give permanent employment. But we lure men with false promises, and they come.

"At the end of four months we lay them off, strangers in a strange country, many of them thousands of miles from their old homes. We wash our hands of them. They come with golden dreams, expecting in many cases to build homes, rear families, become substantial American citizens. After a few weeks, their savings gone, the single men grow restless and start moving; a few weeks more and the married men bid their families good-by. They take to the road hunting for jobs, planning to send for their families when they find steady work. Some of them swing onto the freight-trains and beat their way to the nearest town, are broke when they get there, find the labor market oversupplied, and, as likely as not, are thrown into jail as vagrants. Some of them hit the trail for the woods, the ranches, and the mines.

The "Blanket Stiff"

He built the ROAD—
With others of his CLASS, he built the road,
Now o'er it, many a weary mile, he packs his load,
Chasing a JOB, spurred on by HUNGERS good.
He walks and walks, and wonders why
In H—-L, he built the road.

Many of them never find a stable anchorage again; they become hobos, vagabonds, wayfarers—migratory and intermittent workers, outcasts from society and the industrial machine. . . ."

This is a small but characteristic example of a vast system of human exploitation that has been developed by the powerful suction of our headlong industrial expansion, by the Gargantuan growth of our steel and packing industries, of our logging operations from Florida to the Pacific coast, of our feverish railroad and mining enterprises. Even in ordinary times these gold-brick advertisements are posted not only in the labor market of our great cities, but also in the distant agricultural and mountain villages across the sea. . . . During its recent investigation of labor disturbances in the Arizona copper country, the President's Mediation Commission found as many as thirty-two different nationalities represented in a single mining-camp. In the great mining city of Butte, Montana, one of the wealthiest sources of copper and of precious metals in the world, I recently found a score of alien tongues, but not so much as one night school for the teaching of English to foreigners. In the vast regions traveled by the migratory workers, especially in the states where prohibition has abolished the saloon, practically the only social refuge where these strangers are welcomed . . . is the union hall, and in the lumber and agricultural districts it is almost exclusively the I.W.W. headquarters. . . .

One outstanding result of our national trafficking in human beings has been the growth of a state of abnormal psychological tension between the masters and the strangers in the house. The state of mind I refer to is one which all travelers in foreign lands have mildly experienced. Most of us have felt it in a heightened form since the beginning of our war with Germany. In this time of apprehension and national peril we feel an instinctive suspicion of all persons whose names stamp them as of enemy origin, and we have an instinctive disposition to attribute all manifestations of violence tending to interfere with our defensive activities to the malice of alien enemies. Social and economic conditions in the isolated mining- and lumber-camps and those surrounding the remote farms and ranches of the plains are peculiarly productive of this abnormal psychological tension even in times of international peace.

The typical Arizona . . . mining town . . . is dropped carelessly at the bottom of some cañon between copper-bearing hills, with a main street of stores and hotels and banks, and the wretched little one-, two-, and three-room shacks clinging like lichens to the steep flanks of the barren mountains. In the early spring

School Arts Magazine, MAY, 1923

A 1923 chart of some symbols used by hoboes

the Arizona desert loses its horror and puts on an evanescent veil of green, but the midsummer sun turns on it a fiercer heat . . . and bakes it to a colossal brick. Over against this desolation are set the enormously precious mines under the control of small groups of engineers and their executive staffs whose immediate official responsibility is not to the workers in the mines, but to the owners somewhere in the remote East.

This small group of technical experts stands face to face with the incoherent multitude of aliens—aliens even when they have been recruited back East instead of from across the sea—the muckers who go down into the hot stopes and drifts to blast and shovel out the ore. Between these two extreme groups there is in the Arizona mining towns no middle class to complicate or temper their relations. The few professional men are not, as a rule, free agents: the doctors are associated with the hospitals established by the companies; the bankers and the bank employees are paid by the men who own the mines; the newspaper editors are usually quite frankly subservient to the representatives of the copper companies; the storekeepers run company-owned or subsidized stores; the hotel-keepers entertain the companies' guests; even the clergymen, with rare exceptions, hold somewhat the status of imported feudal retainers. For instance, in one of these mining towns a certain religious body decided to build a church. The dominant mine manager refused to sell them ground on which to build it. Instead he offered them a lease at a normal rental on condition that he should have com-

plete censorship over the pulpit, and it was on this explicit understanding that the church was built.

In times of industrial peace the camps are as cheerfully tranquil as an old Southern plantation. In times of industrial turmoil men's hands are quick to their guns. The atmosphere is charged with the fear of insurrection. Under such conditions the initiative in doing violence will usually be taken by the side that is best prepared, and the records of deportations and other lawless acts during the past year show that it has usually been the guardians of the precious and vulnerable properties—the best citizens, the educated men, the men who in their ordinary personal relationships are the most considerate and delightful of gentlemen—who were best prepared. These emotional outbursts, these sudden releases of abnormal psychological tension, are likely to be most violent where the estrangement between masters and men is sharpened by differences in color, or language, or both, as in Bisbee and neighboring camps along the Mexican border. And of course at this moment the customary tension itself is immensely heightened by the hot strains and pressures of war.

The case of Bisbee, where twelve hundred strikers and their alleged sympathizers who had committed no violence were snatched from their homes and deported at the muzzles of guns into the desert of New Mexico, is notorious. But it is no more noteworthy than scores of less widely heralded instances.

FROM JOYCE L. KORNBLUH, Rebel Voices

Troublemakers

"One of the consequences of all these things," wrote Upton Sinclair, was that his Lithuanian protagonist "was no longer perplexed when he heard men talk of fighting for their rights." Much of the labor movement seemed to be fighting not only for labor rights but for a new social order as well—a revolution with foreign overtones. Thus the involvement in the labor movement of people of recent immigrant origins was overplayed. But there were, for instance, Joel Hägglund, known as Joe Hill, a Swede who wrote songs and organized for the I.W.W.; Arturo Giovannitti, Italian-born organizer for the Wobblies; and thousands of less famous but still foreign instruments of change.

In 1912, textile workers in Lawrence, Massachusetts—most of them foreign-born—went on strike. Early in the strike a woman was killed, and two of the organizers who had come in from outside the Commonwealth were charged as accessories to murder. Joseph Ettor and Arturo Giovannitti had been miles from the scene, but they were said to have fomented disorder and were thus held directly responsible. At the end of the trial, both men addressed the jury. Ettor declared that if the verdict were "Guilty" they should both be sentenced to death, not to prison. Giovannitti agreed. Below is the end of his address, his first public speech in English. The two men were acquitted.

. . . we do not expect you to soothe your conscience and at the same time to give a helping hand to the other side—simply to go and reason and say, "Well, something has happened there and somebody is responsible; let us balance the scales and do half and half." No, gentlemen. We are young. I am twenty-nine years old—not quite, yet; I will be so two months from now. I have a woman that loves me and that I love. I have a mother and father that are waiting for me. I have an ideal that is dearer to me than can be expressed or understood. And life has so many allurements and it is so nice and so bright and so wonderful that I feel the passion of living in my heart and I do want to live.

I don't want to pose to you as a hero. I don't want to pose as a martyr. No, life is dearer to me than it is probably to a good many others. But I say this, that

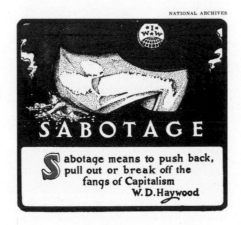

SABOTAGE

Sabotage means to push back, pull out or break off the fangs of Capitalism
W. D. Haywood

A Wobbly sticker, pre-1920

there is something dearer and nobler and holier and grander, something I could never come to terms with, and that is my conscience and that is my loyalty to my class and to my comrades who have come here in this room, and to the working class of the world, who have contributed with a splendid hand penny by penny to my defense and who have all over the world seen that no injustice and no wrong was done to me.

Therefore, I say, weigh both sides and then judge. And if it be, gentlemen of the jury, that your judgment shall be such that this gate will be opened and we shall pass out of it and go back into the sunlit world, then let me assure you what you are doing. Let me tell you that the first strike that breaks again in this Commonwealth or any other place in America where the work and the help and the intelligence of Joseph J. Ettor and Arturo Giovannitti will be needed and necessary, there we shall go again regardless of any fear and of any threat.

We shall return again to our humble efforts, obscure, humble, unknown, misunderstood—soldiers of this mighty army of the working class of the world, which out of the shadows and the darkness of the past is striving towards the destined goal which is the emancipation of human kind, which is the establishment of love and brotherhood and justice for every man and every woman in this earth.

On the other hand, if your verdict shall be the contrary, if it be that we who are so worthless as to deserve neither the infamy nor the glory of the gallows—if it be that these hearts of ours must be stilled on the same death chair and by the same current of fire that has destroyed the life of the wife murderer and the parricide, then I say, gentlemen of the jury, that tomorrow we shall pass into a greater judgment, that tomorrow we shall go from your presence into a presence where history shall give its last word to us.

Whichever way you judge, gentlemen of the jury, I thank you.

On November 19, 1915, Joe Hill was executed by a firing squad at the Utah State Penitentiary. He had been convicted of murder, but many believed he had been framed and was a martyr to the Cause. The funeral service in Chicago featured speakers in ten languages. One of his most popular songs was "The Preacher and the Slave," below, sung to the tune of "In the Sweet Bye and Bye." A key phrase—"pie in the sky"—originated in the Wobbly

movement. The song was published in the third edition of the I.W.W. songbook.

Long-haired preachers come out every night,
Try to tell you what's wrong and what's right;
But when asked how 'bout something to eat
They will answer with voices so sweet:

You will eat, bye and bye,
In that glorious land above the sky;
Work and pray, live on hay,
You'll get pie in the sky when you die.

The starvation army they play,
They sing and they clap and they pray,
Till they get all your coin on the drum,
Then they tell you when you are on the bum:

You will eat, bye and bye,
In that glorious land above the sky;
Work and pray, live on hay,
You'll get pie in the sky when you die.

Holy Rollers and jumpers come out,
They holler, they jump and they shout.
Give your money to Jesus they say,
He will cure all diseases today.

If you fight hard for children and wife—
Try to get something good in this life—
You're a sinner and bad man, they tell,
When you die you will sure go to hell.

Workingmen of all countries unite,
Side by side we for freedom will fight:
When the world and its wealth we
        have gained
To the grafters we'll sing this refrain:

You will eat, bye and bye,
When you've learned how to cook
        and to fry;
Chop some wood, 'twill do you good,
And you'll eat in the sweet bye and bye.

One quality of the movement that particularly troubled the Establishment was the devotion of such men as Hill and Giovannitti—as in the latter's promise to be back if necessary, or as in Hill's farewell telegram to friends: "Don't waste any time in mourning. Organize!" "You gotta stick together," went a union song, and evidence of devoted cohesiveness could be seen in a garment workers' strike that began late in the autumn of 1909. The strikers were mainly young Jewish and Italian women. Sarah Comstock reported on the strike for Collier's Christmas *issue.*

Clara Lembich, a little Russian girl of sixteen with a pompadour behind just like that of any other girl of sixteen, was the one who pressed the button. Because she rose in a labor meeting and moved that the shirt-waist makers strike, between thirty and forty thousand girls quit work in New York City alone, and

news of more going out, more and still more has come in from factories all over the East.

The thing amounts to an uprising such as has never been known since woman entered the Garden of Eden. The strike fever spread like the plague, and organizers belonging to the Woman's Trade Union League have struggled in vain to stop it. Stop Pelée in eruption. An army of girls, turned loose from their shops on the streets, could not be handled; day by day the army increased. From shirt-waist makers the epidemic spread to dressmakers, and it threatened for a time to include all the ladies' garment workers. Remember that the bulk of all this work is done by girls; that even such a small detail as the mere sewing on of buttons gives employment to thousands; and you may gain some conception of what this uprising means to industry. Many employers risked ruin in holding out; already one hundred and seventy shops have signed, agreeing to the girls' terms, and seventeen thousand of the girls are back at work under contract—that is, a half, more or less, have won their fight, the strike being only two and a half weeks old.

. . . We have had girls' strikes before —some appeared big at the time. On the will of the neckwear makers next Easter's scarfs hung for days in the balance. The hat trimmers hindered the stitching of sweat-bands and ribbon bands and postmen's vizors for ten months. But every feminine strike of the past is dwarfed by this. It has passed the point of a battle for one specified demand, such as shorter hours or more pay or no lay-offs or clean shops. It sweeps up all these and more besides into one great Grievance. It says that the girls have borne as much and as long as they will. That they have racked their nerves and risked their health and starved their bodies and suffered insult to the limit of their endurance. But many of these girls are well paid and decently treated. The fever is upon these no less than the others. They have snapped their thread and donned their hats for the sake of the other girls—the girls who earn three, four, five dollars a week perhaps, and feed more mouths than their own.

Joseph J. Ettor   **Arturo Giovannitti**

Strikes in the Coal Fields

Coal mining, an industry that employed large numbers of immigrants from Eastern Europe, was the arena of some memorable strikes during the early decades of the twentieth century. In order to endure the low pay and scandalous working conditions of a coal miner's life at that time, a man had to be both strong and stubborn. When they were finally driven to desperation, the miners had to fight equally strong and stubborn antagonists, the "coal dukes," men so powerful that the regions in which they owned mines virtually amounted to feudal domains. Two strikes involving workers new to the United States—one long and dreary, the other long and above all bloody—are the subjects here.

The material below was published in Collier's *for April 1, 1911, in an article by Richard Lloyd Jones titled "Pennsylvania's Russia"—a reference to Westmoreland County, east of Pittsburgh, where a long strike was then in progress.*

The miners who go into the dark and dangerous holes in the earth to blast and shovel out the coal are paid by car measure. When the standard of wage was set, these cars were five feet long. As the cost of living went up these coal dukes of the Irwin field thought it would be a cute little stunt to [slip] . . . in some larger cars on the miners. The five-foot cars were at first displaced by six-foot cars. Then seven-foot cars appeared; and these cars being good, healthy cars, began to get a little wider and a little higher. No matter how hard the miner bent his back over his No. 3 shovel twelve hours a day, his earnings continued to grow less.

The miner protested, but the coal dukes had no wish to listen to the miners, who are "an ignorant lot of Slavs anyway, and don't know what they want." Nine years ago, during the anthracite strike, President Baer of the Reading Railroad frankly admitted that God in His infinite wisdom had carefully selected these coal dukes to be masters over the bowels of the earth and the fulness thereof.

Strange as it may seem, dissatisfaction among the miners grew, the foreign-born (and most of them are) had heard some foolish stories about these United States—that this country was not like the old countries, that there *was* such a thing as justice and fair play here, that this Government somewhere and somehow protected human rights. The American-born miners were even more stoutly convinced of the truth of this idea. . . .

The miner is a peculiarly unappreciative creature. After all [his] benefits and conveniences had been brought right up to him, he still complained and was discontented. He was allowed to work twelve hours a day, to go into the hole in the ground at dawn and come out at dusk, thus avoiding the annoyance of sunlight; he was given a nice, large car to fill, with no extra financial investments to worry over; the company store and the house rent relieved him of any cash that his pay envelope was supposed to hold. In fact, he usually found that his pay envelope contained a polite little statement that he was under obligations to the company. He was, as he saw it, worse off than the negroes south of the Mason-Dixon line before the big fuss of 1861. He wondered why he came to America.

They began to meet in little groups . . . These little groups began to grow into formal meetings. It is dangerous for men to meet unless they are good men. And the preachers of the nice churches in Pittsburg and Greensburg and Latrobe will tell you that the miners do not know what they want; that they are an ignorant, discontented lot —that the coal dukes are all good men.

The magnates of Pittsburg and vicinity have shown a passion for peace. . . .

They got the county sheriff to hire a lot of deputies to act as company policemen. They paid the sheriff $185,000. He charged the companies $5 a day for each deputy. He paid each deputy $3 a day. He didn't do this dirty work for nothing. For the coal companies he hired a lot of husky thugs and decorated them with a club and a gun and a policeman's star. Miners thereafter were not allowed to gather in groups on any of the companies' grounds, and they were not allowed to walk in more than pairs or in closer file than ten feet apart.

There is a limit to human patience even in Pennsylvania's little Russia, and on the tenth day of March, 1910, twenty thousand miners in the Irwin field struck.

They asked for an eight-hour day, that they might have some time to read and recreate, that they might live American lives.

They asked the right to organize and to have their organization recognized.

They asked the right to employ their own check weigher, whose wages they themselves would pay, that they might know how much coal they dug and what they were being paid for it.

They asked to be allowed to live where they pleased and how they pleased, and to buy their goods where and how they pleased—the commonest right of every American citizen.

Every request was flatly refused. The mine owners claim that the miners were contented and well paid, and that the strike would never have occurred but for the disturbing influence of a union

Workers march during a 1902 coal strike in Shenandoah, Pennsylvania.

leader who was playing a political game.

The strike has held on for over a year. During this time these miners with their brave women and innocent children have been living in tents and the rudest kind of shanties.

The story of this struggle for simple justice has been as effectively suppressed in Pennsylvania's little Russia as it ever could have been under the Czar's twin-headed black eagle. Not a daily newspaper in Westmoreland County has reported it.

The "massacre" at Ludlow, Colorado, in April, 1914, shocked the nation. The American Review of Reviews *for June discussed the tragic event and the "industrial war" that had brought it about.*

The killing of eleven children and two women, on April 20, forcibly drew the attention of the country to an almost unbelievable situation which had existed for more than six months in the great State of Colorado.

Other lives had been lost,—nearly fifty in all,—but the slaughter of innocents furnished the climax to a situation which is now without parallel in the history of industrial strife in this country.

Throughout the extensive coal fields in the south-central part of the State, close to the boundary line of New Mexico, there had been arrayed against each other, ever since October, two radically different classes of armed men. On one side were groups of striking miners, without organization and almost without leaders, but with determination and a common purpose to achieve things to which they believed they were entitled and without which they could not be content. Most of the strikers were recent immigrants from Southeastern Europe. On the other side were the State militia and "professional trouble-lovers," who had been hired by the coal companies, from outside the district, to serve as strike-breakers and as mine guards.

The scene of this recent warfare in Colorado is an eighty-mile strip running due north and south in the foothills of the Rockies. Trinidad, with 10,000 inhabitants, is the only large town in the district. Ludlow, Walsenburg, Aguilar, and the other communities, are mere hamlets with a few hundred inhabitants in each.

The district contains most of the coal deposits of the State, but nothing else; and the inhabitants are entirely dependent upon the mines for their livelihood.

During the long and dreary winter months, while the strike has been in progress, the miners and their families have lived in tents furnished and maintained by the United Mine Workers of America. The houses which they had formerly occupied were, of course, owned by the companies, and when the miners gave up their jobs they simultaneously had to abandon their homes.

As might be expected when armed men face each other, with radically different views and aims, bitter animosities developed and clashes were frequent. . . .

In what would otherwise have been a trivial clash, the strikers' leader—a Greek named Louis Tikas—was shot and killed by the militia at Ludlow on April 20. Who fired the first shot? is a question no one, who can, will answer. Both sides then lost their heads, and a battle began. The militia possessed several machine guns which had been sent to the mines for defensive purposes. These they trained upon the strikers and upon the tent colony, and the miners were forced back into the hills, leaving a dozen of their number lying dead upon the field of battle.

The tents, nearly two hundred in number, were burned to the ground, and in the smouldering débris later were found the bodies of two women and eleven children who had sought refuge in pits dug for the purpose.

Whether the fire among the tents was caused by the shooting, or whether it was deliberately set by order of a militia officer (as has been alleged), is a matter of dispute. . . .

The battle at Ludlow—for such it surely had been—was followed by a series of reprisals by bands of strikers, as a result of which many thousands of dollars' worth of mine property was destroyed. The state of warfare lasted for ten days, resulted in the death of forty-seven persons, and was only ended by the action of President Wilson, . . . who sent several companies of Federal troops to the coal fields on April 28, with specific orders from the Secretary of War to disarm everyone,—militiamen, strikers, mine guards, and deputy sheriffs.

"The Competition of Paupers"

Immigrant labor was attacked from both sides. It was said to be a cause of labor unrest. On the other hand, it was charged with breaking strikes, with passively accepting poor wages and working conditions. The restrictionists argued that the continued unlimited entry of foreign-born workers—who would work for next to nothing because they could live on next to nothing—meant conditions of labor would never improve; unionizing and strikes could always be met by bringing in more foreigners. At a time when the tariff was a pressing issue, one often heard such statements as: "The competition of paupers is far more . . . killing than the competition of pauper-made goods."

The material below is excerpted from Emigration and Immigration, *an 1890 volume by Columbia professor Richmond Mayo-Smith, economist and statistician.*

Protectionists commonly say the tariff is for the protection of American against the poorer-paid labor of Europe. But what avails it to keep out the goods and introduce the laborer and put him side by side with the American in the competition for producing goods at a low price? For the manufacturer it is obviously an advantage to have a monopoly of the market for his goods and a free command of the market in which to buy labor. But the advantage to the working man is not obvious. . . .

The New York commissioner of labor in 1885 found a contractor in Buffalo who admitted that he had furnished four hundred foreigners to railroad companies and other corporations during the preceding year. We hear of similar cases in New Jersey, Kansas, Iowa and Wisconsin. The commissioner of the labor bureau in the last named state asserts that in the year 1886 the state was flooded with circulars from an Italian Labor and Construction company in New York offering to let men "for tunnelling, grading, mining, breaking stone, laying ties, repairing washouts, laying water and gas mains, street cleaning, shovelling snow," or to take such work as subcontractors "at figures that will repay inquiry." "Contractors will find that the authority of this company over the men it furnishes is of special advantage in all dealings it may have with them." It is notorious that the mine owners in Pennsylvania and Ohio have imported laborers to take the places of men at work in the mines.

In New England, French Canadians are brought in to work in the cotton-mills and at brick laying. At the latter trade they work during the summer and return to Canada for the winter. In New York the labor commissioner reported similar cases of masons who were brought over here during the busy season and returned to Europe in the winter.

The testimony before the Ford immigration committee brought to light several cases of the importation of laborers under contract in spite of the law of 1885 against it. That law is extremely difficult to enforce because it is almost impossible to get evidence. The laborer is interested in concealing the fact, and there is no mark by which the inspectors at Castle Garden can tell that he is under contract.

Working men protest against the importation of labor under contract not on account of the small amount of additional competition involved in it, but because it destroys the efficacy of their labor organizations. It renders strikes harmless, and the demand for increased wages or the protest against reduction of wages equally unavailing. It makes the employer master of the situation, for the supply of this imported labor is practically unlimited.

Competition is rendered more diffi-cult for the American laborer and more disastrous for the community because many of the immigrants of recent years represent a very low standard of living. The reason these imported laborers can displace the American by taking lower wages is that they live in a way

Puck, OCTOBER 3, 1888

which it is impossible for the native workman to imitate and which it would be a misfortune for the civilization of the community if he should. It is not merely that the immigrants have received less wages and are less well off in the old country than in this. That would be true of the mass of them since the movement began, and the very fact that they expected better wages in this country has in many cases been the chief inducement to come. But in former times most of them had the desire for a higher style of living and quickly lifted themselves up to the American standard. In recent years, however, a class has come, accustomed to a distinctly lower standard, with no notion of anything else, perfectly content to live as at home, and whose only ambition has been to save enough to return to the old country.

The types of this class of people with which we have become familiar during the last few years are the Italians, the French Canadians, the Poles and the Hungarians. The causes which have contributed to their immigration are the cheapness of transportation, the solicitation of steamship agents and the importation of contract labor.

It is scarcely necessary to describe the standard of living of these people. Attention has been directed to it by newspapers, bureaux of labor statistics, labor organizations and the Congressional committee already mentioned. Italians testified before this committee that they were accustomed to live at home on fifteen cents a day. The committee visited in person the tenement houses in New York city, where these newcomers lodge, and saw sights that almost baffle description. Huddled to-

gether in miserable apartments, in filth and rags, without the slightest regard to decency or health, they present a picture of squalid existence degrading to any civilization and a menace to the health of the whole community. Ignorant, criminal and vicious, eating food that we would not give to dogs, their very stolidity and patience under such conditions show that they lack the faintest appreciation of what civilization means. . . . .

It is this kind of competition that is unfair to our working classes and a danger to the community. It is unfair to ask the working man to compete against labor based on a standard of living which we should be unwilling to see him adopt. It is unwise of the community to allow a competition which, if unchecked, must bring the whole laboring class to a lower standard of civilization.

This cartoon, "The Republican Idea of Protection," was published in 1888, a Presidential election year.

Fair Appraisals

Not surprisingly, the facts and statistics concerning immigrant labor were fairer than the critics of immigrant labor. The foreign-born worker was not generally a rabble-rouser. Nor was he any more susceptible to the messages of rabble-rousers than his native-born counterpart. Some newcomers were indeed imported to break strikes; certainly some were hired at lower wages than native workers. But on the whole they were no more passive about working conditions and no less choosy about how they lived than other men and women employed at like jobs. There were writers who understood these things and came to the aliens' defense during the debate on immigration restriction.

After the Dillingham Commission had given official voice to some of the popular attitudes, a celebrated rebuttal, Immigration and Labor, *was published in 1912 by Isaac A. Hourwich. A political refugee from Russia, a lawyer, and a statistician, Hourwich wrote on various sociological topics—in Yiddish and Russian as well as English. This material is excerpted from his article published in the* Political Science Quarterly *for winter, 1911.*

In summing up the effect of the influx of recent immigrants upon native American wage-earners and upon the earlier immigrants from Great Britain and northern Europe, the Immigration Commission, despite its pronounced bias in favor of restriction, is compelled to concede an "advancement in the scale of occupation" of some portion "of native Americans and of English, Irish, Scotch, Welsh, and members of other races who constituted the wage-earning classes before the arrival of recent immigrants." This readjustment of the working personnel of the nation has been the result of "the remarkable expansion in manufacturing and mining," which has created "additional places for experienced and trained employees in supervisory and skilled positions.". . .

In all arguments in support of restriction it is assumed as axiomatic that the tendency of recent immigration has been to keep down the wages of American labor. The Immigration Commission reluctantly admits, however, that, in the industries covered by its investi-

gation, "as a matter of fact, it has not appeared . . . that it was usual for employers to engage recent immigrants at wages actually lower than those prevailing at the time of their employment in the industry where they were employed." But the development of industry has been attended "by the invention of mechanical devices and processes which have eliminated the skill and experience formerly required in a large number of occupations." . . .

It goes without saying that unskilled labor is cheaper than skilled labor. Since the native American or the earlier immigrant is [now] a skilled worker, while the recent immigrant is an unskilled laborer, the former, of course, commands a higher wage than the latter. But the difference is due to the grade of employment, not to racial characteristics.

William M. Leiserson

The standards of living of the various classes of wage-workers being necessarily determined by their wages, one must expect to find generally a greater degree of congestion and retrenchment in a settlement of unskilled laborers than in a neighborhood where the residents are mostly skilled mechanics. The converse proposition, however, that because the immigrant worker has been accustomed to a lower standard of living at home he will be satisfied with less than the standard wages in the United States, is confuted by the economic make-up of our industrial system.

A Polish peasant may have lived in a straw-thatched cabin at home, but in Chicago he will find none for rent, because the owner of a city lot cannot afford the luxury of maintaining such a cabin. The employer of labor must pay to his hands at least enough to provide for the payment of rent to the landlord. And it must be borne in mind that the immigrants are mostly concentrated in great cities, where rent is high, while the native American workmen predominate in small towns with low rents. So when the article produced by immigrant labor in New York must compete in the market with the article produced by native American labor in a small New England town, it is open to question whether immigrant labor is underbidding American labor, or whether the reverse is the case.

As in the matter of rent, so in the matter of wearing apparel. At home the Lithuanian peasant may have walked barefoot, but when he comes to work in the mines of Pennsylvania he must wear

American shoes. In the backwoods of his native country he wore a sheepskin coat, which he inherited from his father. When he comes to work in the stockyards of Chicago he must wear a suit of American clothes. The prices which the alien workman must pay in an American department store for the cheapest shoes and clothes are fixed, not by his imported individual or racial psychology, but by the American manufacturer, the American railway manager and the American department-store proprietor, everyone of them eager to make an American profit, in order to maintain an American standard of living for themselves.

In the 1920s, the Carnegie Corporation sponsored a study of "methods of Americanization." One of the several volumes resulting from the project was Adjusting Immigrant and Industry, *published in 1924; excerpts from that book follow. Its author, William M. Leiserson, had been born in Estonia in 1883 and was brought to America seven years later. He had a distinguished career as an academician and as an expert in labor relations.*

Because the immigrant industrial population is necessarily so largely an adult population, because it is made up of so many races, and because of the great concentration of immigrants in certain industrial occupations and communities, industry presents at once the greatest need and the greatest difficulty for organized effort to bring about a merging of the native with the foreign born.

In industry . . . the conflict of interests between economic groups, such as employers and employees, skilled mechanics and common laborers, is so bitter that an impersonal conception of Americanism is difficult to maintain.

A native American drove over to the house of a Polish neighbor to inquire if the daughter of the Polish family would accept work as a servant for the American household. The American woman was displeased with the attitude of the Polish girl, but she thought the old Polish woman was "nice." The girl did not seem at all pleased about the oppor-

The pay car at Homestead, Pennsylvania, steel plant

tunity to work as a servant. The mother, however, was quite evidently anxious that the daughter should get the work. The girl asked in good English about the wages offered and the privileges as to days off and evenings out, and she stipulated the kind of work she would do in the household and what she would not do. The mother, in broken English, apologized for her daughter's attitude, apparently fearing that her questions might lose her the job. But the daughter explained that her teacher in the public school told her to be independent like an American and to ask questions like that.

To the American woman seeking a maid this effect of Americanization was quite displeasing, and she preferred the attitude of the un-Americanized Polish mother. It is possible, of course, that the Polish-speaking mother will prove to be a better American than the English-speaking daughter, but apparently it

was the Americanization of the daughter that was most displeasing to her prospective native-born employer.

Similarly the employers in most of the great industries of the country which employ immigrants in such large numbers, object to unionism among their employees on the ground that a union shop itself is un-American; and they have named their policy of maintaining non-union shops, the "American Plan."

On the other hand, the American trade unions and a large section of the public generally condemn the immigrant for not joining labor unions and for being content with conditions which the native born will not accept, and thus lowering the standards of American workers. . . .

If Americans differ thus completely in their conception of Americanism, what confusion there must be in the mind of the immigrant. When he follows the examples of his native fellow wage earners and wishes to join a labor union to improve his conditions and is prevented from doing it, what is he to think? When he is permitted to join a union or organize one, and is condemned as an alien or Bolshevik for this action, what must be his bewilderment? Is he not justified in thinking that we really do not want him to do what a free American may do, that we prefer him to keep his place as an inferior servant? Is not the public exhortation to become Americanized likely to strike him as hypocritical, when he finds the people who urge his Americanization also condemn him when he strives to achieve American standards of living by the methods that American workers use? . . .

No better proof of the Americanizing effects of trade unionism on immigrant labor is needed than the change in the attitude of the public toward the older craft unions affiliated with the American Federation of Labor. It is assumed that these are essentially organizations of American workmen and that the influx of immigrants threatens the existence and the effectiveness of these unions in maintaining American standards. . . . the United States Immigration Commission reported to Congress in 1910 that immigrants were undermining American trade unions and many unofficial writers have taken the same position.

Yet in 1884 the State Department of Labor of New Jersey characterized the trade-union movement as a foreign importation, and its policies and practices as un-American methods developed by immigrant workers to protect themselves against economic evils which they suffer in this country. And in 1893 a writer in the *Century Magazine* charged that trade unions were composed of foreign workmen who kept American boys from learning trades and becoming mechanics.

That most of the national unions which went into the building of the American Federation of Labor in the eighties and nineties were composed mainly of foreign-born wage earners and were organized and led by immigrants

can hardly be doubted. . . .

As far back as 1825, when the Boston House Carpenters struck for a ten-hour day, the organization of the workers was charged with being of foreign origin by the "gentlemen engaged in building." . . .

Both [German-born Adolph] Strasser and [Samuel] Gompers [born in England] were active in the formation of the Federation of Organized Trades and Labor Unions in 1881 and its successor, the American Federation of Labor, five years later. With them were associated many other Irish, Scotch, English, and German leaders. At the second convention of the federated trades it was necessary to elect a German secretary as well as an English secretary, and Hugo Miller of the German-Typographia was chosen for the place. Miller was also a delegate to the first convention of the American Federation of Labor, as was also B. Davis, representing the United German Trades of New York. Of the forty-two delegates at this convention a majority were clearly foreign born. Gompers and Strasser of the Cigar Makers were there. James Duncan, born in Scotland, represented the Granite Cutters. The waiters' and the furniture workers' unions of New York were made up mainly of German immigrants and they sent delegates of their own nationality; the carpenters and the New York boatmen sent Irishmen, and there were other men from England, Scotland, and Ireland.

After the formation of the American Federation of Labor in 1886, it drew native American workmen rapidly to its ranks. So completely were native and immigrant fused in its constituent organizations that by 1909, when the United States Immigration Commission made its investigations, it was generally forgotten that the unions had been formed by immigrants, and the Commission found them to be bulwarks of Americanism and American standards, which were threatened by the more recent immigrants.

Missouri journalist Frederic J. Haskin wrote this tribute to the foreign-born in

his The Immigrant, an Asset and a Liability, *which was published in 1913.*

I am the immigrant.

Since the dawn of creation my restless feet have beaten new paths across the earth.

My uneasy bark has tossed on all seas.

My wanderlust was born of the craving for more liberty and a better wage for the sweat of my face.

I looked towards the United States with eyes kindled by the fire of ambition and heart quickened with a new-born hope.

I approached its gates with great expectation.

I entered in with fine hope.

I have shouldered my burden as the American man-of-all-work.

I contribute eighty-five per cent of all the labor in the slaughtering and meat-packing industries.

I do seven-tenths of the bituminous coal mining.

I do seventy-eight per cent of all the work in the woolen mills.

I contribute nine-tenths of all the labor in the cotton mills.

I make nineteen-twentieths of all the clothing.

I manufacture more than half the shoes.

I build four-fifths of all the furniture.

I make half of the collars, cuffs and shirts.

I turn out four-fifths of all the leather.

I make half the gloves.

I refine nearly nineteen-twentieths of the sugar.

I make half of the tobacco and cigars.

And yet, I am the great American problem.

When I pour out my blood on your altar of labor, and lay down my life as a sacrifice to your god of toil, men make no more comment than at the fall of a sparrow.

But my brawn is woven into the warp and woof of the fabric of your national being.

My children shall be your children and your land shall be my land because my sweat and my blood will cement the foundation of the America of Tomorrow.

In Pursuit of the Dream

Farewell to the Past

Through the 1880s, the 1890s, and the first decade of the twentieth century, more than eighteen million immigrants entered the United States. Most of them were of the "new wave," coming in large numbers for the first time from the countries of Eastern and Southern Europe. The decision to leave friends, family, and ancestral homes was often difficult, even painful to make—as it had always been. But unbearable conditions—economic hardships, political turmoil, and religious persecution like the Czarist-sponsored pogrom in Kishinev, Russia (at right), in which nearly fifty Jews were killed in 1903—eventually hardened minds. The long journey from the Old World to the New began with the securing of a steamship ticket. Sometimes it was sent by relatives or friends already in America, and sometimes it was purchased with meager savings. Then there was a passport to obtain, and an American visa. Departure from home, often a tearful rending, was followed by an arduous trip, on foot or by cart or rail, to a strange and distant port. Finally, after a wait of several days in a port shelter, there came the boarding of the ship and settling in for an eight- to fifteen-day voyage in the steerage section. During the ocean crossing, while all the past—both the good and the bad—receded farther away, fear and expectancy set in. The arrival in New York Harbor and the awesome sight of the Statue of Liberty brought an emotional climax. "Many older persons among us, burdened with a thousand memories of what they were leaving behind, had been openly weeping ever since we entered the narrower waters on our final approach toward the unknown," wrote Edward Corsi, an Italian immigrant of 1907. "Now somehow steadied, I suppose, by the concreteness of the symbol of America's freedom, they dried their tears."

A steerage ticket cost about thirty dollars and usually entitled its bearer to little more than a lumpy mattress in an ill-ventilated, overcrowded area, often below the water line. When they could, passengers sat or slept on the steerage deck, as in the scene, right, on the Red Star Line's S.S. Pennland in 1893. Nearly ninety per cent of the immigrants traveled in the steerage, and it was usually in a state of stunned exhaustion that they stepped ashore on the Promised Land. "Their stolid faces hide frightened, throbbing hearts," wrote one observer who watched them transfer from their ship to the ferryboats that would take them to be examined at Ellis Island (far right). "They obey the signs, gestures and directions of the attendants as dumbly as cattle, and as patiently."

OVERLEAF: *Ellis Island was only one of more than seventy processing centers, but it handled nearly three quarters of all newcomers during its forty years of full operation (it was closed down completely in 1954). Most first- and second-class passengers could land in New York immediately. The others, including all steerage passengers, were taken in quarantine to Ellis Island aboard small ferries like those seen alongside the wharf.*

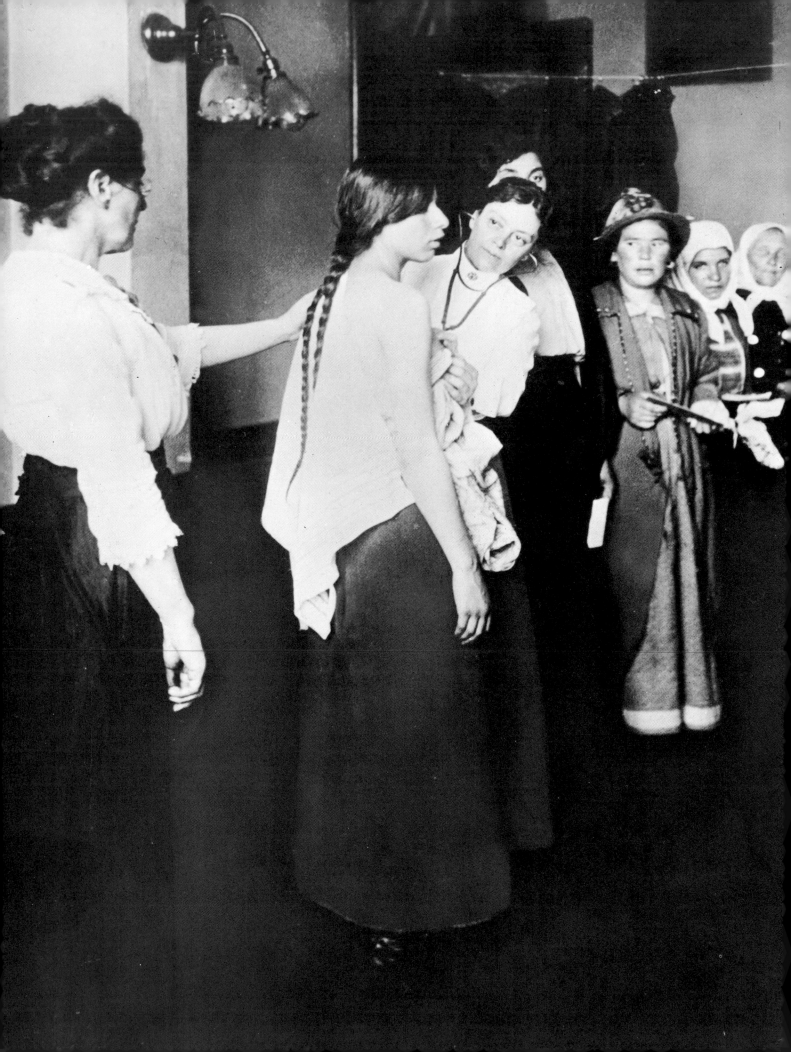

Separated into groups, usually in lots of thirty, arrivals on Ellis Island were processed through a maze of pipe-lined pens in the large, bustling registry room (right), where they were given mental, head, and body examinations (left) and eye inspections by physicians of the United States Public Health Service. If they passed, they went on to inspectors and interpreters who questioned them on such matters as their destinations, their prospects of employment, whether they were anarchists or polygamists, and if they had ever been imprisoned or otherwise institutionalized. Finally, they were either cleared for entry, or detained for further examination, or rejected.

Clearing the Hurdles

Up to five thousand persons a day—sometimes more than a million in a year—moved anxiously through the processing lines in Ellis Island's cavernous registry room. "Here, in the main building," recalled an interpreter who worked with the inspectors, "they were lined up—a motley crowd in colorful costumes . . . Doctors then put them through their medical inspection, and whenever a case aroused suspicion, the alien was set aside in a cage apart from the rest, for all the world like a segregated animal, and his coat lapel or shirt marked with colored chalk, the color indicating why he had been isolated." Those with only minor ailments eventually would be admitted; those with contagious diseases, or with disabling physical or mental defects, or with any of the various "loathsome" diseases (such as ringworm, leprosy, trachoma, or venereal disease), would be deported.

The assembly-line medical inspection was efficient, brusque, and thorough. The young woman above is being examined for trachoma. At right, a Public Health Service official, assisted by an interpreter, is giving a mental test to an immigrant. The objects on the wall were used to test general knowledge.

Those immigrants who were detained at Ellis Island were served meals in the mess hall, as seen at the upper left. The food was provided by the steamship companies, which were responsible for their passengers. The men and boys eat at the long tables in the foreground, while the women and girls sit together at the back of the room. The observance of holidays also helped to cheer those who were marking time. Below at left, a group of immigrants, detained over the Christmas season, gather with Ellis Island officials around a towering tree. Children had special and continuous needs: they had to be cared for and entertained while their parents ironed out the difficulties that were holding up their admittance. Singing was organized for those old enough to participate. The younger children were provided with places to play. At right, happily waving flags of the land they hope will soon be their own, youngsters are seen on a playground atop one of the buildings on the island. Below, a Slavic mother and her children, waiting on Ellis Island in 1905 for clearance to enter the United States, pose for photographer Lewis W. Hine.

Waiting for Admittance

To many immigrants Ellis Island became a temporary home. Aside from those held up for medical reasons, detainees fell into three groups: those briefly delayed, those to be heard by a Board of Special Inquiry, and those designated "likely to become a public charge." The last were deported, as were many in the second group, particularly contract workers. The contracting of cheap foreign labor was strictly illegal, and the alien was usually the victim when the contractor's schemes misfired. Most detainees were in the first category, the "T.D.s," those temporarily detained while they waited for funds to arrive or for a member of the family or friends to meet them. Generally the outcome was a happy one: the son came for his parent, the husband was reunited with his wife and children. It was just a matter of time, and the immigrant was used to waiting.

Cleared finally for entry into the United States, the immigrants above purchase railroad tickets at Ellis Island for the various designations to which they are bound. At the right, a group of Italian immigrants also photographed in 1905 by Hine, wait expectantly with their packed and tied luggage for the moment of their departure for Manhattan. They appear to be eating boxed lunches supplied them by the commissary on Ellis Island. Everything the newcomers owned, all they possessed to get them started in their new life, was in whatever baggage they were able to carry. Below, an immigrant from Poland labors beneath his trunk.

Entry Granted

Having passed the tests and survived the waiting, the new arrivals gathered their bags and bundles. Drachmas, lire, marks, francs, pounds, and rubles were converted to dollars at exchange booths. New York City-bound immigrants boarded ferries for Manhattan; those going elsewhere bought railroad tickets on the island, then crowded onto barges that would take them to various terminals. Addresses were not always easy to decipher in the immigrant's scrawled hand, and officials became adept at decoding such improvised spellings as "Linkinbra" (Lincoln, Nebraska), "Detrayamis" (Detroit, Michigan), and "Deas Moyness Yova" (Des Moines, Iowa). Whatever their destination, most looked forward to life in America confident that it would fulfill its promise. "They did not weigh the price of their coming against the benefits of the New World," wrote 1907 immigrant Edward Corsi, who in 1931 himself became Ellis Island Commissioner. "They were convinced . . . that America had enough and more for all who wished to come. It was only a question of being desired by the strong and wealthy country, of being worthy to be admitted."

For those pictured below, waiting on the Ellis Island wharf for the ferry that will take them across New York Harbor, the great moment has arrived. In the distance, seen dimly through the mist, is Manhattan Island, the goal of their long journey.

OVERLEAF: *The debarkation at the Battery—in America at last.*

Into the "Melting Pot"

"I pledge allegiance to my flag and to the republic for which it stands, one nation, indivisible, with liberty and justice for all."

In the schools of New York City this original version of the Pledge of Allegiance, adopted in 1892 and repeated in assemblies and classrooms each day, was part of the Americanization process for millions of immigrant children, like those shown on the opposite page at the Mott Street Industrial School in that same year.

From the beginning of the 1880s until the start of World War I, Manhattan Island, and particularly its lower East Side, was a phenomenon—a tiny enclave on the eastern coast of America where wave upon wave of foreign-born piled in upon each other and moved no farther into the nation. It was actually a holding point for the masses of newcomers who, without the means or motivation to venture deeper into the continent, clustered together in the fellowship of their own kind, struggling to stay alive and discovering the immediate demands and opportunities of their new land. For many of the adults the teeming tenement districts, some of which were packed with more than half a million people to the square mile, became what the Danish-born Jacob A. Riis called a treadmill. New arrivals—taken by relatives or friends or steered by charitable societies from the ferry slip to neighborhoods of their fellow countrymen—crowded into dingy rooms without enough light or air. They took any job, saved pennies, and literally worked and starved themselves to death, sacrificing for their children or for ticket money for relatives who were still overseas. Some pined away with homesickness: in Italy, Edward Corsi's mother would "sit and gaze for long hours at the quiet beauty of Sulmona's countryside and the towering grandeur of Mount Majella"; in New York, he wrote, she "spent her days, and the waking hours of the night, sitting at . . . one outside window staring up at the little patch of sky above the tenements."

What oppressed the adults exhilarated the children. Because of the public schools, which were the true stirring-spoons of the so-called "Melting Pot," they became assimilated faster than their parents. For many of them, in the din and confusion of the streets, amid peddlers, pushcarts, lumbering wagons, and a thousand and one wonderful things going on at once—as in the scene of an Italian district in the foldout pages—there was no loneliness, only excitement and opportunities in the land of "liberty and justice for all."

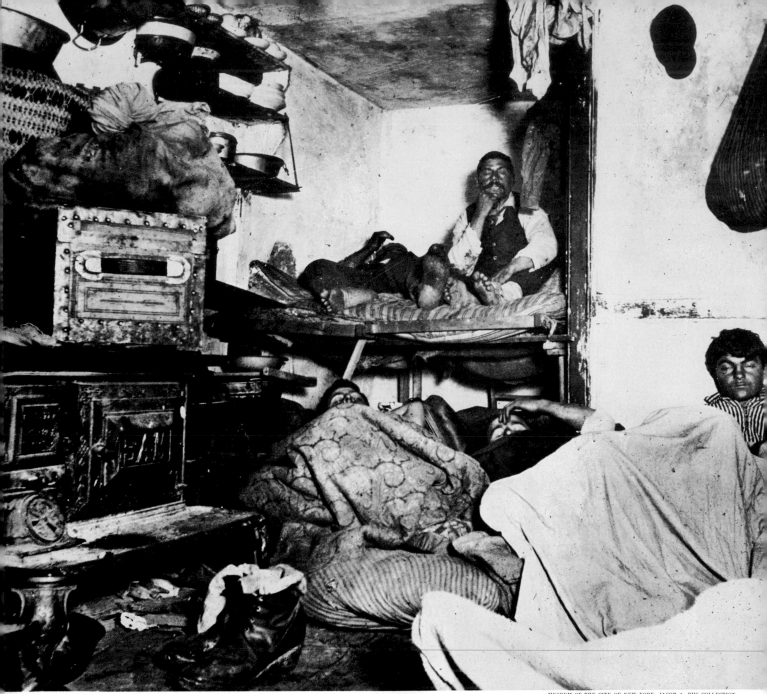

The crowded, unsanitary tenement districts shocked Jacob Riis, who wrote about the "vile" conditions in the immigrant sections and took photographs like the one above of Italians jammed into a "spot" lodging on Bayard Street in lower Manhattan—five cents a night for a spot in which to sleep. It was debatable whether the lot of many of the newcomers to America could have been any more wretched in the lands they had left. To keep their footing in the New World, many of them had to take the hardest, dirtiest, and lowest-paid jobs in the city, becoming ragpickers and working on garbage scows and as pick-and-shovel day laborers.

Many families fought off starvation with the aid of the earnings of their children, who sometimes in tatters and bare feet sold papers (left), peddled wares, or got jobs as lamplighters and messengers. The children's death rate was high. In a single block of tenements in Mulberry Street's "Bend" area (right), which Riis called the "foul core of New York's slums," 155 children younger than five years old died in 1882. Sanitation and health and nutrition workers, like the one visiting an immigrant family (upper right), did their best, but until people began to earn more and move to other places, any significant improvement was impossible.

The Bitter Beginnings

"Dear Mr. Editor. . . . I read the troubles of family life in your 'Bintel Brief' each day very attentively. But my own troubles are so great, so enormous, that I will not even ask for your permission to print my few words in your paper, as others do, but simply, I ask you right on the spot: *Help!*" This plea from an immigrant appeared in 1906 in the *Jewish Daily Forward*, published in Manhattan's lower East Side The writer was not alone in his miseries. Bewildered in an alien culture, most newcomers found survival a grim struggle. They worked long hours for low pay and were often unemployed. Landlords cheated them and provided almost nothing. In cold weather, their children scrounged for lumps of coal to heat their rooms; in summer those rooms were ovens. But if a family could save pennies, spending no more than two or three dollars a week to stay alive, there was hope that the promise of the new land would be fulfilled.

The Way Up

In 1891 a commentator told how Jewish immigrants were beginning to get ahead: ". . . patient toil; zealous application; intelligence infused into labor; frugal thrift and temperance in all things. They have had the self-denial to confine their wants to necessities until the means were provided for comforts; and to limit their desires to these until luxuries could be afforded."

In general, these observations held true for all groups. Hard work, sacrifices and savings, the seizing of opportunities, and the education of the young finally permitted millions of immigrant families to rise above their desperate beginnings in the New World. One way out was to do piecework at home for a manufacturer. The Italian woman at left, carrying home materials on which to work, and the family at the right, shelling nuts at home, would have been paid sweatshop prices; they worked long hours in the hope of being able to save part of what they were paid. The most common piecework was done for the burgeoning ready-made clothing industry. "You are made fully aware of it . . . in any of these East Side streets, by the whir of a thousand sewing-machines, worked at high pressure from earliest dawn till mind and muscle give out together," wrote Jacob Riis. "Every member of the family, from the youngest to the oldest, bears a hand, shut in the qualmy rooms, where meals are cooked and clothing washed and dried. . . . It is not unusual to find a dozen persons—men, women, and children—at work in a single small room." From such beginnings, immigrants were often able to move on to better jobs and to ownership of their own businesses.

To many immigrants, struggling to establish their families in the New World, the full promise of America was for their children. But without education, that promise might be denied. Consequently it was a matter of pride to some parents, like the Italian father at right, to watch their children learn to read and write English and study American history alongside youngsters whose families had long lived in the United States.

OVERLEAF: *Hard work, education, determination, and enthusiasm—the face of a future United States was illuminated in the 1896 photograph of two young bootblacks in New York.*

Seemingly peaceful before its population swelled in the 1920s, Harlem nurtured seeds of the conflicts to come.

URBAN PROMISED LAND

AND SO THE GATES CLOSED on the annual inward surge of European seekers of a new life, and absorption began its work. True, there was a continued influx from the Western Hemisphere, while American nationality itself remained an amalgam of many kinds of "foreign" clay, not yet molded, not yet hardened. But with the damming of the torrents of newcomers, there was space for native and immigrant alike to test, clarify, and reassess the meaning of their encounter.

Americanization, it was evident, was a process acted out largely by the young—the sons and daughters and grandsons and granddaughters of Polotzk and Molfetta and Ljubljana. They were the ones who blended their parents' gift of traditions with the staccato messages of the new environment. If, as many believe, the essence of human experience in the depersonalizing twentieth century is a search for identity, for ties to the past that will strengthen but not confine us, then the story of the second- and third-generation Americans is one of the central sagas of modern American history.

The bits and pieces of transplanted Europe hailed by the cultural pluralists (such as the Swedish newspaper, the Polish clubhouse, the Ukrainian-speaking parish) diminished as the foreign-born aged. The rate of this fading varied for different groups and so set dissimilar styles for each nationality's children. Contrasting patterns of assimilation, moreover, preserved variations in the quality and tone of life among immigrant groups, and kept America a land of noticeable ethnic diversity and color. The offspring of Marco and Isaac and Stefan all did learn to do the same properly American things —to revere the flag, pay taxes promptly, pray in English, save their money, buy homes and insurance, and keep their own young in school. But where they lived and worked and voted—and how—continued to depend in some measure on Old World backgrounds.

One thing was certain: almost all of them were part of the ceaseless swelling of the cities. Furthermore, they were being affected by cultural revolutions of unsuspected scope. During the booming twenties, hungry thirties, war-torn forties, and tense fifties, the whole structure of American social values was under heavy assault. The automobile, the movies, television, Freud, Keynes, suburbia, and all other aspects of an age of technology, leisure, and abundance challenged and upset the moods of respectability and responsibility dominant in 1914, at immigration's high tide. And by the time the newcomers were successful on, say, Calvin Coolidge's terms, many of the terms were obsolete.

Meanwhile, a second part of the story was developing. There was a steady and fateful internal migration of America's black peasantry to the urban frontier. As millions of Negro Americans, after 1910, sought the real and imagined opportunities of the industrial North, they created yet another "new" immigration. This one was not funneled through Ellis Island or blessed by the Statue of Liberty—or suspended in 1924. Like its predecessors, it flowed into the jobs and neighborhoods at the lowest levels of desirability, and displaced their former occupants upward. Black bodies twisted and sweated in the coarse-labor jobs that Irishmen and Italians had held in their turn. Black faces peered from tenement windows vacated by Jewish peddlers. In time, it was hoped, they too would move to better things.

But the black "invaders" soon encountered the seemingly permanent force of racism, both as a barrier

Italian immigrants in America usually banded together in Eastern cities according to their old home province or village. By the early 1900s there were more Italians in New York than in Rome, living in "Little Italys," where sometimes as many as four thousand of them crowded into a single city block. Although some found jobs as bootblacks, barbers, peddlers, furniture makers, and sculptors, the majority were forced at first to accept pick-and-shovel work (left). Italians brought to urban environments their talents for art, enhancing many a subway station, for example, with colorful mosaics.

imposed by whites to their advance and as the source of crippling social damage and inadequacies in black society itself. The hoped-for upward movement of Negro youngsters into professions and property ownership either took place at a heartbreakingly slow rate or not at all. By 1955, black leaders (and white liberals) were straining against the brakes on integration. By 1965, some angry and desperate blacks had given up on integration and were issuing calls for black separatism.

Either way, the black men and women fighting for change found themselves on a collision course with white immigrants' descendants. Irishmen, Italians, Poles, and Jews held the approaches to the stairway upward. They owned the small businesses and were foremen and union leaders in industry; they were teachers and principals in the school system; they were officers and supervisors in the police and fire and sanitation departments and other branches of the civil service; they dominated the neighborhoods adjacent to the slums. They occupied the strong points that advancing black pride would need to possess and fortify. It was an old pattern, except that this time the advance was black against white. The American social stage was set for disturbing confrontations in the 1970s.

Every immigrant group has its own body of "up from Ellis Island" legends, lovingly preserved by ethnic historical societies. The operative word is "up." The values binding American society together in the days of Andrew Jackson, Abraham Lincoln, and Horatio Alger had not changed much in the 1920s, when the former

Commissioner of Immigration in New York, Frederic C. Howe, wrote a piece for a symposium entitled *Civilization in America*. Discontent with the *status quo*, said Howe approvingly, was the power plant of progress for the immigrant as for the old-timer.

. . . the newcomer speedily acquires the wants of those with whom he associates. He becomes dissatisfied with his shack. He demands more and better food and clothes. He almost always wants his children to have a schooling and to rise in the scale, which to him means getting out of the hod-carrying, day-labour, or even artisan class. And the next generation does rise. It rises only less rapidly than did the early immigrant.

The extent and consequences of the upward escalator ride differed according to the culture of each foreign-born community. Boundaries between nationalities in the new land were blurred but not erased. As a perceptive black activist, the Reverend Jesse Jackson, noted in 1969, "There is talk about it [America] being a melting pot. But it really is more like vegetable soup. There are separate pieces of corn, meat, and so on, each with its own identity." He added that blacks, long pushed to the bottom, were going to rise or "turn the pot over." The special talents and traditions of each nationality dictated that some would merge almost totally into American society, as the Germans have done since the two wars against the homeland, or remain highly visible on ceremonial occasions, like the Irish on March 17 each year. America's Italians and Jews—both basically elements in the "new" immigration—offer other interesting examples of contrast.

More than three million Italians landed on American shores between 1900 and 1914. The census of 1960 showed that 1,100,000 people born in Italy still lived in the United States, along with 3,280,000 of their offspring. Third- and fourth-generation Italian-Americans augmented this figure considerably. The Italians became heavily concentrated in New York City, forming between a sixth and a fifth of its population by 1960. Large numbers also went to industrial towns in New Jersey and southern New England.

Italian neighborhoods were quickly formed, duplicating in a few square blocks the supportive closeness of the village. Inevitably these communities were known as "Little Italys." Despite relative prosperity, Italians tended to remain in their original localities. Jewish, Irish, black, Puerto Rican, and, latterly, hippie neighbors might come and go, but the Italians tended to stay on, undismayed by a shabby external appearance in the area, so long as the interiors of their own homes were pleasant.

Italians found these enclaves convenient for perpetuating a style of family solidarity, respect for male elders, and wariness of outsiders. As late as 1968, in the twenty-one-square-block area of Manhattan's Little Italy, there were thirty social clubs whose elderly, dark-clad gentlemen members gravely played cards and *boccie*, sipped *espresso*, and rendered opinions on various problems, most especially on the need to keep the young in line. From such reassuring bastions, new arrivals sallied out into the economy, often armed—like Constantine Panunzio—with shovels. (Mario Puzo, a novelist, says that shovels are as offensive to stuffed-shirt Italian-Americans as watermelons are to stuffed-shirt Negroes.) But they found other sources of their daily *pasta* as well—the needle trades, for example. In 1938, the roving journalist William Seabrook asserted that Italians composed one third of the garment workers of Chicago, Boston, and New York, two thirds of those in Rochester, more than half in Baltimore and in the state of Connecticut, and an incredible ninety-five per cent in Philadelphia.

Italians also went into truck farming in the Northeast, and a few ventured to till the soil of the Far West. Others undertook entrepreneurship and became *prominenti*, neighborhood leaders. In New York alone, such names as La Rosa and Ronzoni in macaroni products and Santini in moving and storage testify to just how successful some were in their chosen lines. And although Italian-Americans are understandably sensitive about it, the presence of many Italian names on the top-level

rosters of organized crime also reflects success of a kind.

Below these major figures were the thousands of Italians who operated barbershops, drugstores, restaurants, bakeries, butcher shops, and, in the old days of iceboxes and coal furnaces, ice and coal dealerships. The realities of the hard-working world of the Italian laborer or shopkeeper were reflected in some of the commonly used words of the Italianized English which served the new immigrant, and which are sometimes fondly recollected by his children. Among them are *sciuppa*, shop; *storo*, store; *giobba*, job; *grosseria*, grocery; and *bosso*, boss. Two other picturesque specimens are *sonomagogna* and *baccauso*, the first readily definable if read aloud quickly, and the latter describing an outdoor sanitary facility in the rear of a dwelling.

Italian clan spirit helped to launch business careers, but it was also a potential handicap to the Italian-American children. The strong dependence on paternal authority made them vulnerable to the peasant concept that education is not of vital import, that intellectual achievement is disloyalty to the past. Large numbers of Italian boys and girls were not encouraged to hold ambitions for academic achievement beyond the high-school diploma, and some drew frowns even for that limited aspiration. Many a dropout of the 1920s bore an Italian name. Working-class Italians, used to the authority of *padroni*, seemed less aggressive unionists than the Irish or the Jews, despite the records of firebrand radicals like Carlo Tresca, Arturo Giovannitti, and Joseph Ettor, not to mention Nicola Sacco and Bartolomeo Vanzetti. Therefore, few of them achieved positions of authority in the national labor movement. In the church, they found the Irish in unyielding command and were not moved in any great numbers to undertake the studies required for the priesthood.

With the passing years, many Italians did enter the ranks of skilled craftsmen (such as electricians and plumbers) through their connections with the building trades. Others enlisted in the civil service's corps of technicians and administrators. But an occupational census of New York City in 1950, for example, showed that among sons of Italian immigrants surveyed, thirty-three per cent were in professional, technical, clerical, and sales fields or were managers, officials, and proprietors. The comparable figure for the Irish was forty-seven per cent; for the male children of Russian (and therefore, in New York, primarily Jewish) immigrants it was seventy-four per cent. More Italian girls than boys had "made it"; forty per cent were in the clerical and sales area alone.

Yet by the 1960s the Italians had moved a considerable distance from a living standard sustained by the shovel, and were justly proud. In neighborhoods where TV antennas sprouted like denuded trees from the ridgepoles and tomorrow's pizza was stored in a late-model freezer, they congratulated themselves on what they had achieved "without help"—a phrase they sometimes used to disparage the Negro's need for public assistance. And on vacation, at places like the Villagio Italia in the Catskills, where strolling minstrels caroled "*O Sole Mio*" in the Stella Alpina Lounge, they showed that one ethnic group could be quite Americanized in certain ways but also quite "unmelted."

Both the Italians and the Russian-Polish Jews reached the shores of opportunity in America at about the same time. The Jews, too, after half a century or so, remained a discernibly separate group. Yet in some ways, not shared by other elements of the mighty 1890–1914 migration, they had been successfully joined to contemporary America—to such an extent that their communal and religious leaders worried over Judaism's possible loss in America of the hardy virtues acquired during centuries of persecution. Or even, thoroughly unlikely as it might appear, of American Jewry's disappearance into the lonely crowd of mass society.

Like the Italians, the Jews had a strong sense of family. But they also traditionally placed a formidable premium on intellectual achievement, especially for males. If this outlook tormented generations of Jewish boys who did not glitter in the classroom, it was a tremendous asset to those offspring of the *shtetl* in whom natural ability was fertilized as well by their own hunger for success. Thousands of boys from New York's lower East Side and other Jewish urban neighborhoods pushed their way through schools of accountancy, pharmacy, education, law, and medicine in the 1920s and 1930s, when those seemed the professions most open to Jews. Often they were financed by a combination of a student's part-time job and parental sacrifice. Their own children and grandchildren attended colleges and graduate schools in record numbers. While Jews were still only about three per cent of the national population, in 1955 it was estimated that they accounted for twenty-three per cent of the student body in Ivy League colleges. A survey taken in Providence, Rhode Island, in the mid-1960s showed that a third of all Jewish men twenty-five years old and older had had four years of college or more. Forty-one per cent of them had gone to college for a while at least, compared to thirteen per cent for the general population. A study of another Jewish community showed more than a third of its youth with graduate-school training.

Even armed with diplomas, Jews were not able to pry open every door closed by historic prejudice. In leading industrial corporations, as of 1960 they formed less than half of one per cent of executive personnel, although the post-1945 industrial and scientific boom had brought great numbers of Jewish engineers and research specialists onto corporate and government payrolls. But in entertainment, journalism, literature, and the performing arts the efflorescence of Jews was universally noted. And professorships, formerly the near-monopoly of old-stock Americans, had become available to aspiring Jewish youth to such an extent that one estimate in the late 1960s counted thirty thousand Jewish faculty members. Approximately half of all American Jews, it was estimated, were involved in wholesale or retail trades, as against twenty-eight per cent of the total white population. Almost half were self-employed; the national average was ten per cent. Almost three fourths were white-collar workers, compared to thirty-three per cent of American Catholics and forty-three per cent of the Protestants. The image of the American Jew as a basically middle-class type was justified by the facts. But some were still blue-collar workers, especially in New York City, where half of the country's Jews lived and accounted for a fourth of the city's population. Most of the rest were concentrated in some nine other major metropolitan areas in the country. In New York, Jews still worked in garment factories, drove taxis, wore police uniforms, and served as house painters, plumbers, and carpenters. Thousands of others were in white-collar occupations whose incomes probably did not exceed those of skilled laborers—for example, teaching. Half of New York City's teachers in 1970 were Jewish; and every year, schools closed on the High Holidays out of sheer necessity as well as deference to the ethnic vote. This predominance produced an ominous conflict in 1968 between teachers' demands for job security and the clamor of many blacks and Puerto Ricans for control of their neighborhood schools; a bitter strike resulted. It was disturbing for New York's future that Negroes had traditionally known Jews only as "superiors"—landlords, shopkeepers, social workers, doctors, lawyers, and employers.

Rich or poor, the Jews retained their visibility. Most of those in New York had long since moved out of their bastions on the East Side, but they created identifiable neighborhoods in Bensonhurst, the West Bronx, and Washington Heights in the 1920s and 1930s, and in suburban towns in Long Island, New Jersey, and Westchester after World War II—communities with counterparts around other large cities. In suburbia, their synagogues, designed by expensive architects, rose amid landscaped parking lots—a far cry from the store-front *shuls* of urban Jewry forty years before. Alleged Jewish ostentation, vulgarity, and lack of genuine piety had been assailed, not least by Jewish intellectuals themselves. Rabbis, commentators, and novelists asked whether Professor Goldstein, with his summer home, sailboat, hi-fi, son at Harvard Law, and daughter in the Peace Corps, was as whole and as self-aware as his pants-pressing grandfather.

But the question itself implied a curious tribute to the United States. The descendants of the Russian pants presser might agonize over whether they still needed his specifically Judaic faith and folkways; whether they were being disloyal to Grandfather by substituting the purchase of Israel bonds for the multitude of religious observances that once concerned him. But their "problem" arose from a society that took the pants presser from the *shtetl* and gave his children a chance. That they used it so effectively said something complimentary about them and about America.

Ethnic groups of all kinds continued to exist on the national scene. Most occupied the middle ground—somewhere between totally divorcing themselves from their Old World customs and clinging to them so rigidly as to become isolated from any meaningful participation in modern life—like the Amish. In the industrial cities where the immigrants gathered years ago, Polish, Italian, Hungarian, and other "unassimilated" neighborhoods still stood, complete with their own grocery stores and churches. Though they, too, were changing, one key to identifying those that changed most slowly was the persistence of the foreign-language paper. The immigrant press had been in decline since its zenith in 1914. There were then some 1,300 foreign-language newspapers and periodicals published in the continental United States, forty per cent of them in German. Between 1914 and 1940 the number diminished by a fourth and then plummeted. In the late 1960s there were just seventy-five such journals in the United States—islets of a surviving past in the mass-culture sea. Twenty-five of these had their offices in New York, eleven in Chicago, ten more in San Francisco and Los Angeles, and others in Cleveland, Detroit, Pittsburgh, Philadelphia, and Watertown and New Bedford, Massachusetts. The languages represented were Chinese and Japanese—which together made up the largest number—as well as Spanish, Greek, Arabic, Finnish, Rumanian, Ukrainian, Serbian, Czech, Slovenian, Russian, Polish, Yiddish, Lithuanian, Latvian, Italian, Armenian, Hungarian, and Portuguese. As a sign of the "new" immigration replacing the "old," only three of the papers were printed in German.

Nowhere could one get so strong a sense of ethnic

Though many Jewish weddings in America appeared by mid-century to be similar in most respects to marriages in other faiths, on occasion the rites were performed in the traditional way. At right, guests dance the hora at the New York marriage of a rabbi's daughter. Note that there are no men in the circle of dancers; men and women danced in different rooms, as Jewish orthodoxy directs. The father of the bride was a Hungarian "miracle rabbi" who had brought his family to America in 1948. The succession of Zaddikim—miracle workers—from which he came originated in the 1400s.

persistence as in New York—where groceries might change nationalities and aromas every few blocks. Oriental youngsters from Chinatown ate pizza in the adjoining Italian neighborhood along Mulberry Street. Puerto Ricans, Haitians, Dominicans, and Cubans clustered on the West Side, mingling with Koreans and Japanese in the same neighborhoods. Ukrainians patronized the Akra Discount Store for "native" clothing, and feasted on pigs' feet and mushroom dumplings at the Odessa Restaurant.

Thus in the great metropolis, the peasants who came from a dozen cultures sixty and seventy years before and helped make the United States a modern nation had left enduring legacies. American children sprung from their loins carried their inheritance forward, conscious of that past as well as what they might become. American social institutions, still malleable, were being shaped as much by the presence of those immigrants' children as by anything that happened on the frontier or in the "Saxon" past.

One arena in which the process was most apparent, naturally, was the political. Partisan politics in the United States specialized in mediating among diverse groups, often groups with really conflicting interests. Immigrants have been among the most readily identifiable of groups, and therefore American urban politics developed what is known as the ethnic ticket. In New York, for example, ward bosses still spoke in the 1970s of "the Three-I League"—Israel, Ireland, and Italy—and took it seriously, as they did in 1965, when the regular Democratic candidates for the offices of mayor, president of the city council, and controller were Abe Beame, Frank O'Connor, and Mario Procaccino.

At first glimpse, such ethnic back scratching might have seemed foolish and trivial. But more than a quarter of a century had elapsed since the New Deal drew a deep dividing line across American political history. As the political analyst Samuel Lubell has pointed out, the 1930s were just about the time when the children of the new immigration came of voting age. Two great forces, the city and the immigrant, made it inevitable that the national political center of gravity would settle amid an electorate that was largely urban and non-Protestant. It would be the Irish story again, in one sense, but far wider in scope and impact, as the nation of the 1930s was far more complex than that of the 1890s. Those who were most sensitive to the needs of the new voting masses would have ready-made majorities at their command.

Lubell discovered this pattern in scrutinizing the Presidential votes of the country's twelve largest cities. In 1920 they gave the Republicans a plurality of 1,540,000. But eight years later, they gave the losing

candidate, Alfred E. Smith, a 210,000 plurality. "What Smith really embodied," Lubell wrote, "was the revolt of the underdog, urban immigrant against the top dog of 'old American' stock." His Catholicism lost him crucial rural votes, but his religion was an essential element in that revolt. Brown-derbied, speaking with an accent unabashedly New York, he was quintessentially urban. He was a genuinely productive and progressive governor in Albany, but the heart of his appeal to the voters was symbolized when the band struck up his theme song, "The Sidewalks of New York." He pushed the Democratic Party away from one of its historic bases— the Bible-thumping crossroads towns beloved of William Jennings Bryan—and this momentum endured. The key metropolitan areas included in Lubell's investigation gave Franklin D. Roosevelt a 3,479,000 plurality in 1936, and later piled up victory margins for John F. Kennedy and Lyndon B. Johnson.

Under the lash of depression, Roosevelt and his aides formulated programs of public assistance to the aged, the jobless, the unorganized, the untrained, and the ill cared-for—programs that met the basic needs of a new generation of city-bred Americans disenchanted with unrestricted free enterprise. The quarterdecks of state and local Democratic organizations were manned at the

Sitting beside United Nations Secretary General U Thant, Ambassador Arthur Goldberg, left, addresses the Security Council in 1966. Goldberg, the son of Russian-Jewish immigrants, was born on Chicago's West Side and was educated in public schools there. By working nights in the post office and vacations on construction gangs, he was able to study law at Northwestern University. In 1961 President John Kennedy named Goldberg, then a leading labor lawyer, Secretary of Labor. The following year he was appointed to the Supreme Court, from which he resigned in 1965 to become United States Ambassador at the United Nations.

beginning of this movement by old-timers from the reform establishment and by a few machine veterans. But it was only a question of time before the rising young public leaders of the second-generation immigrant communities would aspire to visible and prestigious roles. And it was inevitable that they should achieve these roles, especially after many returned with honorable records from World War II service.

The story of Rhode Island's John Pastore is highly illustrative. When he was born, in 1907, one of a tailor's five children, Italians constituted one thirteenth of his state's population. They voted for the Republican Party, the supposed provider of prosperity and the full dinner pail, but got little by way of political reward. In 1910, Providence had only one schoolteacher, one policeman, and one fireman of Italian descent. In 1912 the Republicans named Antonio A. Capotosto as assistant to the state attorney general, and that completed the Italian patronage list.

If the Pastore family, for one, felt any resentment at such slights, it was overshadowed by personal tragedy in 1916, when John's father died suddenly. Mrs. Pastore went to work full time as a seamstress, never permitting her children to stray from the path of respectability, even when it demanded the utmost from her,

such as ironing twenty shirts a week so that her boys would never appear at school without a fresh one.

Young John worked his way through night law school. When he passed the state bar examinations, in 1932, only four or five Italian-Americans a year were doing so. Also in 1932, F.D.R. was elected. The ethnic urban vote was noticed. The Italians were suddenly, visibly more important, and by 1938 every fifth Rhode Island voter was of their stock. The Democrats moved in, and showed themselves ready to improve on Republican parsimony by sharing the spoils more liberally. And so, one Sunday, John Pastore waited outside St. Bartholomew's Church for Tommy Testa, the Democratic boss of his ward, and gave his oath of allegiance. By 1944, his credentials were so good that he was given a spot on the state Democratic ticket—candidate for lieutenant governor. The ticket won, and when Governor J. Howard McGrath resigned to take a Federal post, John Pastore was governor. He ran for another term in 1946 and won. Then, in 1950, a proven vote getter, John Pastore became the first Italian-American to sit in the United States Senate.

It was also in the 1950s that Foster Furcolo became the governor of Massachusetts, Abraham Ribicoff the first Jewish governor of Connecticut, and Edmund Sixtus Muskie, Polish-American, the governor of Maine. The 1950s were the decade of arrival. At the outset of that decade, New York City saw a three-way race for its mayoralty, often considered the second most important and trying political job in the United States, in which all the candidates—Vincent Impellitteri, Edward Corsi, and Ferdinand Pecora—were Italian, and so was the boss of Tammany, Carmine De Sapio. As the next decade began, a Catholic heir of Irish immigrants in Massachusetts won the Presidential office that Al Smith had vainly tried to reach. Part of the explanation for all this could be found in the words of a Buffalo Polish ward leader in 1940 predicting the ultimate election of a Polish mayor (which happened in 1949): "Out in ritzy Humboldt Park they get two voters to a family. I get six out of my house. I got neighbors who give me eight." But there was something else, too—a change of attitude, a softening of heart, since the days of the restrictionist crusade.

By no means had the millennium of universal tolerance arrived. As the 1970s began, there were still underrepresented minority groups, mostly nonwhite, and their urgent pressure for admission to the feast of office was mercilessly straining the joints of the traditional New Deal alliance. The 1960s had witnessed the election of black mayors in Gary, Indiana, Cleveland, Ohio, and Fayette, Mississippi, but also a great backlash and the nationalizing of the appeal of demagogic conservatives. Moreover, to win office is not necessarily to find a path into such major strongholds of social and economic power as banks, corporations, and communications networks and universities—all of which at the end of the 1960s had few directors from the "new" immigration's offspring. And finally, the Italian or Polish or Jewish or Negro mayor or governor could stay in office only by spreading favors with reasonable even-handedness. He could not offer much to his own ethnic group that he did not offer to others, except perhaps the honor inherent in his election.

Yet men live by such symbols as honor, and in the long run the symbolic meaning of an election can be as influential as its immediate impact on parties. The election of John Kennedy as President was a genuine landmark, but little notice has been given to the sequel. Only eight years later, the two Vice-Presidential candidates were of recent East European roots. Spiro Agnew did not parade his Greek background; on the other hand, the fact that his original family name was Anagnostopoulos caused him no embarrassment. As for Edmund Muskie, his father's surname in Poland had been Marciszewski; it was changed by an Ellis Island official in 1903 who found it too much to spell. Agnew is an Episcopalian, but Muskie's middle name is proudly that of five Popes.

During the campaign, everyone was aware that the Vice Presidency was an important office. Of the five most recent Presidents, two had died in office—one by assassination; one had been the intended victim of an assassination attempt, and one had been seriously ill several times. Yet there was no major outcry over the prospect of putting a second-generation American a heartbeat away from the most powerful office in the world. The bodies of the old Klan, the American Protective Association, and the Immigration Restriction League may have turned over in their graves, but if so, that caused no earthquakes. Society had, in fact, come a long way in seventy years.

While the offspring of the steamship immigrants were working their ways into American life, black families were moving northward. Their journey was not unique. Everywhere in developing nations, rural people pricked up their ears at the sound of the factory whistle. And the nearly nine million American Negroes who lived in the South in 1910 (and made up ninety per cent of the nation's total black population) were predominantly a peasantry, living on farms, confronting permanent tenantry, poverty, ignorance, and disease. A government commission studying farm labor crisply summarized their plight that year: "There is absolutely nothing before them on the farm . . . no prospect . . . but to continue until they die." From this desperation they began to flee, in a movement that still continued in the 1970s. By 1920, fifteen per cent of the nation's Negroes lived outside the South. By 1940 it was twenty-three per cent, by 1960 forty per cent, and 1970 about half of black America lived outside what might well be called their "old country."

They came to the cities by train in the early days, pouring onto the platforms with their bundles and their boxes, looking around, filling their eyes with the sights of Mecca. They came in response to letters and messages from relatives—sometimes in response to nothing more than ads clipped from the Pittsburgh *Courier*, the *Amsterdam News*, the Baltimore *Afro-American*, or the Chicago *Defender*, that said things like "3000 laborers to work on railroad. Factory hires all race help. More positions open than men for them." It was very encouraging. True, the unions would not easily accept black men, so the factory jobs turned out many times to be the hardest, the dirtiest, the ones offering the smallest promise of advancement. Or else they were for strike-breakers, which was a dangerous way to earn a living. Even a scab's work was not always available, so black men (and their women) had to do the traditional chores of their people in America: cooking, cleaning, fetching, and grooming for white men.

Still, it was the North. Schools were better than what the South offered. The coarser humiliations of legalized segregation were somewhat muted. Voting was possible, and there might be a future for the young. There was an air of promise. Some black men in the cities, members of Booker T. Washington's National Negro Business League, were making money as owners of their own barbershops, funeral parlors, and livery stables. Washington's well-known antagonist, W. E. B. DuBois, was talking about a "talented tenth" of the Negro race, which would save its future. In 1909, DuBois and other Negro leaders had helped to found the National Association for the Advancement of Colored People, then a "radical" force fighting courtroom battles for black rights. At their side were sympathetic and brilliant whites like Mary White Ovington, Joel Spingarn, Oswald Garrison Villard, and Moorfield Storey. In 1910, the National Urban League was founded to set about opening job opportunities for blacks. A new day did seem on the way.

There were drawbacks, of course. Living quarters were scarce. Northern whites would seldom accept black neighbors except perhaps along the alleys behind their houses; so old Negro districts, cramped for expansion, grew desperately crowded. The poet Langston

New York mayoralty candidate Procaccino at a rally in 1969

Hughes, born in 1902, remembered that his family in Cleveland always seemed to inhabit attics or basements and to pay a lot for them. When white people did finally rent to Negroes, they would cut up their houses into five or six apartments and charge gold-rush prices for each—and for garages and sheds, too.

But a Northern city offered a little acceptance to Negroes when they were still definitely a minority. Hughes went to Central High School. Once it had taught the children of proper Clevelanders; by 1916 it was full of the children of the foreign-born, divided mainly between mutually suspicious Jews and Catholics. When elections were held for class officers, Hughes often won as the "compromise candidate," having apparently the advantage of being considered neither Jew

nor Gentile. On a summer vacation he visited Chicago, which was exciting. South State Street was "in its glory" in 1918, "a teeming Negro street with crowded theaters, restaurants and cabarets. And excitement from noon to noon. Midnight was like day. The street was full of workers and gamblers, prostitutes and pimps, church folks and sinners. The tenements on either side were very congested. For neither love nor money could you find a decent place to live."

More attractive than Chicago for many a bright young Negro was a place that had once been a quiet Manhattan suburb, "the rural retreat of the aristocratic New Yorker"—a place called Harlem. After 1900, Negro real-estate operators began to buy buildings there, hoping to open the ownership of tidy homes to worthy blacks. They undoubtedly had profits in mind, but they also hoped to avoid the creation in New York of a "Niggertown," a "Buzzard's Alley," a "Bronzeville," as Negro slums were already called in other cities. And, though New York's Negro population began to increase markedly after 1910, they seemed for a while to be succeeding. White residents, unsurprisingly, fled before the migrants, who were described by one newspaper as "black hordes . . . eating through the very heart of Harlem." But they left behind a Harlem that suddenly became a magnet for black artists and intellectuals, who made it their cultural capital.

Young whites reveled in Mencken, Eliot, Pound, Hemingway, Stravinsky, Cubism, and Dadaism, while black poets and writers like James Weldon Johnson and Claude McKay and Countee Cullen, black scholars like Carter G. Woodson, Alain Locke, and E. Franklin Frazier, and black musicians like Bessie Smith and Duke Ellington, sang their various lyrics of emancipation. Not all of them lived in Harlem, but for most it was at least their spiritual home. Langston Hughes spoke for a whole black generation when he described how it was to come up from the subway under Harlem after a long absence. "I stood there, dropped my bags, took a deep breath and felt happy again."

And yet there was another side to Harlem in the 1920s. It might float the mirage of a "new Negro" before the eyes of intellectuals—who, even so, quickly perceived that New York was a place where good jobs for blacks were scarce and pay skimpy. And when, between 1920 and 1930, the city's black population rose by another 115 per cent, good will and hope collapsed. Black and white slumlords found that milking decayed buildings for a few years was more profitable than long-time investments in repairs, and so black Harlemites endured falling plaster, exposed wiring, malfunctioning plumbing and heating systems, and rats and roaches.

"*For years now, I have heard the word, 'Wait!,'*" *wrote the Reverend Martin Luther King, Jr., right, from his jail cell after the Birmingham antisegregation demonstrations in 1963. The subservient role of blacks, stereotyped in the picture above, taken in 1899, could no longer be tolerated. Said King: "We have waited for more than three hundred and forty years for our Constitutional and God-given rights. . . . when your first name becomes 'Nigger' and your middle name becomes 'Boy' (however old you are) . . . when your wife and mother are never given the respected title, 'Mrs.,' . . . when you are forever fighting a degenerating sense of 'nobodiness'—then you will understand why we find it difficult to wait.*"

Disease flourished in Harlem. Negro death rates from rickets, tuberculosis, childbed fever, venereal disease, and respiratory infections climbed and stayed high. Doctors were few and expensive; folk remedies and charlatanry were relied on. The white visitors who taxied to Harlem to listen to jazz at the Cotton Club neither saw nor wanted to see this Harlem. They wanted to see the black as an exotic, who could laugh and dance spontaneously in a land "flowing with Socony and Bryan and pristine Rotary purity." If they sensed black agony, they made it part of a fashionable Negrophilia. Carl Van Vechten, author of a best-selling 1926 novel, *Nigger Heaven*, wrote that the "squalor of Negro life, the vice of Negro life, offer a wealth of . . . picturesque materials to the artist." That had a familiar ring: the Noble Savage now lived in a tenement instead of a jungle.

But the squalor of Negro life was scarcely "picturesque" to those who endured it. They sought everywhere for escape. A few turned to political radicalism; more to red-hot religion—Christianity melted in the crucible of memory and pain. Sometimes they pursued the anodyne of hope by gambling on a "hit" in the numbers game. Sometimes they clutched the transient solace of liquor or drugs. Each night the squeals and swoops of jazz mingled with the exhortations of preachers in store-front churches, while the pushers and whores and gamblers—black themselves—separated other blacks from what cash the grocer and landlord had left them.

And, slowly, many of the children whose parents had moved north to give them a second chance died spiritually. Small dark wraiths wandered the streets with keys on strings around their necks, while fathers who had given up the fight drifted, somewhere, and mothers scrubbed kitchens in white people's homes. Those black youngsters who made it to school were bowed by psychological burdens that few white teachers understood. If they were recent "immigrants," they also suffered from the inadequacy of Southern preparation.

Despite the glamor of the "Harlem Renaissance," the nation's best-known black community had become by 1930 what it would remain for forty years at least—a place of enmity between policeman and community; where many local businessmen were outsiders and enemies. It was a pit of dilapidation and fury, often turned inward by blacks to become self-destruction, a center of narcotics traffic and crime. The crash and the Depression merely sealed its fate. For blacks, the hard times had started early. As Langston Hughes put it, "The Depression brought everybody down a peg or two. And the Negroes had but few pegs to fall."

Behind the immediate crisis of Negro poverty lay a question that ran deeper. The newly urbanized Negro raised as a sharecropper faced the same problem as his grandfather just out of slavery. How could he take a comfortable and dignified place in a rejecting society? Would the task require that he transform himself? If so, what would be the cost, if any, to his sense of identity? These were questions that every immigrant group faced, but the issues were bitterly complicated for the black not only by the unchangeable fact of his color but also by the passionate intensity of the feelings that race provoked. Could any metamorphosis of black life take place without massive white help, and would that help be encumbered by impossible reservations and conditions? Was it worth it? Would any such improvement really overcome white fears and open the way to a livable common future for both races in America?

Thinking blacks weighed such questions, and their answers took either of two general directions. One was toward black separatism, and in Harlem in the 1920s, separatism raised up a prophet in the stout figure of Marcus Garvey. Born in the West Indies in 1887, he had been trained in youth as a printer, a trade congenial to the upsetters of applecarts long before Benjamin Franklin's time. He drifted around the Caribbean and then to London, where he met rebellious "colored"

students from various parts of the British Empire. Back in Jamaica, Garvey founded the Universal Negro Improvement and Conservation Association and African Communities League. There was a steady, economically motivated West Indian migration to the United States, and in 1916 he joined it. In Harlem he founded a paper, the *Negro World*, to bring redemption to his people.

Garvey was the first to take up the cause that black is beautiful. "Up, you mighty race!" *Negro World* exhorted. "You can accomplish what you will." And Garvey also told them: "When Europe was inhabited by a race of cannibals, a race of savages, naked men, heathens and pagans, Africa was peopled with a race of cultured black men, who were masters in arts, science and literature; men who were cultured and refined; men who, it was said, were like the gods."

By 1919 the black community was more than ready for his message. In that so-called "Red Summer," as the pressure of the Negro migration increased and black servicemen returned from France more impatient than ever with the old ways, race riots tore half a dozen cities. In Washington, troops had to be called out. In Chicago, street fighting lasted more than a week, leaving twenty-two blacks and sixteen whites dead, and five hundred injured. Black emotions surged high, and Garvey fed some of their needs with pageants. He decked himself in gaudy uniforms. He devised a flag—a black star on a red and green background: black for the race, red for its blood, green for its hopes. He collected, mostly from the poor, ten million dollars for a "Back to Africa" movement. Negroes who were working toward improving conditions in America, such as the fiery union leader A. Philip Randolph of the Pullman Car Porters, denounced Garvey as a fool and a fraud, but Garvey stirred a pot that still boils. His organization founded a Black Star Line of ships to carry the pilgrims back to the homeland, as well as a Negro Factories Corporation, an African Orthodox Church and Court of Ethiopia, a Universal Black Cross Nurses association, Black Eagle Flying Corps, an African Legion. None of this got beyond the paper stage except for the Black Star Line, whose first ship nearly sank off Newport News on her maiden voyage. Yet despite white snickers, this was much more than minstrel-show foolery. National flags and national histories and institutions and insignia were part of the paraphernalia that buttressed white self-confidence. For blacks they had to be rediscovered and even invented.

Garvey distrusted integrationists and mulattoes (whom he called "hybrids of the Negro race"), and he was even baited into kind words about Klansmen for their comparative "honesty" about racial feelings. Con-

Fleeing Southern poverty and discrimination, Negroes looking for work moved North and added to the unskilled labor force.

servative blacks believed he was milking the community for his own aggrandizement. In time, leading Harlemites took up the slogan "Garvey Must Go." Finally, Garvey went—in shackles—to a Federal penitentiary on a charge of using the mails to defraud. In 1927 he was pardoned and deported to Jamaica; he died in London in 1940.

Was Garvey a charlatan and false Messiah? Many blacks came to believe that he was a ground breaker for the militants of the 1960s who demanded black economic self-sufficiency, black control of black institutions, black pride, black power. In any case, Garveyism was moribund by 1930. At that point, the curtain rose on a period of some thirty-five years during which Negro Americans appeared to take the alternative road, away from black isolation. They used a combination of legal argument, moral suasion, economic pressure, and political influence to quicken white America's conscience. They walked the path of coalition and integration.

The compass needle of Negro policy swung in that

The "colorful" Negro slum, a profit maker for writer, painter, and real-estate owner, was for its residents a sink of disillusionment and despair. Many blacks found the only lasting joy of their existence in religion: OVERLEAF, *a gospel tent in Brooklyn, New York.*

direction as a result of historic paradox. The Democratic Party, ancient bastion of Southern segregationism, became the sponsor of the New Deal, whose programs for public relief, employment, and housing did not discriminate. The Federal government under Franklin Roosevelt did not bring blacks into the Promised Land, but it did feed them some manna in the wilderness. In 1933, more than two million Negroes were receiving some form of public aid. In 1935 the figure ran to 3,500,000. About a third of the 120,000 dwelling units built by the United States Housing Administration up to 1941 were for Negroes. Ten per cent of the Civilian Conservation Corps' youthful membership was black. The Works Progress Administration had a marked effect on black employment rates.

So the Negro was swept into the New Deal coalition, along with white farmers, workers, homeowners, and small businessmen, and gave thanks at the voting machine for AAA, TVA, homeowners' loans, bank deposit insurance, Social Security, and the Wagner Labor Relations Act. Then World War II and postwar prosperity opened economic doors wider. Between 1940 and 1950, the number of Negro males in nonfarm labor went from 1.8 million to 2.8 million; ten years later it had risen to more than 3.5 million. In those twenty years the number of blacks in white-collar occupations rose from 149,000 to more than half a million, in skilled workers' and foremen's slots from 130,000 to 407,000. In 1950 only 0.3 per cent of Negro families earned more than $6,000 a year. By 1960 that had risen to 19.9 per cent. In 1940, 4.5 per cent of blacks finished high school and 1.3 per cent completed college. Twenty years later, those percentages had nearly tripled. Blacks might see some of these figures—legitimately—as puny, but forward movement was visible.

Meanwhile, legal and political victories made the headlines—integration of the armed forces during and after the Korean War, the Supreme Court's school-desegregation decision of 1954, the bus boycotts and the lunch-counter sit-ins and the freedom rides of the 1950s

and 1960s, the breaking of a Senate filibuster to pass the Federal Civil Rights Act of 1964, and the historic Voting Rights Act as a legislative climax in 1965. The continued shift of blacks to the cities began to produce, in the customary way of immigrant groups, black faces in city government. In seven of the twelve most populous cities in the United States in 1960, Negroes formed more than twenty per cent of the population. After 1962, five such cities were sending Negro Congressmen—all Democrats—to Washington. In the mid-1960s, one Negro, Robert Weaver, was appointed Secretary of Housing and Urban Development, and another, Thurgood Marshall, was named to a Supreme Court seat. Black voting strength was receiving traditional forms of recognition.

Yet by that time the picture was not at all rosy. Blacks had made definite gains in an absolute sense, but relatively they were well behind the rest of the society. A white youngster was much more likely to go to college than a black. Negro professional, managerial, and clerical workers had median incomes of $3,700 in 1965, with a figure of $5,400 for comparable whites. Only one Negro high-school graduate in three landed a skilled or white-collar job, while two out of three white graduates did. The likelihood that a white college graduate would become a manager or an official or a proprietor was three times greater than it was for a college-educated black. And at the base of the economic pyramid, black unemployment, especially among young males, always far exceeded that of whites. Civil rights or no civil rights, it was still Depression time for millions of black Americans.

The Negro, in short, was getting a smaller slice of a growing pie. The frustration of the black masses seemed to melt very slowly in the intermittent sunshine of white "benevolence." Impatience fed on aroused expectations. "It is precisely because this is a period of high mobility that it is a period of high tension," said historian Oscar Handlin.

Heartsick Negroes were reaching a crossroad. At best, integration had a faint suggestion that for blacks redemption could be found only by a change of skin. "Nobody demanded of the the Irish, Italians or Jews," said Handlin, ". . . that they become a vanishing element." So once more the appeal of separation was sounded in the streets, by Black Muslims and Black Panthers. Yet it was hard to know if a black community that isolated itself from the major tides of surrounding American society would fare any better psychologically or economically than it had in the "integrated," underdog role.

In a sense the situation presented separate problems for blacks and whites; blacks had to achieve some unity to develop a solution to their dilemma, and whites had to make their accommodation to the undying reality of black aspiration. Yet it was also a crisis for the nation as a whole, and it was, once again, an ethnic conflict presenting a familiar pattern. The union workers, the low-income homeowners on the margins of the black inner cities, the people who would literally have to move over to make room for oncoming blacks, were by and large of recent immigrant stock. They were now the "native Americans," confronting the barbarians at the gate. Many of them felt resentful. They were asked to bear, in taxes, a burden of reparation for an original sin—enslavement—that was not of their making. They were asked to commit their children to a new order that, even if they were being unreasonable, they desperately feared. They were asked to rework their values on behalf of people who appeared to lag far behind them in the cleanly and parsimonious virtues of good Americanism—and people moreover that they disliked as if by instinct and who were now sufficiently self-aware to return the dislike openly. In many ways, particularly economically, these whites were closer as a class to poor blacks than they were to the affluent liberals who preached racial equality at them; this seemed only to deepen their sense of betrayal.

It had happened before. But the circumstances were more dangerous in 1970 than they had been in 1910. There was a steadily contracting market for unskilled labor, little room for growth within the major cities, a huge public budget that kept much of the individual's surplus revenue from being used in entrepreneurial activities. In short, there was no frontier—literally, less room for maneuver and, it seemed, less time to maneuver in. There seemed to be no consensus of social values to which newcomer and old-timer could both conform. It was a violent, anxious era. The nation was fused in a way by mass media but not cohesive in beliefs—performers and audience, not a community. The prospects seemed ominous.

Yet despair is always slow to see the first edge of sunlight on the morning horizon. Solving the dilemmas of human diversity had been a task the American people had met reasonably well during a long period of unrestricted immigration. There was no reason to think that the assets the nation then had brought to the work had somehow disappeared. The restrictionists of the 1920s had been foolish to believe that by barring the doors they would solve the problems brought on by ethnic variety. It might be equally foolish for crowded America a half century later to believe that the problems could not be solved at all.

The Element of Hate

On December 21, 1919, 249 aliens were deported to Russia on the
army transport Buford, victims of the "Red Scare" that gripped
the nation after the First World War. Among those deported was
Alexander Berkman, a Polish-born radical, shown at right addressing a labor rally in New York in 1914. Although Berkman
had a criminal record (he had been convicted of an attempt on
the life of Henry Clay Frick of Carnegie Steel during the 1892
Homestead strike), most of those aboard the Buford were guilty
only of being radicals. Echoing the feelings of many Americans,
the evangelist Billy Sunday preached, "If I had my way with
these ornery wild-eyed Socialists and I.W.W.'s, I would stand
them up before a firing squad and save space on our ships."
Such, in essence, was the fate of two famous victims of the nation's first bout with anti-Red hysteria. Officially charged with
robbery and murder, Bartolomeo Vanzetti and Nicola Sacco
(opposite) seemed to many to be on trial because they were foreign-born radicals. In an atmosphere of unabashed hatred,
where even the presiding judge was heard to refer to the de-
fendants as "anarchist bastards," Sacco and Vanzetti were
sentenced to death for crimes they may never have committed.

Radical Bogeymen

In the days immediately after World War I, America suffered an attack of a recurrent illness—xenophobia. Disguised and dignified as a cleansing of the unpatriotic and anti-American elements in society, the newest outbreak of fear and hatred was nothing more than a campaign to weed out and deport foreign-born "agitators." Just as the Know-Nothing movement of the 1850s was precipitated by the influx of starving Irish peasants, so this latest attack of prejudice had its roots in the migration of thousands of Southern and Eastern Europeans at the turn of the century. These "new" immigrants were not only poor, uneducated, unskilled, and for the most part Catholic or Jewish; some of them were also advocates of socialism, anarchism, and militant industrial unionism. America's entry into the war, coupled with the overthrow of Russia's Czar and the formation of American Communist parties, created an atmosphere of increased tensions. *All* aliens became, in the popular mind, radicals; *all* radicals, bomb-throwing Bolsheviks. "There is hardly a respectable citizen of my acquaintance," wrote one businessman, "who does not believe that we are on the verge of armed conflict in this country." "Face to Face" (as in the cartoon at far left), Lady Liberty prepared to meet her newest "foe."

OVERLEAF: *Proudly waving the Stars and Stripes, citizens of New Jersey celebrate July Fourth, 1924, in Long Branch.*

BROWN BROTHERS

317

A Pride of Blood

In the 1920s, old and new America met in a head-on collision as every tradition was tested, and in many cases discarded, by a society that could not return to "normalcy." One defender of old-time ruralism was the resurrected Ku Klux Klan, whose strength, said one historian, "derived from an exploitation of regional prejudices. . . . Negro in the South, Jew in New York, Oriental on the West Coast and Catholic in the Bible Belt." Atrocities against Negroes were committed with shocking regularity and widespread public indifference. Anti-Catholicism, however, tended to be less violent. Its most prominent victim was Al Smith, the Irish Catholic governor of New York, above. In 1924, K.K.K. opposition denied Smith the Democratic Presidential nomination; four years later, as the party's candidate, he was the target of vicious attacks. Protestants, said one magazine, would not tolerate "the seating of a representative of an alien culture, of a mediaeval Latin mentality, of an undemocratic hierarchy and of a foreign potentate in the great office of President. . . ."

The tableau at the left was photographed in the South in 1932. During the first half of the twentieth century, more than 1,700 American blacks died at the hands of lynch mobs.

When "Amos 'n Andy" moved to television, the white creators of the original radio show, Freeman Gosden and Charles Correll (above), were replaced by black actors. In the 1960s Negroes were powerful enough to force the offensive program off the air.

Popular Stereotypes

The face of racism is not always violent. Often it is covert and subtle—a joke or thoughtless expression intended neither to insult the victim nor brand the speaker a bigot. But no matter how gentle it may be, ethnic humor is, in fact, demeaning to those against whom it is directed, and it has always been evident in popular American taste. From the early 1800s well into the twentieth century, blackface minstrel shows entertained audiences with grotesque imitations of Negro songs and dances. The Katzenjammer Kids, Hans and Fritz (top right in 1905), in 1970 still diverted millions, as they had for generations. In many moving pictures Harry Green (middle) had demonstrated that the "typical" Jew was a peddler, and Henry Armetta (bottom) symbolized Italians perpetually mangling the English language. Even in 1970 a newspaper editor could write: "It is not good business to make fun of Negroes any more. But it still seems to be good business to poke fun at other minority groups. . . . It would startle most of us now to encounter a television commercial showing a pickaninny eating watermelon and grinning from ear to ear, but we still see Indian braves selling cigarets with smoke signals and slothful Mexican bandits selling corn chips."

For a nation whose opinions were notably influenced by what it saw in motion pictures, characterization by ethnic types could easily turn into racial symbols. Probably the quintessence of the derisive self-stereotype was bumbling, stuttering Stepin Fetchit (left), who shuffled his way through many a "B" movie.

Prejudice in a Uniform

"Every realist knows," said President Franklin Roosevelt in January, 1941, "that the democratic way of life is at this moment being directly assailed in every part of the world—assailed either by arms, or by secret spreading of poisonous propaganda by those who seek to destroy unity and promote discord in nations that are still at peace." When he spoke, the United States was not being assailed by arms, but the purveyors of hatred were busily at work. Not all groups were as obvious as Fritz Kuhn's German-American Bund (below); however, in most isolationist organizations there ran an undercurrent of anti-Semitism. Many Americans agreed privately with those who declared publicly that Jews were "a danger to the country." The attack on Pearl Harbor made "a danger to the country" of 126,000 native and foreign-born Japanese-Americans. In what Justice Frank Murphy called "one of the most sweeping and complete deprivations of constitutional rights" in the history of the United States, 112,000 people, most of them American citizens, were imprisoned as potential spies and saboteurs, although they had committed no crimes.

To millions of radio listeners, Father Charles E. Coughlin (below) was "the greatest priest in America." Using the air waves and his periodical Social Justice as forums, "the radio priest" spread his doctrines of isolationism and fascism across the nation. Coughlin began his polemical career as a supporter of F.D.R., but he soon soured on the New Deal (he called it the "Jew Deal"); by the time war broke out in Europe he was an all-out anti-Semite and a staunch supporter of the Axis. Coughlin remained an influential force until 1942, when Social Justice was charged with violation of the Espionage Act and the church silenced him.

Discrimination was not new to the Japanese living in America. Even in 1941, Orientals were still ineligible for naturalization; only those of them born in America were actually citizens. The owner of the store at left was one of 93,000 Japanese living in California when this picture was taken on December 8, 1941. Unfortunately for him, for the family below being evacuated, and for the many others who waited out the war in barbed-wired "detention" camps, just proclaiming patriotism was no protection against race hatred.

Hate Dies Hard

From the end of Reconstruction until after World War II, America ignored and avoided the issue of equal rights for Negroes. But the demands of war, coupled with the mass exodus of Southern blacks to Northern industrial cities, forced the nation to face its problem squarely. The first attempt by the Federal government was made by Harry Truman in 1948. Calling for new legislation, the President said, "We cannot be satisfied until all our people have equal opportunities for jobs, for homes, for education, for health and for political expression. . . ." Truman's appeal failed, but at least it was a beginning. The death knell of government-sanctioned segregation in public schools was sounded in 1954, when the Supreme Court ruled that "separate" was "inherently unequal." Values do not change so easily, and implementing the decision took the forces of the United States Army, shown above in Little Rock, Arkansas, in 1957. Another bastion of white Protestant America gave way in 1960 when John F. Kennedy was elected the nation's first Catholic President. In the campaign, faced with the threat of anti-Catholic invective, Kennedy approached the problem forthrightly. Addressing a meeting of ministers in Houston, Texas (top right), the future President said, ". . . I believe in an America where religious intolerance will someday end." The Presidency, he declared, is "a great office that must be neither humbled by making it the instrument of any religious group, nor tarnished by arbitrarily withholding it . . . from the members of any religious group."

"Negroes looked a little different and acted a little different when James Meredith was graduated," Dick Gregory wrote, "because they all graduated with him, graduated from the derogatory stigma that all Negroes are ignorant, that all Negroes are lazy, that all Negroes stink." At right, Meredith is shown as he entered the University of Mississippi in 1962. Despite the presence of three hundred Federal marshals, there were riots that led to two deaths; once more a President had to send regular troops and federalize a state's National Guard.

OVERLEAF: For all the gains made in the 1960s, life in America did not seem to be really improving for those whose needs were greatest—the minority groups at the bottom of the social and economic scale. The frustration, desperation, and hate that had been building up for so long in ghettos across the country finally exploded with terrifying fury in the latter half of the decade (Newark is shown here in 1967). "Social justice and progress," said Martin Luther King, Jr., "are the absolute guarantors of riot prevention. There is no other answer."

BENEDICT J. FERNANDEZ

327

Europeans came to Princeton (above) and other American universities in search of academic freedom and independence.

BRAIN DRAIN

IN THE 1930s, WALTER W. S. COOK, then director of New York University's Institute of Fine Arts, delivered an apparently insane judgment: "Hitler is my best friend." Before his listeners could explode, Cook added: "He shakes the tree and I collect the apples," meaning that the institute had grown into an important center of art studies, thanks to the work of European refugee scholars. In that respect, Hitler was all America's "friend." First the movement that brought him to power, and then his regime, uprooted tens of thousands of Europe's best thinkers and forced them to flee and serve the brain-power needs of other countries, notably the United States. It was a mistake made by other totalitarian governments. Laura Fermi, wife of a Nobel Prize-winning physicist who left Mussolini's Italy, compared the 1930s to "the fifteenth century, when the learned men of the dying Byzantine empire, fleeing from the barbarian invasion, sowed seeds of the old Hellenistic culture in European centers."

On a May morning in 1933, England's *Manchester Guardian Weekly* ran a story headlined "Nazi 'Purge' of the Universities." More than three columns of small type listed dismissals of professors between April 13 and May 4, including such luminaries as the philosopher and theologian Paul Tillich, the artist Paul Klee, and Fritz Haber, a chemist and inventor of the synthetic-ammonia manufacturing process on which Germany had depended for nitrates to produce explosives in the First World War. By April of 1936, more than sixteen hundred persons had been fired from universities and scientific institutions. They were a Who's Who of German intellect. They included Jews, Socialists, and a variety of hard-to-herd intellectuals. Some were migrants to Germany from other European countries. Some were among the artists and thinkers who had given Germany's postwar Weimar Republic an outstanding cultural life, and so many were promising scientists that the Hungarian-born mathematician John Von Neumann wrote to a friend, speaking of the Nazis, that "if these boys continue for only two more years . . . they will ruin German science for a generation—at least." Self-mutilation was one of Joseph Paul Goebbels' first gifts to the fatherland.

British intellectuals, at the onset of Nazism in 1933, had quickly created an Academic Assistance Council to try to place some of the ousted scholars in university posts. On the American side of the Atlantic, a similar organization, the Emergency Committee in Aid of Displaced German [later Foreign] Scholars, was founded by Stephen Duggan, then director of the Institute of International Education.

One of the Emergency Committee's wheelhorses was a scholar-journalist then nearly sixty years of age, a friend of Duggan's named Alvin Saunders Johnson. Johnson was a Westerner, born in 1874 to Danish settlers in northeastern Nebraska. As a boy, he had more or less taught himself Greek and Latin. He had planned to be a doctor, but the grind of memorizing muscle names and doing laboratory work was not enough food for his restless spirit. Johnson quit college to fight in the Spanish-American War, then settled down to graduate study in economics. He took his doctorate at Columbia University in 1901.

For sixteen years he lived the peripatetic life of a professor—Bryn Mawr, Columbia, Nebraska, Cornell, Chicago, Stanford—while writing crisply and successfully on a variety of public issues. He became an editor of the *New Republic* in 1917 and of the *Encyclopedia of the Social Sciences* in the 1920s, when he also was appointed director of New York's New School for Social Research, which specialized in offering advanced study to adults. In 1933 he was intellectually alive, tough, adventurous, and full of a prairie individualist's anger at any kind of forced orthodoxy. His reaction to reading the list of dismissed German professors was that it contained "the names of nearly all the social scientists who had any creative spirit in them."

Quickly, Johnson emerged as a major formulator of plans for bringing these creative spirits to America. He had more than a touch of the academic impresario about him, and delighted in assembling a star array of minds. His first impulse was to bid for a single refugee economist, but that gave way to a much more ambitious idea. In the United States it was easier to get money for a large project than for a small one. On April 24, 1933, Johnson wrote to a number of friends, proposing to hire fifteen men for two years at $4,000 a year each and assign them as graduate faculty at the New School. He would call them the University in Exile. "I want to make what return I can," he said, "for liberties I have enjoyed." A benefactor, Hiram Halle, offered to guarantee the required funds for two years, and Johnson was promptly off to London to assemble his faculty. By the beginning of summer, they were "arriving ship by ship," and he was meeting them at the gangplank. Meanwhile he continued his labors with the Emergency Committee in Aid of Displaced Foreign Scholars. Working with him were Walter Cook of N.Y.U.'s Institute of Fine Arts and Abraham Flexner, head of Princeton's new Institute for Advanced Study. As the 1930s—and Nazism—advanced, they and a number of museum directors, major librarians, and university presidents rescued group after group of scholars, scientists, artists, writers, and musicians from under the shadow of the swastika as it fell over Austria, Czechoslovakia, Poland, Norway, Denmark, Holland, Belgium, and France. Committees and conferences pro-

liferated to handle the flow of refugees—not only academics but those from every walk of life. The Joint Distribution Committee, the National Council of Jewish Women, the American Friends Service Committee, the Hebrew Sheltering and Immigrant Aid Society, the War Relief Services of the National Catholic Welfare Conference, and the Emergency Committee in Aid of Foreign Physicians were a few of the names on a lengthy roster of such agencies. Their inevitable overlaps and conflicts were partially harmonized by a National Coordinating Committee, ultimately called the United Service for New Americans.

Of all the organizations for dealing with refugees, perhaps none had annals so full of dramas as those of the Emergency Rescue Committee, created in 1940 to face the situation brought about when the Germans subjugated France in six weeks.

One condition of the Franco-German armistice was that the Vichy government surrender on demand all antifascist refugees wanted by the Gestapo. Thousands of Hitler's enemies, chased from all parts of Central Europe, had found a temporary haven in France. The speed of her collapse now trapped them. The Emergency Rescue Committee was formed to save as many of them as possible.

The committee soon learned from contacts in the German underground that it would need an agent in Marseilles. The man whom the directors named to the job was a young scholar and an editor of the Foreign Policy Association, Varian Fry. Fry had a month's vacation due him. He agreed, at the committee's urging, to spend it in France organizing rescue work, under the cover of operating a Centre Américain de Secours, a free food-distribution center for needy refugees.

Varian Fry's one month stretched into thirteen, each as taut as any spy-novel aficionado could wish. He and his assistants first had to locate those on the Nazi "wanted" list. Many were in hiding; rescue teams had to find them. Some were in French detention camps; their releases had to be secured. Finally, they had to be smuggled to the coast and onto outgoing ships. The

 *Walter Gropius*

 *Otto Klemperer*

 *Ludwig Mies van der Rohe*

 *Bruno Walter*

 *George Grosz*

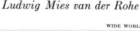

academically oriented Fry became adept at dealing with the grubby underworld of a Mediterranean port—where he found, for example, forgers of passports and visas; he learned to trace men living under aliases in cheap hotels, to bluster and lie to Vichy bureaucrats.

Fry and his associates were tailed, spied on, raided by the police, and harassed by Marshal Henri Pétain's collaborationist government. But they had the help of other agencies such as the American Friends Service Committee and the Unitarian Service Committee. Before Fry was expelled by the Vichy government in September of 1941, he had aided in almost fifteen hundred departures. A successor added another three hundred before the committee ended its French operation in June, 1942.

Not all of the escapees went to the United States. Yet Fry's work must have made an impression, even beyond the *Scarlet Pimpernel* heroics of the mission. Hans Sahl, a refugee writer, put it in moving terms. Sahl had been in concentration camps, been marched out of Paris to southern France, ducked Nazi bombs and strafings, been in jail for a while in Marseilles, and was let out but believed that he was at a dead end there. Sitting despondently in a café, he was approached by someone who whispered the name of a Mr. Fry, Hôtel Splendide. Sahl went there. He wrote:

Imagine the situation: the borders closed; you are caught in a trap, might be arrested again at any moment; life is as good as over—and suddenly a young American in shirt sleeves is stuffing your pockets full of money, putting his arm around your shoulders, and whispering with the conspiratorial expression of a ham actor: "Oh there are ways to get you out of here," while, damn it all, the tears were streaming down my face, actual tears, big, round, and wet; and that pleasant fellow . . . takes a silk handkerchief from his jacket and says: "Here, have this. Sorry it isn't cleaner." You know, since that day I have loved America.

For the United States, those years of Hitlerism marked new beginnings in immigration policy. Nineteen thirty-three was only the fourth year after the national-origins quota system had gone into full effect. Almost from the start, events had a more powerful effect on the actual flow of immigrants than the fine print in the lawbooks. As soon as the Depression set in, immigration dwindled. There was, therefore, a chance to see what actually happened when virtually no immigrants were arriving—to think afresh about laws whose basic pattern had been set in the martial atmosphere of 1917 and the "Red scare" of 1919–21. The arrival of the European refugees spurred further reflections on what a truly wise and modern immigration-control policy should be.

The refugees were far different in number and kind from the peasants and villagers of the earlier waves at the beginning of the century. Not even determined disparagers, for one thing, could describe them as "hordes." Less than half of the 580,000 visas issued to persons from Germany and German-held areas between 1933 and 1943 were actually used to come to the United States. Immigration to America *from all countries* in that period was 528,549. Less than seventeen per cent of the total European quota was taken up, and only in 1939 and 1940 was the generous German quota near full utilization. Moreover, an extraordinary percentage of the more than a quarter million refugees consisted of professionals and self-employed men who had had from eight to fourteen years of education. They were cosmopolites and heads of families, multilingual and cultivated—the kind of successful people who in America would be found at PTA meetings, in political caucuses, and on the advisory committees of churches and charity drives. They were inclined to remain in cities, where openings for them were comparatively plentiful, and surprising numbers (after the fumbling confusion of readjustment) found their way back into their fields of specialization.

Maurice R. Davie, director of the study *Refugees in America*, recorded that managers, bankers, architects, and lawyers had hard times in finding jobs like those they had left. But eventually more than three fourths of the chemists, dentists, and physicians surveyed re-

Paul Tillich   *Thomas Mann*   *Albert Einstein*   *Hans Morgenthau*   *Bertolt Brecht*

entered their professions. So did some 72 per cent of the clergymen, 68 per cent of the musicians, 61 per cent of the professors and teachers, and 55 per cent of the engineers. In Davie's sample of more than eleven thousand refugees, about half of the artists and a third of the writers were back at their old occupations by 1944. The same was true of about two thirds of those described as "skilled workers." Often there was an upward climb in the best American Horatio Alger rhythm. A bookkeeper might begin as a stock clerk and, as he acquired English, get back into his calling. A female dressmaker might "graduate" from domestic service to a sales job as she mastered the new tongue, and from there return to *couture*. Hundreds of refugee scholars were placed in colleges and universities scattered throughout the country. Interesting things happened in small college towns—where, outside of the faculty, sophistication usually reached its peak in *vin rosé* for dinner and the "1812 Overture" at a band concert, and where intellectuals were generally regarded as "men who wouldn't be able to make a living if they didn't find someone willing to pay them for talking." Authentic philosophers, musicians, and scientists, speaking the language of Kant and Beethoven and Roentgen, appeared at grocery stores and garages, still wearing clothes tailored in Berlin or shoes made in Munich. They inevitably made friends and learned their way around. At Winston-Salem and at Erskine, and at the University of Kansas City, aristocratic European males learned to play (or at least to watch) softball, while their wives taught white neighbors and black cooks the secret of thin strudel dough, and in turn were initiated into corn bread.

Not all encounters of native and alien were warm. Some refugees were stiff-necked and demanding, and had a hard time suppressing an ingrained contempt for America. Some American professionals consistently depreciated their European colleagues. Yet the fugitives remained and, as had so often happened before, adjusted to the American scene. By 1970 their children were grown, and their grandchildren doubtless found the story of the 1930s as remote as tales of the potato famine must have been to the youngest Kennedys.

Thousands of men and women in the refugee migration were ordinary souls. But there were among them some truly outstanding figures: in music, Darius Milhaud, Béla Bartók, Arnold Schönberg, Igor Stravinsky, Bruno Walter, Otto Klemperer, and George Szell; in art and art history, Willem de Kooning, Paul Klee, Erwin J. Panofsky, Marcel Duchamp, Marc Chagall, George Grosz, and Vasili Kandinski; in architecture, Ludwig Mies van der Rohe and Walter Gropius; in lit-

FRITZ GORO

erature, Heinrich and Thomas Mann, Bertolt Brecht, Stefan Zweig; in philosophy, history, and the social sciences, Ernst Cassirer, Werner Jaeger, Joseph Schumpeter, Hannah Arendt, Hans J. Morgenthau.

In the sciences, and particularly in the field of psychoanalysis, the honor roll would run to vast length, its names recognized primarily by specialists. But one story of émigré scientists is of absolutely overpowering significance. Essentially it was a handful of refugee physicists that gave to the United States the tip-off to the possibility of the atomic bomb, and who thereby started the nation on the road to Hiroshima.

European physicists had been drifting into the United States for nearly a decade before World War II began. Some were in flight from dictators; some, trained by Europe's outstanding theoreticians, needed to use the high-powered and high-priced experimental machinery available here. In the United States at the beginning of 1939 were Russia's George Gamow; the German Hans A. Bethe; three Hungarians, Edward Teller, Leo Szilard, and Eugene P. Wigner; and the Roman-born Enrico Fermi, who by then already had a Nobel Prize. They had come to stay. The American physicist J. Robert

In the fall of 1938, when Enrico Fermi, a Nobel Prize-winning physicist, realized that he could no longer remain in his native Italy, he let a hint drop to four American universities that he would be willing to accept an invitation; he received replies from five. The following year, Fermi (flanked by two colleagues, beside a cyclotron, left) became a professor at Columbia University. In December, 1942, he produced history's first self-sustaining nuclear chain reaction. The coded telegram informing Washington of his achievement read, "The Italian navigator has just entered the new world."

Oppenheimer later recalled that "they were all very good and yet wonderfully adaptable . . . they genuinely came to this country not as a temporary and resented alternative but as something that could be lived with and enjoyed."

In January, 1939, the Danish physicist Niels Bohr, on a visit to New York, sat down for a round of professional gossip with his friend Fermi, then at Columbia. Among his bits of news was an account of an experiment by two German scientists, who had bombarded uranium with neutrons—the noncharged particles in the nucleus of the atom—and produced a lighter element, barium. Bohr's information came from one of the Germans' former associates, Lise Meitner, who was brilliant but Jewish, and was therefore in exile in Sweden. She interpreted the result to mean that the neutrons had actually split the unstable uranium atom to produce the barium, with its different atomic weight.

Fermi drew the same conclusion, and was thunderstruck. If such a reaction had taken place, he reasoned, then the tremendous energy binding the particles of the nucleus together had been liberated. And if, in this "nuclear fission," additional neutrons were released to split

other atoms, liberating more neutrons to split still more atoms, a chain reaction could result that would free incredible amounts of energy. In harness it could perform prodigious work—or create devastating explosives. Fermi quickly revealed his apprehensions to scientific friends, including Szilard, who was between teaching appointments and was visiting with Wigner at Princeton.

Szilard, too, was alarmed. In Berlin, in 1933, he had kept two bags packed in his living quarters, and within a few weeks of Hitler's accession to power, he had picked them up and fled first to Austria, then to England. Szilard and Fermi, though differing on many matters, were both haunted by what Laura Fermi described as "this vision of Hitler with an atomic bomb in his hand." Szilard joined Fermi at Columbia University (without benefit of an academic appointment) to study the theoretical foundations and possibilities of chain reactions. By the summer of 1939, Frédéric Joliot-Curie was already on the trail in France; German physicists —even those certified 100 per cent pure by the Nazis— would not be far behind. Hitler now held the uranium mines of Czechoslovakia and had just forbidden exports of the material. Did he know something?

Fermi was away for the summer. Szilard and Wigner, worrying at their problem, suddenly devised a plan. The world's most distinguished refugee scientist, Albert Einstein, who came to the United States in 1933 and had been a member of the Institute for Advanced Study since that year, was much admired by the dowager Queen Elisabeth of the Belgians. The Belgian Congo had large deposits of uranium. Perhaps he could write to her, warning of the danger of letting uranium fall into Nazi hands. Impulsively the two scientists jumped into Wigner's car and drove out to Peconic, Long Island, where Einstein was vacationing in the cottage of a friend. Once on the rural roads around Peconic, they realized that they had no idea of the cottage's exact location. It was fortunate that Albert Einstein's sunburst of white hair and swoop of mustache were unforgettable. Wigner and Szilard spied a boy alongside the road, and asked if he knew where Dr. Einstein lived. They immediately got directions.

Einstein was willing to co-operate; he fully understood the possible horror. But there was still the problem of arousing the United States. Szilard took it to an influential friend, Alexander Sachs, an economist with the Lehman Brothers banking firm. Sachs had access to President Roosevelt through his Lehman connections (it was Herbert H. Lehman who succeeded Roosevelt as New York's Democratic governor); he promptly advised Szilard to forget the Belgian Queen. If Einstein would sign his prestigious name to a letter explaining

(Text continued on page 339)

"Could I Repay This Country?"

Only a small number of the refugees from fascism were famous when they arrived, or became famous after they reached the United States. A great many more had ordinary backgrounds and settled down to relatively inconspicuous existences. They became independent businessmen, teachers, technicians, farmers. They raised families and joined Lions Clubs and volunteer fire departments. Among this mass of the unsung was, for instance, Kurt Julius Burger, a Berliner. He and his wife Charlotte and their young son Ralph escaped from Germany in one of those hair-raising nick-of-time adventures that were commonplace during the late 1930s in Europe. Once in America, they put down roots in Casper, Wyoming, where a second child, Dorothy, was born in 1942. In a modest way, the family prospered, as Kurt Burger's moving letter, excerpted below, indicates. It was written to his son, who was working in New York City, in the summer of 1969.

Dear Ralph,

Thank you for your letter . . . in which you are asking for some notes regarding our emigration from Germany. . . . it is not too pleasant to recall those crucial years preceeding our arrival in this country. It might be advisable to give a short background to the happenings before the 30s. My father was a traveling salesman. Due to his quiet, sincere personality he was respected and appreciated by all his customers in Southern Germany, in Holland and Switzerland. He died after a minor surgery in 1910 at the young age of 43. Together with my sisters and brothers I had to quit school at 18 to help my mother to make a living. For 28 years I was employed at the Berlin garment center with the exception of the 44 months I served in the first world war, first as a fortification worker and later as a radio monitor on the French front. For several years I have spent some of my after office hours as an unpaid welfare worker for the city of Berlin. I was well liked and did not have any enemies, until [the 30th of January, 1933], 17 days before you were born, the Nazis came into power. It was a terrible shock to all cultivated and peace loving people. As the loud, frightening drum-beat in Tchaikovsky's "1812" overture interrupts the peaceful Russian country life our and many other families' civilized development came to a halt. Like in the "1812" overture the stunned victims of the assault tried to recover. But slowly and steadily the Nazis increased the pressure on the German people and especially on the so-called non-Arian part of the population and in 1938 I lost my job and was not allowed to accept any other employment except the lowest labor. At this point grandma (my wife's mother) contacted her brother Richard Lindstaedt, a rancher in Wyoming for help. Uncle Dick soon gave an affidavit that he would be able to assist us that we would not fall a burden to the authorities. We probably could have been on our way to the United States after a short time, if that affidavit would not have gotten lost or more likely was stolen by another desperate person trying to get out of Nazi-Germany. The second affidavit arrived in Berlin in 1939 when the chances to get out of Germany were already almost hopeless. There were thousands of applicants for an American visa registered at the Berlin Consulate of the United States, but the American quota for immigrants from Germany was filled. . . . I could only show one Christian grandmother and Mother, although baptized a Lutheran had a Jewish father, so, together with you, Ralph, we were doomed. In our dearest need the Lindstaedts came to Berlin. On their way to their boat in New York they stopped at the office of the Wyoming Senator Joseph O'Mahoney, who gave them a letter of recommendation for the American Consul in Berlin. Uncle Dick as an American citizen was able to see the consul who dug out our application from the pile of others and it looked we were safe now. . . .

The Lindstaedts hurried to Norway where they got a freighter for their return home, because the German passenger traffic was halted. On September 21st we received our visa but still could not leave. We would not get any foreign money for a passage from another country. Again our hopes were gone. In the 12th hour, the Nazis were already at the Dutch border, we got through the Berlin Jewish Hilfs-Verein Tickets for the "Rotterdam" of the Holland-American Line. I believe the sponsor of our free passage was the Montefiore Society, because at their office in the city of Rotterdam we were supposed to register for our boat. It makes me sick thinking of these good people. I am afraid their office in the center of Rotterdam certainly was destroyed by the massive Luft-Waffe assault shortly after we were safe in America. And the people itselves?

The Statue of Liberty was passed by the "Rotterdam" December the 2nd 1939 on her way to the Hoboken docks. You are right, Ralph, you were only 6 then but you can be sure your parents got the meaning of the Statue's greeting to the poor and the persecuted of the world. We were poor all right, poor for the first time in our lives because the Nazis did not allow us to take more than $2.50 a person along from our savings. But we were not desperate. We had

7 big boxes with our household belongings and clothing along and we knew that the Lindstaedts were sincere in their wish to help us to get on our own [in Casper]. 1939 was the time of WPA and foodstamps in America. We did not have a very good chance for a start. I was 46, had a family and no practical schooling, so I took whatever I could find in the line of a job. And I became a retail-clerk for 3 (three) dollars a week, Mother worked in the Henning Hotel as a chamber-maid for $2.-a day. The Lindstaedts rented us one of their small apartments for $15.- and helped us out with groceries, so we never went hungry. We sent you into one of Casper's wonderful gradeschools and soon you talked a better English then we did.

Then came our big chance. We were able to take over a rundown neighborhood grocery store worth $200.- worth of merchandise. . . . With our place open for business from 6.45 AM until 9.30 PM we soon were able to pay for the property and (with the Lindstaedts help again) build two more houses on our corner to be used as rentals.

We never had the ambition to get rich. We were more than happy to live in a peaceful little town in contact with the most wonderful neighbors in the world and to be appreciated by customers and tenants as well. Still from our earnings we were able to get more relatives to this country who all found work since there was a demand for employees

I had to retire from my business with 71, on account of frequent illnesses and receiving now the benefits of Social Security and Medicare I have asked myself am I or was I ever of use to this country? Could I repay this country for

giving me and my family refuge and the salvation from an unspeakable end? I believe I have something to my credit after all:

This country pays for the education of a native American through High School and College a considerable amount of money. I forgot how much. Mother and I brought no money but our education along and could start paying income taxes, however moderate, right away.

Although we have not been paying income tax after our retirement anymore, we still pay our property tax and participated with $1600. on Casper's street improvement program.

As long as Grandpa still lived he and I brought into this country $500.- a month on foreign (German) money for our old age pension. For me alone it still amounts to $200.- a month.

Of the people we helped to come to America four have their master degrees and are holding essential jobs in Defense, Industry and College Education. If I dont pay any income tax anymore they sure do.

We are providing four decent homes to the Casper people for a more than reasonable rent. And we are keeping our corner neat and clean like anyone would want to see it.

Last but not least we have given you and Dorothy a family background, a home and school education that should give you both a chance to do your part in the life of our new homeland, . . .

Best Wishes
Yours Dad

Kurt Burger poses in front of the family grocery store in 1948 with his daughter Dorothy—"the first American Citizen of the family"—who was then six years old. When he bought the property, he told his son, he "read in our abstract of title that President Theodore Roosevelt handed over the land on which we live to Mr. Robert White as a homestead. It is requested on the deed that 'Trees should be planted on the Western Plains.' Aha, I said to myself, if that's what I'm supposed to do, then I will have 10 shade trees on the curbing around our corner! They were baby-trees at first, now they are big and fat, the branches reach out on the street and the people of the printing office park their cars under them to keep them cool."

LEON GIERLOWSKI.
Mscr. o'Dwyer. Los Angeles
California.

Gierlowski.
o Dwyer
Angeles

the peril, Sachs would deliver it personally to the President. So, after a drafting conference (which by now included Edward Teller), the letter was prepared. It described the concept of nuclear energy's release, and warned that it could lead to the manufacture of bombs so powerful that a single one, "exploded in a port, might very well destroy the whole port together with some of the surrounding territory." The President was asked to take steps to secure a uranium supply for the United States and money for further experimentation.

The immediate action initiated by the letter was minimal. An Advisory Committee on Uranium was appointed, and the tiny sum of six thousand dollars was allotted for research. Not until 1940 was the pace accelerated appreciably; not until after Pearl Harbor was the basic decision taken to proceed with the bomb, and the financing provided to enter the race in earnest.

In the end, there really was no race. The Germans had not worked intensively on nuclear explosives. Hitler died in his bunker while the atomic bomb was still two and a half months away from its first test at Alamogordo, New Mexico. Japan endured the fury of the bomb in August, 1945, by which time some of the weapon's fathers were regretting their work and trying to persuade the United States to forgo its use and further development. But they had, in Oppenheimer's brilliant phrase, "known sin," and the consequences were to be as inexorable as when Adam made the same mistake. Yet they had begun with the intention of sparing mankind horror, through trusting the United States with their knowledge. It was in a way their repayment to the land of their liberation.

Pearl Harbor opened a period of nearly four years when practically all transoceanic travelers wore uniforms. Yet new developments were in the making. The war, which allied us with one Asian nation and against another, led to contradictory steps on the home front. On the one hand, there was a savage anti-Oriental outburst when, early in 1942, approximately 112,000 Japanese-Americans from the West Coast were summarily hustled into bleak, remote "relocation centers" that were, in fact, prison camps. Those born in the United States as well as those born abroad were uprooted and detained, sometimes for years before release. The excuse was that the government had to protect California against spies and saboteurs in the event of a Japanese naval attack, yet Americans of German and Italian ex

In the aftermath of an abortive uprising against the Communist regime in Poland in June, 1956, a young refugee—headed west in hope, like so many people before him—waits with his trunk.

traction were not treated in the same way—confined wholesale merely on the basis of race. But the American tradition of civil liberties was always wobbly where nonwhites were concerned.

In the next year, Congress opened a door that had been slammed shut by the Chinese Exclusion Acts. But just a crack. Sending Americans to fight alongside "yellow" people who were not allowed to enter the United States was an incongruity obvious even to West Coast legislators, and Representative Warren G. Magnuson of Washington State sponsored a repeal bill. But the act scarcely spread open arms to the Chinese. It gave them an annual quota of 105—105 members of "the Chinese race" from the entire world. Moreover, it reserved half of the entry visas for those with skills needed in the United States. Still, it was a first step; and later the Chinese, like other nationalities, were allowed to take advantage of various ways of getting around the official quotas, so that between 1944 and 1965 the total number of Chinese entering the United States was 52,959. One such method was embodied in the War Brides Act of 1945, under which Congress allowed returned soldiers who had married foreign girls to bring their wives and children into the country without regard to quotas. More than 5,000 Chinese women and infants entered in this way—as did 9,046 brides and babies from Italy, 14,175 from Germany, and 36,390 from the United Kingdom.

The common sense compassion that permitted overseas wartime romances to continue happily ever after in the United States was also one reason for the Displaced Persons Act of 1948. Refugees were a problem of the entire world community, and the United Nations took responsibility for feeding, sheltering, and otherwise caring for millions of homeless and jobless families. But three years after the war, the problem was still acute. It was clear that the unscarred and wealthy United States should fulfill its United Nations obligations in this situation not only with cash—which it had been doing—but with refuge.

The response of Congress was something less than wholehearted. It authorized a four-year quota credit plan to accommodate the overflow of visa-seeking applicants. During that period, a country could "borrow" extra visas and later "repay" the loan by accepting reductions of up to half of its future quotas. In this way, enormous waiting lists of applicants (773,465 long in 1951) were pared down. Of course the greatest need was precisely in devastated Eastern Europe, against which the national-origins policy had been aimed in the first place. War-torn Poland had an annual quota of only 6,524. Because of the many thousands of Poles admitted during the life of the Displaced Persons Act, subsequent Polish quotas were diminished by half, and would remain at half quota until the year 2000. Tiny Latvia, with a quota of 236, had been in the track of both Soviet and Nazi armies. Its half-quota mortgage was supposed to run until the year 2274. But it had been swallowed up by the Soviet Union, and American consuls simply charged visas issued to its nationals against its hypothetical account. These bookkeeping devices, in which the columns represented suffering human beings, were simple-minded and repugnant. Even so, some 400,000 refugees were taken into the United States under the law—a rescue that drew heroic efforts from American assistance agencies, which had to find jobs and housing for the immigrants before entries could be authorized. Congress measured out its hospitality by the teaspoon.

The game of quota stretching continued beyond 1952. Special enactments measured the spread of global disaster, natural and artificial. In 1953—the year of an unsuccessful East German uprising against the Russians, and four years after the Communist triumph in China —a Refugee Relief Act authorized the issuance, beyond quotas, of 205,000 temporary visas to "refugees, escapees, and expellees." It was expected that the "temporary" visa period would probably never be terminated while the immigrant was on his good behavior. In effect, he was on parole, and was sometimes even referred to as a "parolee."

In 1957 and 1958, two new acts allowed provisional entry to about 39,000 of the nearly 179,000 people who fled Hungary after the failure of the October, 1956, revolt against the Stalinist government in Budapest. Still other legislation between 1958 and 1962 opened the doors to victims of earthquakes in the Azores; to Dutch settlers dislocated by purges of "colonialists" following Indonesia's independence; to 15,000 Greek, Italian, Japanese, and Korean orphans adopted by Americans; and to 15,000 fugitives from Communist China who had been crammed into British Hong Kong. There was also the matter of the hundreds of thousands of Cubans who had left Castro's island by 1965. As Western Hemisphere immigrants they were not restricted by quotas, but special bills committed the Federal government to help with their transportation and resettlement in the United States.

Total immigration did not rise spectacularly in the first two decades after the war. The publicity given to some oversubscribed quotas obscured the fact that many countries, such as England, were not utilizing theirs to anywhere near the full. Between 1945 and 1965 some 4,800,000 immigrants, all told, were admitted.

The biggest single year was 1957, with 326,867. The total number for the period 1951–60 was 2,515,479; excluding the 1940s, when the world was at war, that was the smallest decade's ingathering since the 1860s.

Nevertheless, the old fear of inundating hordes existed throughout that period, and it certainly underlay the McCarran-Walter Immigration and Nationality Act of 1952. There was indeed a need for an overhaul of the patched and red-taped immigration system, but it was unfortunate that the overhaul should be done in the middle of one of the periodic national fits of xenophobic anxiety. The McCarran-Walter measure was not only intended as a tightening and unifying of legislation; it was aimed at insulating the United States from the dangers of the post-1945 revolutions in world order.

The national-origins quotas were preserved at the old levels. Countries in the Asia-Pacific triangle did receive small quotas, but all persons with even one Asian parent, no matter where they were born or lived, went on an Asian quota. (A Cambodian's son, for example, might have been born in Paris and gone to school there and never left; still, if he chose to resettle in the United States, he was not counted on the French annual quota of more than 3,000 but rather against Cambodia's one hundred.) Further, whereas immigration from all Western Hemisphere countries had in the past always been free, now colonial dependencies in the Western Hemisphere were given subquotas of their "parent" nations. The effect was to curtail the immigration of colored people from such places as the British West Indies. The law also was loaded with harassments for aliens who were suspected subversives. There would be a series of inquiries. Did the alien have a criminal record? That might even mean a record incurred by resistance to a dictator's police or by some childhood misdemeanor long forgotten. Had the alien ever been a member of a Communist party? It did not matter that such membership was virtually obligatory in some Iron Curtain countries: a Communist is a Communist is a Communist. If all these barriers were overcome and the alien were admitted, he might still be deported virtually without a hearing, if he were deemed by the U.S. Attorney General to be engaged in activities "prejudicial to the public interest." (The Alien Act, in 1798, had contained a similar provision, but the phrasing was "dangerous to the peace and safety of the United States.") Even foreign-born persons who had achieved citizenship were vulnerable to this arbitrary denaturalization.

The McCarran-Walter bill also proposed the creation of a Congressional Committee on Immigration and Naturalization Policy, which was to keep a suspicious eye on the State and Justice Departments to make sure that the Executive branch was sufficiently zealous in enforcement of the law. This provision in particular was a clear challenge to the White House, whose occupant, Harry Truman, was no man to let a flung gauntlet lie at his feet. He vetoed the bill on June 25, 1952, with a message that denounced the national-origins idea as "utterly unworthy of our traditions and our ideals. . . . It repudiates our basic religious concepts, our belief in the brotherhood of man. . . . It is a slur on the patriotism, the capacity and the decency of a large part of our citizenry."

Senator Pat McCarran of Nevada, a vigorous conservative who was the bill's public defender as well as its cosponsor, had his way as Congress quickly overrode the veto. But the long-run tide was against the McCarran principles. His measure would stand up for only thirteen years.

Consider what had happened since the passage of the Johnson-Reed Act, which had closed the doors in 1924. The German "Aryan" racial-superiority myth had been blasted by a war; that put American exponents of race superiority on the defensive. Furthermore, the high economic and intellectual quality of the refugees of that war suggested that some immigrants could be as valuable as gold to a nation, and that national-origins quotas that took no account of special skills and talents demonstrated not only poor ethics but poor sense. This became increasingly a factor as the age turned to nuclear and jet power, transistors, computers, rockets, satellites, wonder drugs, and miracle synthetics. Advanced industrial nations found that they needed now not just muscle power but alert, trained minds to program, to devise, to measure. A talent hunt swept the world's laboratories, and rich America started with a big advantage.

Simultaneously a black, brown, and yellow "third world" emerged from the wreckage of Europe's Asian and African empires, and was wooed by Soviet and American foreign offices. This diplomatic courtship helped further to undercut racist thought in the United States. The concepts of Anglo-Saxon or Northern European "superiority," so firmly lodged in 1910, were almost entirely discarded by the educated community of half a century later. Gradually, therefore, America's immigration laws were reworked.

A Truman-appointed immigration study commission dug zestfully into the national statistics. Between 1924 and 1951, while the total population went from 114 million to 154 million, the gross national product of the United States had soared from $140 billion to $329 billion, based on the value of the dollar in 1951. The labor force had increased from 41.2 million in 1920 to 66 mil-

On October 23, 1956, Hungarian students and workers protested in the streets of Budapest demanding liberalization of the government; a revolution had begun. Above, one victim of the conflict.

lion in 1951. More hands and minds than ever were required on the production line. In the nation's first modern industrial boom, from 1880 to 1920, the labor pool had been fed by the massive European migrations. In the quarter century after the restriction act of 1924, the slack in the labor market had been taken up by rural migration to the cities and by nonquota Western Hemisphere immigration. When these streams failed to fill certain needs for manpower, temporary immigration programs had been set up. For example, in wartime, 135,283 Mexican nationals had been admitted to sweat on the railroads at substandard wages. In 1951 another 191,000 or so were allowed, supposedly temporarily, to come in for agricultural work—at substandard wages. (Thousands more entered illegally, swimming the Rio

341

Grande, thereby earning the name of "wetbacks.") Special legislation in 1951 also admitted 10,000 Canadian woodsmen.

Loophole making could take time, and there was now a fast-growing demand for the superskills of engineers, designers, and research scientists. One basic reason for liberalizing immigration policy was expressed to the commission by Dr. Alan T. Waterman, director of the National Science Foundation, who said that visa delays had "a seriously detrimental effect on the strength of science in this country."

The national need, the commission decided, was for a policy that would regard immigration not as a problem but as a potential resource to be utilized judiciously, humanely, and with an eye to self-interest. America had been approaching the problem of control from the wrong end. As Dr. Vannevar Bush, a former scientific adviser to President Roosevelt, put it, "Instead of placing our emphasis on the desirability of attracting the right individuals, most of our emphasis has been on the problem of keeping the wrong ones out."

The commission therefore developed a set of recommendations that would completely overturn the McCarran-Walter Act. (Senator McCarran sputtered that the report resembled "the current series of articles attacking the Act in the Communist *Daily Worker*.") It was proposed that a total annual immigration ceiling be set at one sixth of one per cent of the entire American population as of the most recent census. At the time, the existing legal limit was based only on the white population and only as of the 1920 census. Also suggested were mechanisms for streamlining application procedures, co-ordinating various agencies' work, and providing avenues for immigrants to appeal deportation orders.

The Eisenhower administration did not push immigration reform, but John F. Kennedy had new legislation introduced in July of 1963. That year, Congress allowed the measure to die, but Lyndon Johnson, in January of 1965, resumed the work of reform and succeeded. On October 3, 1965, a liberalized Immigration Act became law, providing a new framework in which the United States could continue its centuries-old history of accommodating some of the world's wanderers. With his eye for the conjunctions of history, politics, and public relations, President Johnson chose to sign it at the base of the Statue of Liberty.

The foremost novelty lay in the abandonment of the national-origins quota system. It is not coincidental that the year of the act marked the peak of a legislative assault on racism. That assault also produced the Voting Rights Act of 1965. A lid remained on immigration:

170,000 a year from outside the Western Hemisphere. Furthermore, as of July 1, 1968, immigration from Western Hemisphere countries was limited to 120,000 a year until a special study of the impact of immigration from the Americas was completed. But gone at last were the mortgaged quotas of the Cold War and the knotty questions of assigning nationality. The only reservation was that no more than 20,000 might be admitted from a single country in a given year.

There were official ranks of preferability—a continuation of practices already long formalized and written into pre-1965 laws. First preference went to unmarried grown sons and daughters of United States citizens (spouses, minor children, and parents were already permitted entry without quota). Second, fourth, and fifth preferences went to other relatives of citizens and resident aliens; seventy-four per cent of visas were initially reserved for such kinfolk. But third on the list of preferences were members of professions and persons with exceptional ability in the sciences or the arts, who received ten per cent. Sixth on the list and also permitted ten per cent was "skilled labor in great demand." Seventh in preference were specially designated refugees, for whom six per cent of the spaces were saved. There was, therefore, room each year for at least 34,000 engineers, teachers, doctors, nurses, performers, craftsmen, and their families. There would be more when higher-preference categories went unfilled, because the 1965 act permitted unused visas from high-preference categories to be transferred downward. The potential newcomers still were required to pass many tests of economic self-sufficiency and moral character as official America defined these qualities. Western Hemisphere immigrants coming to the United States to take work, as an instance, had to secure certificates stating that their specialties were genuinely needed, and that they would neither displace American workers nor adversely affect wages and working conditions. Yet these demands were at least capable of fulfillment, where under previous law a man might be irrevocably doomed to exclusion because he could not change his birthplace.

After only two full fiscal years had elapsed since the act took effect, the statistics for July 1, 1967, to June 30, 1968, hinted at an interesting profile of new Americans in the 1970s.

Fiscal 1968 had produced 454,448 "immigrants." Not all of them arrived at sea- and airports; the number, by a convention of immigration figures, included 130,455 who were already in the United States and had their temporary status adjusted by the Immigration and Naturalization Service of the Department of Justice. That is, instead of visitors they became settlers.

Restrictive immigration laws provided visas immediately for only 5,000 of the Hungarians who fled their country following the ill-fated revolution in 1956. But President Eisenhower intervened and issued invitations to 30,000 others, who were thus able to enter as provisional immigrants. Among the oldest refugees was fifty-seven-year-old Sandor Blau of Budapest, below, who arrived on one of the military transports provided by the American government. One group of escapees made the trip Christmas Day on the Presidential plane, the Columbine. Above, they are shown with their pilot, Lieutenant Colonel William C. Draper, after landing at McGuire Air Force Base, New Jersey. The children hold up gifts they received from the President and the plane's crew at a party held during the flight.

OVERLEAF: Clearing customs at New York International Airport (later renamed John F. Kennedy International) in 1960. For the immigrant, arrival was by then a far cry from the old procedure—which had sometimes kept a newcomer waiting at Ellis Island for days or even weeks. Those who traveled by sea were now cleared by officials of the United States Immigration and Naturalization Service on board ship before it docked. Those entering the country at an air terminal were routed through a special immigration desk, where agents checked to make sure that the newcomer had the necessary documents and health certificates. This process, which was supposed to require only a few minutes to complete, ended the immigrant's "ordeal." He then took his luggage through customs like any other airline passenger.

343

More than 105,000 of the newcomers were natives of Western Hemisphere countries—with 41,290 from Mexico, 27,018 from Canada, and 17,414 from Jamaica leading the list. Those people entering the United States from Puerto Rico, of course, did not count as immigrants.

From countries outside the Western Hemisphere came 156,212 immigrants, who were subject to the numerical limitations of the law; 8,153 were professional men, scientists, and artists, and 7,940 workers came to fill needed jobs, and brought spouses and children with them.

The proportion of skilled people in the total may seem small, but a study of the 102,726 persons *naturalized* in 1967–68 adds some highlights to the picture. Of these new citizens, most had come from Germany, Italy, Great Britain, Canada, Cuba, or Mexico. About 45,000 of them were men—roughly 11,000 professionals, 20,000 skilled craftsmen and technicians, 4,000 managers and foremen, 11,000 sales and service workers. Only 3,379 were classed as laborers, 948 as household workers, and 487 as farmers or farm laborers. It was a long way from the days of the steerage.

Specific nationality-group examples multiplied. Of the Hungarian refugees to the United States after 1956, about three quarters were well educated and possessed skills or professional background. Chinese arrivals from Formosa and Hong Kong between 1956 and 1965 totaled about 46,000; the 20,000 men included 6,000 professionals and technicians; an approximately equal number were officials, proprietors, and service workers; very few were laborers. The "coolie" was gone with the buffalo, a legend of the Far Western past.

In August, 1968, a pair of events—the Soviet invasion of Czechoslovakia and a fresh wave of anti-Semitism in Poland—led to a rush of petitions by Czech, Polish, and other Eastern European scientists and artists for immigration visas to the United States, Canada, and Australia. Many of them had been "involuntary Communists," who needed—and got—special waivers for entry to America. In one month, American officials in Vienna processed 1,500 prospective immigrants, including Ida Kaminska, former director of the famous Warsaw Yiddish Theater; János Kende, conductor of the Košice Symphony Orchestra in Czechoslovakia; Rumanian opera singer Yolanda Malanescu and her husband, Sandu Stern, first violinist of the Bucharest Symphony Orchestra; and Dr. Jan Kemplenyi, a Czech heart specialist.

There might have been surviving restrictionists who continued to have bad dreams of an immigrant inundation. But by the late 1960s the rest of the world worried that America and other growing modern countries were taking the cream of the world's talent. A study printed in 1966 showed that 2.2 million of the 4.7 million immigrants to the United States between 1947 and 1965 had work experience and were in the prime productive years. Other nations had borne the expense of raising and educating them; America would get the finished products. Seventeen per cent of these occupational veterans had been professionals, one in six a craftsman, one in five a clerical, sales or managerial employee. Between 1956 and 1965, nearly 7,000 chemists were admitted, along with more than 35,000 engineers, almost 38,000 nurses, and more than 18,000 physicians. They came to sharpen and use their skills, as Americans.

The "brain drain" problem was an old one, going back to at least as far as the Ptolemaic dynasty in Egypt; the Ptolemies enticed scholars to Egypt from all over the Hellenistic world. But the losing countries took little comfort from historical perspective. In Scotland, birthplace of the steam engine and the Industrial Revolution, a newspaper complained in 1967 that red tape and wage-and-spending freezes were driving intelligent Scots to Canada, South Africa, and the United States in record numbers. At least 47,000 had left the country in the preceding two years. Between 1952 and 1961, Great Britain lost sixteen per cent of her Ph.D.s down the brain drain; half of those who left went to the United States. Between 1955 and 1960, an average of 483 British medical doctors emigrated each year, with one sixth going to the United States.

If the problem was serious for sophisticated Britain, it could be life and death for underdeveloped nations. A cultural attaché in a Middle Eastern embassy estimated in 1966 that only half of Iran's six thousand students in the United States would return to Iran; the rest would inevitably be drawn to the greater opportunities of the Western world. In 1961 the United States "absorbed" nearly a third of the medical graduates of Greece; five years later it was taking more than a fifth of the Greek crop of engineers. Such figures haunted the thoughts of Ministers of Education in the capitals of many a country.

There was a certain irony in the possibility, but the day might well come when the governments of "backward" nations would fight as enthusiastically as the Immigration Restriction League once did to keep their people away from America's shores.

Once thronged daily with thousands of people passing through to become Americans, in 1969 the reception center on Ellis Island was deserted, its many offices now only tombs for broken furniture and its walls slowly shedding flakes of paint.
WILTON TIFFT

Store signs and a theater marquee reflect Spanish influences on an American city street.

THE SPANIARD'S CHILDREN

IN THE EARLY MORNING HOURS OF July 3, 1898, bugles rang out across the harbor of Santiago de Cuba. They sounded from the deck of the Spanish battle cruiser *Infanta María Teresa*, one of six warships penned up by a United States blockading squadron; they summoned the Spaniards to a brave but ill-fated dash for the open sea, in a climactic and decisive moment in the Spanish-American War. Within four weeks, Madrid would sue for the peace that stripped her of her last New World possessions. The *María Teresa*'s captain, Victor M. Concas y Palau, later wrote mournfully that his buglers' notes were "the signal that the history of four centuries of grandeur was at an end. . . ."

Yet it was not the end of Spain in the Americas, only of her jurisdiction there. A nation's power may die, but its imprint on history survives. In four centuries Spain and Portugal had stamped an Iberian image on the greater part of the Western Hemisphere. From Cape Horn all the way up to the southern tips of Texas and Florida at the 25th parallel of north latitude, mountains, jungles, lakes, rivers, seas, and islands are part of what we still call Latin America. Most of its people and place names are a blend of the Indian and the Hispanic, with a strong infusion, particularly in the Caribbean region, of the African strain created by the importation of slaves.

Hundreds of thousands of the children of this Latin culture formed the backbone of one of the twentieth century's great migrations into the continental United States. By 1970 they and their sons and daughters constituted a bloc of perhaps nine million Spanish-speaking Americans. The descendants of the conquistadors were thus encountering and modifying the folkways of the nation to the north that grew from seeds planted by England, Spain's mortal enemy when she was at the height of her glory in the 1500s. Long after the armor had rusted and the flags faded, heavily modified remnants of the two nations' traditions still confronted each other, as if some historical cycle beyond our comprehension had to be fulfilled.

The greatest numbers of these latest Hispanic settlers in the United States came from Mexico, which won independence from Spain in 1821, and from Puerto Rico and Cuba, both of which Spain lost in 1898. It is ironic that these generally poor and undereducated dark-complexioned Catholic immigrants arrived mostly after the passage of the laws of the 1920s that had the aim, among others, of reducing the inflow of poor, undereducated, dark-complexioned Catholics. But Congress did not foresee the increasing demand for cheap labor in the fields and orchards of the Southwest, which acted as a magnet for Mexicans. It did not anticipate that hundreds of thousands of Puerto Ricans, already under the American flag in their home island, would move without restraint or red tape to seek new opportunities on the mainland of the United States. Nor did it forecast a revolution in Cuba, sixty years after the Spanish left, that would fill certain neighborhoods in Miami with refugees from Communism.

The migrations that resulted furnish the occasion for a summarizing scrutiny of America's role as world asylum, and for some analysis and speculation concerning the future. For these latest immigrants came, in good measure, from unusually "primitive" localities to a modernized United States. They came to a nation more powerful than it had ever been, more richly endowed with miraculous inventions—and more self-conscious, divided, and hamstrung by its problems than at any time in its history. Inevitably, this affected the reception accorded the Latin-Americans, their prospects, and their hopes for themselves. In one way, they could not avoid re-experiencing what the Germans, Irishmen, Swedes, Italians, Africans, Poles, and others who came before them experienced. But they would do so in a radically different setting. Old theories might not apply to them; repetition of earlier immigrant behavior on their part might have no value. In any event, they would test, under new conditions, what had been said by exclusionists, assimilators, pluralists, Anglo-Saxonizers, those who still denounced the American past as ever flawed by racism, and those who insisted that meritorious men of every race and tongue had always prospered in the United States, given a little time. In the end, Spain's children might show Americans where the nation had been and where it was going. At least as far as the next bend in the road.

The first "Mexicans" to live within the boundaries of the United States were not immigrants at all but members of old Spanish-descended families in the territories taken from Mexico by conquest—the future states of Texas, California, Nevada, Utah, and parts of Arizona, New Mexico, and Colorado. These sons of the Spaniard were good copy for writers of romantic fiction, among them Helen Hunt Jackson, whose *Ramona* (in 1884) glamorized the *Californios* and their world of missions, horseflesh, wine, and hospitality. They were also the distant vanguard of less aristocratic legions who began to trek northward from Mexico around 1900.

As always, jobs were the attraction. The Southwest pulsed with booms in mining and railroad construction from 1880 onward; then in 1910, as the region's cattle-based agrarian economy was being broadened with the help of irrigation to include large-scale general farming, there was a revolution in Mexico. In the Southwest, hands were needed to plant and to pick cotton, beans, lettuce, beets, artichokes, grapefruit, oranges, spinach, grapes, tomatoes, and melons. Native American "hoboes," "bindle stiffs," "fruit tramps," and other picturesquely named migrant workers furnished much of the necessary labor, but the Mexicans fleeing their homeland were hired, too. World War I and the industrial expansion of the 1920s drew many American workers to army camps, factories, and cities—and created an even more urgent demand for Mexicans to fill the vacated places.

The true dimensions of Mexican immigration are hard to draw. The border was long and ineffectively patrolled, and thousands slipped back and forth unre-

A cotton picker in California's San Joaquin Valley in 1936

corded by statisticians. The official figures alone, however, showed a Mexican influx of 185,000 in the period 1910 through 1919, and nearly 500,000 from 1920 through 1929. Even the Mexican who reported himself to United States officials, furthermore, and intended to remain in his new homeland, did not quite fit the category of the uprooted. His journey might be only a few miles in length; the cactus-strewn deserts and mountainous horizons around Santa Fe or Los Angeles were like what he had left behind; he moved in what Carey McWilliams, a leading student of Mexicans in the United States, has called "an environment that was geographically, culturally, and historically familiar."

What he sought and found in the United States was, first of all, freedom from the uncertainties and dangers of internal warfare that plagued Mexico during the long period of revolutionary upheaval that began in 1910; and, secondly, a wage that was higher than any he could command on his native ground: in the 1920s, for example, it was about $105 a month in the United States and $18 in Mexico. A popular *corrido*, or ballad, about a Mexican youth who emigrated caught the essence of things.

Vámanos, madre, que allá está el *dollar*
y mucho, juro, que he de ganar.

(Let's go, Mother, over there is the dollar,
And I swear I am going to earn a lot of them.)

The dollars did not come easily, however. The work was brutally hard. Cesar Chavez, who in 1969 was leading the United Farm Workers Organizing Committee in the fourth year of a strike against California grape growers, recalled for a reporter his own boyhood as a sugar-beet harvester in the 1930s. "That was work for an animal, not a man. Stooping and digging all day. And the beets are *heavy*. Oh, that's brutal work. . . . *that* is how a man is crucified. *Crucified*." And the camps in which the farm laborers were put up were often horrible collections of unshaded tents and shacks, inadequately supplied with water and open-ditch latrines. Moving from one such camp to another in boxcars, trucks, or rusted jalopies piled high with bedsprings, chicken coops, and children, the Mexicans knew they were in no Promised Land. This was particularly so after the Depression began, when wages plummeted to as low as fifty-six cents a day; when families of four, with every member working, toiled to earn cash incomes that averaged $340 a year for the family; when a Mexican father spoke for thousands when he cried, "It is work or starve for my children"; and when, in the off seasons, sheriffs' deputies, state troopers, and the border patrol would round up and deport Mexicans by the hundreds to save relief costs.

Along with economic exploitation—which the white migrant farmer also endured, especially in the Depression era—went anti-Mexican prejudice. All the traditional charges that had been leveled at immigrants in the past were sounded anew. Typical remarks were those of the Archbishop of San Francisco, Edward J. Hanna, who declared that the Mexicans "drain our charities," formed "a large part of our jail population," and were of "low mentality."

"You can americanize the man from the southeastern

Working under conditions not much changed from those in the 1930s, Mexican migrant workers in 1968 harvest onions in New Mexico.

and southern Europe," said another Catholic clergyman, before a Rotary Club audience, "but can't americanize a Mexican."

Yet while labor unions and civic boosters in Texas and California denounced the policy of allowing unchecked Mexican immigration, the growers, who held the Southwest's highest political cards, saw to it that the supply of cheap and manageable Mexican labor was not reduced. During World War II, when there was a generally acute labor shortage, the United States government entered into an agreement with Mexico for the temporary admission of workers called *braceros*, who were trucked across the border during harvest months and trucked back later. Thus the restriction-minded Americans who had denounced Southern and Eastern European immigrants twenty-five years earlier for allegedly being "birds of passage" were treated to the sight of their own government providing Mexican "birds" with temporary nests and grain. The *bracero* program, a testimony to the strength of the Southwestern farm lobby, was supplemented during the 1950s as unregistered workers slipped into the country by—among other methods—swimming the Rio Grande. No one knows how many of them came and went before the border patrols were tightened, but as many as 447,000 *braceros* were imported in 1959. In 1964 the utilization of *braceros* ended, but in the late 1960s it was still possible, under a clause of the McCarran-Walter Act, for individual foreigners to retain their foreign citizenship while entering the United States for periods of temporary work. The Mexican holders of such "green card" visas earned in the United States an estimated $15,000,000 in wages in 1967; presumably, much of this cash left the country with them.

A good many Mexicans, then, had never considered themselves, or ever been considered, immigrants in the ordinary sense. Yet as the decades rolled by, more and more of them remained in the towns and cities intermittently between farming jobs, and some of them settled into industrial or service work or small businesses. Somewhat more than half a century after 1910, when the heavy Mexican surge northward had begun, there were some five million Americans of Mexican birth or parentage in the Southwest, adding color to the national demographic patchwork and creating fresh data for the students of assimilation patterns.

They were an almost unknown minority, in one sense. They were poor, with a third of their families earning less than $3,000 per year. They were crowded into *barrios* (literally, "neighborhoods") in major cities, in squalor bearing the usual marks and scars of poverty— broken homes, high rates of infant mortality, frequent

Robert Kennedy offered bread to Cesar Chavez as the Mexican-

arrests, much disease, a tendency toward narcotics addiction, a staggering school dropout rate—and, with all these discouragements, a birth rate as much as fifty per cent higher than that of the general population. Yet the Mexicans had not attracted the kind of anxious attention from domestic critics of America's shortcomings that other minority groups had. One student of the problem went so far as to say, "For the Mexican-American, there are no liberals."

Part of the reason for this state of affairs might have been found in the fact that the Mexicans, while as eager as any other people for a decent livelihood, had not sought much help from non-Mexicans, or shown any eagerness to adopt American life styles as part of breaking poverty's grip. They did not practice the self-rejection implicit in some of the earlier immigrant groups' struggles to "Americanize." There was in them a kind of Indian stoicism and Spanish pride, expressed in Cesar Chavez's reply to the question *cómo está*, namely, *batallando con la vida:* "I am still struggling with life." The Mexican sometimes struggled with life by singing in the face of adversity, confirming in hostile minds the stereotype of the "lazy, happy greaser." Sometimes he sought strength for the struggle in wine or in marijuana or in intense religious exercises, to the neglect of what the Puritan-based national culture called "useful work." Sometimes he struck an aggressive "I am myself" pose, and suffered for it. That happened, for instance, to some Mexican youths in Los Angeles during World War II. They called themselves *pachucos*—roughly "regular guys," or "swingers"—trying to maintain their treas-

American leader of the grape pickers ended a fast in 1968.

ured masculinity and arrogant freedom, *machismo*, despite their impoverished minority status. They adopted as a uniform the "zoot suit," a costume consisting of broad-brimmed hat, finger-length jacket, and billowing pants pinched tight at the ankles—a costume that cried "Hey, look at me," just as did the beaded chaps and gorgeous leather boots of the Mexican cowboy. But American servicemen in Los Angeles, despite the fact that thousands of Mexican-Americans were in service, regarded the zoot-suiters as draft dodgers and delinquents. Young arrogance met young self-righteousness; insults were traded; fights broke out, and finally, from June 3 to June 8, 1943, thousands of sailors and soldiers rampaged through the Mexican *barrio* of Los Angeles, beating up and stripping zoot-suit wearers, often with the amiable acquiescence of the police.

Decades later, the sons and nephews of some of the Mexican-Americans involved in those riots were still attempting to find a comfortable place in the national life. Again, the paths they sought might not be the same as those trodden by the "newcomers" from Europe in the first half of the twentieth century. Those older immigrants had fought their way upward by successful performance in the schools, by group involvement in American party politics, and by individual adaptation to the prevalent social demand for success in business and the professions. But Mexican-American children, to begin with, seemed unwilling to meet a school's demands if they perceived in those demands a threat to Hispanic identity. Often the teacher's first requirement was that pupils abandon the speaking of Spanish during school hours. Unlike earlier "foreign" children, the young Mexican found that this change set up an unacceptable tension between himself and his family. To follow the rule was to turn his back on his own. Yet to reject it was to be punished. "It's always my parents telling me to be proud I'm Mexican and the school telling me to be American," one junior-high boy complained. Often the dilemma was solved by dropping out—which elicited harsh reactions of the sort expressed by one Los Angeles high-school principal: "They don't belong here anyway—they belong in the fields." Ultimately, both child and society were losers in that sort of battle.

Dr. Manuel Guerra, an educator of Mexican background, made a plea for bilingual instruction and raised the familiar flag of cultural pluralism. "We do not want," he said, "to give up the Spanish language, pray to God in English, substitute mashed potatoes for *frijoles* or 'junk' our *piñatas*. Rather we want to bring all of these values to American society as our contribution to the diversity and wealth of our country. Rather than the melting pot, we believe in the heterogeneity of American society, including the give and take with other peoples and other cultures."

Even setting aside the language question, the schools might also have failed to make contact with large parts of the Mexican-American community because the educators focused on the preparation of youngsters for a middle-class status, which few of them desired. In 1967, for example, there were only thirty thousand Mexican-Americans in the entire Southwest—a very small percentage of their population—who were in "professional, technical and similar work": doctors, lawyers, teachers, accountants, engineers, draftsmen, and the like. That might have been due to lack of opportunity and preparation, but it was also possible that Mexican-Americans by and large were not eager to accept the constraints on dress and behavior, the rigid time schedules, the emphasis on such symbols of security as insurance policies, bank accounts, expensive automobiles, homes, gadgets, and vacations—in short, all the appurtenances of a life style that even successful middle-class Americans term a "rat race."

On the other hand, Mexican-Americans seemed to be slowly and belatedly exerting some of the bloc voting power that had advanced so many Irishmen and Italians. As of 1967, they had elected three Representatives and one Senator to the Congress of the United States, a handful of representatives to the legislatures of Arizona, Texas, and Colorado, and a fairly sizable delegation—thirty-three—to the New Mexico legislature. A few Mexican-Americans sat on the judicial benches of

The majority of Puerto Rican migrants to New York had at one time lived in a San Juan slum. La Perla, shown above, was

typical of the squalid conditions from which most tried to escape.

Arizona and Texas, and there had been several Mexican-American appointments to Federal posts, though to be sure these were posts of more honor than responsibility. And Mexicans sat, in increasing numbers, on city councils and boards of education in the five states where they were most concentrated. Time might well bring more Mexican names onto party slates. But it was not unlikely that young Mexican-Americans (the median age for the entire group was several years younger than for the population as a whole) would find the traditional climb to party influence too slow for their communities' urgent economic, medical, and educational needs. Even minority-group officeholders, under our system of coalition politics, must undertake expensive campaigns, make numerous concessions, and worry about their public images in order to win election; once in office, they must make compromises to secure even marginal gains. It is a basically conservative system that may work best in a smaller and simpler society.

Young Mexican-Americans who were convinced that traditional political practices were irrelevant might see the way out for them in other action. Two possible varieties of it are suggested by the careers of Cesar Chavez and Reies López Tijerina.

Chavez was born in 1927, the grandson of a successful Mexican immigrant who owned substantial property in Arizona. But his parents lost everything in the Depression, and Chavez spent his youth in the movable hell of the migrant camps. In 1952 he was an apricot picker, living in the Mexican *barrio* of San Jose that was grimly named *Sal Si Puedes*, "Escape If You Can." While there he was recruited into the Community Service Organization, a grass-roots pressure-and-action group of and for the poor, started under the leadership of Saul Alinsky, a Chicago-based self-styled radical who specialized in such work. Through the CSO, Chavez rose to leadership. Chavez in the 1960s was not a politician in the ordinary sense, and he would even have denied that he was particularly a leader of Mexicans; his constituency was agricultural labor. Yet the bulk of his followers were Mexican-born or of Mexican parentage. And if politics is the art of securing group objectives in a pluralistic society through persuasive leadership, then politics was the primary gift of Chavez. He had organized the grape pickers, whose earlier brave attempts at unionization had been ignored by established labor organizations — and been broken with ease by the growers. Chavez had earned national attention, publicity, and donations, and had inspired a nation-wide liberal boycott of table grapes. He had gradually begun to win concessions from the growers.

Despite the influence of the tough world in which he

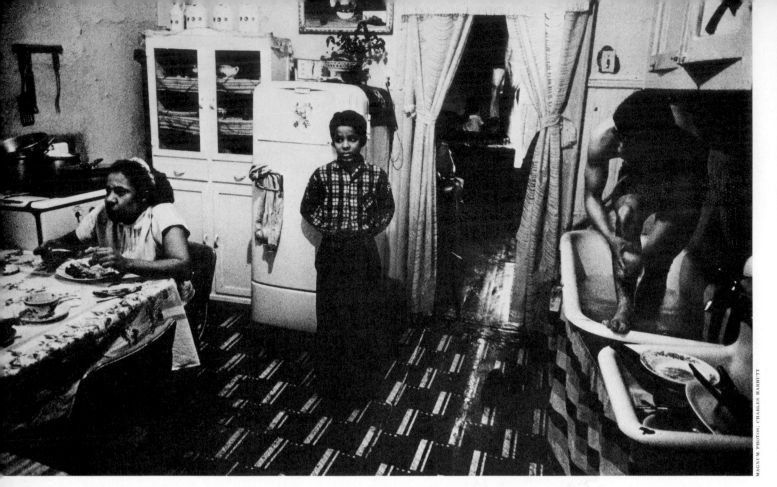

For most of the self-uprooted Puerto Ricans (such as those shown here in tenement flats), chronic poverty, the language barrier, and the burden of large families meant merely the substitution for tropical of northern slums in mainland American cities.

grew up, Chavez preached nonviolence and adopted Gandhi-like techniques, including fasts, peaceful mass pilgrimages to legislative halls, and constant exhortations to his followers to practice love and brotherhood. His career bore a clear resemblance to that of Martin Luther King, Jr.

In contrast, Tijerina might have been characterized as a middle-aged equivalent of Stokely Carmichael. He preached "brown power" to cheering students who wore buttons inscribed CHICANO POWER and VIVA LA RAZA. Flanked by guards in brown berets, he shouted such charges as "If the Anglo is frightened it is because his historical crimes are catching up with him." Tijerina claimed that certain government-owned forests in the Southwest were in fact the property of the Mexican-Americans under pre-1848 grants, and his "confrontations" with the authorities over the disputed soil led to prison sentences.

Chavez deplored talk of *la raza*, "the race." "To-day," he warned in 1969, "it's anti-gringo, tomorrow it will be anti-Negro, and the day after it will be anti-Filipino, anti-Puerto Rican. And then it will be anti-poor Mexican, and anti-darker-skinned Mexican." And yet Chavez himself, with his contemplative withdrawals, stubborn individualism as a leader, and strangely

contrasting appeals to the mystique of community spirit, seemed quintessentially Mexican. He and Tijerina shared with many black leaders the goal of autonomy for the ghettos, and with young Indian activists, too, the demand that the government stop trying to impose on the minority poor the cultural values of the majority; thus money for improvement should be spent as the affected groups saw fit. All such spokesmen preached the worth of the minority group; all aimed to bring their people into the sunlight by strengthening, not discarding, the customs that made them different. For Chavez, the cultivation of such group consciousness among Mexican-Americans was only a first step toward a larger concept of brotherhood, while for Tijerina and those like him, it might be an end in itself. But both viewpoints were a long way from preachments of salvation through assimilation.

Many of the problems and responses visible among the Hispanic-Americans of the Southwest were strikingly similar to, almost duplicated by, the next largest Spanish-speaking group in contemporary America, the Puerto Ricans, who were primarily in and of New York.

The Puerto Rican migration began, like so many others, with the modernization of the homeland. In 1940 the island was impoverished, its economy wrecked

Puerto Ricans arriving in New York found East Harlem a place where more and more of the signs, goods, and foods were geared to their wants. While the young began acclimatization, going to school, playing traditional games of the city streets (below), their parents fell into the time-honored paths of migrants—learning trades, earning money, dreaming of the return home. But many stayed, and filled a vacuum as the old middle class stampeded to the suburbs. They may have stayed because they could not afford to do anything else, but, again, the paths they trod were well worn: puertorriqueños moved up in their jobs; they formed small businesses; they improved their homes when they could. "I always thought I would go back," said one old man in the late 1960s. "But it was too expensive, too long a trip. I finally went in 1958, with my son, who paid for the airplane ticket. In three days I was ready to come home. I had been away too long and I was a New Yorker, not a real Puerto Rican anymore."

by long years of heavy dependence on sugar and to-bacco cultivation. Then the government undertook a series of development programs to bring diversified industries to the land, resettle impoverished farmers, increase cash incomes, encourage tourism, modernize cities, and raise the level of literacy and of public health. The programs were remarkably successful, but one consequence was a population boom. In 1968 some 2,700,000 Puerto Ricans were clustered on their island—an average of close to eight hundred per square mile—making Puerto Rico one of the world's most crowded areas This furnished one stimulus for emigration. Another was added not by the poverty that survived in the midst of progress but by the improvement in national living standards. The phenomenon of rising expectations set in. "Even in the 'thirties," a Puerto Rican explained to a reporter, "many of the basic commodities were imported from the mainland. The people began to yearn first for a radio, then for an automobile, and eventually for a TV set. . . . Their desires were aroused; cash became more and more important to them, and New York was the place to get it."

New York did offer attractions after World War II, primarily jobs that paid an average of thirty-five or forty dollars a week, almost twice as much as island jobs did, with unionization, health benefits, pensions, and Social Security sometimes included. Moreover, New York was easy to reach. There were no problems of immigration visas. Puerto Ricans had been American citizens ever since the Jones Act of 1917 created the framework of government for the Caribbean colony. They retained that status when Puerto Rico became an almost completely independent self-governing commonwealth in 1952. And, just as the transatlantic steamer of the 1890s offered the European migrant cheap passage to the Promised Land, the postwar transport plane furnished the same to the hopeful Puerto Rican. Price wars among major carriers and a number of nonscheduled lines reduced fares to as little as $35 per person, and the aircraft flying at 250 miles an hour ate up 1,000 air miles in no time. A family could board a "thrift flight" at San Juan at eleven at night, carrying coats to put on over their light clothing when they got off in the northern climate, and be deposited at Idlewild (now Kennedy) air terminal when dawn was silhouetting the New York skyline. So the steerage had become airborne. Thousands of Puerto Ricans made the journey. Some were "birds of passage" and did not stay long, but by 1953 the average net gain was about forty thousand a year, with the flow swelling or diminishing in response to business conditions in the United States.

Not many of the newest immigrants were *jíbaros*,

cane-field peasants. They were already partially urbanized. A 1950 sociological study of a sample group of Puerto Ricans in New York showed that they were on the whole older, better educated, and more likely to be skilled than those who had stayed behind. About eight out of ten went to work immediately upon their arrival, in jobs overwhelmingly concentrated in the light manufacturing and service occupations. The men became "pressers and floor boys in garment factories, dishwashers, bus boys, pantrymen, laundry workers, [and] porters"; the women were likely to end up as "domestics, in hospitals, and in laundries . . . as hand sewers, floor girls, cleaners, [and] sewing-machine operators."

In some cases, the Puerto Ricans actually lost job status, though gaining in salary, as a result of migration. An experienced machine operator unable to understand complicated instructions given in a new language might at first have to accept a job pushing a hand truck between departments in a plant. In many cases the lost ground was made up, occasionally with the help of the unions, particularly in the garment industry. Puerto Ricans were not readily accepted, however, into the skilled-labor unions like those of the painters, carpenters, electricians, and bricklayers. Not many, therefore, were able to attain such employment. At the same time, few moved into the white-collar classes. Even those who qualified for that sociological label were apt to be marginal small businessmen, operating barbershops, cleaning establishments, lunch counters, beauty parlors, radio repair shops and groceries. Like the owners of "Mom and Pop" candy stores and delicatessens in older ethnic neighborhoods of New York, they fended off bankruptcy only by using their families as unpaid and overworked help.

Some Puerto Ricans were placed by the Migrant Division of the Commonwealth of Puerto Rico's Department of Labor in jobs as far to the northwest as Milwaukee. But the overwhelming concentration was in the low wage brackets in New York. That was the mecca, though a tarnished one. The Puerto Ricans hit the city in the early years of what was to become an apparently permanent shortage of low-income housing. The median income of $36.28 a week for a Puerto Rican family in 1950 bought little in the way of residential space. Most of the newcomers were confined to a few neighborhoods. They lived in Brooklyn, in a district known as Morrisania in the Bronx, or, most of them, in East Harlem. Also known as Spanish Harlem, or simply *El Barrio* to the Puerto Ricans, East Harlem ran from 100th Street northward, bounded on one side by the East River and on the other (roughly) by central, or black, Harlem. The quality of accommodation offered

In a scene from "Rebels of Sierra Maestra," a CBS special report in 1957 on Cuba's guerrilla fighters, revolutionary leader Fidel Castro, above, leads his men in a cheer. Opposite: Cuban refugees arrive in Miami, fleeing the successful revolution.

in these Hispanic enclaves was reflected when, in the early 1950s, a church group in East Harlem circulated a questionnaire among 1,000 tenants asking them to list their housing problems. There were 721 cases of defective wiring, 612 of inadequate plumbing, 571 of broken windows, 895 of rats in the building, 696 of gas leaks, 778 of no heat, 553 of no hot water, and 308 of leaks in the roof. It went without saying that the victims of these housing-code violations, lacking political influence, lacking command of English, without money for lawyers, and having no comprehension of bureaucratic byways, were almost powerless to compel landlords to make repairs.

Life had not been any more gracious in the slums of San Juan, it was true. And yet in familiar surroundings, misery had perhaps been less threatening. A Puerto Rican named Piri Thomas grew up in *El Barrio*, experiencing early in his life poverty, drug addiction, and prison. In a deeply moving memoir entitled *Down These Mean Streets*, he recalled his mother comparing the lot of the lowly in two cultures:

. . . in Puerto Rico those around you share *la pobreza* with you and they love you, because only poor people can understand poor people. I like *los Estados Unidos*, but it's sometimes a cold place to live—not because of the winter and the landlord not giving heat but because of the snow in the hearts of the people.

Similar observations by Puerto Ricans are plentiful in the anthropologist Oscar Lewis's *La Vida*, a study of the culture of poverty in San Juan and New York.

Puerto Ricans in the United States also found themselves coping with a problem that was relatively new to them, racial discrimination. Some of the islanders were quite "white," many were dark-skinned like the majority of Mexicans, but about twenty-five per cent were *negritos* and *grifos*, blacks and mulattoes, descended from slaves brought in by the Spaniards. In a general way, social and economic advancement in Puerto Rico, as in the United States, came more quickly and easily to the light-skinned. But black Puerto Ricans, and especially those with only a few "negroid" characteristics, were unprepared for the shock of being taken for "niggers" in the United States and treated accordingly. For them, the choices were agonizing. They might deny their blackness, assume the white man's attitude of hostility to Negroes (often thoroughly reciprocated by American blacks), and live in a twilight zone between the races. Or they might seek co-operation with Negroes, individually or in organizations, and even positively accept their own color and define their own loyalties by it. Very few made this choice. Piri Thomas did, and it imposed on him the ache of a painful separation from his father, who was likewise black but who cried out to his son: "I don't like feeling to be a black man. Can you understand it's a pride to me being a Puerto Rican?" To which Piri replied with cruel honesty, "What kind, Poppa, black or white?"

For some Puerto Ricans, the escape from this and other traps was a return flight to San Juan. But thousands stayed to rear families, and each child born in the United States was a tie to the new land. By 1968 the Puerto Rican community of New York City had grown to nearly a million. The majority of its members were young, the group's median age as a whole being only nineteen.

The children often suffered the same initial linguistic problem in the schools as did the Mexican-American youngsters. A majority of Puerto Rican parents might want their children to attend college; a survey in 1950 indicated this ambition. But it was a vain hope for most of them. Puerto Rican children had a high dropout rate in the 1950s and 1960s. Bewildered by the strange tongue, the first- and second-graders would drop behind the class, would sometimes be labeled "unco-operative" or "stupid," would retreat into fantasy, aggression, or truancy, and would begin a long downward slide. To combat this sequence, some teachers in the New York City system suggested a new approach: that the Puerto Rican beginner be taught in Spanish and gradually in-

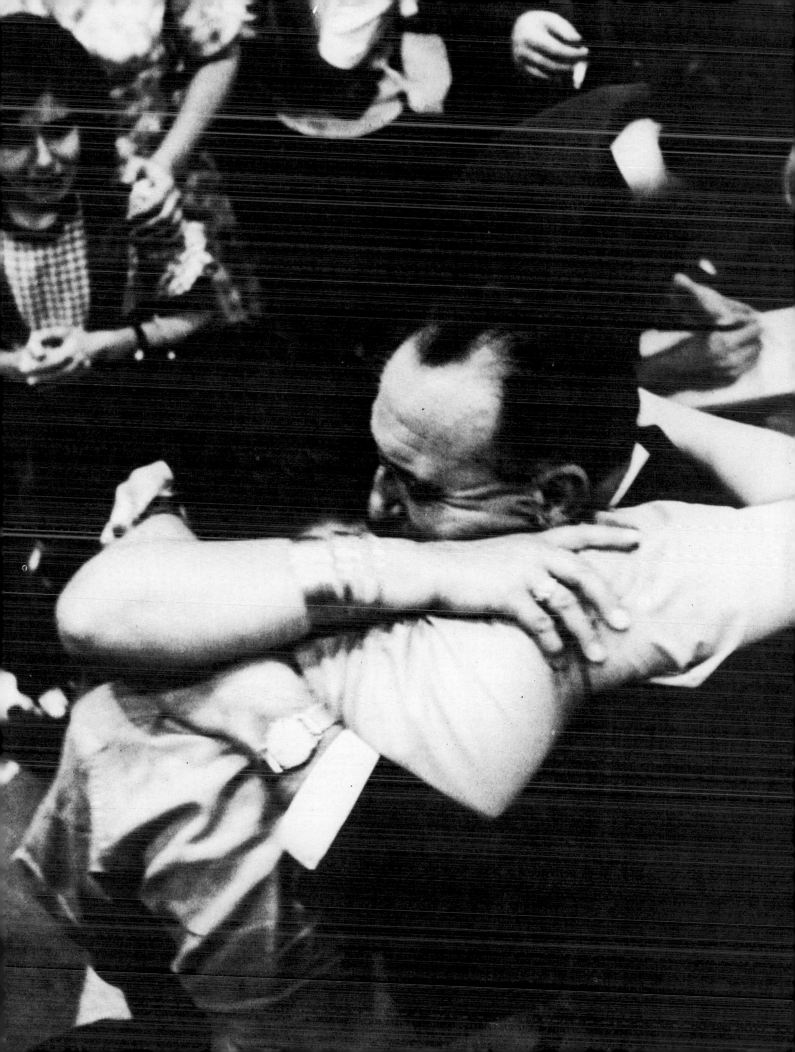

troduced to bilingualism. It was assumed that whatever benefits this might produce, an improvement in the child's competence in Spanish was itself a worthwhile educational goal.

Such an approach, of course, would set the pupils marching to a different drumbeat from the one sounded for the immigrant children of the early 1900s, and would rest frankly on what one writer has called "the philosophy of the multiethnic society in which all groups are identifiable," a philosophy that "attacks the middle-class value system on many fronts. . . ." Undeniably it was arousing the wrath of tradition-minded teachers, one of whom denounced multiethnicity as a gimmick, and declared in a newspaper interview that schools must "organize parents to cooperate, to send their children to school on time, to behave in school." The battle was joined, and it was a long way from being decided.

Again like the Mexicans, the Puerto Ricans appeared to be moving into political office on a slower timetable than the older nationality groups. This was, of course, a subjective and preliminary judgment. The New York Puerto Ricans were so youthful, in the most literal sense of the word, that in 1969 eighty-five per cent of those born in the United States were still under fourteen years of age. Patently, this helps to account for that state of affairs described in the headline of a New York *Times* story written on the eve of the 1969 city elections: "Puerto Rican Prospect: 10% of Population, 0% of Political Power." The article noted that while the Puerto Ricans could boast of one borough president and two of the thirty-seven city councilmen, all three leaders would leave office at the end of the year. Moreover, of 246 candidates running for municipal office in that election, only five were of Puerto Rican origin and none of these was on the regular Democratic ticket, which was the one that most Puerto Ricans normally voted. In Albany there were only three Puerto Rican legislators, all from the Bronx.

Inexperience and a certain amount of dispersion through many neighborhoods and districts might explain Puerto Rican political weakness in New York. But it was also possible that Frank Espada, a Puerto Rican who was vice-president of the New York Urban Coalition, had come very near the truth when he stated: "We are in the process of losing our second generation in terms of political involvement. The only Puerto Ricans that can break into the system are those who break into machine politics, which doesn't reflect our aspirations and goals."

The new breed of Puerto Rican, under twenty-five years of age, confronted a number of hurdles in the

In a Cuban neighborhood in Miami Beach, a blindfolded child attempts to break open the gift-filled Christmas piñata.

way of his goals—perhaps including an ambivalence about what goals to choose. There were obvious crises to be solved: a median Puerto Rican income in New York City of only $3,949 in 1968, rising numbers on the relief rolls, an unemployment rate sometimes equal to three times the national average. But the Puerto Rican had also to define himself, to decide what relationship he would try to create with whites and Negroes. He had to consider whether he would look for models in urban American patterns of family life and consumption, or in Latin styles. He had to choose between individual and group action, and between militants and traditionalists, if he wished to exert political pressure. Above all, he had to decide upon what emotional and geographic foundations he would build.

That was, paradoxically, both hard and easy, for the Puerto Ricans had never entirely left home. The first generation of Puerto Ricans on the mainland drew comfort from the fact that they could visit the island often and cheaply. Oscar Handlin believes that this may be the key to their failure to create separate institutions right away, such as ethnic churches and private schools, to cushion the shock of separation. Like the French-Canadians of New England as well as the Mexicans of the Southwest, they were "never altogether detached from the lands of their birth" in the fashion of the European immigrant who knew that he had "decisively severed his ties with his old home . . . and that his future was entirely in the United States."

But the children born to Puerto Ricans in New York did not share their parents' hopes of return. For them, "home isn't a dusty plaza on a tropical island, but a New York block where smells of fried fish and hamburgers mingle with the Latin beat drifting from the corner record store. . . ." Yet they were not ready to disappear entirely into the theoretical Melting Pot. They might turn out to be both old-countrymen and Americans in a deeper sense than most "hyphenated Americans" of the past. Through such organizations as the Puerto Rican Citizens Committee for Unity (which has a counterpart in MAPA, Mexican-American Political Action, and another in PUMA, Political Unity for Mexican-Americans), they might find a special strength, resting, according to a Fordham University student of Puerto Rican affairs, "not on the continuation of a traditional culture in the form of an immigrant community, but on the solidarity which results from organizing their efforts for the pursuit of group interests in the political arena." *Puertorriqueno* power, as one might say, would be more than a dwindling fortuitous product of their common background. They would use it, too, to perpetuate that identity—to encourage, for example, Spanish-speaking schools and Spanish neighborhoods.

Meanwhile, the Puerto Ricans were leaving their mark, like those who had gone before—in little *bodegas* selling plantains, in restaurants dishing up *asopao* (a chicken or sea-food stew with rice and vegetables), in papers like *La Prensa* and *El Diario de Nueva York*, which converted Blondie into Pepita and Mickey Mouse into El Ratón Miguelito, in billboards advertising a popular brandy as endowed with *alma española*.

Though Mexicans and Puerto Ricans came from, and settled in, widely different areas—one agricultural, one urban-industrial—there was enough similarity in their American experience to tempt an observer into speculating about the influence of innate Latin qualities. Such a racial theory would collapse into rubble, however, as soon as it was tested against the amazing experience of the Cuban refugees of 1959 to 1969. For the exiles from

Castro's revolution seem to epitomize the traditional success story of the foreign boy who makes good.

While the first year's refugee wave, forty thousand strong, was arriving by boat and plane in 1959, United States officials laid plans for the future. Almost from the beginning, Washington provided Federal temporary assistance funds of up to a hundred dollars a month for refugee families—whom the Cuban revolutionary government allowed to take only five pesos, one watch, one ring, and the clothes on their backs out of Cuba. Washington also allocated special funds to the Miami school system to help handle the influx of Cuban children, whose numbers grew by as many as a thousand a week. In 1965 the Federal government started to provide Cubans with air transport to the United States. The Department of Health, Education and Welfare also made grants to experienced social-work agencies, such as the National Catholic Welfare Conference and the International Rescue Committee, to help them maintain Cubans in special resettlement centers and then move them into jobs throughout the country. Under vigorous administration, approximately 109,000 Cubans were placed outside of the Miami area, and as far from the Caribbean as Chicago and southern California.

A heavy proportion of the more than 285,000 Cubans who had arrived by early 1967, however, remained in Dade County, which includes Miami. It was a natural debarkation point not far from Havana, and it had a thriving Hispanic colony even before 1959, composed of Puerto Ricans, Cubans, and other Latin-Americans. Miami had long been in the business of welcoming tourists from the southern continent to the United States. By 1969 it was estimated that Cubans made up ten per cent of greater Miami's population. As an index to their concentration in certain neighborhoods, by February of 1966 the local Catholic dioceses had to furnish eighty Spanish-speaking priests just for the Cubans; sixteen parishes said the Mass in Spanish; more than five thousand Cuban children were enrolled in parochial schools. Unlike the Mexicans and Puerto Ricans, whose nominal Catholicism did not seem to have a tight hold on them once they were transplanted to America, the Cubans were in the main active church supporters.

They were diligent in their own business as well as the Lord's. The Miami *Herald* referred to them as "the cream of a nation in exile," a somewhat biased judgment, suggesting that everyone who remained within Fidel Castro's jurisdiction was skimmed milk. But it was true that these refugees were endowed with ability, experience, and middle-class concepts of achievement. Most of them were soon off relief and paying back, in taxes, a substantial portion of the hundreds of millions of government dollars spent on the refugee program.

Men like Raul G. Menocal were among the new Cubans of Miami. Menocal had twice been mayor of Havana, and by 1967 he was vice-president in charge of the Latin-American division of a Coral Gables bank. There were also men like Angel Aixala and the Luis Encheniquis, father and son, who began a marine construction company named International Boats that by 1966 had annual gross sales of $1,500,000. And Raul and Jesus Gutierrez, who built a small company into the million-dollar-a-year Calmaquip, selling American products to Latin America. And Manuel Fernandez, who was stripped of his cattle ranch and packing house when he fled at the age of seventy in 1961—but who five years afterward was the contented owner of the Wajay Crackers Company.

Such individuals undoubtedly had head starts in the form of business contacts in the United States. These guaranteed them access to credit, and some had probably found ways to transfer assets out of Cuba despite Castro's laws. But there were also thousands of Cubans like Jose Simon, an attorney. He arrived in Miami so poor that his first, gratefully accepted job was as door-to-door salesman for a milk company. Simon studied English at night, and by early 1967 was a professor of Spanish at Emory University in Atlanta. At that time 2,500 Cubans were teaching in United States schools and colleges, and 1,900 Cuban physicians were working in United States hospitals.

By the end of Castroism's first decade, the Cuban community in Miami showed a respectable top layer of affluence, demonstrated in the expensive and handsome homes of refugees who owned automobile dealerships and garages, restaurants and hotels, small factories, real-estate agencies, and the like. Many of the Cubans still eagerly awaited the day when the usurper would be overthrown and they would return to their rightful homeland. But thousands were discovering that children born in the house of strangers create blood ties to those strangers and their house. Increasingly, Cubans who had children enrolled in American schools—where they were becoming "more American than Cuban"—were applying for citizenship papers and settling in for good. "The Cubans," said one Dade County Chamber of Commerce official, "have put a lot more into this community than they have taken out." As time went by, they were beginning to add their own lives to their investments in America.

The Cubans may have shaken the belief of many native Americans in the laziness and ineptitude of Latin-Americans, long contemptuously referred to as "spicks," "dagos," and "greasers." They may equally have punctured romantic notions that the Latin-American soul is too poetic to be fettered to the office stool. In any event, these particular Cubans represented a picked group of elite immigrants—educated, and supremely able to manipulate the machines, the blueprints, the bank figures, and the statutes that add up to power in the modern world.

They had their historical counterparts in many earlier immigrants to America who came well educated or well heeled or both, or who came with skills in metallurgy or glassblowing, for example, comfortably aware that they would be hired by industry as soon as they stepped ashore. They, too, were part of the immigrant procession through America's history.

Such people as the Castro refugees cannot fairly be compared to Mexican farm hands or Puerto Rican bellboys. Yet there was possible meaning for the lives of all of them if they simply *believed* in a Hispanic identity. For every twentieth-century American, as a child of the machine age, seemed to need an identity; and for minorities, both privileged and underprivileged, the search was invested with particular urgency. There was in New York in the late 1950s a Federación de Sociedades Hispanas, Inc., which hoped to unite Latin-Americans in the area. At first Puerto Ricans tended to stay clear of such efforts, apparently because they cherished their American status. But by the end of the 1960s numbers of them were joining in the activities of the federation, because it offered them a path to self-respect safer than "Americanism," which bigots could deny to them. "Their self-image is better served as Latinos than as Puerto-riqueños," wrote one sociologist some years earlier, and "who can say but that such elements are a proud thing, and necessary in order to bear their kind of life?"

One of the activities of the Hispanic Societies in New York was to celebrate Columbus Day as a *día de la raza*. The holiday was marked in New York by a widely publicized parade, and traditionally the emphasis was on the discoverer's Genoese background. It was a day to woo the Italian vote. The Spanish-Americans of New York, however, had a special ceremony of their own. They would gather at the statue of Columbus on the Mall in Central Park. There, fittingly, they would lay flowers at the feet of the man who, under the Spanish flag, began it all nearly five centuries ago. With the flowers were placards that managed to link the destinies of Spain, Spain's children, America, and the world:

AMERICA WAS DISCOVERED
FOR THE GLORY OF SPAIN
AND THE GOOD OF ALL PEOPLE.

The Old and the Young

IN THEIR WORDS

Within the not-so-sheltering confines of the family, immigrant parents strove sometimes to shed their foreignness, but they were more apt to cling to accustomed patterns as a source of identification and protection. The normal conflict of generations could be given a tragic sharpness by the immigrant experience. True, the sense of a shared goal—Americanization—might bind family members more tightly together; mutual affection might bridge a "generation gap" that was also a language and culture gap, as children felt the full impact of American ways while their parents could not escape Old World patterns. One Italian-American wrote of his immigrant father, "He regretted that progress seemed to lead away from the kind of life he had lived. Yet he could not be quite certain that were he given the power, he would want his children to undergo similar experiences. . . . He wanted his children to experience the discipline of physical labor, to learn the value of money, to avoid the disgrace of waste, to become intimate with the soil; but he found himself in a world of central heating and labor-saving devices." Or rebellious youngsters and angry parents might deliberately accentuate their differences so as to hurt each other. So the normal emotional turbulence of growing up was heightened for the child of the immigrant home. And from such homes children would emerge whose feelings about the United States would always be closely bound up with memories, sweet or bitter, of their parents as perplexed human beings.

"You Should Have Left It Behind"

To be an immigrant before the Civil War was to be part of an experiment in which all whites, in a way, took the same chances and shared the rewards and penalties. When the experiment succeeded, however, the "new" immigrant to industrial America no longer was regarded as co-pioneer but as an intruder trying to horn in on a good thing. In spasms of defensiveness, some newcomers tried to rid themselves of remnants of their old lives that supposedly branded them as "green." Fathers and sons alike might feel this impulse toward rejection, though rarely at the same time. What they cast off might be a trivial habit, or a fundamental value. Each time there was a price in suffering.

In the 1934 novel Call It Sleep, *Henry Roth wrote about his experiences as the son of immigrants in Brooklyn. In the following passage he portrayed a man's bitter distaste for signs of the outlander in his newly arrived wife and son.*

. . . All those steerage passengers of the ships that had docked that day who were permitted to enter had already entered—except two, a woman and a young child she carried in her arms. They had just come aboard escorted by a man.

About the appearance of these late comers there was very little that was unusual. The man had evidently spent some time in America and was now bringing his wife and child over from the other side. . . . As for his wife, one guessed that she was a European more by the timid wondering look in her eyes as she gazed from her husband to the harbor, than by her clothes. For her clothes were American—a black skirt, a white shirt-waist and a black jacket. Obviously her husband had either taken the precaution of sending them to her while she was still in Europe or had brought them with him to Ellis Island where she had slipped them on before she left.

Only the small child in her arms wore a distinctly foreign costume, an impression one got chiefly from the odd, outlandish, blue straw hat on his head with its polka dot ribbons of the same color dangling over each shoulder.

Except for this hat, had the three newcomers been in a crowd, no one probably, could have singled out the woman and child as newly arrived immigrants. They carried no sheets tied up in huge bundles, no bulky wicker baskets, no prized feather beds, no boxes of delicacies, sausages, virgin-olive oils, rare cheeses; the large black satchel beside them was their only luggage. But despite this, despite their even less than commonplace appearance, . . . there was something quite untypical about their behavior. . . .

They had been standing in this strange and silent manner for several minutes, when the woman, as if driven by the strain into action, tried to smile, and touching her husband's arm said timidly, "And this is the Golden Land." She spoke in Yiddish.

The man grunted, but made no answer.

She took a breath as if taking courage, and tremulously, "I'm sorry, Albert, I was so stupid." She paused waiting for some flicker of unbending, some word, which never came. "But you look so lean, Albert, so haggard. And your mustache—you've shaved."

His brusque glance stabbed and withdrew. "Even so."

"You must have suffered in this land." She continued gentle despite his rebuke. "You never wrote me. You're thin. Ach! Then here in the new land is the same old poverty. You've gone without food. I can see it. You've changed."

"Well that don't matter," he snapped, ignoring her sympathy. "It's no excuse for your not recognizing me. Who else would call for you? Do you know anyone else in this land? . . .

"And as if those blue-coated mongrels in there weren't mocking me enough, you give them that brat's right age. Didn't I write you to say seventeen months because it would save the half fare? Didn't you hear me inside when I told them?". . .

The western wind that raked the harbor into brilliant clods blew fresh and clear—a salt tang in the lull of its veerings. It whipped the polka-dot ribbons on the child's hat straight out behind him. They caught his father's eye.

"Where did you find that crown?"

Startled by his sudden question his wife looked down. "That? That was Maria's parting gift. The old nurse.

She bought it herself and then sewed the ribbons on. You don't think it's pretty?"

"Pretty? Do you still ask?" His lean jaws hardly moved as he spoke. "Can't you see that those idiots lying back there are watching us already? They're mocking us! What will the others do on the train? He looks like a clown in it. He's the cause of all this trouble anyway!" . . .

While his wife looked on aghast, his long fingers scooped the hat from the child's head. The next instant it was

sailing over the ship's side to the green waters below. The overalled men in the stern grinned at each other. The old orange-peddler shook her head and clucked.

"Albert!" his wife caught her breath. "How could you?"

"I could!" he rapped out. "You should have left it behind!"

When Shmelka Glickstein, small son of immigrant parents in New York, announced that his name was now Sammy Glick, he took his first step in a headlong drive to imitate Americans. In his battle with life, the tough hero of Budd Schulberg's novel What Makes Sammy Run? *used as one of his weapons a cynicism that destroyed his pious father's authority.*

Sammy lugged his papers up and down Fourteenth Street yelling about a war in Europe. He used to come home with a hoarse throat and thirty or forty cents in pennies. He would count the money and say, "God dammit, I'm yellin' my brains out for nuttin'."

Papa Glick would look up from his prayer book. "Please, in this house we do not bring such language."

"Look who's talkin'," Sammy said. "Know what Foxy Four Eyes tol' me—he says I wouldn' hafta peddle papers if you wasn't such a dope and quit your job. He says his ol' man tol' him."

"Silence," said Papa Glick.

"He says that strike screwed us up good," said Sammy.

Papa Glick's hand clapped against Sammy's cheek. It left a red imprint on his white skin but he made no sound. By the time he was six he had learned how to be sullen.

"Papa, please," Mrs. Glickstein pleaded. "He's so small, how should he know what he's saying—he hears it on the street."

"That's so he should forget what he hears," said Papa. . . .

Life moved faster for Sammy. He was learning. The Glicksteins' poverty possessed him . . . He was always on the lookout to make a dollar. The way the little Christians put on Jewish hats and mingled with the Jewish boys to get free hand-outs in the synagogue on the holy days gave him an idea. On Saturday he went down to the Missions on the Bowery and let the Christ-spouters convert him. At two-bits a conversion. He came home rich with seventy-five cents jingling in his pockets. His father, struggling to maintain his last shred of authority, the patriarchy of his own home, demanded to know why he was not at *cheder*. Sammy hated *cheder*. Three hours a day in a stinking back room with a sour-faced old Reb who taught you a lot of crap about the Hebrew laws. You don't go to jail if you break the Hebrew laws. Only if you got no money and get caught stealing, or don't pay your rent.

"I hadda chance to make a dollar," Sammy said.

"Sammy!" his father bellowed.

"Touching money on the Sabbath! God should strike you dead!"

The old man snatched the money and flung it down the stairs. . . .

"You big dope!" Sammy screamed at him, his voice shrill with rage. "You lazy son-of-a-bitch."

The old man did not respond. His eyes were closed and his lips were moving. He looked as if he had had a stroke. He was praying.

Sammy went down and searched for the money until he found it.

His mother came down and sat on the stairs above him. She could never scold Sammy. She was sorry for Papa but she was sorry for Sammy too. She understood. Here in America life moves too fast for the Jews. There is not time enough to pray and survive. The old laws like not touching money or riding on the Sabbath—it was hard to make them work. . . . Sammy was not a real Jew any more. He was no different from the little wops and micks who cursed and fought and cheated. Sometimes she could not believe he grew out of her belly. He grew out of the belly of Rivington Street.

On the Way to Learning

Leaving a past filled with problems and restrictions in search of betterment in America, the new immigrant was likely to arrive with intensified emotions—the love of freedom, the fear of ridicule, and an eagerness to succeed and belong. Aware that they were considered "undesirables," many immigrant parents struggled to help their children rise above undesirability to become, in fact, indispensable, through the best opportunity the new country offered—formal education. For the immigrant family, the experience of sending the children to school was exhilarating, demanding, and bewildering all at once. But learning was the unavoidable highroad to acceptance.

A music class, including guitarist, pianist, violinist, and a mandolin chorus

Nine-year-old Angelo Pellegrini and his brothers and sisters came to America with their Italian mother in 1913 and settled in McCleary, Washington. Later Angelo became a university professor and wrote his autobiography, Immigrant's Return, *in which he described a typical and vividly memorable experience at school.*

. . . I could not achieve the kind of harmony with my parents which I so much desired. The relationship was actually disturbing rather than unpleasant. I was a rather serious student. Each day I became more and more in-volved in the life of the school. I wanted so much that they should share my en-thusiasm and understand what I was doing. I wished so ardently that they might be able to give me guidance and encouragement. But they were unable to do any of these things; and I felt deeply the deficiency in our relationship.

. . . all extracurricular activities were immensely important to me. Nothing was done in the school in which I did not manage to intrude. I participated in all the sports. . . . When I tried to ex-plain to . . . [my parents] in Italian why it was important that I should play on the baseball team and participate in school programs, the language not only proved inadequate to my needs; it made my preoccupations sound silly. The glory of a home run was simply not transmissible in Italian.

What disturbed me most profoundly, however, and occasionally brought tears to my eyes, was the fact that I could not go to my parents for aid and guid-ance on the many occasions when the need seemed desperate. Never once did I know the pleasure of having Father or Mother resolve one of the many difficul-ties a child encounters during his first years at school. I felt very much alone, deserted, isolated as I heard some of the pupils report in the classroom what their fathers, or mothers had said on a given problem to which we had been asked to seek an answer. I wondered how it would be possible to continue in school and to make the marks which meant so much to me, without aid from my parents.

I remember a trifling incident which dramatizes the isolation I felt so bitterly. One day in the hygiene class we were discussing the care of the teeth. That led quite naturally to an appraisal of the sets of teeth in the classroom. Everyone talked glibly of visits to the dentist, of a certain number of cavities filled, of the excruciating pain bravely endured in the dentist's chair, etc. What did Angelo have to report? Nothing. Absolutely nothing. I had never heard of a dentist up to that day. . . . I felt very much embarrassed—an alien, an inferior breed who had never had what everybody could boast of: a tooth cavity drilled and filled by a dentist.

For a brief while I felt like an oddity. And then, quite unexpectedly, I became a hero. The teacher asked me if I would let her look at my teeth. . . . When she had completed the examination she announced to the class with considerable and undisguised excitement that she had seen a miracle: a perfect set of teeth. . . .

Had the matter been dropped at that stage it would not have been so bad. But apparently even miracles must have an explanation. What did I do to my teeth to keep them so perfect? Would I consult with my parents and share the secret with the class the next day? Of course I would; and I promised a complete report. . . .

That evening, during the dinner hour, I related what had happened in class. They were both amazed and amused at the vagaries of American education. What had the quality of one's teeth to do with grammar and arithmetic? But, since I insisted, they told me what they knew about the care of the teeth: that an uncle, who had notoriously strong, sound teeth, occasionally rinsed his mouth with his own urine. I knew that

to be gospel truth. . . .

I was in a very embarrassing situation, and I had to find a way out. I had the one opportunity to quote my parents in the classroom, and all I could say was that they advised rinsing the teeth with urine! . . .

After much thought and more worry I found a solution which was no solution at all. I went to the druggist and asked for the best tooth paste available —regardless of cost. When I appeared in class to make my report, to reveal the great secret, I flashed a tube of a famous brand of tooth paste and solemnly lied that brushing the teeth twice daily with that stuff would do the trick.

Immigrant parents relentlessly prodded their offspring—even the reluctant ones —along the thorny pathways to an education and gentility. In this selection from his book Everything But Money, *Sam Levenson, teacher, humorist, and popular sage, recalled the sacredness of musical instruction to his parents' generation.*

Culture was not optional. In a era when heads of families earned ten to twelve dollars a week there was hardly a family in our building that did not have a piano with a hand-knit shawl on it, and/or a violin. Practice was compulsory. "Practice! I'm spending Papa's bloodstained money on you!" All day long one could hear the voices of mothers screaming from windows: "Your music teacher is here!" If the reluctant virtuoso didn't show up, the kid brother had to take the lesson for him. Those kids who practiced willingly weren't safe on the street. There were trios and quartets waiting for them at the corner to teach them a lesson or two.

I was given violin lessons, and I knew where Mama got the money. She stole it from the "table money"! "Some day you'll appreciate." I appreciated Mama even more than I appreciated music, so I practiced. Since I played so badly that one melody was almost indistinguishable from another, she knew I was practicing only if she heard screeching sounds from the bedroom. I could bounce rhythmically on the mattress for

a half hour and satisfy Mama's soul in the kitchen. I suffered for my art, too. Whenever Papa read in the paper that Jascha Heifetz got five thousand dollars for a concert, I got hit. "Practice!" Even the street musicians played better than I did. I used to give them a penny to move away from our window before Mama heard them and made me practice harder.

Along with most of the kids on the block I took my music lessons at the neighborhood "Y." At the end of each year the school gave a student recital at which we displayed the progress we had made. Most of us sounded no better than the previous year, but we were now making weird sounds from Book II rather than Book I.

We each brought home tickets for the concert. Mama didn't boast. She merely informed the neighbors that Sammy was going to "give a concert." There wasn't a single neighbor who thought that Sammy had any talent, but if he was going to "give a concert," maybe they had underestimated his ability.

These student-recital audiences were the best in the world. They loved every performer, that is, each family loved its own, but applauded sympathetically for all. The program was longer than a Wagnerian opera as originally scored, without intermission. It usually opened with "Flow Gently, Sweet Afton" performed on the violin by Paul Berkowitz, age nine, six months' instruction. The music flowed neither gently nor sweetly. He started without waiting for the piano introduction, covered the Afton in thirty seconds flat, and tore the house down when he bowed so low that his head touched the floor. He then exited the wrong way and bumped into a young cellist coming on stage. Grand ovation for both.

Then came more Berkowitzes, Murphys, Kowalskis, Angelinis, Thompsons, and Hoffritzes plowing through polonaises, Valses, Etudes, Caprices for one hand, two hands, four hands and no hands. By this time the audience was cadenza-happy and tone-deaf.

As a reward for appearing in the concert, Mama told me I didn't have to practice for a whole week.

Becoming Something New

Education helped lead the children of immigrant families into American styles of life. But such entering was often accompanied by the pangs of departure—from parents, even from brothers and sisters. Not all children could be sent to school; family economics might well demand that the older siblings work, permitting the younger ones to forge ahead in the new country. And as they learned a strange language, as they perhaps gained a knowledge of history or arithmetic that their parents did not have, they also absorbed—through the pores—new ways of thinking, new ways of behaving. Their differences might or might not be agonizing, depending on the family's ability to adjust.

Because Mary Antin's immigrant father could not support his family of six alone, it was decided that in America the youngest children—Dora, Joseph, and Mary—would go to school, while the eldest, Frieda, would help to earn a living. In these passages from her memoirs, The Promised Land, *Mary Antin tells of her schooling and of the changing relationships with her father, her sister, and her new home.*

Our initiation into American ways began with the first step on the new soil. My father found occasion to instruct or correct us even on the way from the pier to Wall Street, which journey we made crowded together in a rickety cab. He told us not to lean out of the windows, not to point, and explained the word "greenhorn." We did not want to be "greenhorns," and gave the strictest attention to my father's instructions. . . .

Education was free. That subject my father had written about repeatedly, as comprising his chief hope for us children, the essence of American opportunity, the treasure that no thief could touch, not even misfortune or poverty. It was the one thing that he was able to promise us when he sent for us; surer, safer than bread or shelter. On our second day I was thrilled with the realization of what this freedom of education meant. A little girl from across the alley came and offered to conduct us to school. My father was out, but we five between us had a few words of English by this time. We knew the word school. We understood. This child, who had never seen us till yesterday, who could not pronounce our names, who was not much better dressed than we, was able to offer us the freedom of the schools of Boston! No application made, no questions asked, no examinations, rulings, exclusions; no machinations, no fees. . . . The smallest child could show us the way. . . .

It was a great disappointment to be told by my father that we were not to enter upon our school career at once. It was too near the end of the term, he said, and we were going to move to Crescent Beach in a week or so. We had to wait until the opening of the schools in September. What a loss of precious time—from May till September! . . .

Who were my companions on my first day at school? Whose hand was in mine, as I stood, overcome with awe, by the teacher's desk, and whispered my name as my father prompted? Was it Frieda's steady, capable hand? Was it her loyal heart that throbbed, beat for beat with mine, as it had done through all our childish adventures? Frieda's heart did throb that day, but not with my emotions. My heart pulsed with joy and pride and ambition; in her heart longing fought with abnegation. For I was led to the schoolroom, with its sunshine and its singing and the teacher's cheery smile; while she was led to the workshop, with its foul air, care-lined faces, and the foreman's stern command. Our going to school was the fulfilment of my father's best promises to us, and Frieda's share in it was to fashion and fit the calico frocks in which the baby sister and I made our first appearance in a public schoolroom.

I remember to this day the gray pattern of the calico, so affectionately did I regard it as it hung upon the wall—my consecration robe awaiting the beatific day. . . . And when the momentous day arrived, and the little sister and I stood up to be arrayed, it was Frieda herself who patted and smoothed my stiff new

School children line up for

calico; who made me turn round and round, to see that I was perfect; who stooped to pull out a disfiguring basting thread. If there was anything in her heart besides sisterly love and pride and good-will, as we parted that morning, it was a sense of loss and a woman's ac quiescence in her fate, for we had been close friends, and now our ways would lie apart. Longing she felt, but no envy. She did not grudge me what she was denied. Until that morning we had been children together, but now, at the fiat of her destiny, she became a woman, with all a woman's cares; whilst I, so little younger than she, was bidden to dance at the May festival of untroubled childhood. . . .

. . . It was understood, even before we reached Boston, that she would go to work and I to school. In view of the family prejudices, it was the inevitable course. No injustice was intended. My father sent us hand in hand to school, before he had ever thought of America. If, in America, he had been able to support his family unaided, it would have been the culmination of his best hopes to see all his children at school, with equal advantages at home. But, when he had done his best, and was still unable to provide even bread and shelter for us all, he was compelled to make us children self-supporting as fast as it was practicable. There was no choosing possible; Frieda was the oldest, the strongest, the best prepared, and the only one who was of legal age to be put to work.

. . . it was with a heart full of longing and hope that my father led us to school on that first day. He took long strides in his eagerness, the rest of us running and hopping to keep up.

At last the four of us stood around the teacher's desk; and my father, in his impossible English, gave us over in her charge, with some broken word of his hopes for us that his swelling heart could no longer contain. . . .

All three children carried themselves rather better than the common run of "green" pupils that were brought to Miss Nixon. But the figure that challenged attention to the group was the tall, straight father, with his earnest face and fine forehead, nervous hands eloquent in gesture, and a voice full of feeling. This foreigner, who brought his children to school as if it were an act of consecration, who regarded the teacher of the primer class with reverence, who spoke of visions, like a man inspired, in a common schoolroom, was not like other aliens, who brought their children in dull obedience to the law; was not like the native fathers, who brought their unmanageable boys, glad to be relieved of their care. I think Miss Nixon guessed what my father's best English could not convey. I think she divined that by the simple act of delivering our school certificates to her he took possession of America. . . .

We [Frieda and I] continued to have part of our life in common for some time after she went to work. We formed ourselves into an evening school, she and I and the two youngsters, for the study of English and arithmetic. As soon as the supper dishes were put away, we gathered around the kitchen table, with books borrowed from school, and pencils supplied by my father with eager willingness. I was the teacher, the others the diligent pupils; and the earnestness with which we labored was worthy of the great things we meant to achieve. Whether the results were commensurate with our efforts I cannot say. I only know that Frieda's cheeks flamed with the excitement of reading English monosyllables; and her eyes shone like stars on a moonless night when I explained to her how she and I and George Washington were Fellow Citizens . . .

At bedtime she and I chatted as we used to do when we were little girls in Polotzk; only now, instead of closing our eyes to see imaginary wonders, according to a bedtime game of ours, we exchanged anecdotes about the marvellous adventures of our American life.

lunch in this photograph taken about 1914 by Jessie Tarbox Beals.

Some reminiscences of a Sicilian up-bringing in Rochester, New York, appear in Jerre Mangione's book Mount Allegro. *Like countless other children from immigrant families, Jerre was often called upon to assist his elders with the English language and experienced mixed feelings about his family and its place in America.*

So elated was my father with the amount of English he absorbed in a half-year that he stopped learning the language then and there and never made any further conscious effort to add to his vocabulary or improve his grammar. . . .

The little English my mother knew she acquired from my father. But she spoke the language without any system, groping for nearly all the words she used, without any of my father's wonderful sureness. . . .

My Uncle Luigi, more than any other of my relatives, had to depend on his smiles and charms to maintain good relations with Americans. His English was so rudimentary that it could be understood only by Sicilians. In view of his burning ambition to marry a slim widow with a fat bank account, his scant knowledge of the language proved something of a handicap. Most of the Italian widows he knew were fat and had very slim bank accounts. The few widows he met who qualified did not know a word of Italian. . . .

There was the time he fell in love with an Australian-born widow who lived on a five-hundred-acre farm . . . and was said to own seven cows. . . .

One evening he cornered me alone. "My nephew," he said gravely, "I want you to do me a brotherly favor. I will pay you well for it. Do you think you could write a passionate love letter for me?"

At the mention of pay I became thoroughly interested and assured him I could write such a letter, if he told me what he wanted to say.

He became a little impatient. "You, a young man with eleven years of life behind you, at least six of which have been squandered watching countless movies, have the gall to tell me that you don't know what to say in a love letter? Very well, I shall describe what I want

said." He paused to take a pinch of snuff.

"Her name is Belle. After I marry her I shall call her Bella. Tell Belle I love her, of course. It might be a good idea to repeat that in the letter a few times. Tell her, too, that I like the country and fresh vegetables and have a great fondness for cows—I detest milk, but don't mention that. You might reminisce a bit —women like nostalgic men—and let her know that I used to milk goats in my youth and probably would have no difficulty at all with cows. Have I made myself clear?"

I wrote the letter and promptly received my first fee as a ghost writer, twenty-five cents. But Uncle Luigi never received a reply to the letter, and when he saw the Australian widow at the church the following Sunday she turned crimson and lifted her nose as high as it would go.

"What in God's name did you say in that letter, squash head?" he asked. "Why, I could almost see the froth gathering at her lips when she caught sight of me!"

I mumbled that I had only written what he had asked me to. It was not until a few years later, when I was more qualified to think of the opposite sex as such, that I realized you could not woo a lady effectively by devoting most of your first letter to a discourse on your passion for milking cows. . . .

If the children had had their own way, my parents would have dropped all their Sicilian ideas and customs and behaved more like other Americans. That was our childhood dream. Yet, as much as we wanted them to be Americans and as much as we wanted to live an American life, we did not have the vaguest notion as to how to go about it.

. . . The more aware I became of the great differences between their Latin world and the Anglo-Saxon world (I thought of it as "American" then) the more disturbed I was; nor was I the only child of Sicilian parents who was disturbed. We sensed the conflict between the two worlds in almost everything our parents did or said. Yet we had to adjust ourselves to their world if we wanted any peace. At the bottom of our dis-

satisfaction, of course, was the normal child's passion for conventionality. It wasn't that we wanted to be Americans so much as we wanted to be like most people. Most people, we realized as we grew older, were not Sicilians. So we fretted inside.

I was embarrassed by the things my relatives did when in public; most of all by their total indifference to what Americans might be thinking of them. I mistook their high spirits, their easy naturalness, and their extraverted love of life for vulgarity, never dreaming that these were qualities many Americans envied. I had a particular dread of picnics in public parks. Spaghetti, chicken, and wine were consumed with pagan abandon then and the talk and laughter of my relatives filled the park like a warm summer breeze.

A few feet away would be an American family quietly munching neatly cut sandwiches that came out of neatly packed baskets—and drinking, not wine of course, but iced tea with trim slices of lemon stuck into the brims of their glasses to make them look pretty. It would make me blush to realize how shocked these subdued, well-mannered Americans must be by the circus din of our Sicilian eating festival. . . .

Our general attitude toward all Americans was bound to be distorted, for, not knowing any of them well, we could not make independent judgments and were influenced by the confused opinions our elders had of them. On one hand, my relatives were cynical about *Americani:* they had no manners; they licked their fingers after a meal and they chewed gum and then played with it as though it were a rubber band. Also, *Americani* were *superbi* (snobs) and looked down on people who didn't speak their language fluently. On the other hand, they feared and respected *Americani* and there were times when they emulated them.

If a Sicilian began to behave like an *Americano*, they said he was putting on airs but, actually, they had great admiration for anyone who achieved any degree of Americanization. After all, to be an *Americano* was a sign that you were getting on in the world.

A Visible Diversity

Americans All

The promise of a forward motion in life has drawn people across the oceans to America from every corner of the world. Native and newcomer have, headlong, pursued wealth and individual freedom and progress, and this has given a special vitality to American existence. Part of the spirit of the pursuit has also been flight, an emancipation from the past. Swept along in this current, many of the immigrants who poured into the country not only gratefully accepted the chance to make better lives for themselves, but also could not wait to put on Yankee clothes and attitudes.

By the 1970s, however, Americans were making a rediscovery: roots firmly anchored in the past might be the surest guarantee of a healthy future. The Irish-American, the Jewish-American, the Armenian-American apologized less and less for a hyphenated status. In fact—inspired partly by the American blacks' aggressive drive toward race pride—many ethnic groups were making concerted efforts to reassert their own special, traditional characteristics, qualities denied just a few decades before in the scramble to Americanize. Denied now was that unlikely ideal of homogeneity, the Melting Pot. Whether one was a descendant of the First Families of Virginia or came from a centuries-old line of Polish Catholics or Russian Jews, an honorable connection with the past was essential to the self-assured individuality that Americans most admired in themselves as a nation.

The third-generation Eastern and Southern Europeans who began to meet regularly to speak the language of their grandfathers and to do the old dances, the blacks whose "Afro" hair styles emphatically advertised their different race and past, the Puerto Ricans campaigning to get Spanish-language public-school education for their children, were saying not that they were immutably aliens but that they were ready to take part in another American demonstration of the ability of different people to get along with each other. The question "What is the American?" was still specifically unanswerable, but one could note that the individuals whose pictures follow were each of them American.

Acknowledgments

The Editors appreciate the generous assistance provided by many individuals and institutions during the preparation of this book. They especially wish to thank the following:

AMERICAN COUNCIL FOR EMIGRÉS IN THE PROFESSIONS, NEW YORK CITY, Mrs. Lenore Parker

BANCROFT LIBRARY, UNIVERSITY OF CALIFORNIA AT BERKELEY; John Barr Tompkins

BROWN BROTHERS, NEW YORK CITY; Mr. and Mrs. Harry Collins

KURT JULIUS BURGER

RALPH BURGER

CALIFORNIA HISTORICAL SOCIETY; Lee Burtis

MRS. AUDREY CATUZZI

CINCINNATI HISTORICAL SOCIETY; Mrs. Lee Jordan, Mrs. Carolyn LeaMond

COLUMBIANA COLLECTION, COLUMBIA UNIVERSITY; Susan Bilton

CULVER PICTURES, NEW YORK CITY; Sol Novin

MICHAEL E. DuBOIS

GEORGE EASTMAN HOUSE, ROCHESTER, NEW YORK; Tom Barrow

JAY JACOBS

LIBRARY OF CONGRESS; Virginia Daiker, James Goode

LOS ANGELES COUNTY MUSEUM; Ruth Mahood

MAGNUM PICTURES, NEW YORK CITY; Jerry Rosencrantz

MINNESOTA HISTORICAL SOCIETY; Mrs. Dorothy Gimmestad

MUSEUM OF THE CITY OF NEW YORK; Charlotte La Rue

MUSEUM OF PRIMITIVE ART, NEW YORK CITY; Herbert Bronstein

NATIONAL BROADCASTING COMPANY, NEW YORK CITY; Daniel Jones

NATIONAL PARK SERVICE; Cecil Stoughton, M. V. Williams

NATIONAL PORTRAIT GALLERY; Monroe H. Fabian

NEW-YORK HISTORICAL SOCIETY; Wilson Duprey, Jan Hudgens

NEW YORK PUBLIC LIBRARY; Picture Collection, Rare Book Room

PATRICIA RECTOR

STAATSBIBLIOTHEK, HANDKE BILDARCHIV, BERLIN; Dr. Hans Klempig

STATE HISTORICAL SOCIETY OF WISCONSIN; Paul Vanderbilt, Mrs. Judy Topaz

STATEN ISLAND HISTORICAL SOCIETY; Raymond Fingado

MR. AND MRS. PAUL TISHMAN

UNITED STATES IMMIGRATION AND NATURALIZATION SERVICE; Sol Marks

ROBERT WEINSTEIN

WELLS FARGO BANK, HISTORY ROOM, SAN FRANCISCO; Mrs. Irene Simpson Neasham

YIVO INSTITUTE FOR JEWISH RESEARCH; Ezekiel Lifshutz

The Editors also make grateful acknowledgment for permission to use material from the following works:

Adjusting Immigrant and Industry, by William M. Leiserson. Copyright 1924 by Harper & Brothers, assigned to the Carnegie Corporation, 1925. The excerpt on pages 271–72 reprinted by permission of the Carnegie Corporation and of Arno Press Inc. (1969 edition).

Call It Sleep, by Henry Roth. Copyright 1934, 1962, by Henry Roth. The excerpt on pages 366–67 reprinted by permission of Cooper Square Publishers.

Everything But Money, by Sam Levenson. Copyright 1949, 1951, 1952, 1953, 1955, 1956, 1958, 1959, 1961, 1966 by Sam Levenson. The excerpt on page 369 reprinted by permission of Simon & Schuster, Inc.

The First Americans, 1607–1690, by Thomas Jefferson Wertenbaker. Copyright 1927 by The Macmillan Company. The excerpt on page 62 reprinted by permission of The Macmillan Company.

Immigrant's Return, by Angelo M. Pellegrini. Copyright 1951 by Angelo M. Pellegrini. The excerpt on pages 368–69 reprinted by permission of The Macmillan Company.

"The Industrial Workers of the World," by Robert W. Bruere. Copyright © 1918 by Harper's Magazine, Inc. The excerpt on pages 262–63 reprinted from the July, 1918, issue of *Harper's Magazine* by special permission.

Land of Their Choice, The Immigrants Write Home, edited by Theodore C. Blegen. Copyright © 1955 by the University of Minnesota. The excerpt on page 152 reprinted by permission of the University of Minnesota Press.

"Letters of the Rev. and Mrs. Olof Olsson, 1869–1873, Pioneer Founders of Lindsborg," translated and edited by Emory Lindquist, from the *Kansas Historical Quarterly*, Vol. XXI, No. 7, 1955. The excerpt on pages 154–55 reprinted by permission of the Kansas State Historical Society and Dr. Emory Lindquist.

Memoirs of American Jews, 1775–1865, Vol. III, by Jacob R. Marcus. Copyright 1955 by The Jewish Publication Society of America. Excerpt on pages 152–54 reprinted by permission of The Jewish Publication Society of America.

Mount Allegro, by Jerre Mangione. Copyright 1943, 1952 by Jerre Mangione. The excerpt on page 372 reprinted by permission of Alfred A. Knopf, Inc.

Original Narratives of Early American History, edited by J. Franklin Jameson. Copyright 1907–1912 by Charles Scribner's Sons, assigned to Barnes & Noble, Inc., 1946. Excerpts on pages 51–57, 59, and 61–63 reprinted by permission of Barnes & Noble, Inc.

"The Preacher and the Slave," by Joe Hill, from *Rebel Voices: An I.W.W. Anthology*, edited by Joyce L. Kornbluh. Copyright © 1964 by the University of Michigan Press. The excerpt on page 265 reprinted by permission of the Industrial Workers of the World.

The Promised Land, by Mary Antin. Copyright 1940 by Mary Antin. The excerpt on pages 370–71 reprinted by permission of Houghton Mifflin Company.

"The Schramm Letters, Written by Jacob Schramm and Members of His Family From Indiana to Germany in the Year 1836," translated and edited by Emma S. Vonnegut, from the *Indiana Historical Society Publications*, Vol. 11, No. 4, 1935. The excerpt on pages 150–51 reprinted by permission of the Indiana Historical Society.

The Story of the "Old Colony" of New Plymouth, by Samuel Eliot Morison. Copyright © 1956 by Priscilla Barton Morison. The excerpt on page 59 reprinted by permission of Alfred A. Knopf, Inc.

The Thirty Years War, by C. V. Wedgwood. Copyright 1938 by C. V. Wedgwood. The excerpt on pages 23–24 reprinted by permission of Humanities Press, Inc.

Western Star, by Stephen Vincent Benét. Holt, Rinehart and Winston, Inc. Copyright 1943 by Rosemary Carr Benét. The excerpt on page 36 reprinted by permission of Brandt & Brandt.

What Makes Sammy Run?, by Budd Schulberg. Copyright 1941 and renewed 1969 by Budd Schulberg. The excerpt on page 367 reprinted by permission of Random House, Inc.

Index

NOTE: *Page numbers in italic type indicate that the subject is illustrated.*

174, *175*, 176

CLEVELAND, GROVER: on white man's hunger for Indian land, 227

CLINTON, DEWITT, 105

CLOTHING INDUSTRY: 152–54, 259, *294;* strikes, *257*, 265

COAL MINING. *See* Mining

COKE, SIR EDWARD: 37

COLLOT, VICTOR: 111

COLONISTS: distinguished from immigrants, 19

COLORADO: Ludlow coal strike, 267

COLUMBIA COLLEGE: *102–103*

COLUMBUS, CHRISTOPHER: on Bahama Indians, 25; Italian and Hispanic homage to, 364

COMMUNISTS: entry banned, then eased, 340, 346; "Red Scare," 316, *316–17*

COMMUNITARIAN SETTLEMENTS: 121 ff., *126*, 127–28

COMSTOCK, SARAH: on 1909 garment workers' strike, 265

CONCORD (ship); 69

CONCORD, MASSACHUSETTS: bridge, *96*

CONFEDERATE STATES: foreign-born troops, 176. *See also* Civil War, U.S.

CONGRESS, U.S.: enactment of Alien and Sedition Laws, 110–111; exclusionist legislation, 221, 255, 339–41; qualifications for membership debated at Constitutional Convention, 103–105; report on Chinese, 220; restrictive legislation, 1917–24, 250

CONNECTICUT: Dutch vs. English, 32

CONSTITUTION, U.S.: Convention, 1787, debated qualifications for Congress, 103–105; defied on Negroes' rights, 227, 228

CONSTRUCTION: Chinese workers, 218, 219, *236–37*, *236–37;* Irish workers, 122, 203; Italian workers, 203, *300*

CONTRACT LABOR: Chinese, 219; white foreigners, 268. *See also* Servants

COOK, WALTER S.: 331, 332

"COOLIE": term misused, 219, 220

CO-OPERATIVES: ethnic groups', 249

COPLEY, JOHN SINGLETON: portrait of Henry Laurens, *105*

COPPER: miners' strike in Arizona and Montana, 263

CORONADO, FRANCISCO VÁSQUEZ DE: 20

CORSI, EDWARD: on immigrant life, 274, 287

COTTON, JOHN: on settlers' right to Indians' land, 42

COUGHLIN, CHARLES E.: *324*

CRABTREE, SAMUEL: 115

CRÈVECOEUR, MICHEL-GUILLAUME DE: *Letters from an American Farmer* quoted or cited, 16, 67, 82

CRIME: in England, 17th century, *51;* immigrants as victims and perpetrators, 149, 156–57, 301

CROCKER, CHARLES: 218

CROKER, RICHARD: 171, *182*, 183, *183*

CROMWELL, OLIVER: 37

CUBA: Castro revolution, *360*, 363;

Spanish-American War, 349

CUBANS: in New York, 304; refugees, 340, 346, 349, *361–62*, 363–64

CUSHMAN, ROBERT: supposed tract on England quoted, 50

CZECHOSLOVAKIA: 346

D

DALE, SIR THOMAS: 44

DANCKAERTS, JASPER: on treatment of early New York Indians, 57

DARWIN, CHARLES: evolutionary doctrines used by racists, 35, 232, 248

DAVIDSON, BASIL: on early African cultures, 92

DAVIE, MAURICE R.: on refugees in America, 333–34

DAWES ACT: 226–27

DE LANCEY FAMILY: 101 ff.

DEMOCRATIC PARTY: beneficiary of urban votes, 304–305; Negro vote, 311; shaken by Klan, 254. *See also* Tammany Hall

DEPRESSION (1930s): fall in immigration, 256, 333; Mexican farm workers in, 351; Negroes in, 309, 311

DEVERY, WILLIAM: *189*, 190–91

DE VRIES, DAVID: description of New Netherland, 22

DEW, THOMAS: on fate of black slave, *229*

DILLINGHAM COMMISSION: 254

DISEASE: among homeworkers in U.S., 259; in 19th-century Ireland, 118; in 19th-century New York, 292; in 17th-century England, 37–38, *39;* in 17th-century Europe, 24; in 20th-century Harlem, 309

DISPLACED PERSONS ACT, 1948: 339–40

DOCTORS. *See* Medicine

DOUGLASS, FREDERICK: on persecution of Negro, 232

DRAYTON, MICHAEL: poem on Virginia quoted, 53

DUBOIS, W. E. B.: 232, 306

DUGGAN, STEPHEN: 331

DUNKARDS: 70

DUNNE, FINLEY PETER ("MR. DOOLEY"): on Anglo-Saxon pretensions, 35

DU PONT DE NEMOURS, PIERRE S.: 111

DUTCH. *See* Netherlands, The

DUTCH WEST INDIA COMPANY. *See* New Netherland

E

EDUCATION: desegregation of, 314, *326–27;* effect of immigrants on, and vice versa, 206, 249–50, 294, *294*, 301, 302; European refugees' contributions, 332 ff.; Germans' interest in,

130, 135; middle-class standards not appealing to many Mexican-Americans and Puerto Ricans, 350, 360, 362, 374; naturalization class, *253;* Negroes' struggle for after Civil War, 227 ff.; New York industrial school, *205;* reservation Indians', 226; urban elementary school, *370–71*

EGMONT, JOHN, EARL OF: 71

EINSTEIN, ALBERT: *333*, 335, 338

ELIOT, CHARLES W.: on multiracial America, 252

ELIZABETH I OF ENGLAND: 36

ELLIS ISLAND: reception center, *16–17*, 19, 116, *193*, 194, 256, *274–85*, 346, *347–48*

EMERGENCY COMMITTEE IN AID OF DISPLACED FOREIGN SCHOLARS: 331–33

EMERGENCY RESCUE COMMITTEE: 332–33

ENCLOSURE ACTS (England): 50

ENGLAND. *See* Great Britain

ENGLAND, JOHN: Catholic Bishop of Charleston, 166; on assimilation of Irish, 166

EQUIANO, OLAUDAH: on being captured as a slave, 90

ERICSON, LEIF. *See* Norsemen

ESPADA, FRANK: on Puerto Ricans in U.S. politics, 362

ETTOR, JOSEPH: 264, *265*, 301

EUROPE: social conditions, 17th century, 22–24; social conditions, 19th century, 18 ff., 123 ff., 193 ff.

EXPLORATION OF AMERICAS: 20–32

F

FAIRCHILD, HENRY PRATT: 243–44

FARMING. *See* Agriculture

FEDERALIST PARTY: backed Alien and Sedition Acts, 109–110

FERMI, ENRICO: 334, 335, *335*

FERMI, LAURA: quoted, 331, 335

FETCHIT, STEPIN: *323*

FFRETHORNE, RICHARD: on sufferings in Virginia, 60

FILLMORE, MILLARD: *168*, 174

FISKE, JOHN: 249

FITZGERALD, F. SCOTT: on American promise, 19

FITZHUGH, WILLIAM: description of Virginia estate, 62

FLEXNER, ABRAHAM: 332

FLORA AND FAUNA: abundance in colonies, 58–59, *58*, *59;* armadillo, *22;* corn (maize), *23;* forest, 34; gulls, *18;* of New Netherland, 22; of Virginia, 21–22; tobacco, *40*

FLORIDA: Cubans in, *348*, *361–62*, 363–64; Spanish in, 22

FOLLEN, PAUL: 121

FORAN ACT OF 1885: 219

FRANCE: intellectuals rescued from during German occupation, 332–33;